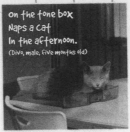

on the fone box
Naps a cat
In the afternoon.
(Divo, male, five months old)

樋 口 大 輔

Stumbling along, I've been diligently cranking out this series for four years. My heart is moved when I see the results of my labors stacked up in the bookstore.

Working solely in the confines of my small world, I started to worry about whether I was really communicating what I was trying to draw. But just then, I met many people involved in turning it into an anime, and even though it was only a vague conviction, I got the feeling for a moment that my message was getting through to others. That feeling made me feel a fountain of renewed energy bursting forth. How simple-minded I am. Just as my spirits are returning to me, the World Cup is about to begin. So let's enjoy soccer!!

– Daisuke Higuchi

Daisuke Higuchi's manga career began in 1992 when the artist was honored with third prize in the 43rd Osamu Tezuka Award. In that same year, Higuchi debuted as creator of a romantic action story titled *Itaru*. In 1998, *Weekly Shonen Jump* began serializing *Whistle!* Higuchi's realistic soccer manga became an instant hit with readers and eventually inspired an anime series, debuting on Japanese TV in May of 2002.

WHISTLE!
VOL. 21: TRY ON MY DREAMS

The SHONEN JUMP Manga Edition

STORY AND ART BY
DAISUKE HIGUCHI

English Adaptation/Heidi Alayne
Translation/Naomi Kokubo
Touch-up Art & Lettering/Jim Keefe
Design/Matt Hinrichs
Editor/Jonathan Tarbox

Editor in Chief, Books/Alvin Lu
Editor in Chief, Magazines/Marc Weidenbaum
VP, Publishing Licensing/Rika Inouye
VP, Sales & Product Marketing/Gonzalo Ferreyra
VP, Creative/Linda Espinosa
Publisher/Hyoe Narita

Printed in the U.S.A.

Published by VIZ Media, LLC
P.O. Box 77010
San Francisco, CA 94107

SHONEN JUMP Manga Edition
10 9 8 7 6 5 4 3 2 1
First printing, January 2009

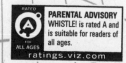

PARENTAL ADVISORY
WHISTLE! is rated A and
is suitable for readers of
all ages.
ratings.viz.com

THE WORLD'S
MOST POPULAR MANGA

www.viz.com

www.shonenjump.com

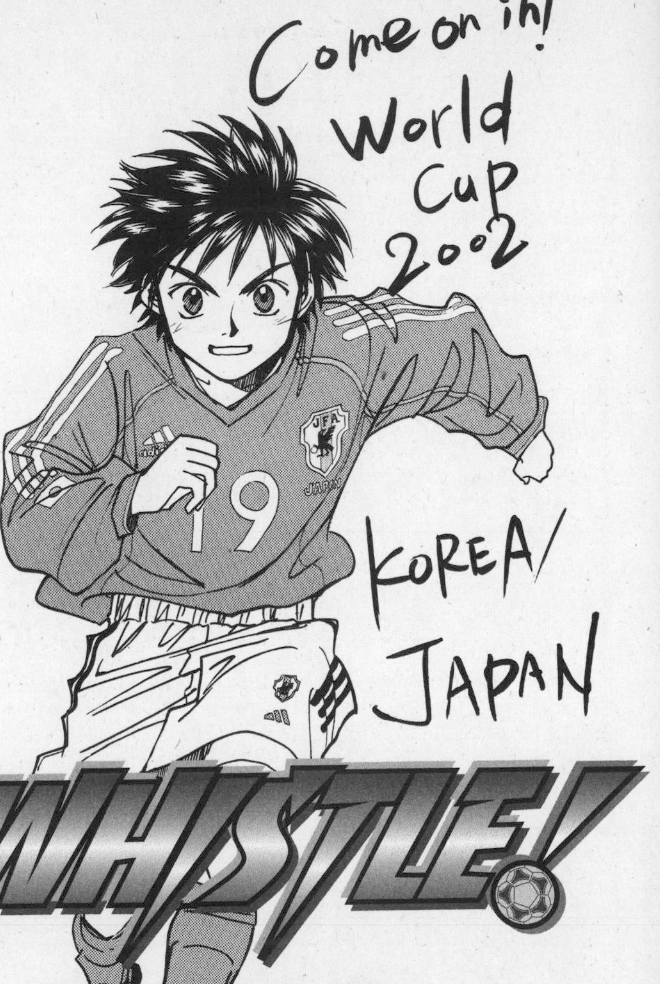
Come on in!
World Cup 2002
KOREA/ JAPAN
19

WHISTLE!

Vol. 21

TRY ON MY DREAMS

Story and Art by
Daisuke Higuchi

CHARACTERS

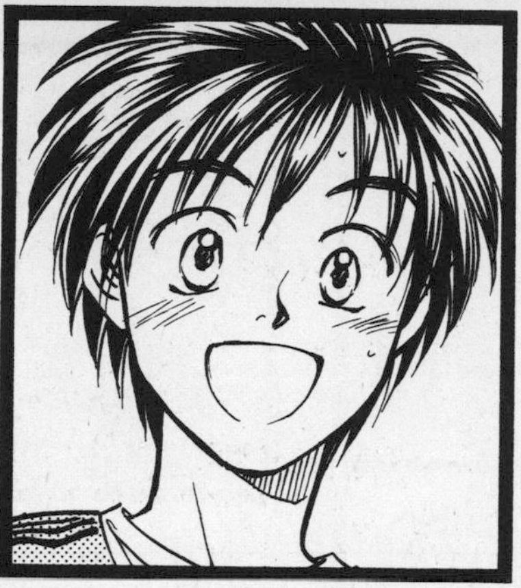

SHŌ KAZAMATSURI

● JOSUI JUNIOR HIGH SOCCER TEAM FORWARD

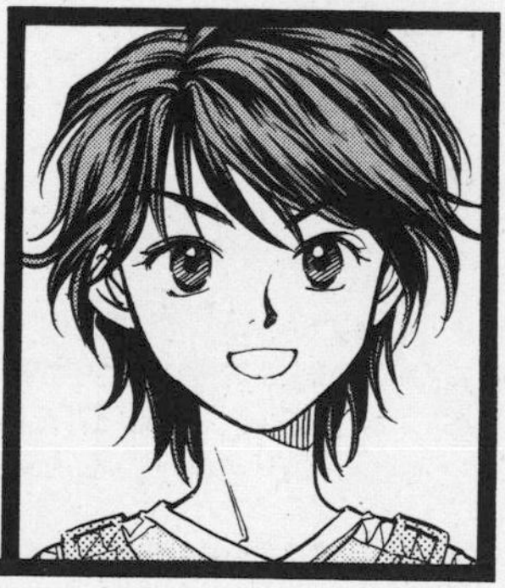

AKIRA SAIONJI

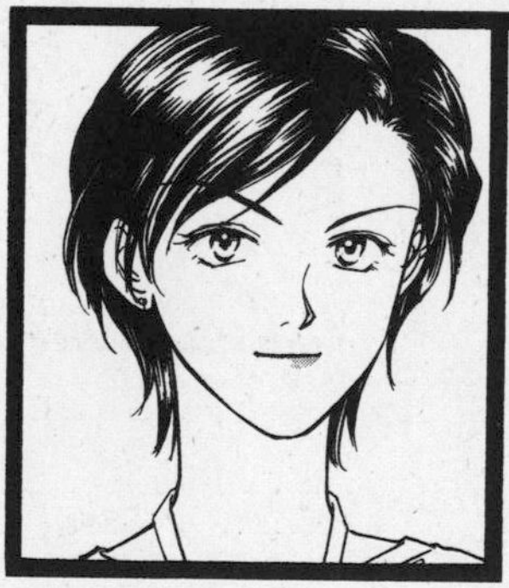

TSUBASA SHIINA

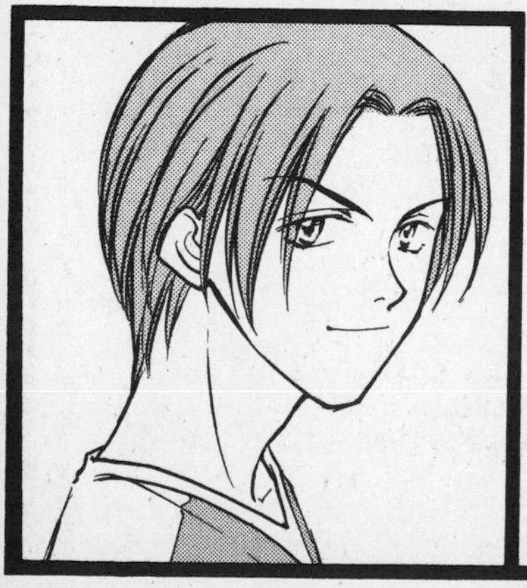

TATSUYA MIZUNO

● JOSUI JUNIOR HIGH SOCCER TEAM MIDFIELDER

SHŌEI TAKAYAMA

KYUSHU SELECT TEAM

DEFENDER SIDE BACK

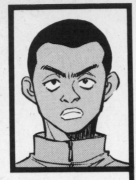

KOTARŌ ABE

TOHOKU SELECT TEAM

RIGHT WING

MITSUHIRO HINASE

TOHOKU SELECT TEAM

LEFT WING

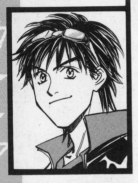

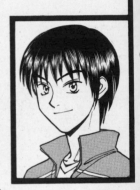

STORY

TO REALIZE HIS DREAM, SHŌ KAZAMATSURI, A BENCHWARMER AT SOCCER POWERHOUSE MUSASHINOMORI, TRANSFERRED TO JOSUI JUNIOR HIGH SO HE COULD PLAY THE GAME HE LOVES.

SHŌ'S IMPRESSIVE PLAY FOR JOSUI EVENTUALLY LEADS TO A SUBSTITUTE POSITION ON THE WORLD-TRAVELING TOKYO SELECT TEAM.

TOKYO SELECT TEAM HAS NOW JOINED THE NATIONAL TORESEN--A TRAINING EVENT WHERE THE BEST PLAYERS FROM EACH DISTRICT GO HEAD-TO-HEAD IN AN INTENSE ELIMINATION TOURNAMENT.

IN THE SECOND ROUND, TSUBASA BECAME THE VICTIM OF TOHOKU'S VICIOUS PSYCHOLOGICAL TACTICS. OVERLY FOCUSED ON HIS LACK OF SIZE AND STRENGTH, HE STARTS TO CRACK UNDER THE PRESSURE. THAT'S WHEN SHŌ COMES TO THE RESCUE!

WHISTLE!

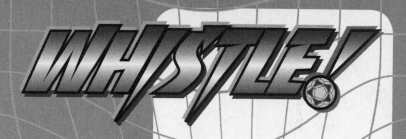

Vol. 21
TRY ON MY DREAMS

STAGE.183 Unspoken Support

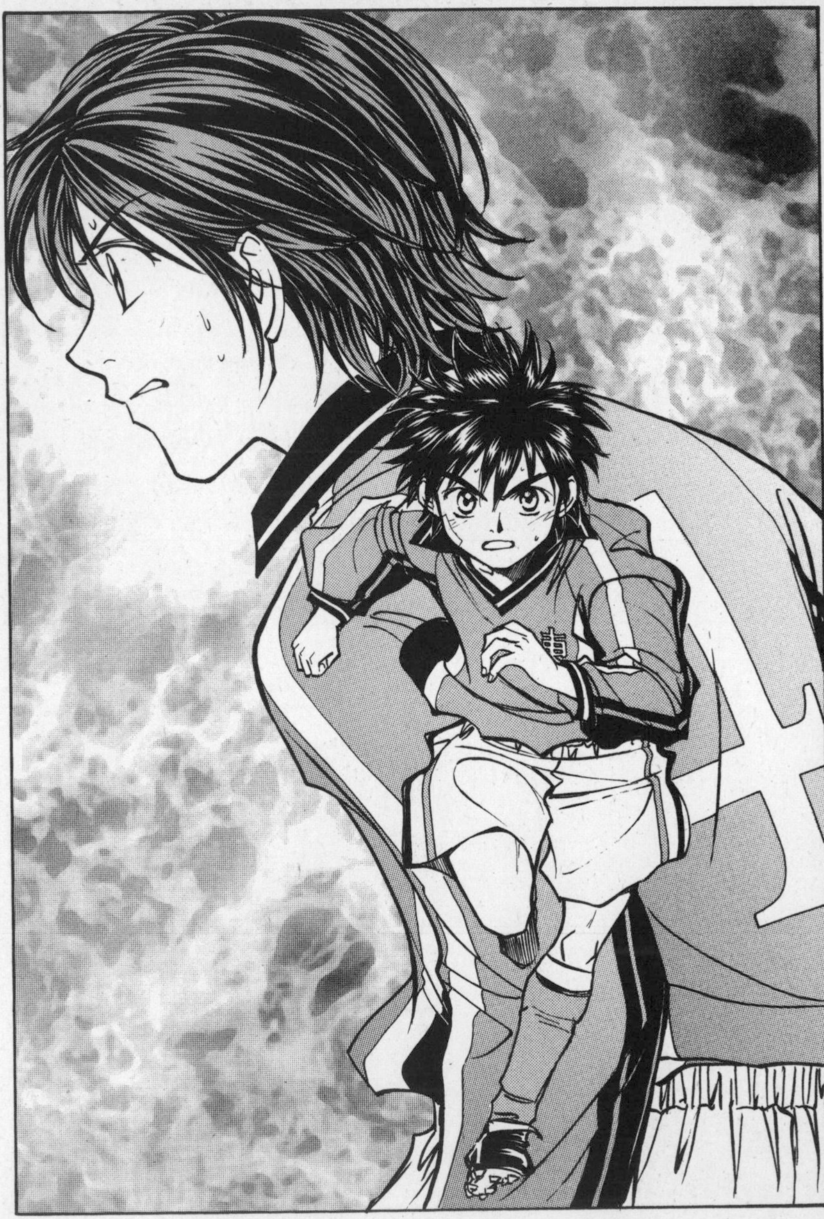

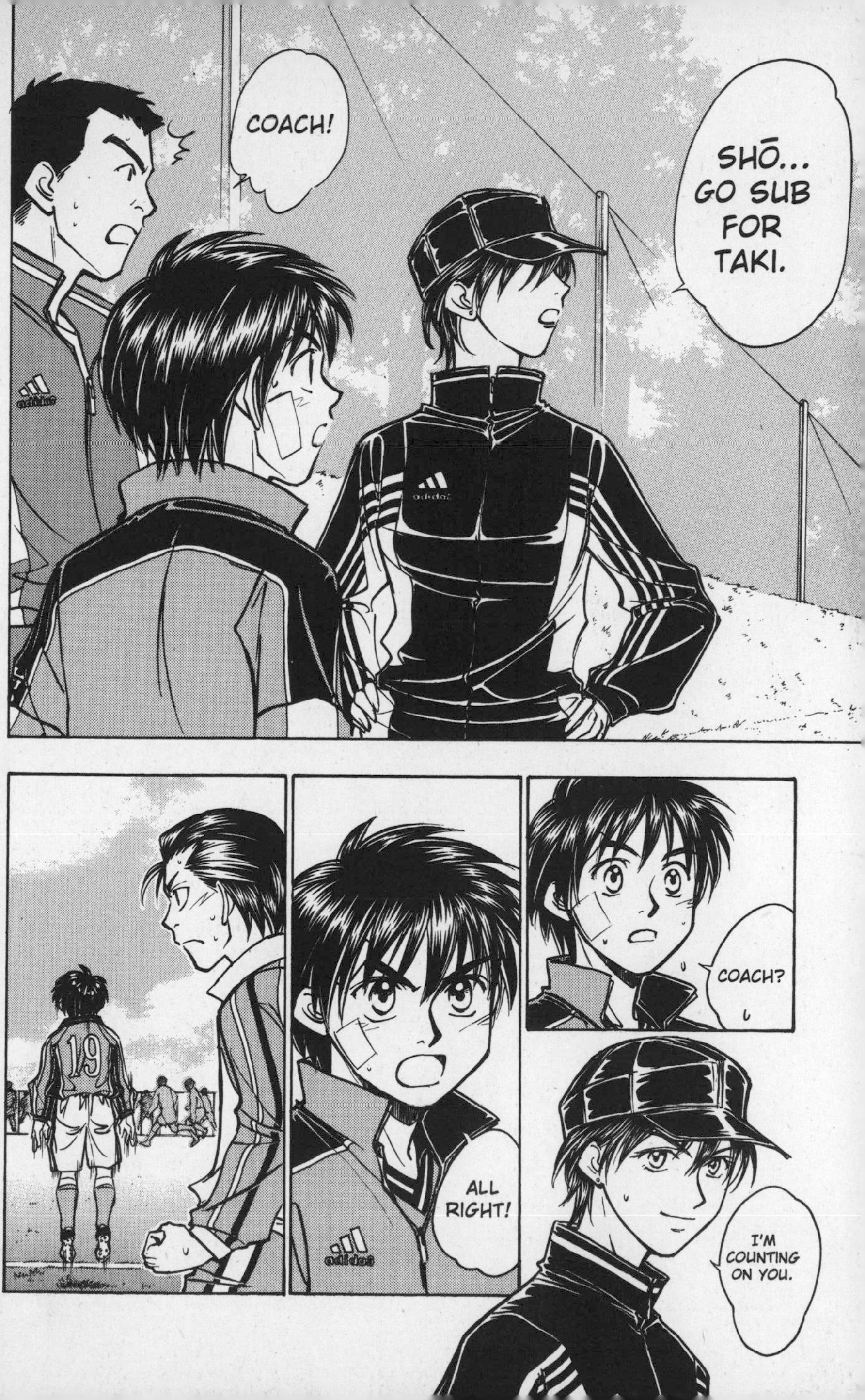
SHŌ... GO SUB FOR TAKI.
COACH!
COACH?
I'M COUNTING ON YOU.
ALL RIGHT!

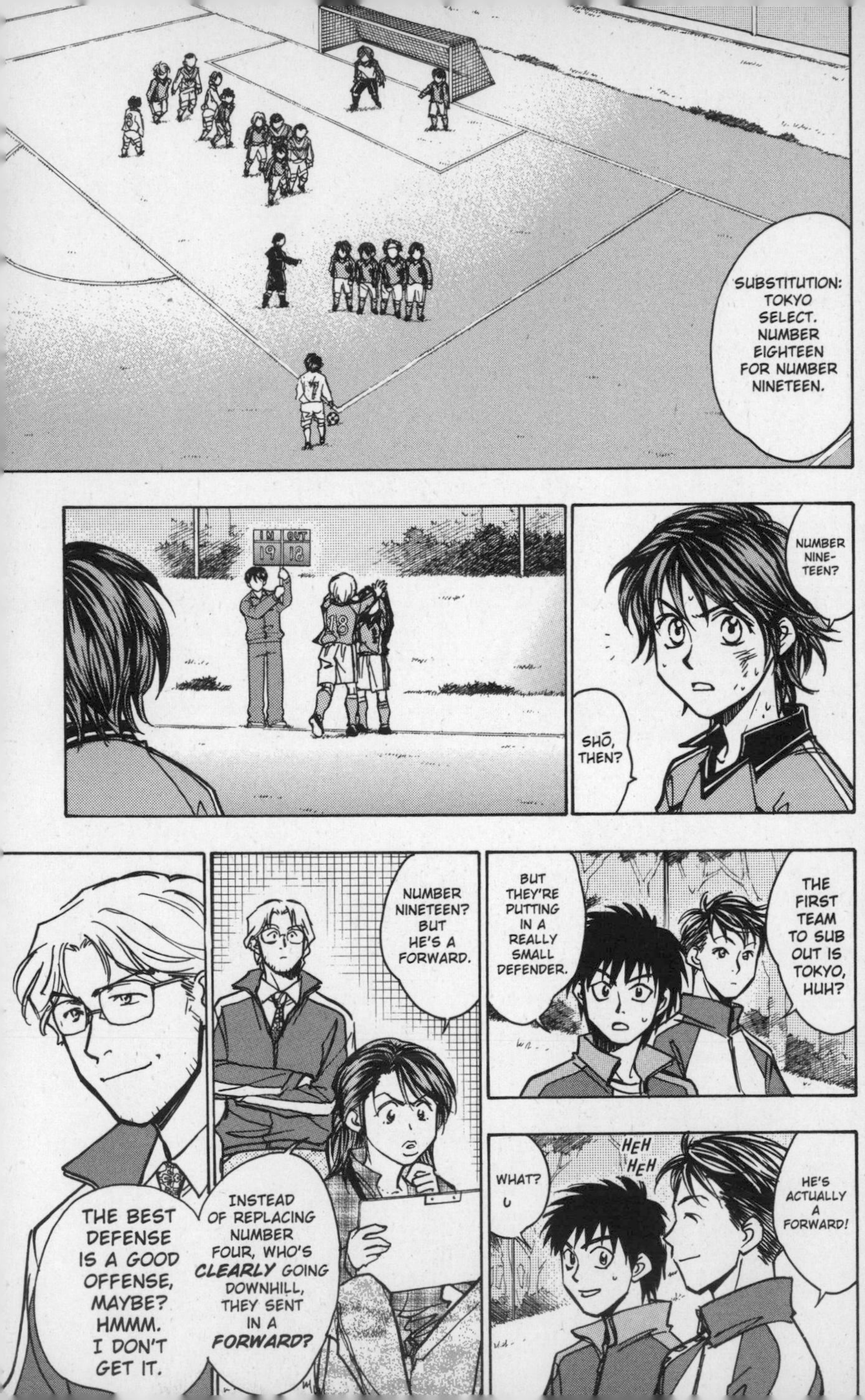
SUBSTITUTION: TOKYO SELECT. NUMBER EIGHTEEN FOR NUMBER NINETEEN.
NUMBER NINE-TEEN?
SHŌ, THEN?
IN OUT
19 18
THE FIRST TEAM TO SUB OUT IS TOKYO, HUH?
BUT THEY'RE PUTTING IN A REALLY SMALL DEFENDER.
HE'S ACTUALLY A FORWARD!
HEH HEH
WHAT?
NUMBER NINETEEN? BUT HE'S A FORWARD.
INSTEAD OF REPLACING NUMBER FOUR, WHO'S *CLEARLY* GOING DOWNHILL, THEY SENT IN A *FORWARD?*
THE BEST DEFENSE IS A GOOD OFFENSE, MAYBE? HMMM. I DON'T GET IT.

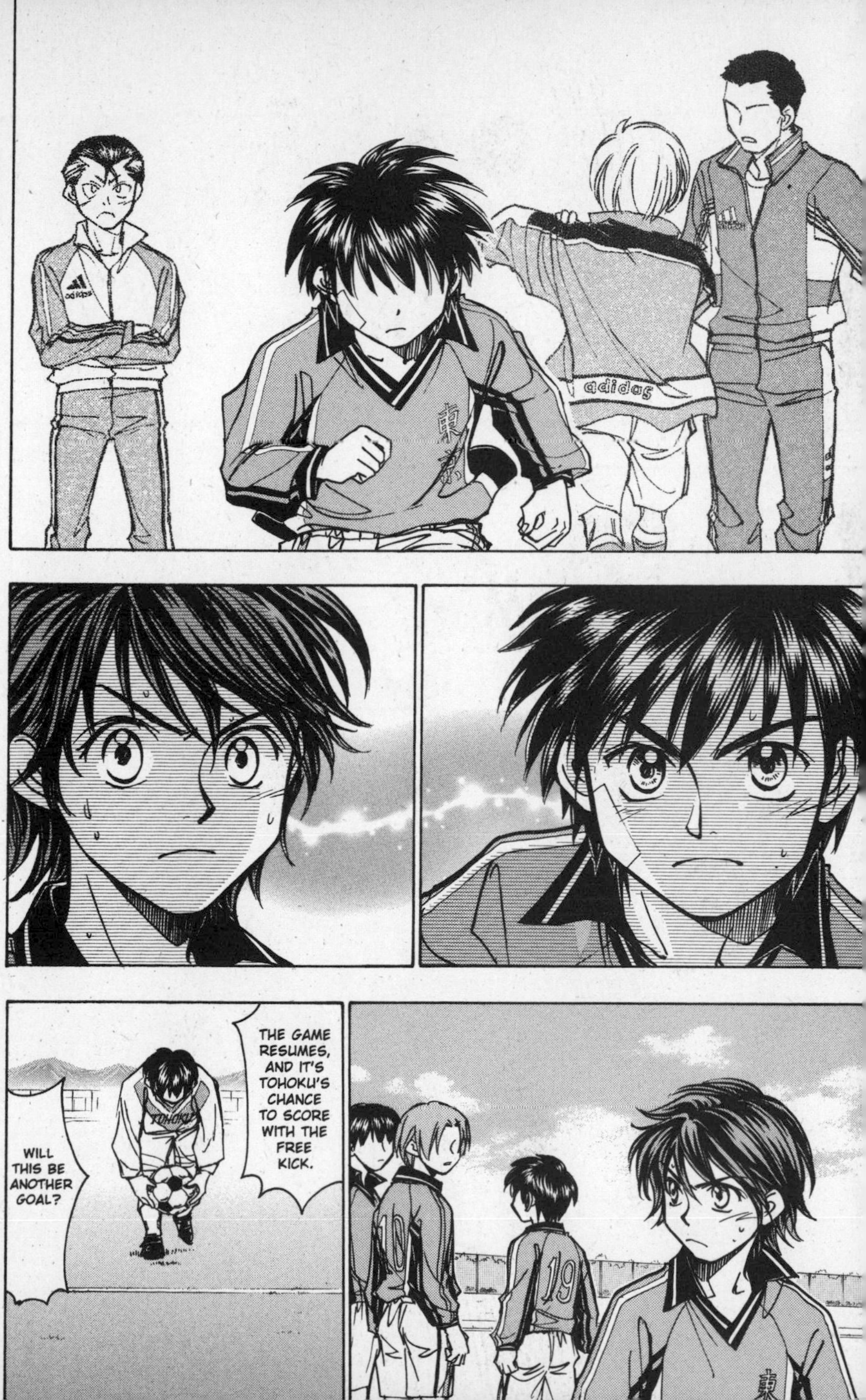
THE GAME RESUMES, AND IT'S TOHOKU'S CHANCE TO SCORE WITH THE FREE KICK.
WILL THIS BE ANOTHER GOAL?

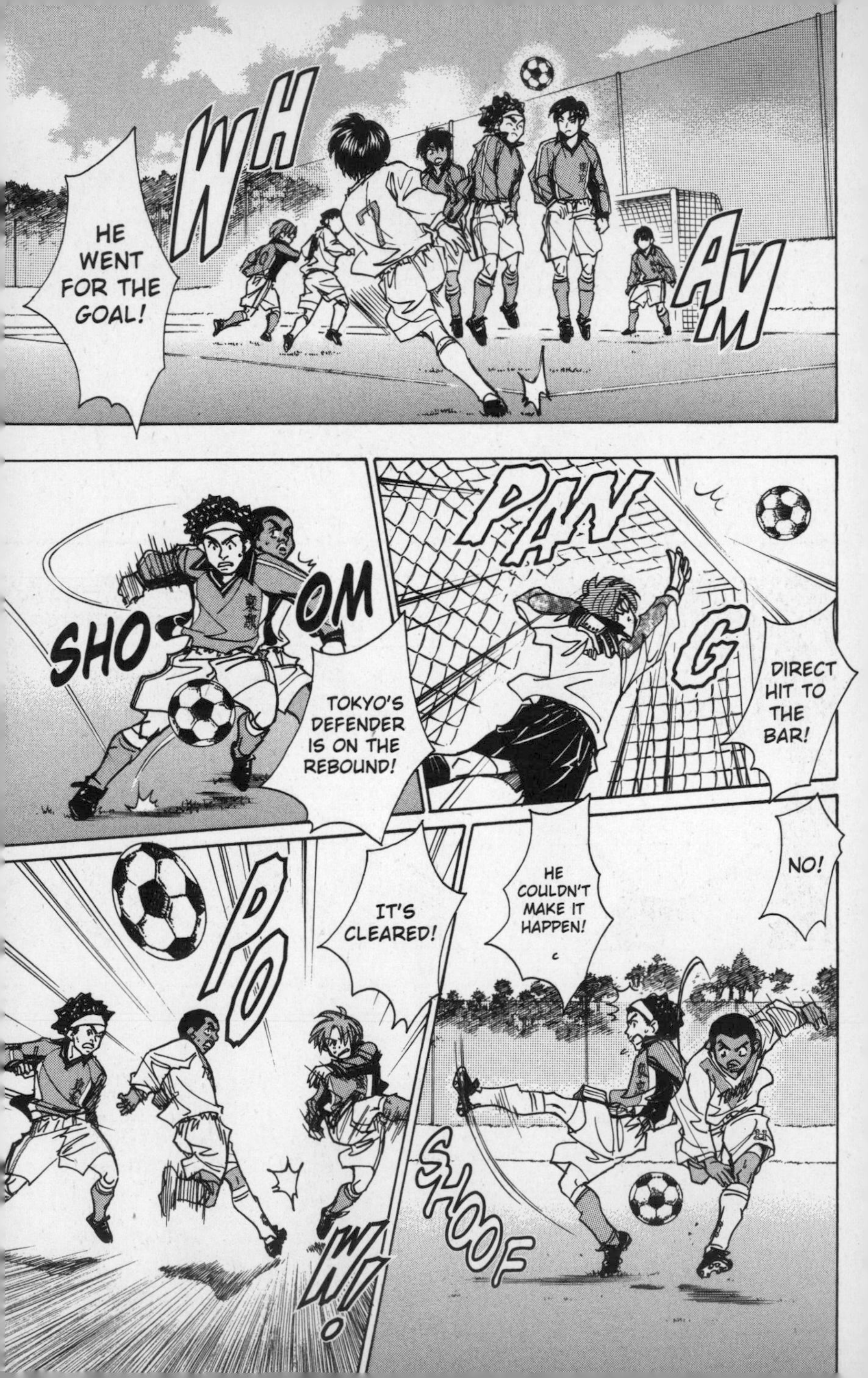
WH
AM
HE WENT FOR THE GOAL!
PAN
G
DIRECT HIT TO THE BAR!
SHO
OM
TOKYO'S DEFENDER IS ON THE REBOUND!
NO!
HE COULDN'T MAKE IT HAPPEN!
SHOOF
IT'S CLEARED!
PO
WH!

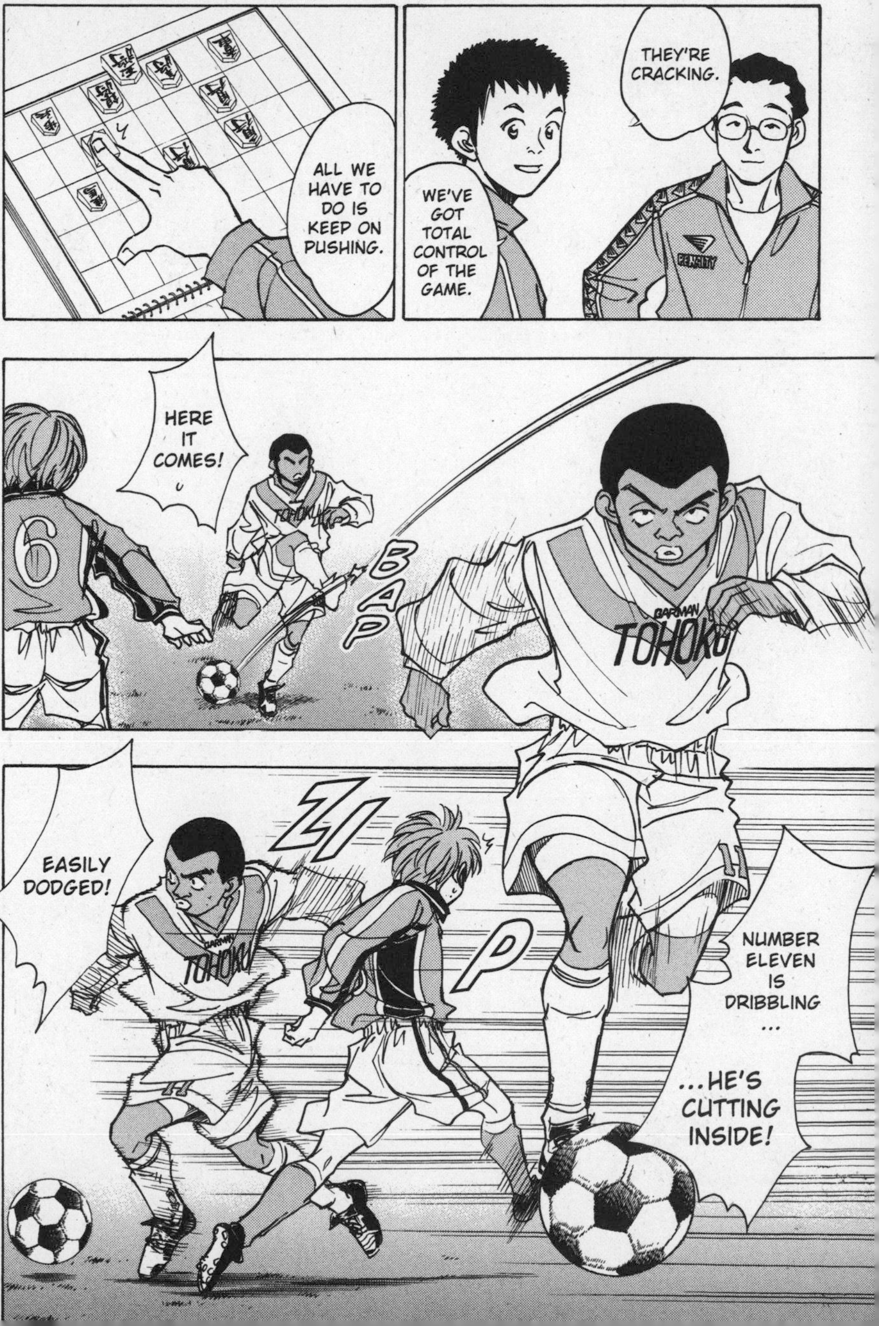
THEY'RE CRACKING.
WE'VE GOT TOTAL CONTROL OF THE GAME.
ALL WE HAVE TO DO IS KEEP ON PUSHING.
HERE IT COMES!
BAP
TOHOKU
NUMBER ELEVEN IS DRIBBLING...
...HE'S CUTTING INSIDE!
ZIP
EASILY DODGED!

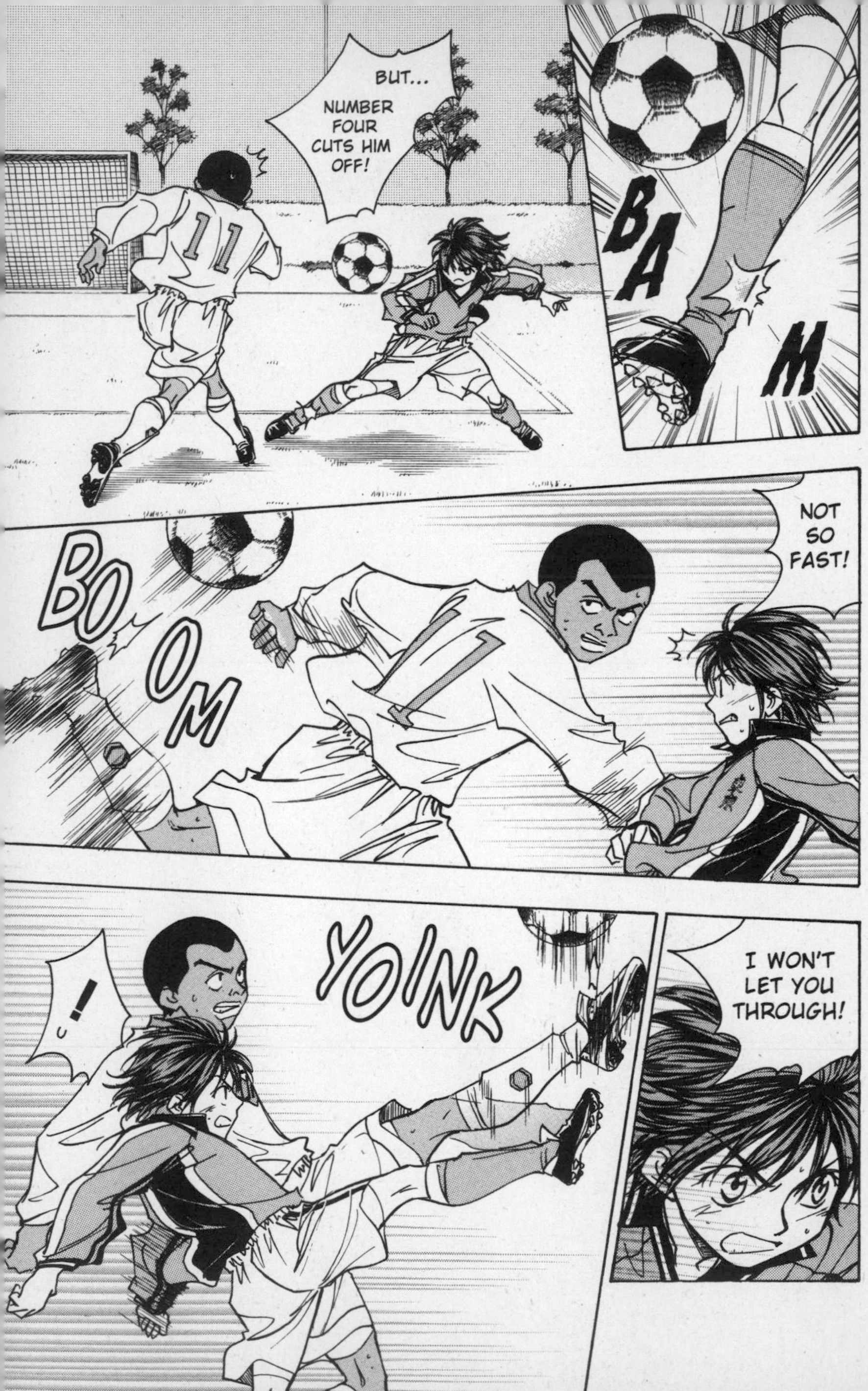
BAM
BUT...
NUMBER FOUR CUTS HIM OFF!
NOT SO FAST!
BOOM
I WON'T LET YOU THROUGH!
YOINK
!

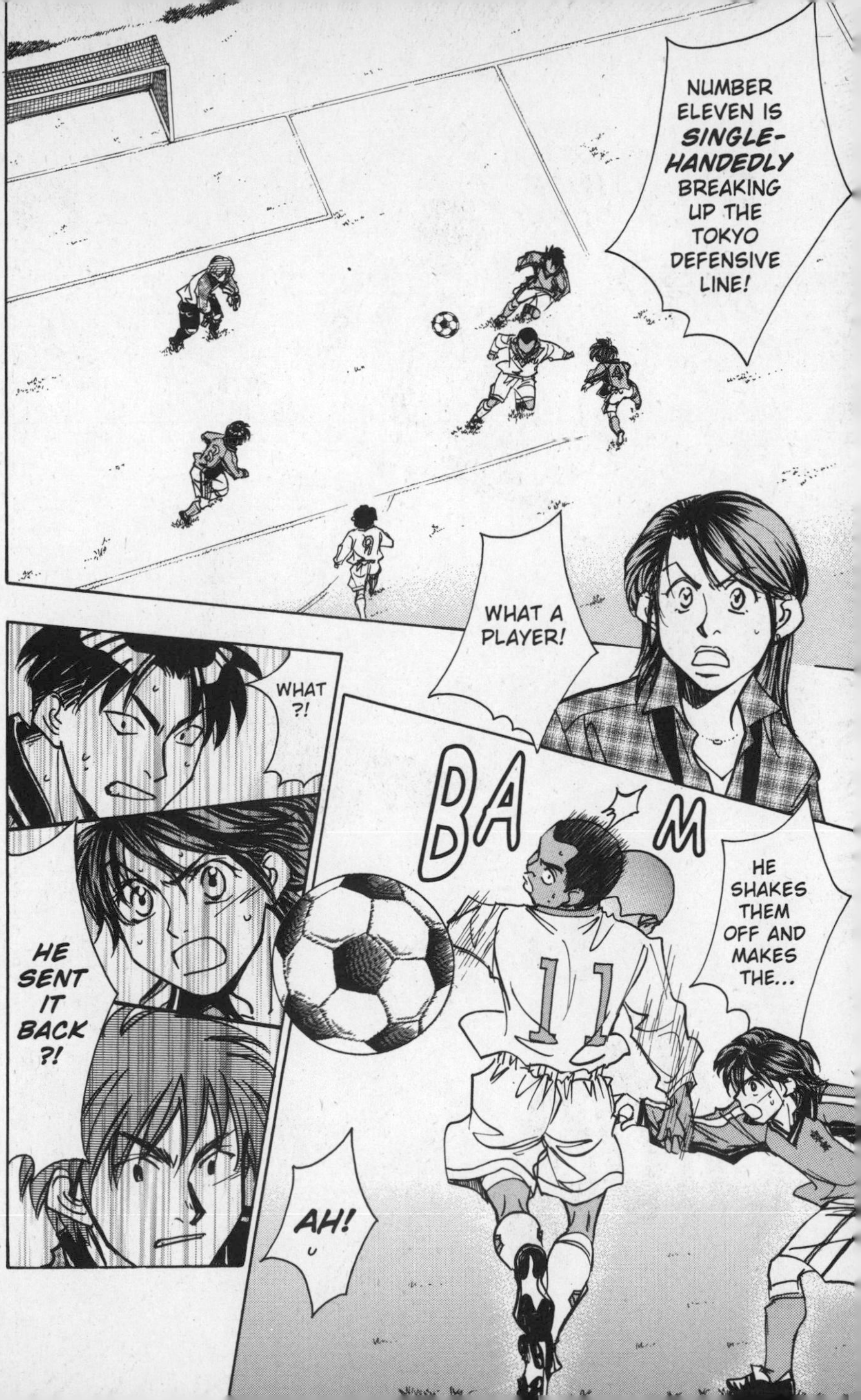
NUMBER ELEVEN IS SINGLE-HANDEDLY BREAKING UP THE TOKYO DEFENSIVE LINE!
WHAT A PLAYER!
BAM
HE SHAKES THEM OFF AND MAKES THE...
AH!
WHAT ?!
HE SENT IT BACK ?!

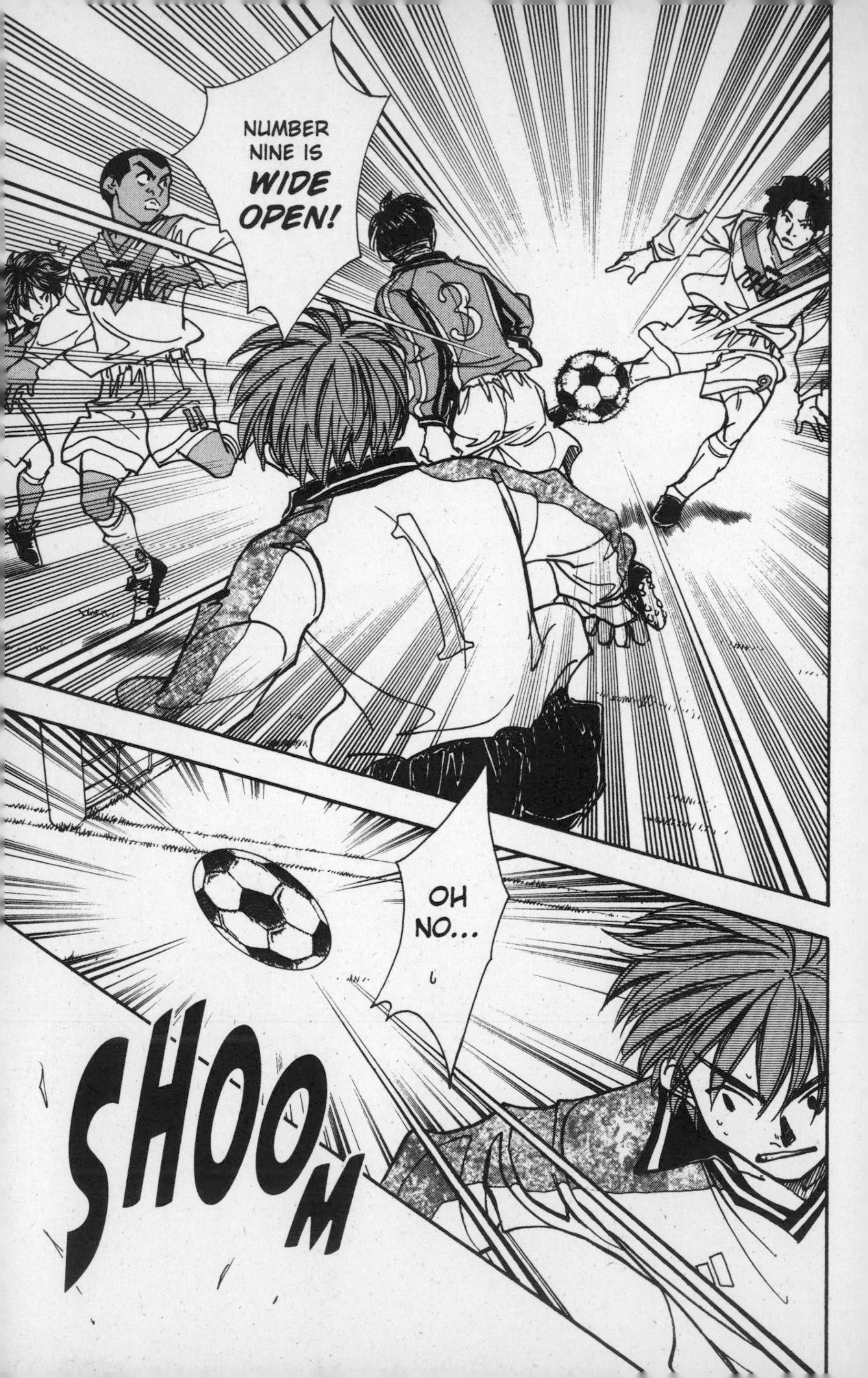
NUMBER NINE IS WIDE OPEN!
OH NO...
SHOOM

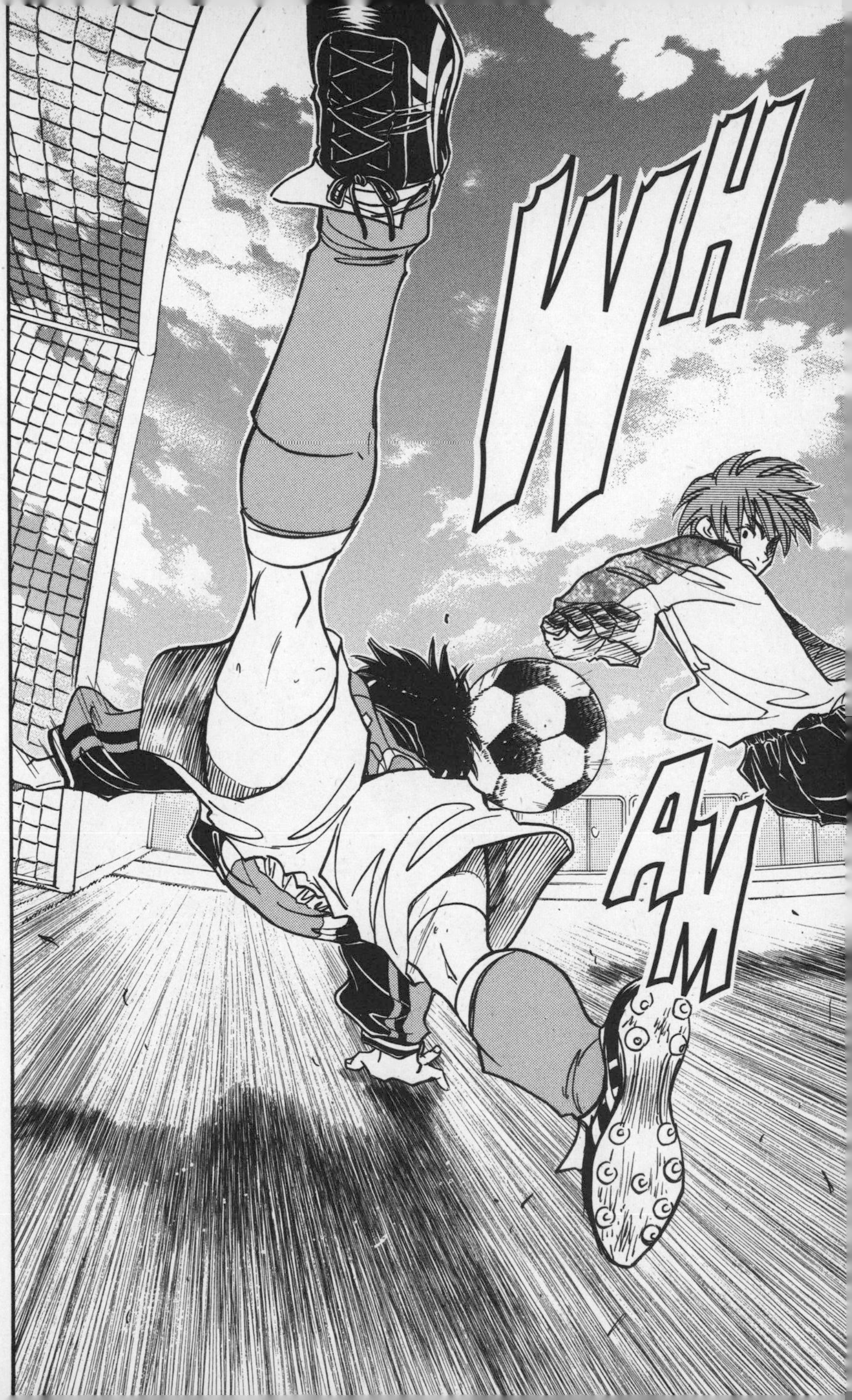
WHAMM

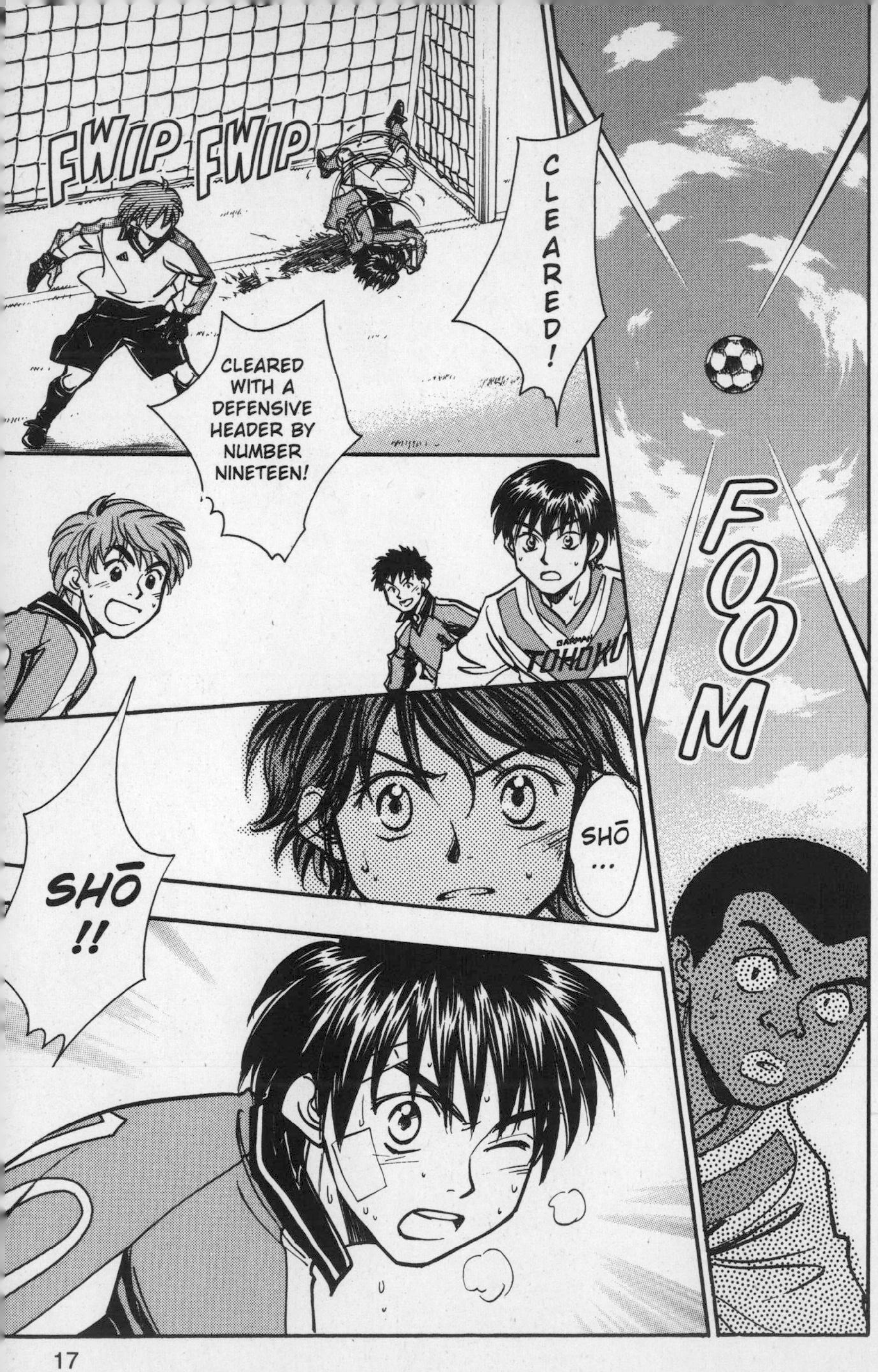

FOOM
CLEARED!
FWIP FWIP
CLEARED WITH A DEFENSIVE HEADER BY NUMBER NINETEEN!
TOHOKU
SHŌ ...
SHŌ !!

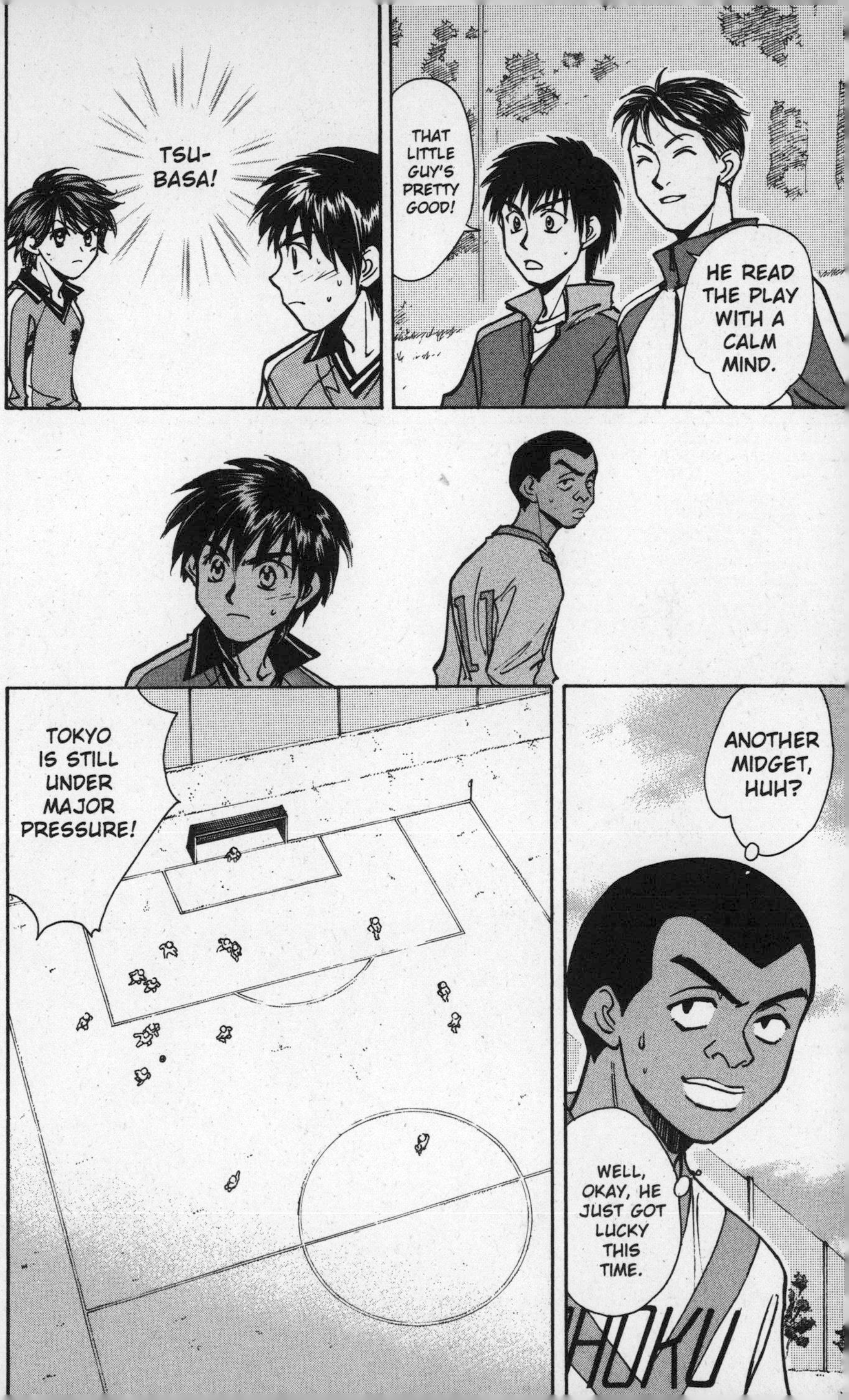
THAT LITTLE GUY'S PRETTY GOOD!
HE READ THE PLAY WITH A CALM MIND.
TSU-BASA!
ANOTHER MIDGET, HUH?
WELL, OKAY, HE JUST GOT LUCKY THIS TIME.
TOKYO IS STILL UNDER MAJOR PRESSURE!

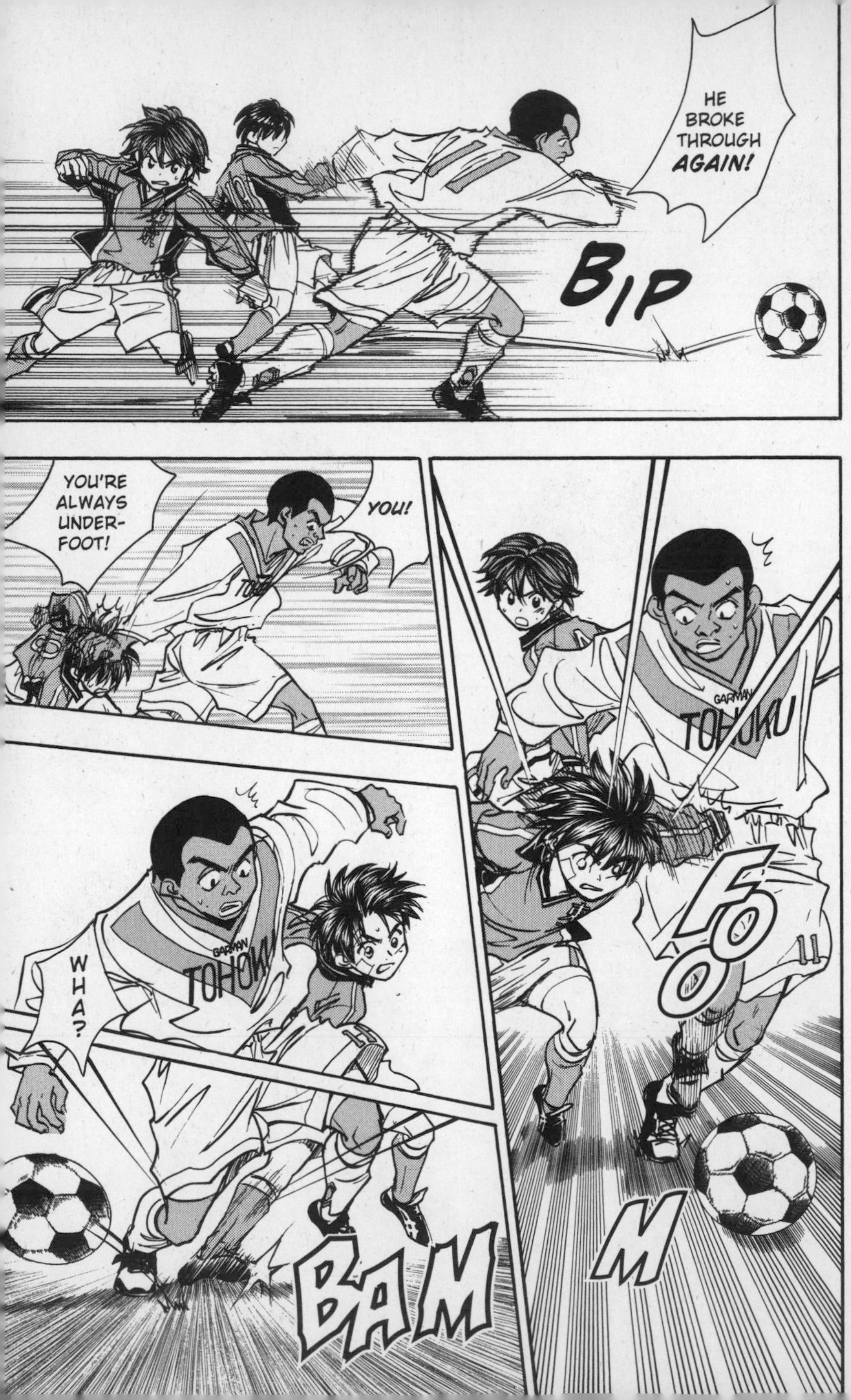
HE BROKE THROUGH AGAIN!
BIP
M
YOU!
YOU'RE ALWAYS UNDER-FOOT!
WHA?
BAM

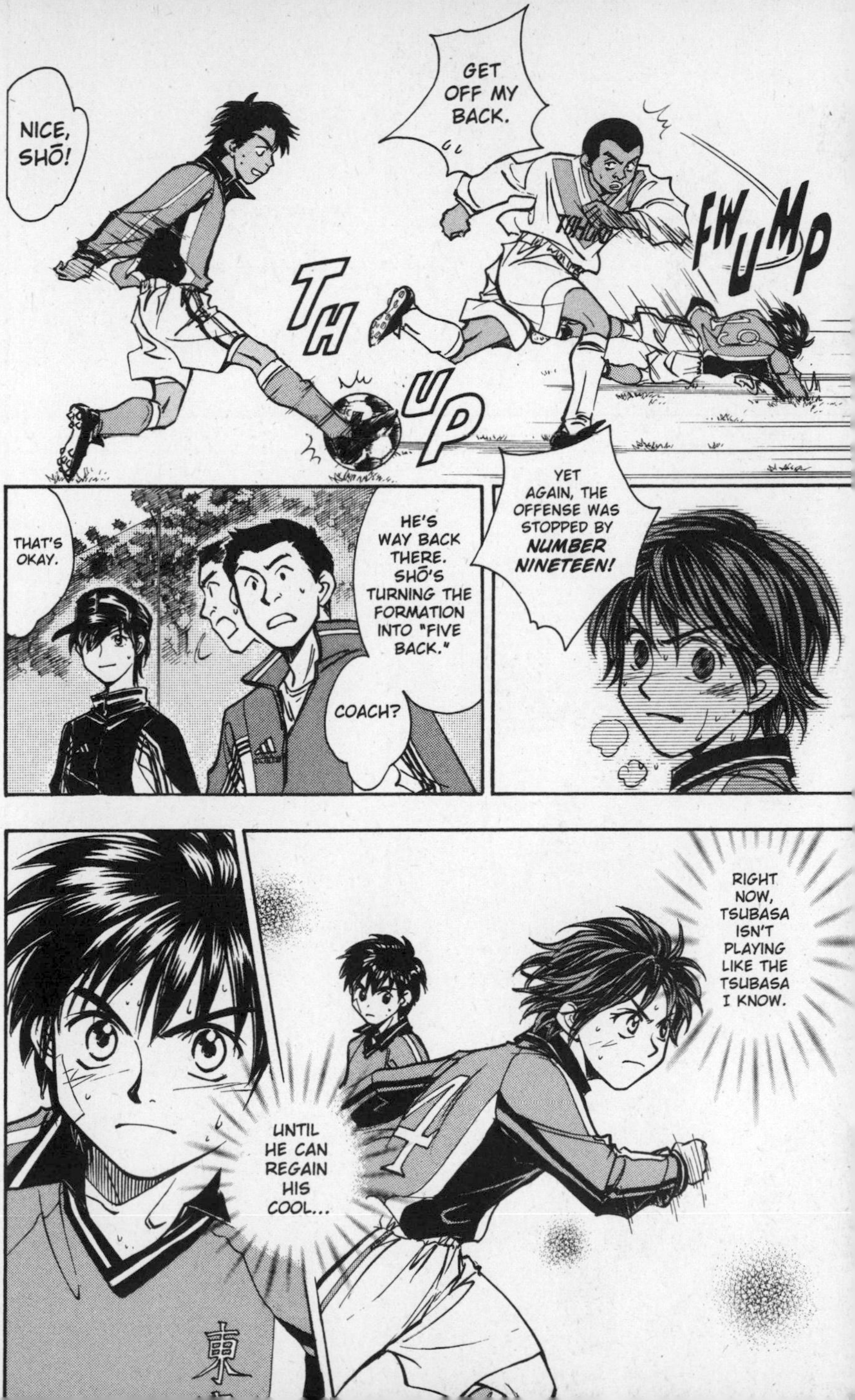
GET OFF MY BACK.
FWUMP
THUP
NICE, SHŌ!
YET AGAIN, THE OFFENSE WAS STOPPED BY **NUMBER NINETEEN!**
HE'S WAY BACK THERE. SHŌ'S TURNING THE FORMATION INTO "FIVE BACK."
COACH?
THAT'S OKAY.
RIGHT NOW, TSUBASA ISN'T PLAYING LIKE THE TSUBASA I KNOW.
UNTIL HE CAN REGAIN HIS COOL...

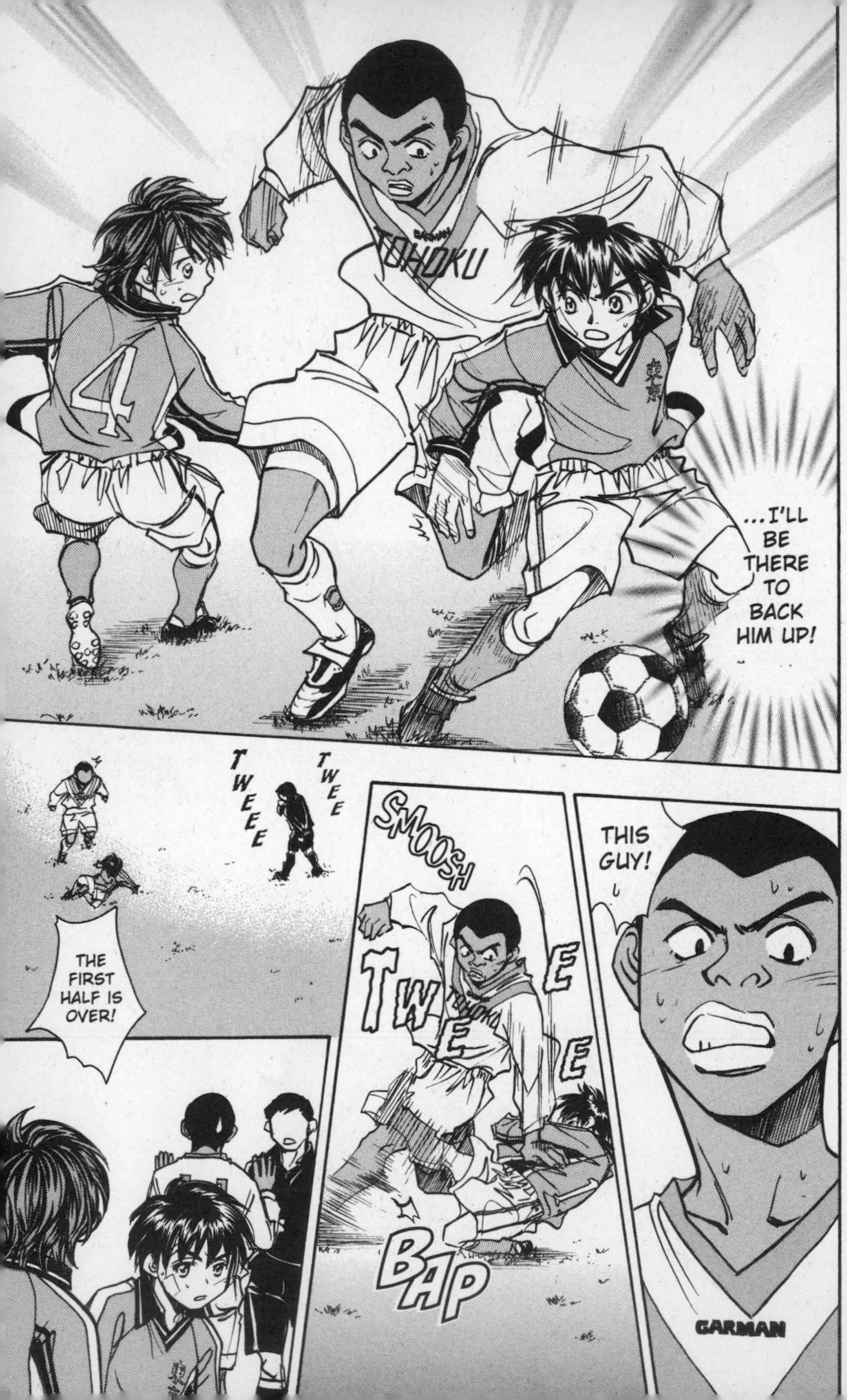
TOHOKU
...I'LL BE THERE TO BACK HIM UP!
THIS GUY!
GARMAN
SMOOSH
TWEEEE
TOHOKU
BAP
TWEEE
TWEEE
THE FIRST HALF IS OVER!

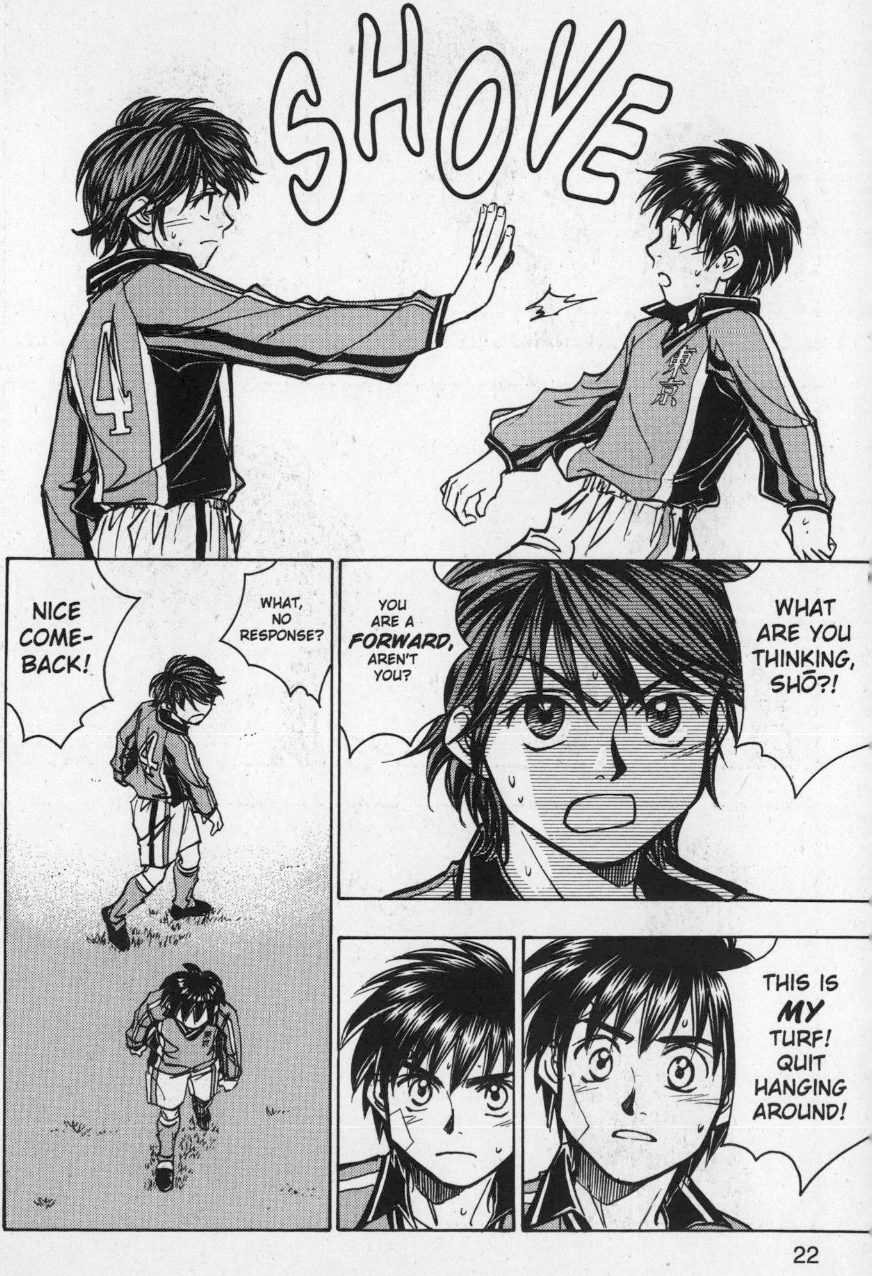
SHOVE
WHAT ARE YOU THINKING, SHŌ?!
YOU ARE A FORWARD, AREN'T YOU?
THIS IS MY TURF! QUIT HANGING AROUND!
WHAT, NO RESPONSE?
NICE COME-BACK!

READ THIS WAY

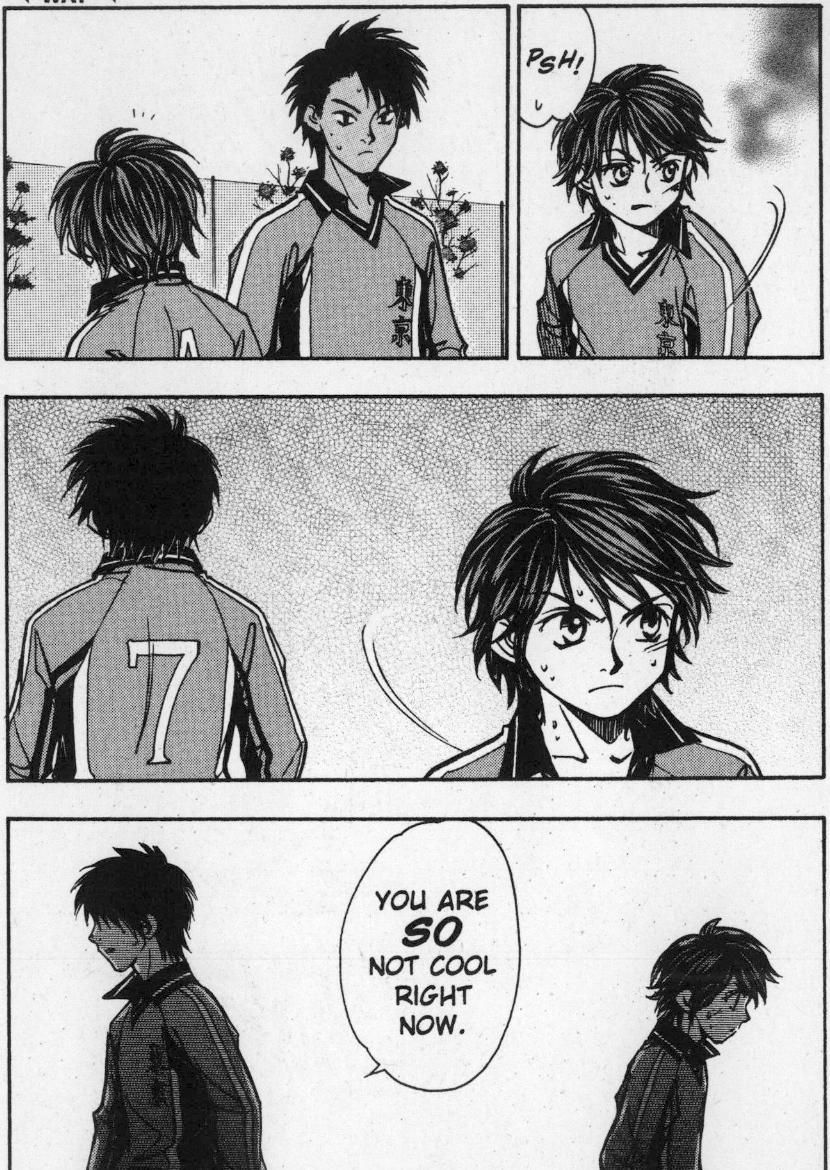
PSH!
YOU ARE SO NOT COOL RIGHT NOW.

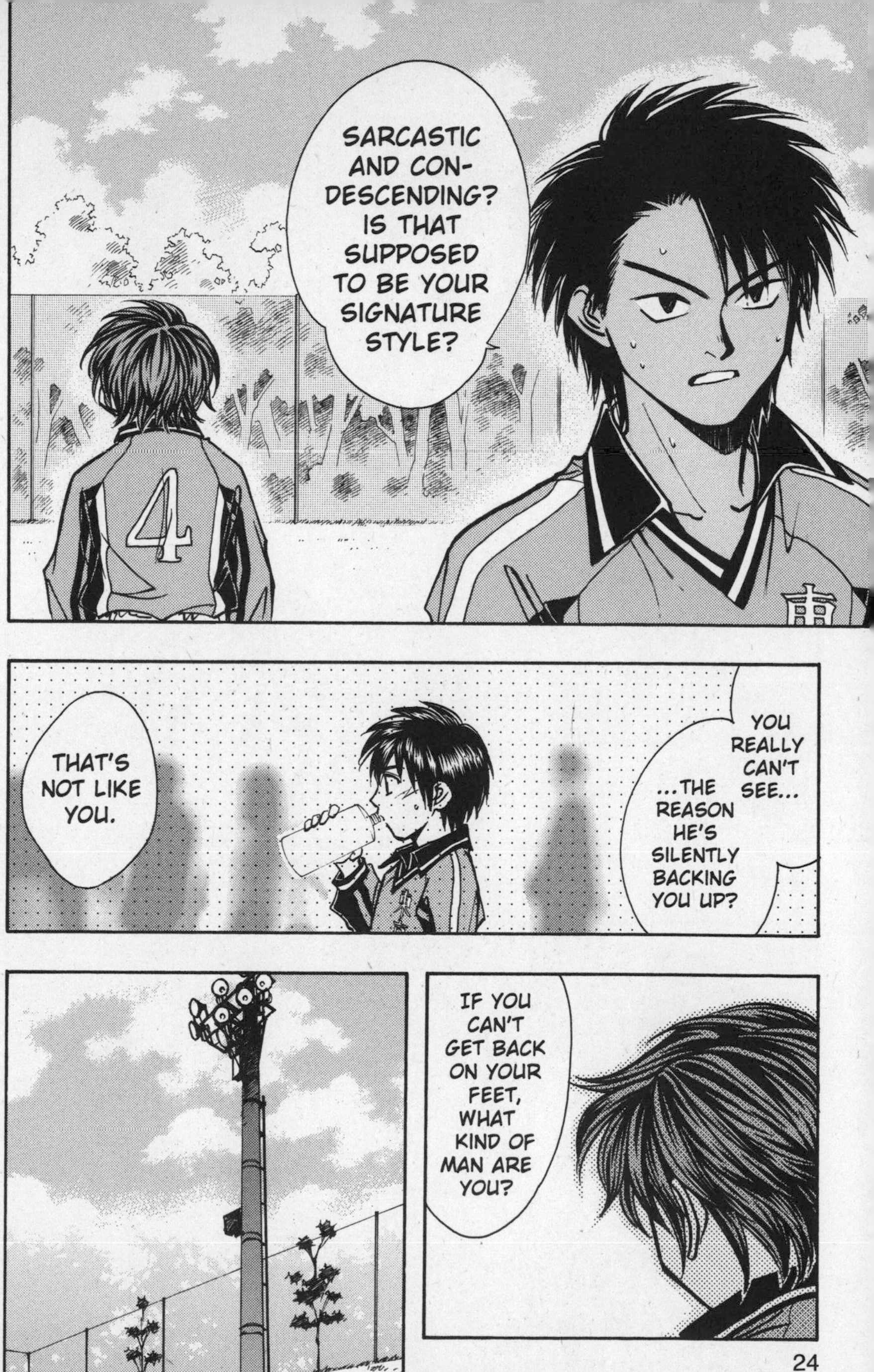
SARCASTIC AND CON-DESCENDING? IS THAT SUPPOSED TO BE YOUR SIGNATURE STYLE?
YOU REALLY CAN'T SEE...
...THE REASON HE'S SILENTLY BACKING YOU UP?
THAT'S NOT LIKE YOU.
IF YOU CAN'T GET BACK ON YOUR FEET, WHAT KIND OF MAN ARE YOU?

READ THIS WAY

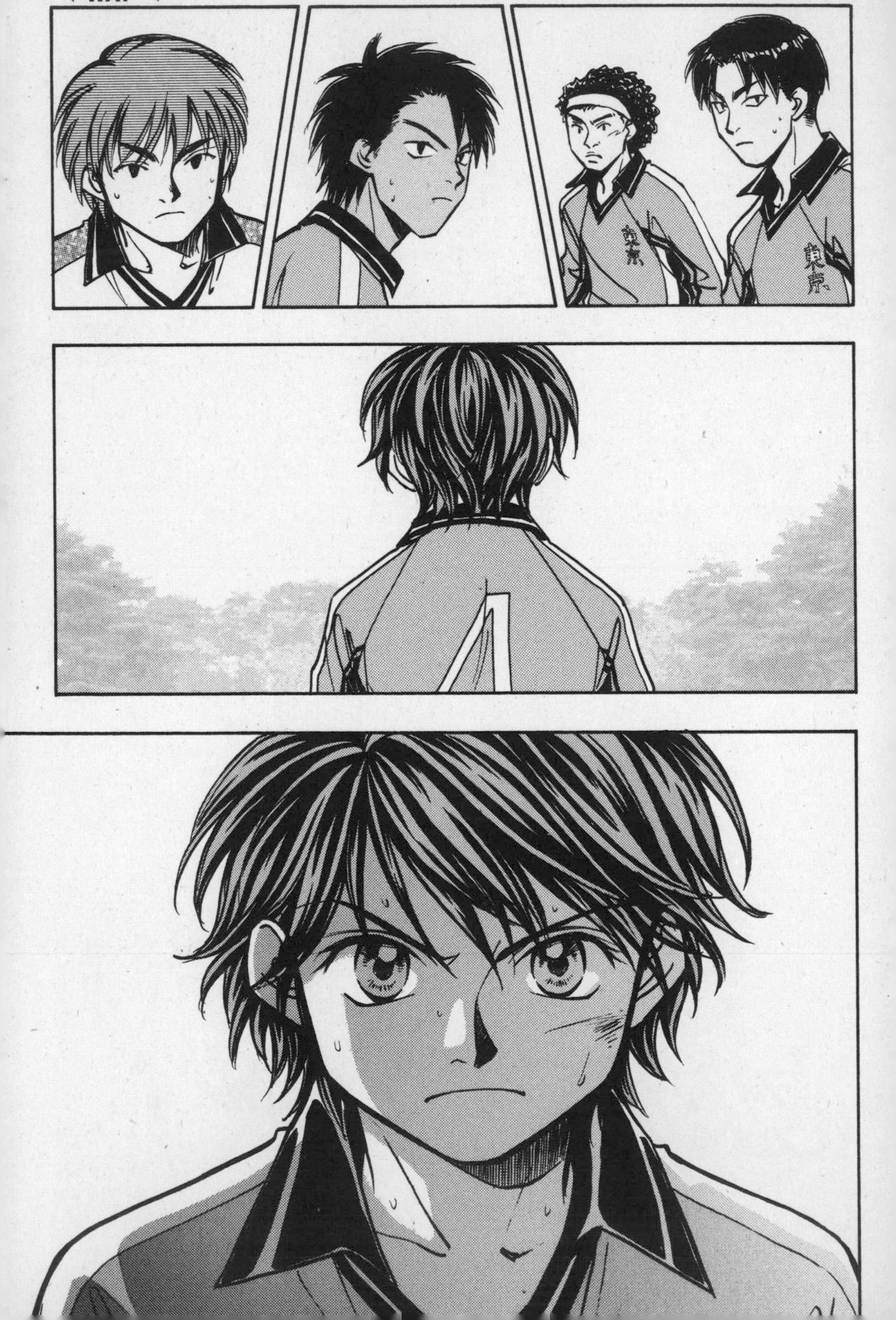
東京
東京

WHISTLE!

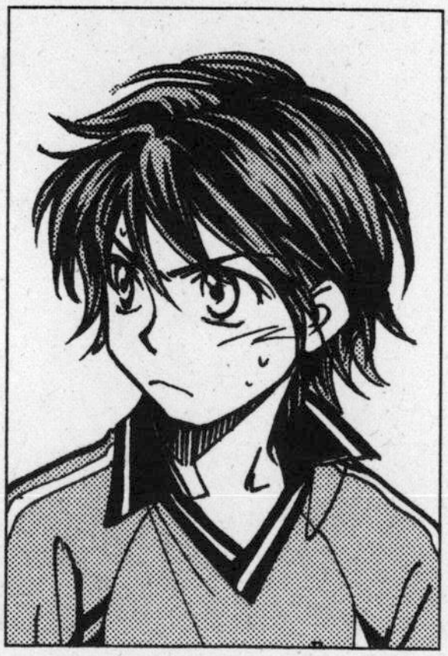

STAGE.184

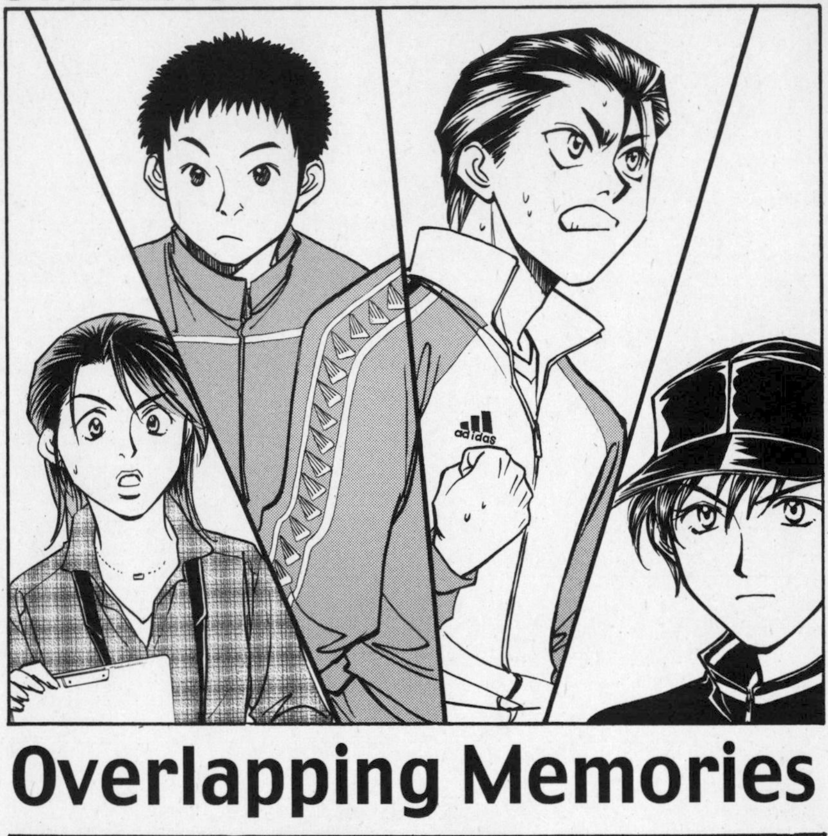

Overlapping Memories

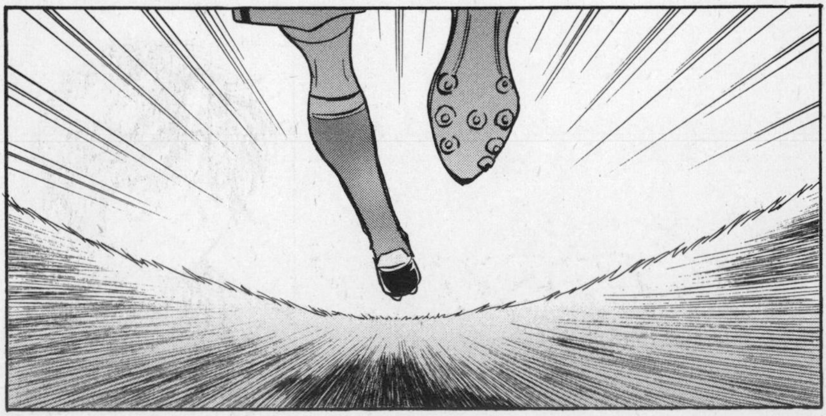

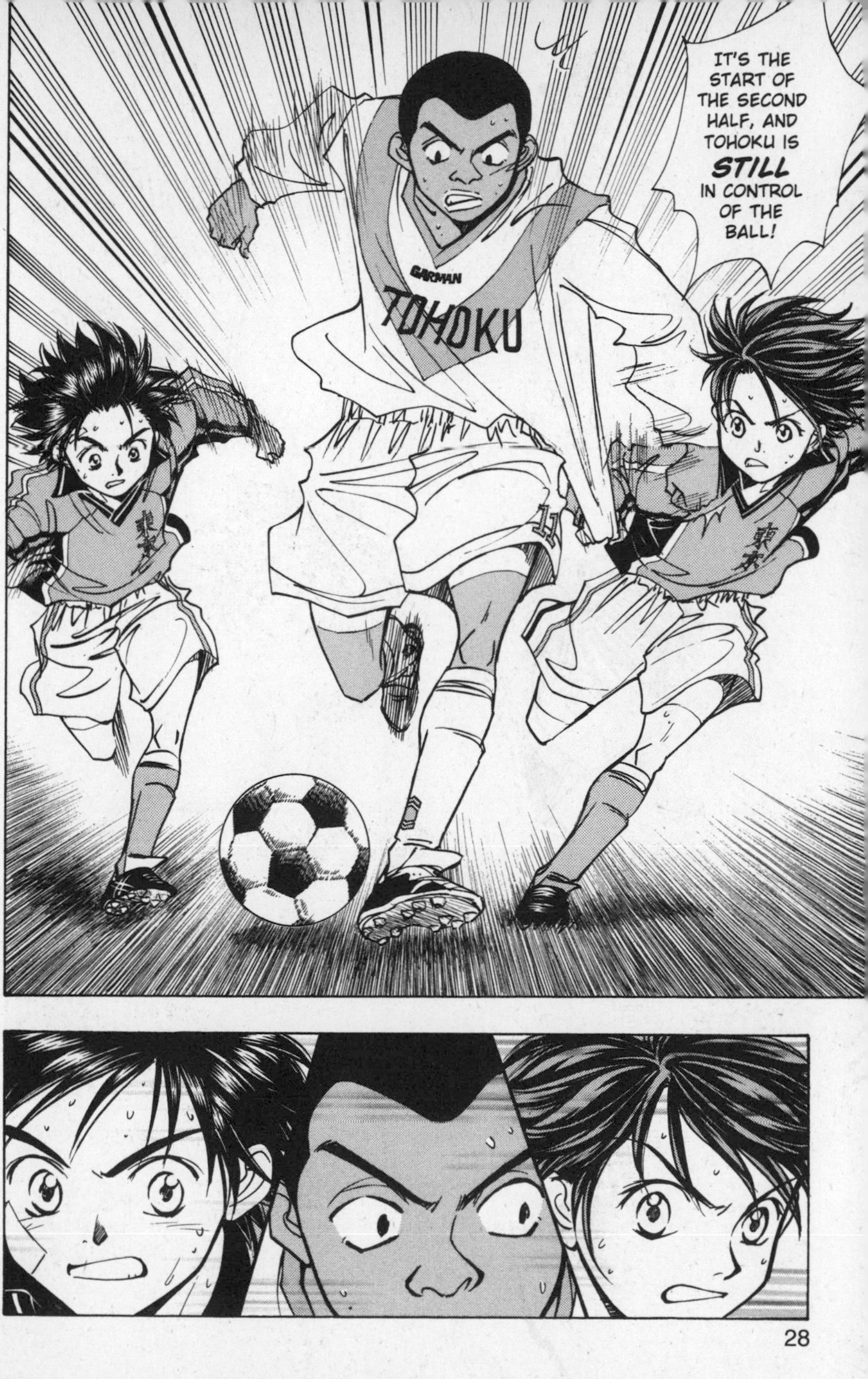
IT'S THE START OF THE SECOND HALF, AND TOHOKU IS **STILL** IN CONTROL OF THE BALL!
GARMAN
TOHOKU

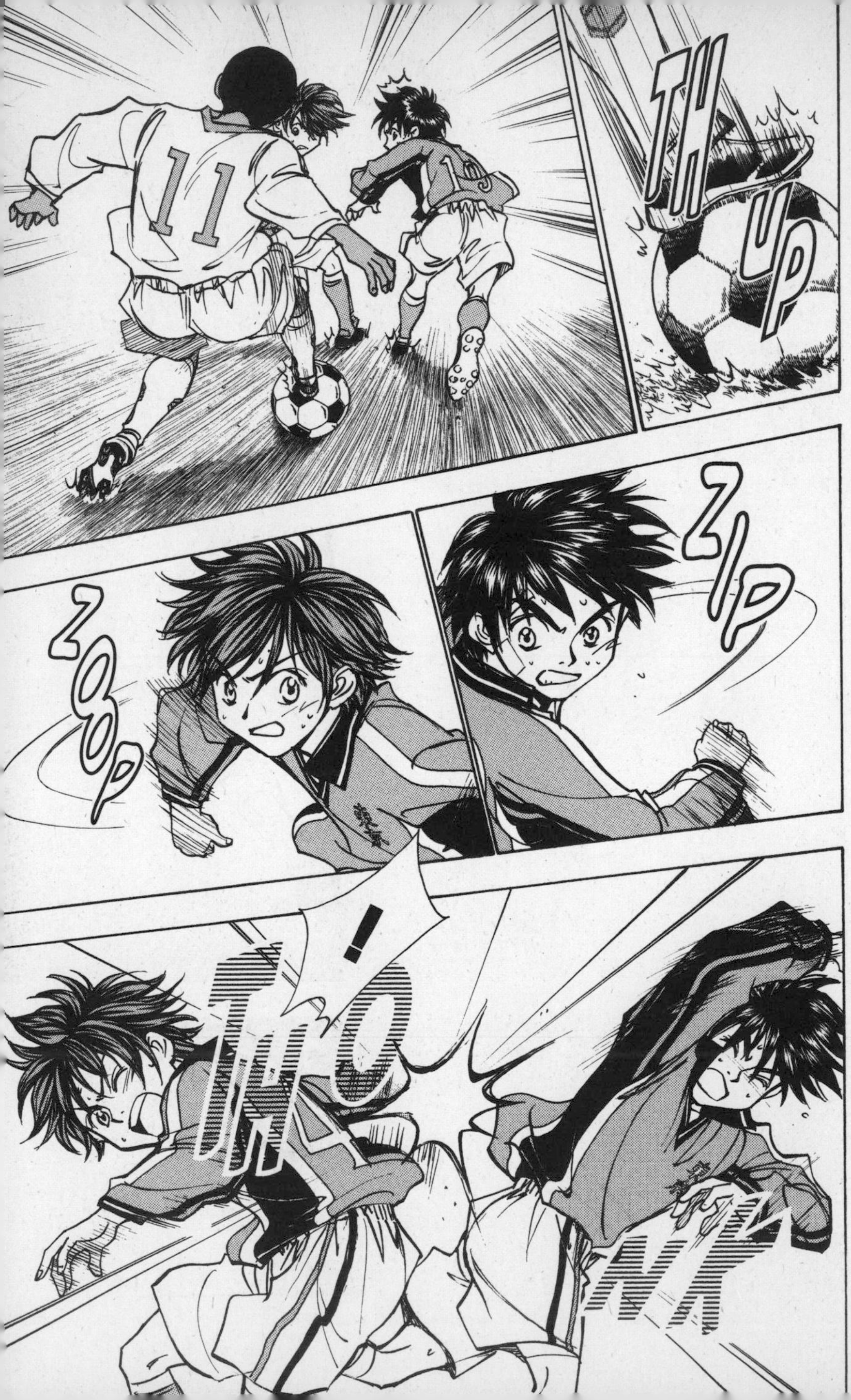
THUP
ZIP
ZOOP
!
THONK

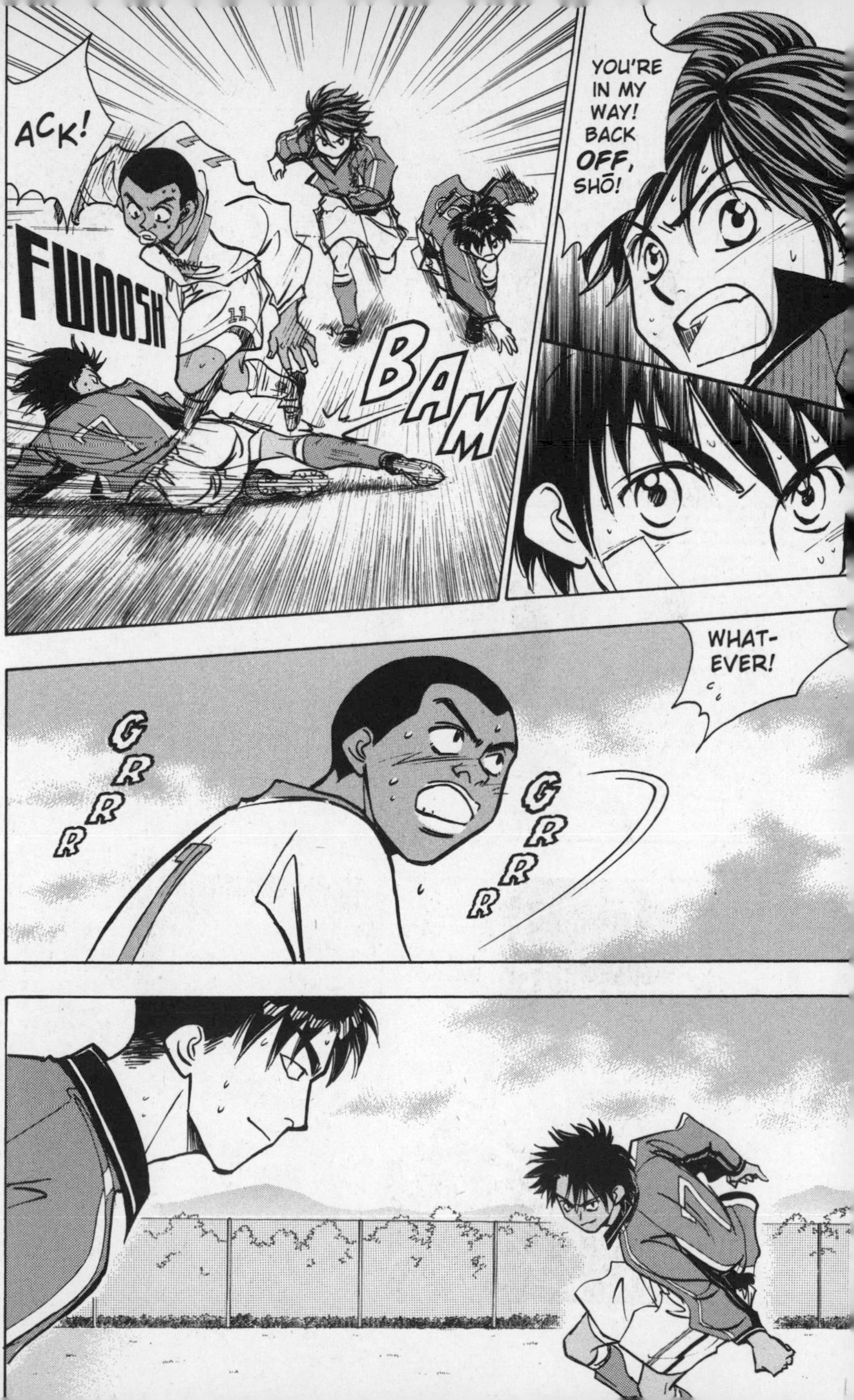
YOU'RE IN MY WAY! BACK OFF, SHŌ!
ACK!
BAM
FWOOSH
WHAT-EVER!
GRRRR
GRRRR

READ THIS WAY

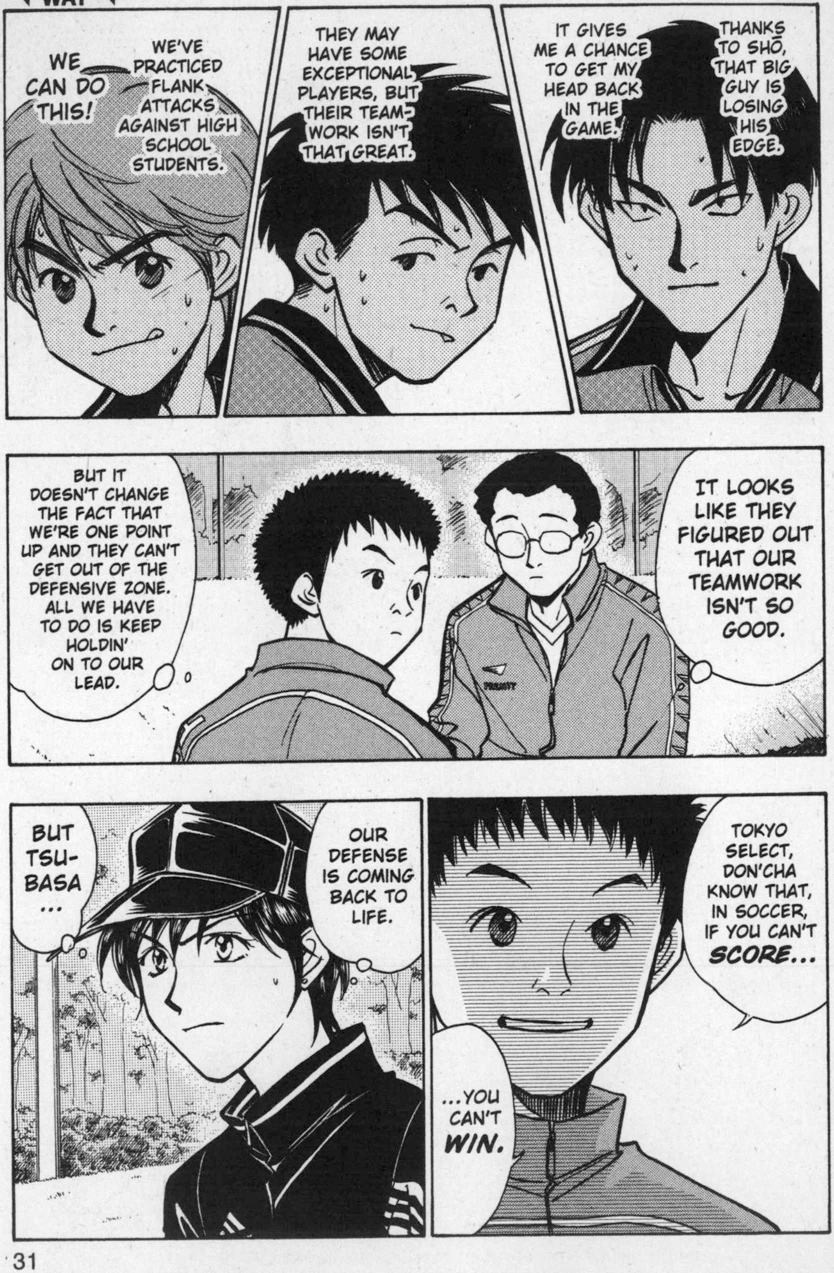
THANKS TO SHŌ, THAT BIG GUY IS LOSING HIS EDGE.
IT GIVES ME A CHANCE TO GET MY HEAD BACK IN THE GAME.
THEY MAY HAVE SOME EXCEPTIONAL PLAYERS, BUT THEIR TEAM-WORK ISN'T THAT GREAT.
WE'VE PRACTICED FLANK ATTACKS AGAINST HIGH SCHOOL STUDENTS.
WE CAN DO THIS!
IT LOOKS LIKE THEY FIGURED OUT THAT OUR TEAMWORK ISN'T SO GOOD.
BUT IT DOESN'T CHANGE THE FACT THAT WE'RE ONE POINT UP AND THEY CAN'T GET OUT OF THE DEFENSIVE ZONE. ALL WE HAVE TO DO IS KEEP HOLDIN' ON TO OUR LEAD.
TOKYO SELECT, DON'CHA KNOW THAT, IN SOCCER, IF YOU CAN'T SCORE...
...YOU CAN'T WIN.
OUR DEFENSE IS COMING BACK TO LIFE.
BUT TSU-BASA ...

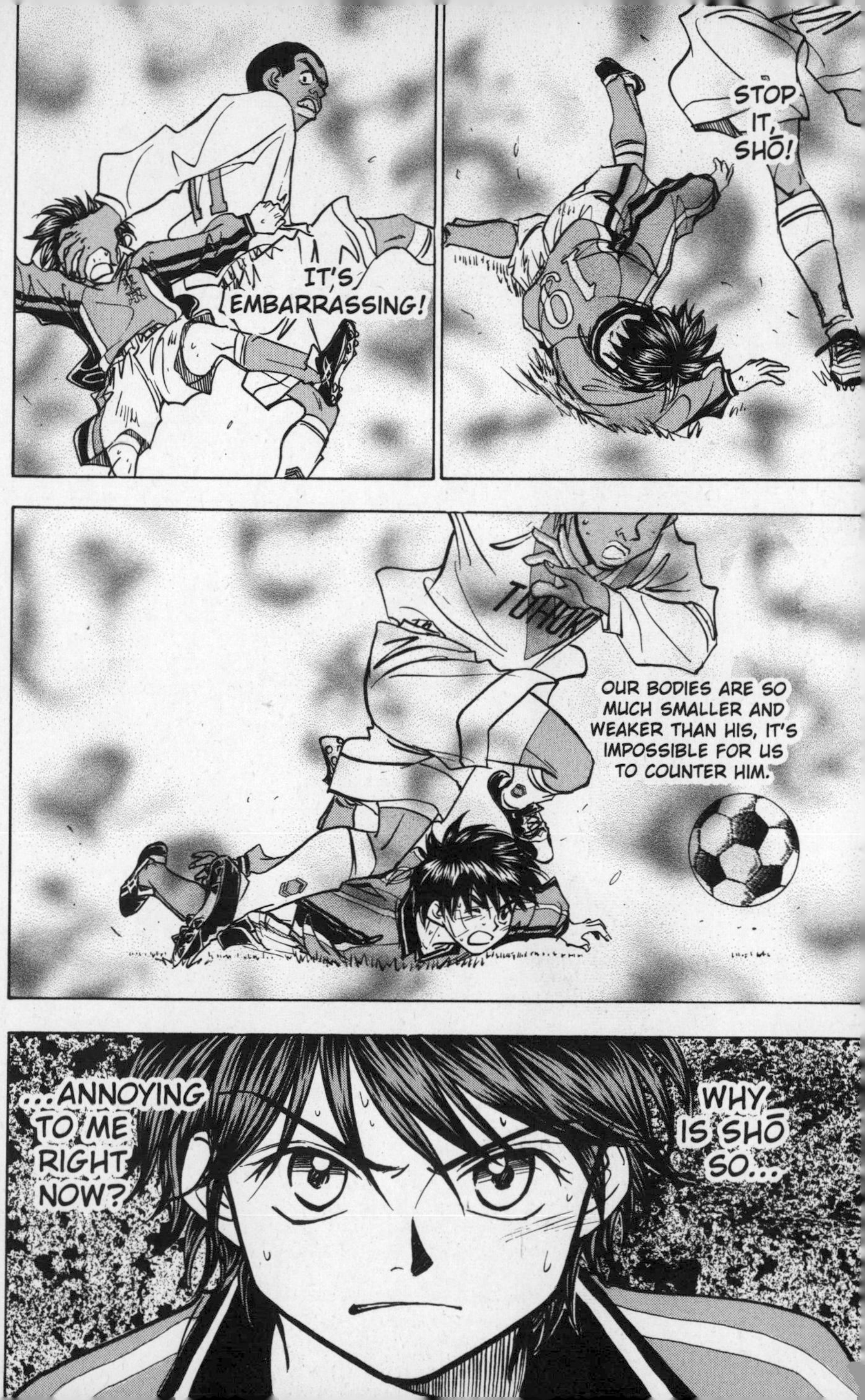
STOP IT, SHŌ!
IT'S EMBARRASSING!
OUR BODIES ARE SO MUCH SMALLER AND WEAKER THAN HIS, IT'S IMPOSSIBLE FOR US TO COUNTER HIM.
WHY IS SHŌ SO...
...ANNOYING TO ME RIGHT NOW?

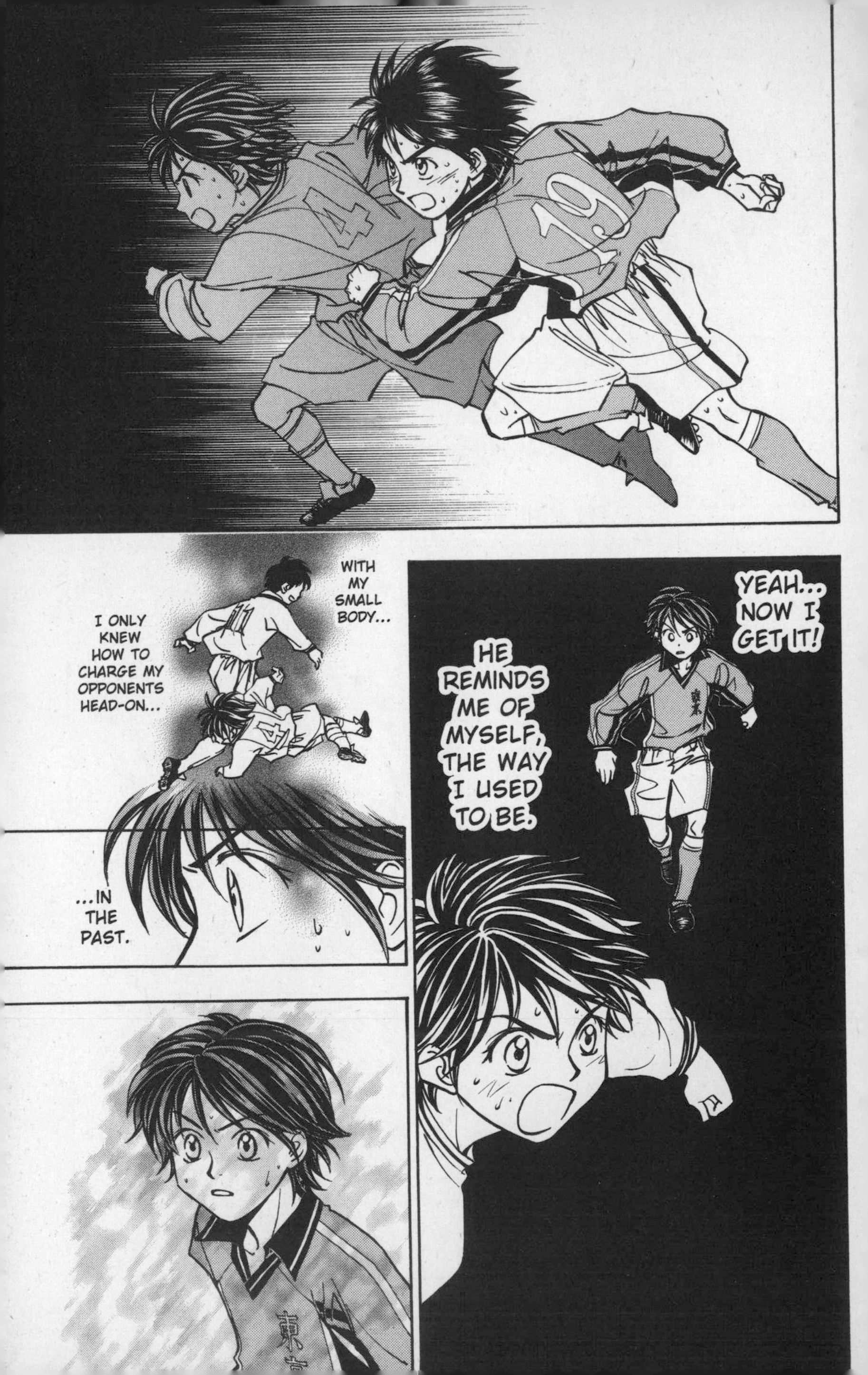
YEAH... NOW I GET IT!
HE REMINDS ME OF MYSELF, THE WAY I USED TO BE.
WITH MY SMALL BODY...
I ONLY KNEW HOW TO CHARGE MY OPPONENTS HEAD-ON...
...IN THE PAST.

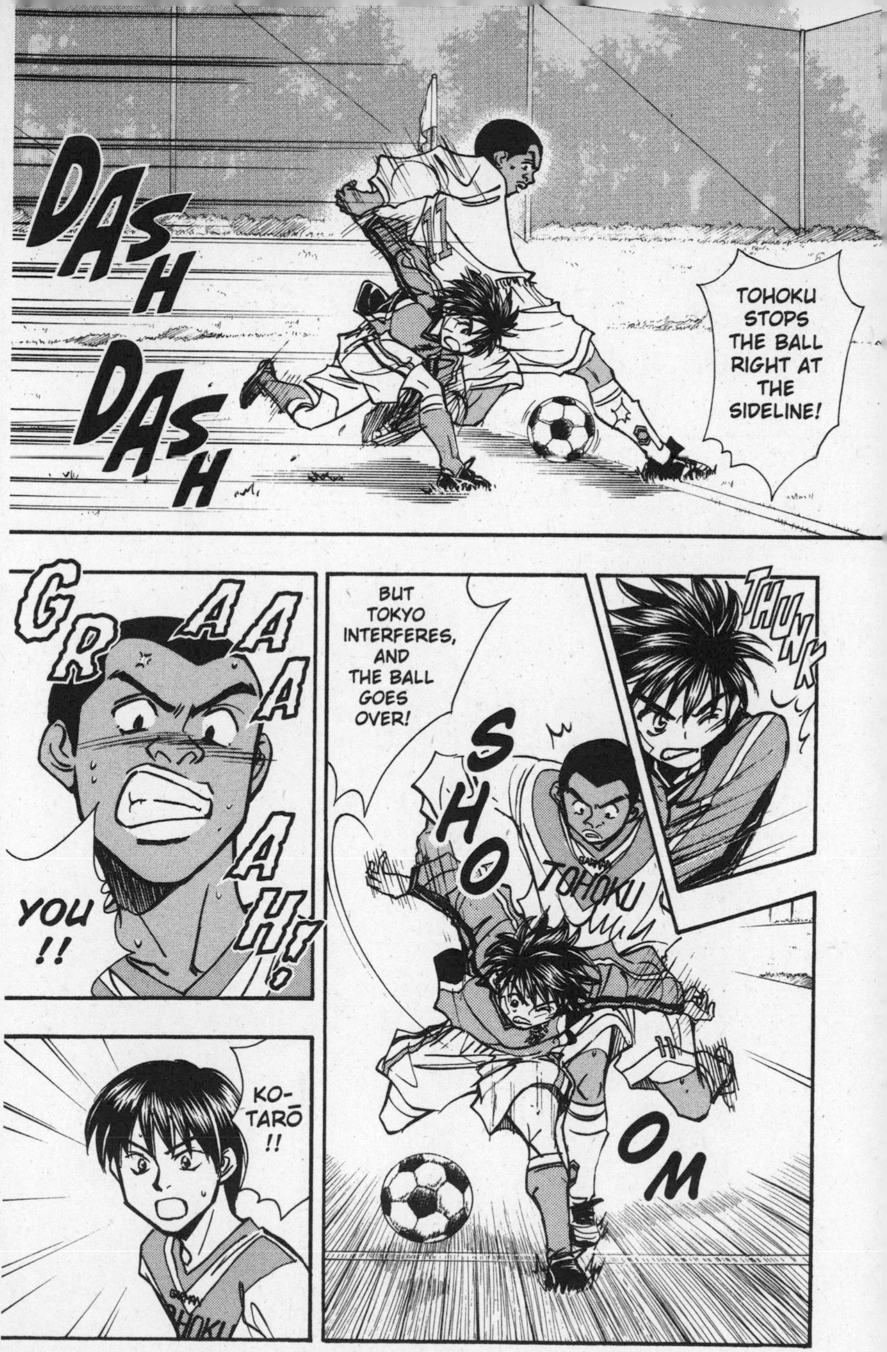
TOHOKU STOPS THE BALL RIGHT AT THE SIDELINE!
DASH
DASH
THUNK
BUT TOKYO INTERFERES, AND THE BALL GOES OVER!
SHO-OM
TOHOKU
GRAAAAAH!
YOU!!
KO-TARŌ!!

READ THIS WAY

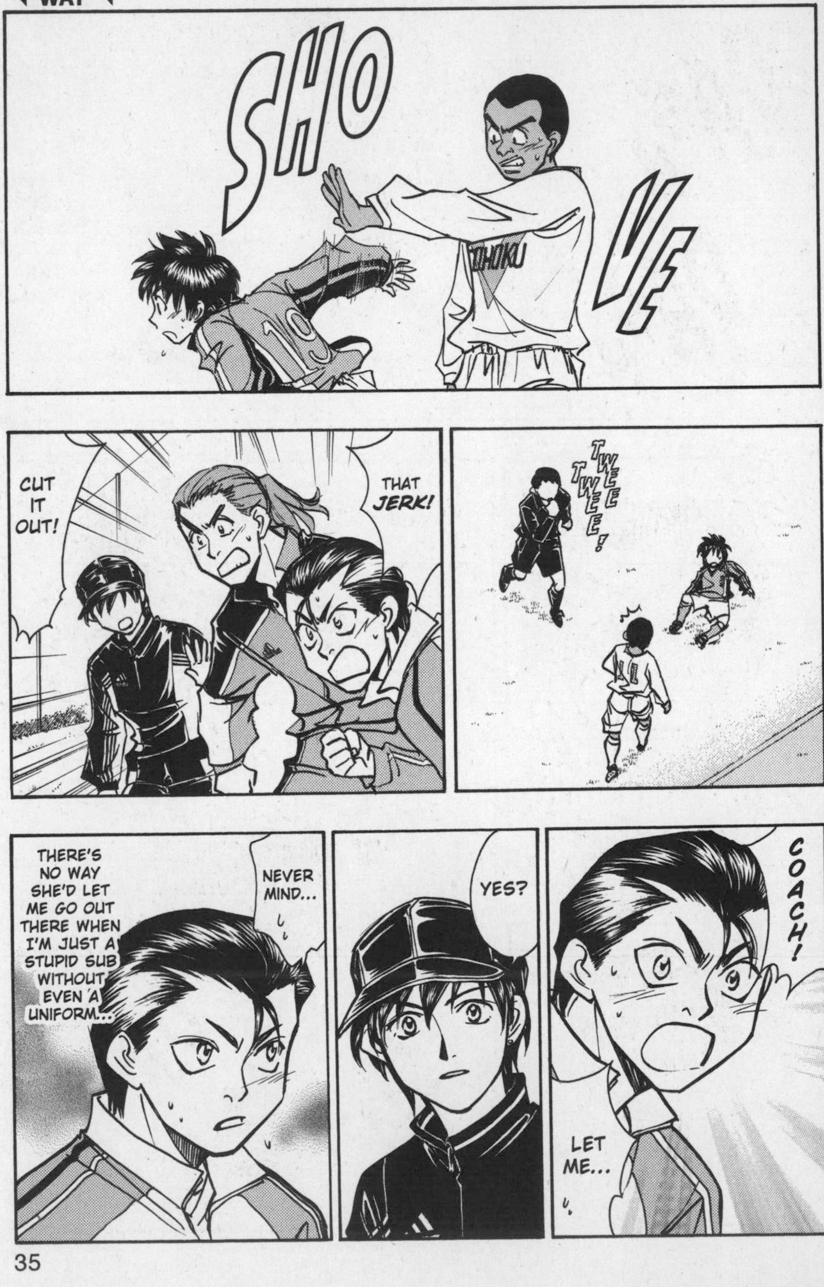
SHO
VE
TOHOKU
TWEE
TWEE!
THAT JERK!
CUT IT OUT!
COACH!
LET ME...
YES?
NEVER MIND...
THERE'S NO WAY SHE'D LET ME GO OUT THERE WHEN I'M JUST A STUPID SUB WITHOUT EVEN A UNIFORM...

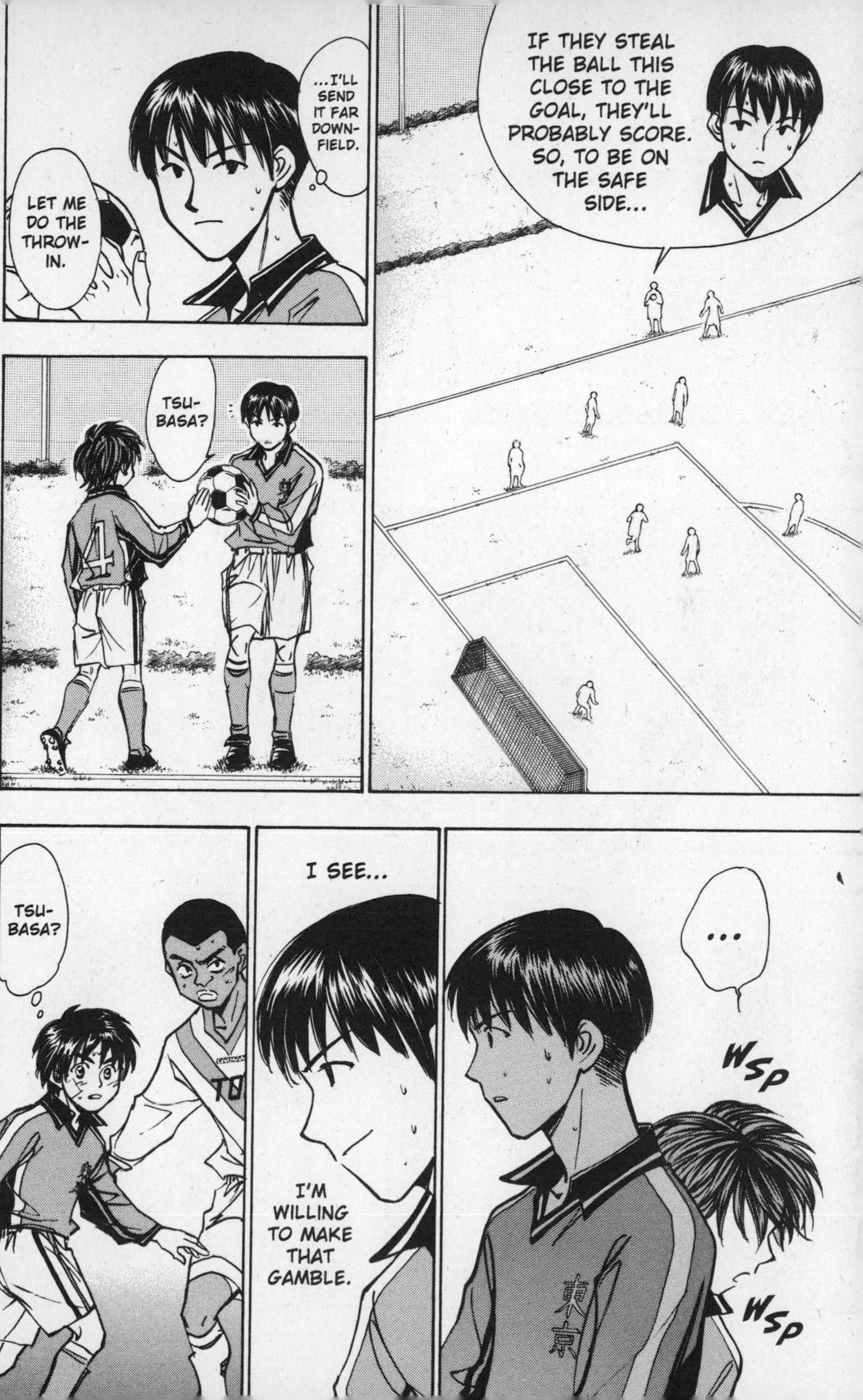
IF THEY STEAL THE BALL THIS CLOSE TO THE GOAL, THEY'LL PROBABLY SCORE. SO, TO BE ON THE SAFE SIDE...
...I'LL SEND IT FAR DOWNFIELD.
LET ME DO THE THROW-IN.
TSUBASA?
...
WSP
WSP
I SEE...
I'M WILLING TO MAKE THAT GAMBLE.
TSUBASA?

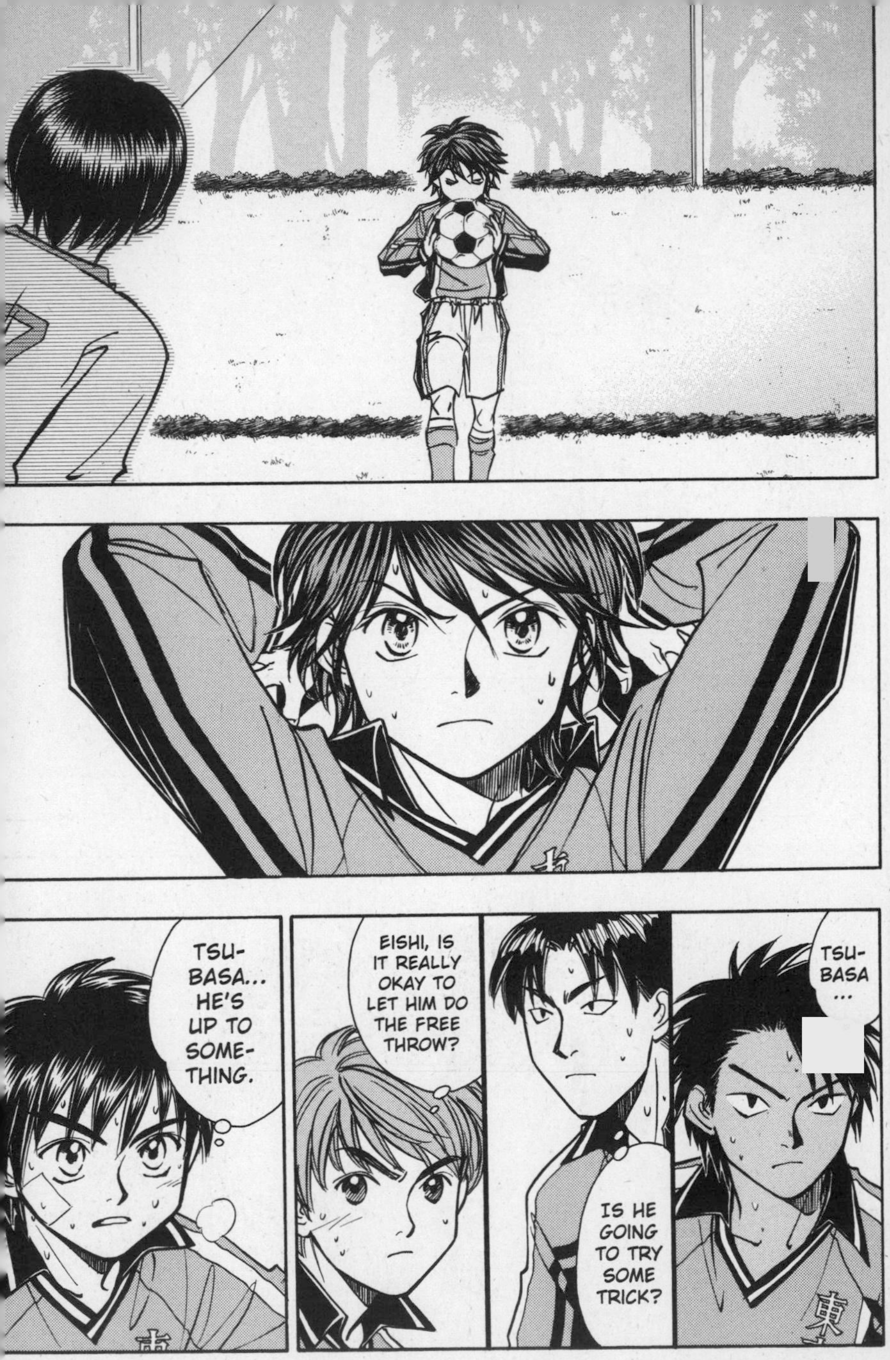
TSU-BASA...
IS HE GOING TO TRY SOME TRICK?
EISHI, IS IT REALLY OKAY TO LET HIM DO THE FREE THROW?
TSU-BASA... HE'S UP TO SOME-THING.

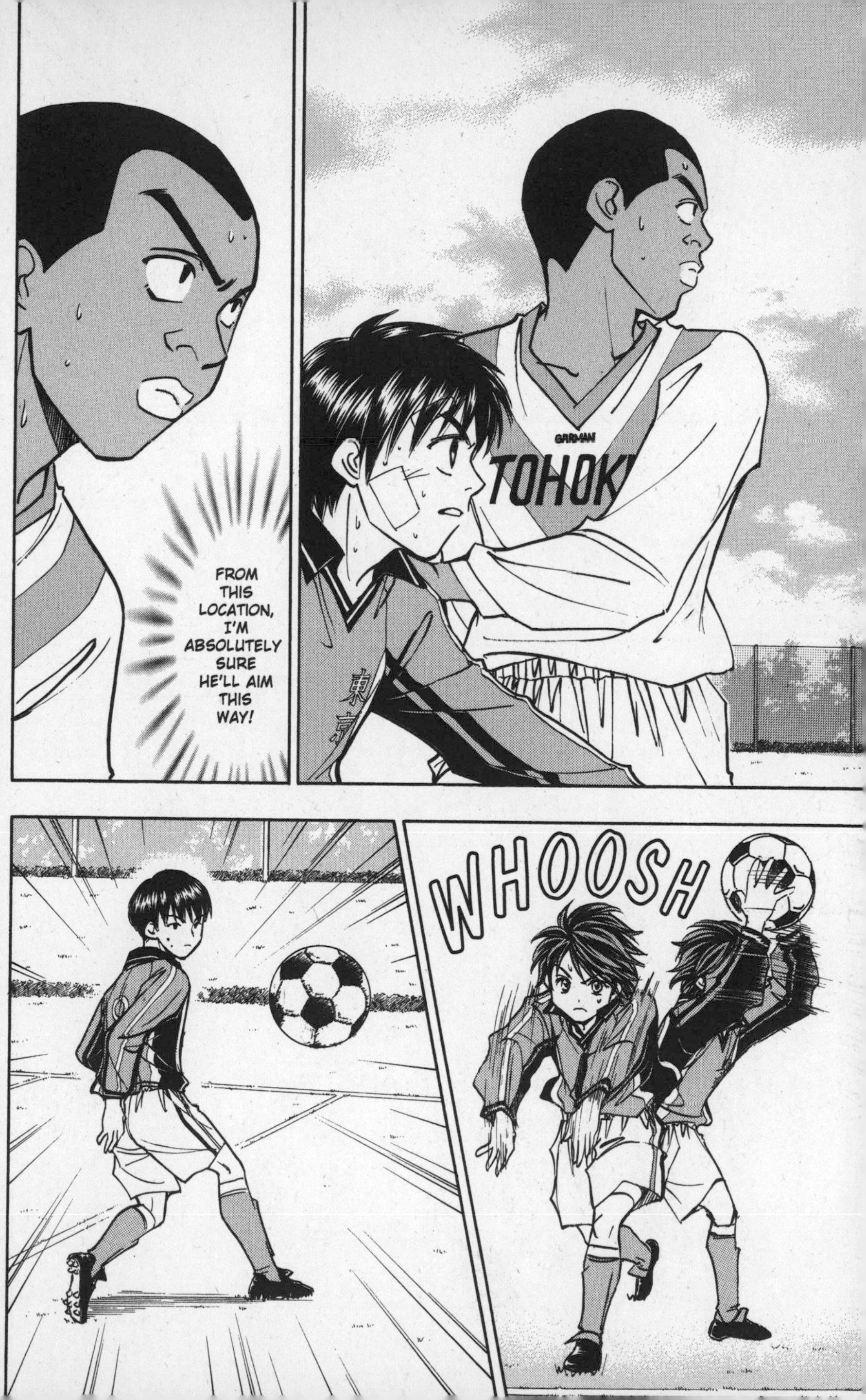
FROM THIS LOCATION, I'M ABSOLUTELY SURE HE'LL AIM THIS WAY!
WHOOSH

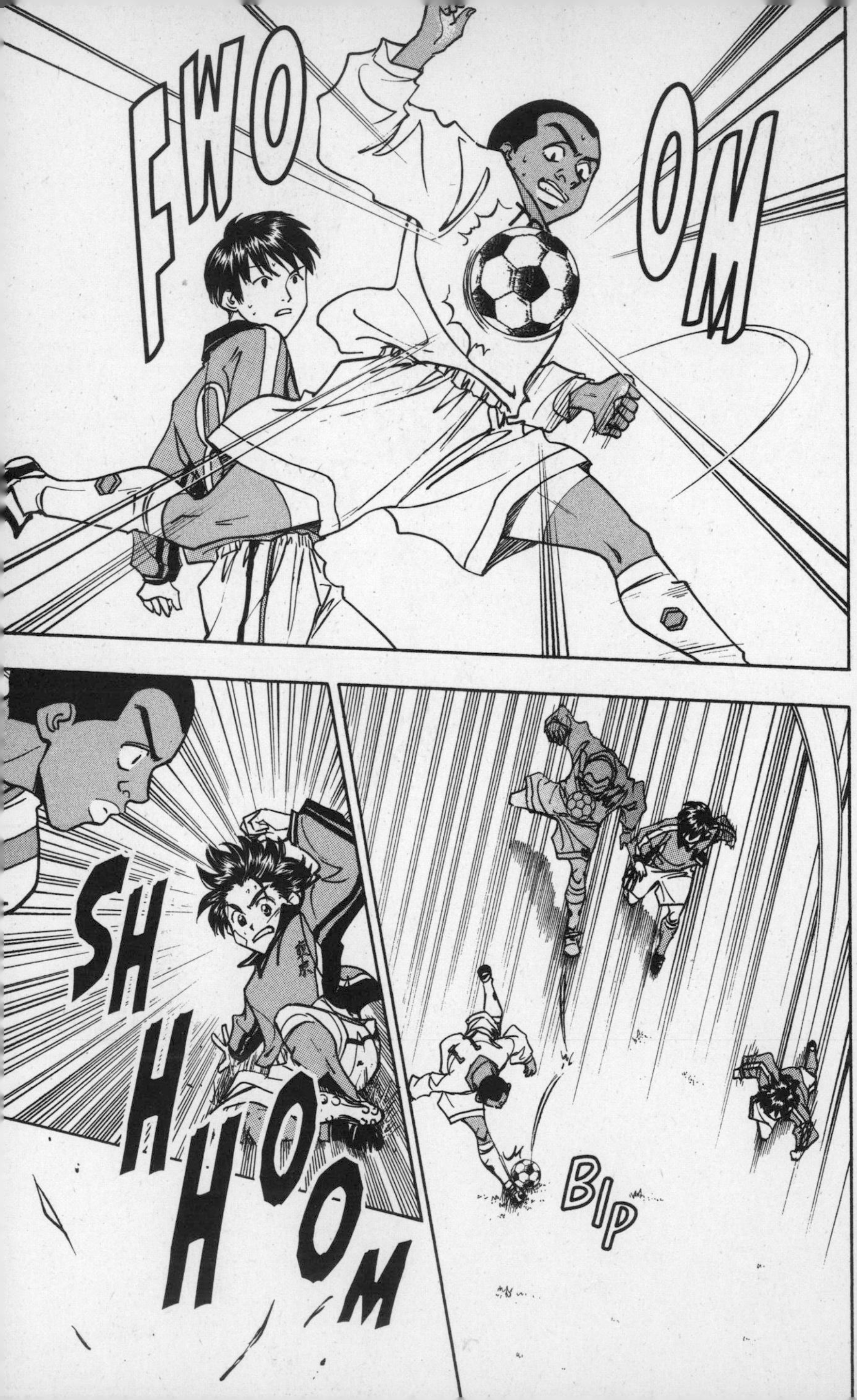
FWOOM
BIP
SHHOOM

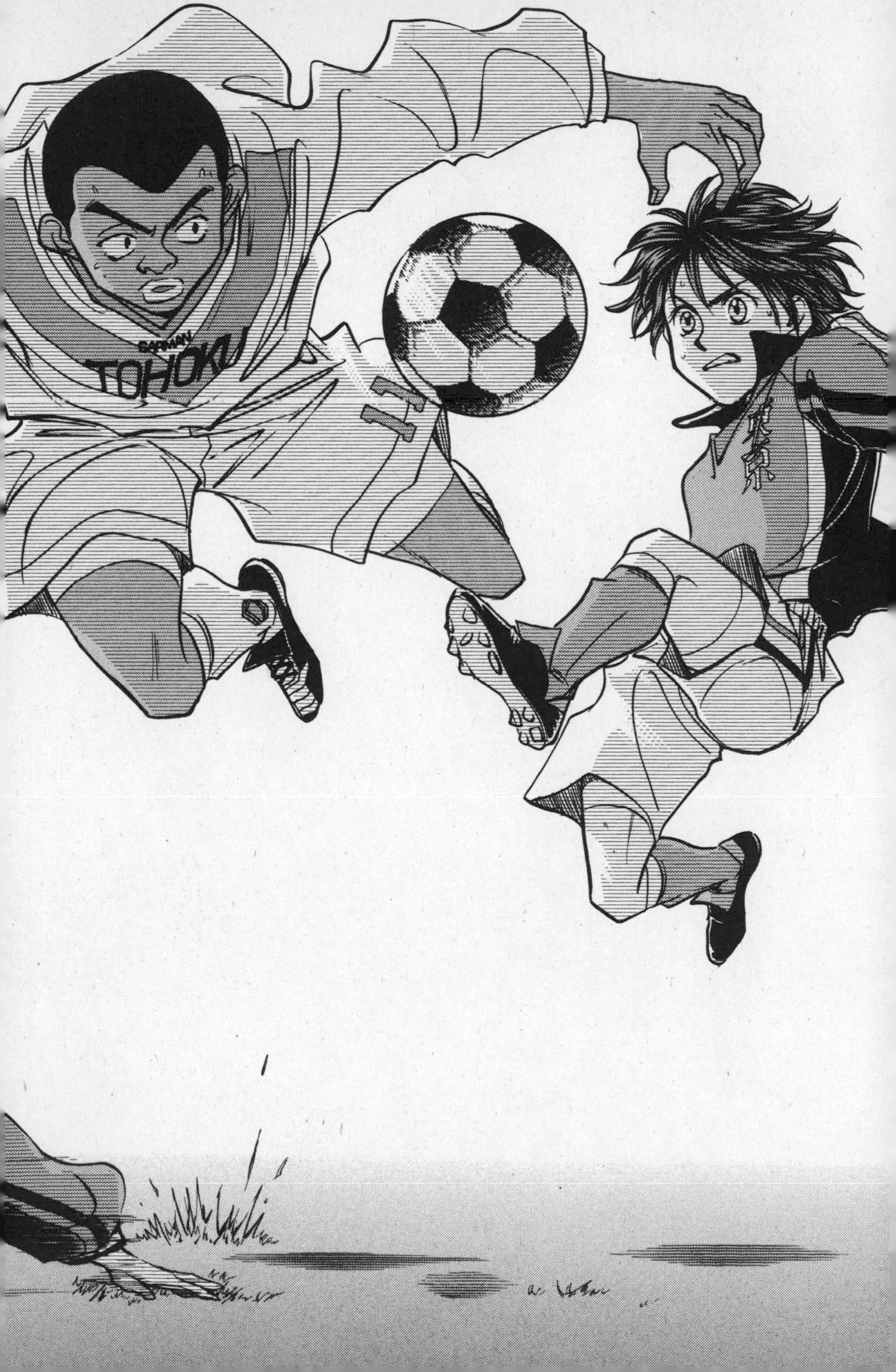
TOHOKU

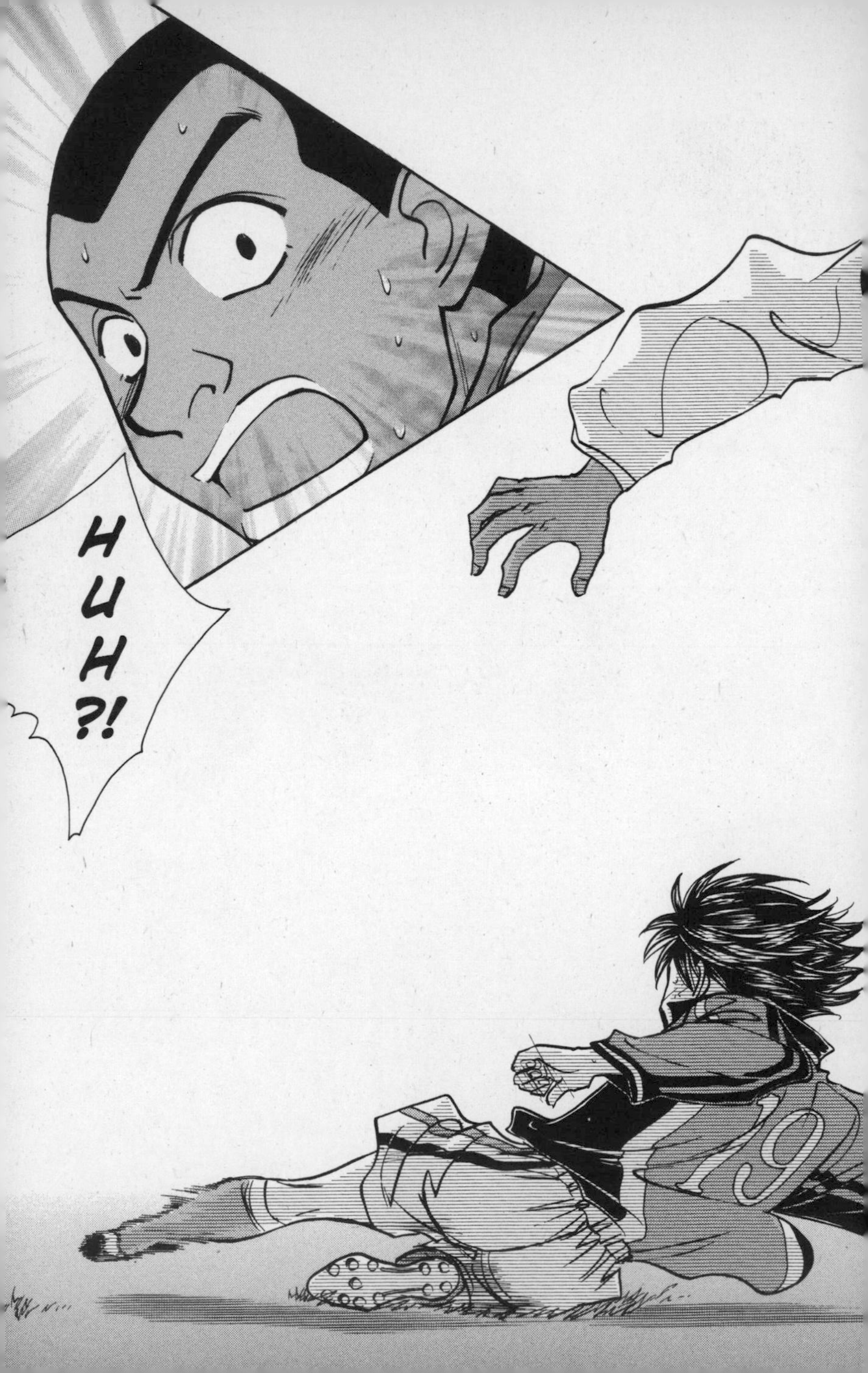
HUH?!

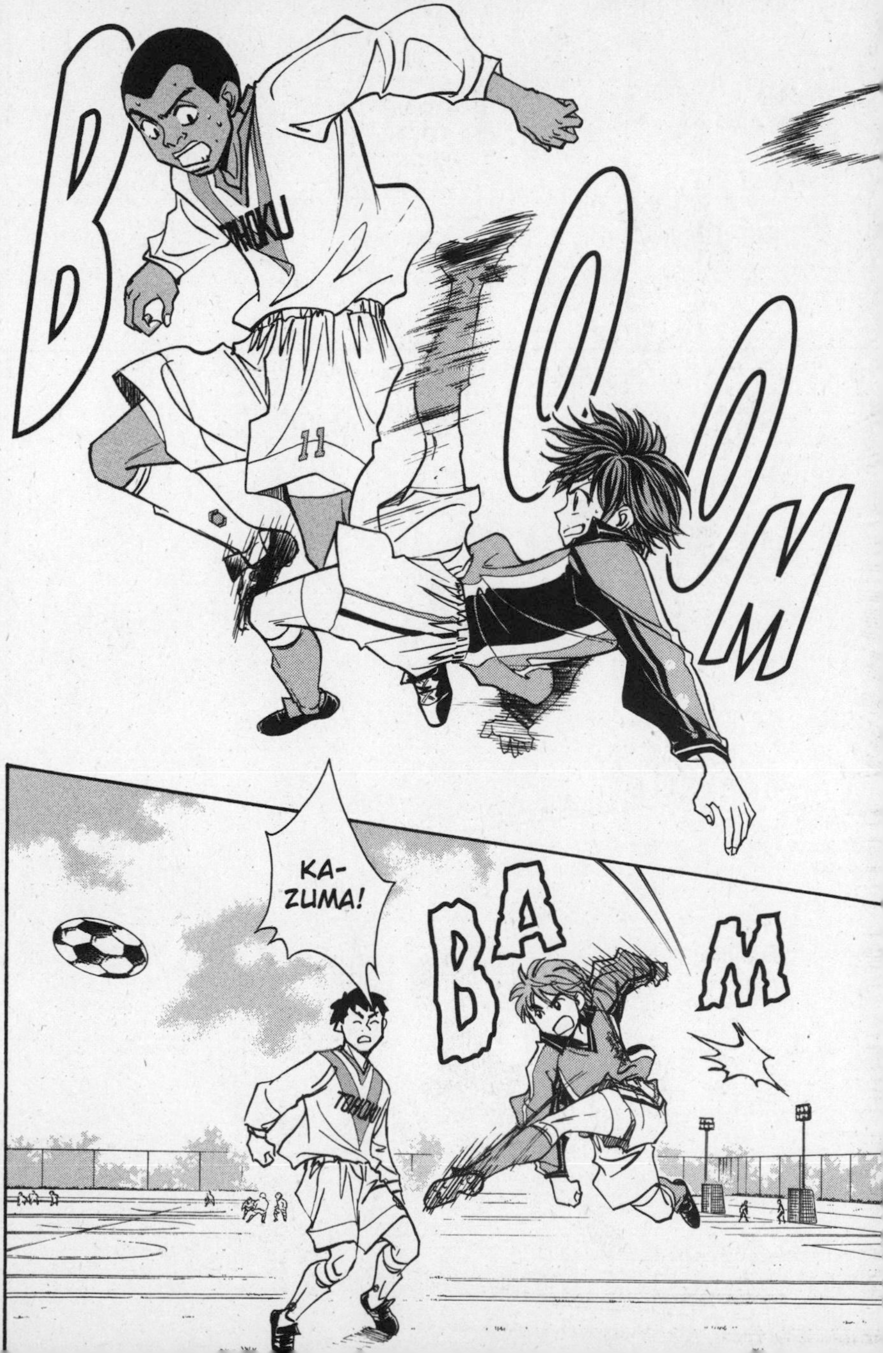
BOOM
BAM
KA-ZUMA!

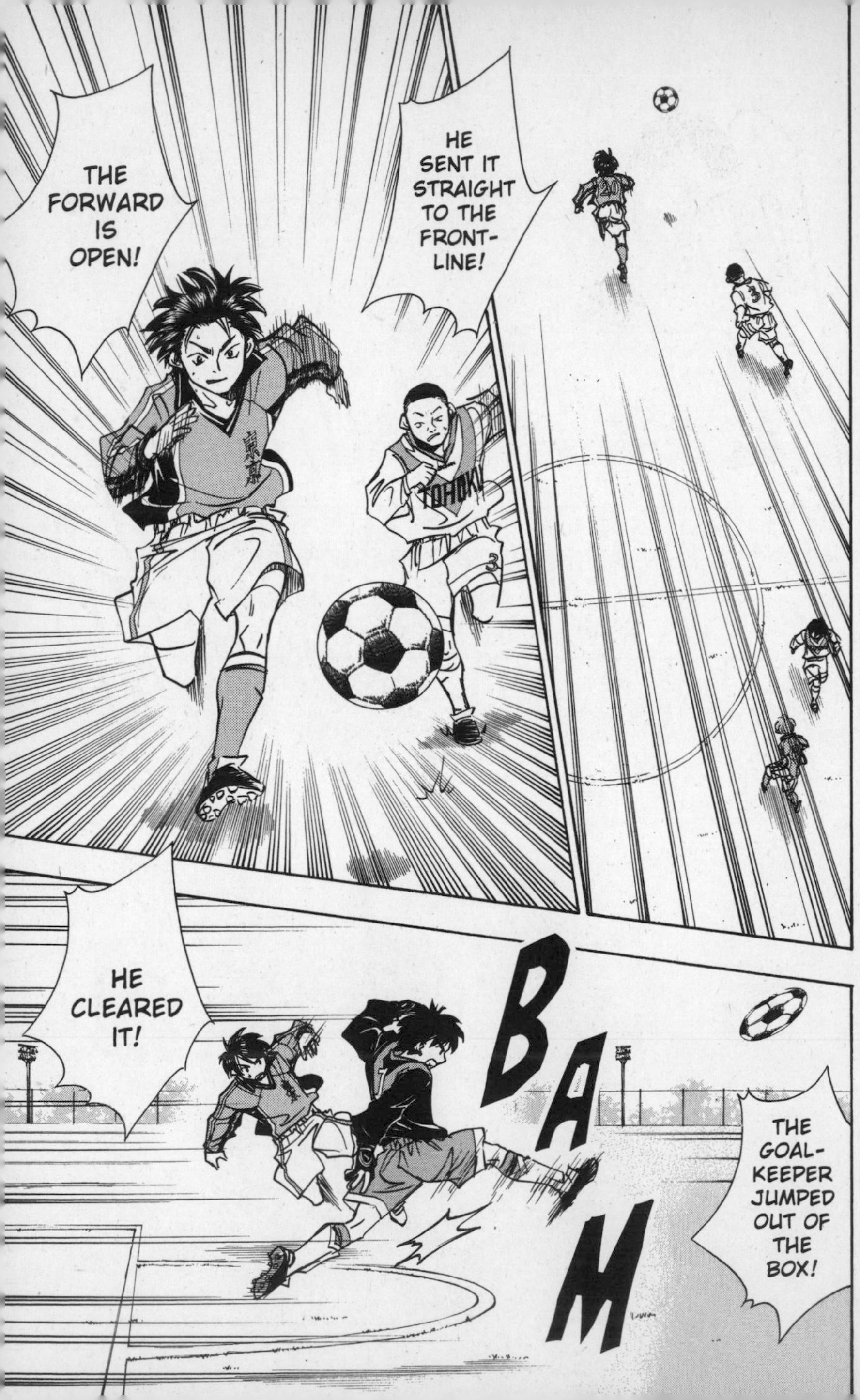
HE SENT IT STRAIGHT TO THE FRONT-LINE!
THE FORWARD IS OPEN!
TOHOKU
THE GOAL-KEEPER JUMPED OUT OF THE BOX!
BAM
HE CLEARED IT!

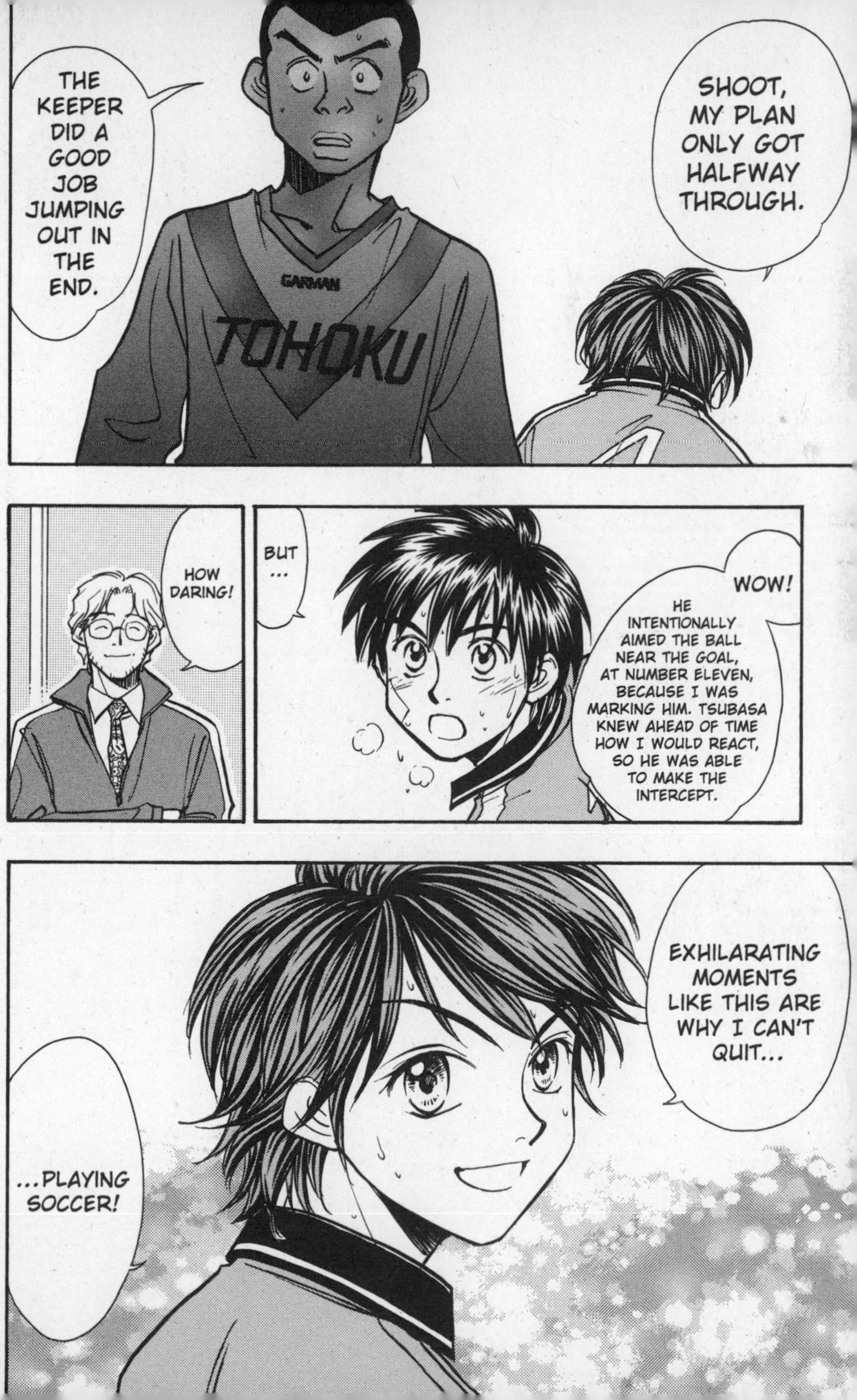
SHOOT, MY PLAN ONLY GOT HALFWAY THROUGH.
THE KEEPER DID A GOOD JOB JUMPING OUT IN THE END.
GARMAN
TOHOKU
WOW!
HE INTENTIONALLY AIMED THE BALL NEAR THE GOAL, AT NUMBER ELEVEN, BECAUSE I WAS MARKING HIM. TSUBASA KNEW AHEAD OF TIME HOW I WOULD REACT, SO HE WAS ABLE TO MAKE THE INTERCEPT.
BUT ...
HOW DARING!
EXHILARATING MOMENTS LIKE THIS ARE WHY I CAN'T QUIT...
...PLAYING SOCCER!

READ THIS WAY

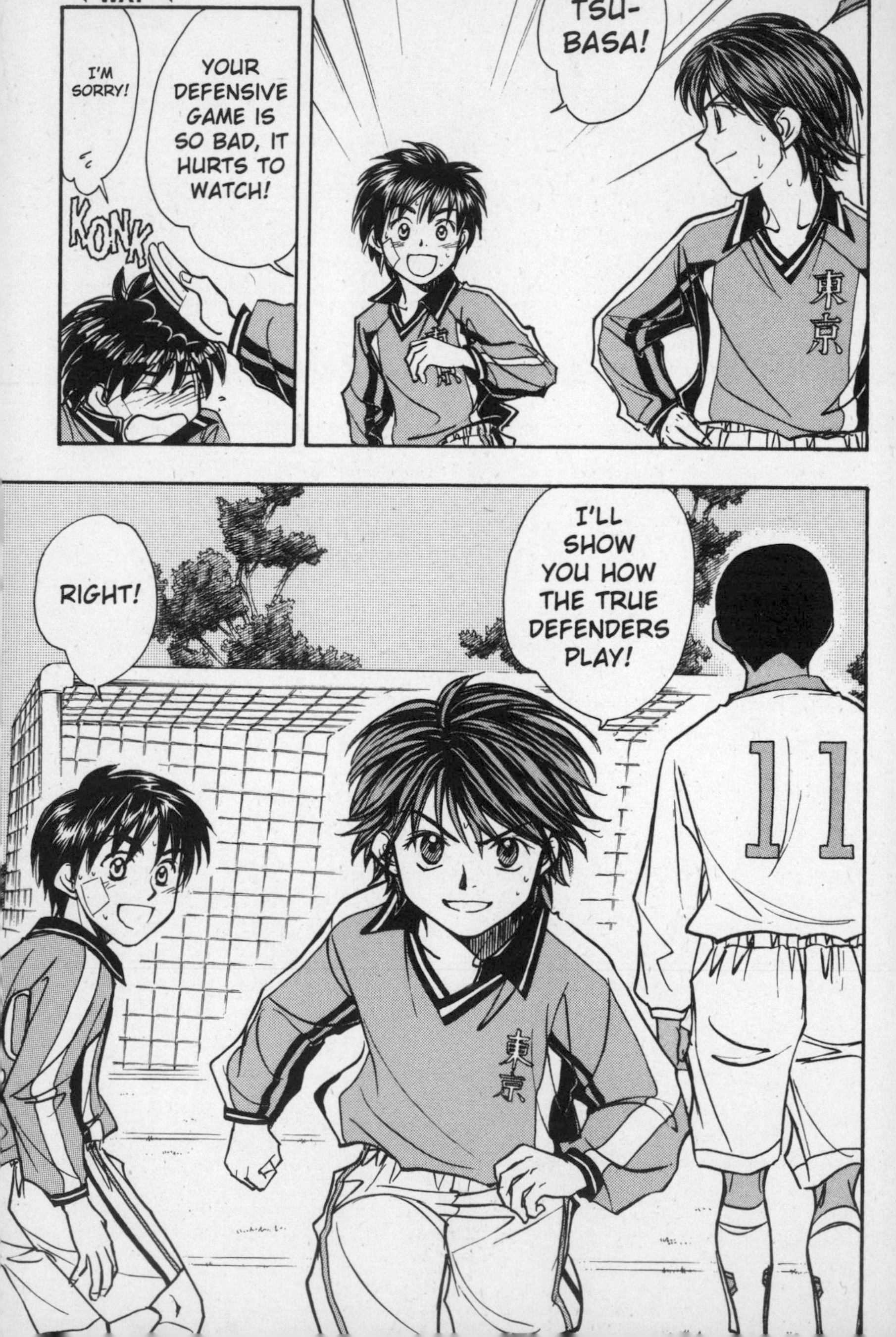
TSU-BASA!
YOUR DEFENSIVE GAME IS SO BAD, IT HURTS TO WATCH!
I'M SORRY!
KONK
I'LL SHOW YOU HOW THE TRUE DEFENDERS PLAY!
RIGHT!

WHISTLE!

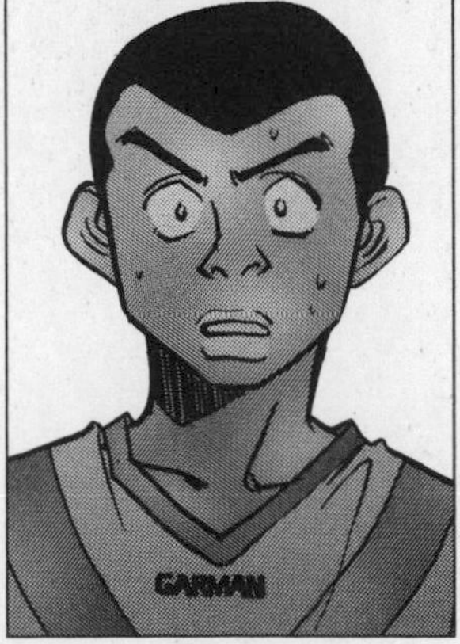
GARMAN

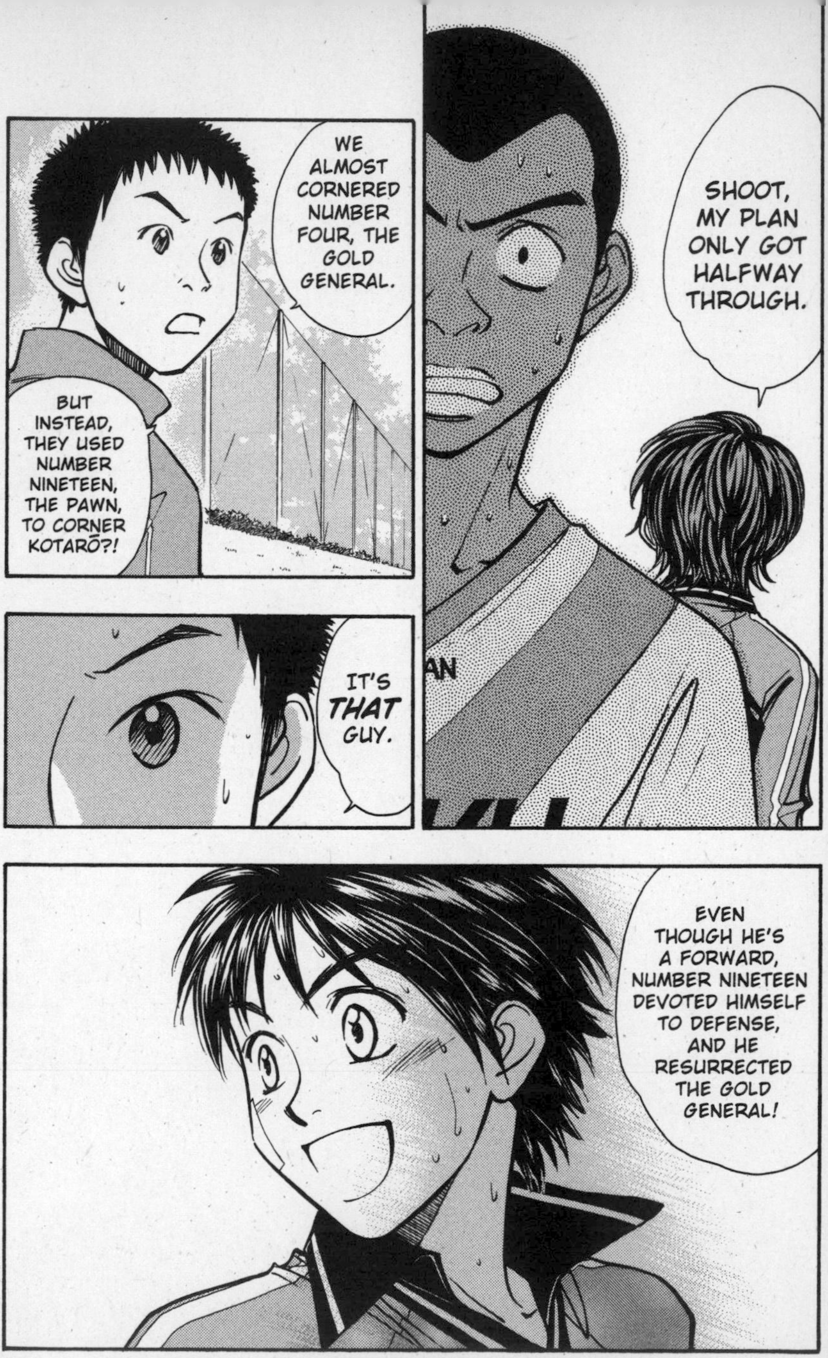
SHOOT, MY PLAN ONLY GOT HALFWAY THROUGH.
WE ALMOST CORNERED NUMBER FOUR, THE GOLD GENERAL.
BUT INSTEAD, THEY USED NUMBER NINETEEN, THE PAWN, TO CORNER KOTARŌ?!
IT'S *THAT* GUY.
EVEN THOUGH HE'S A FORWARD, NUMBER NINETEEN DEVOTED HIMSELF TO DEFENSE, AND HE RESURRECTED THE GOLD GENERAL!

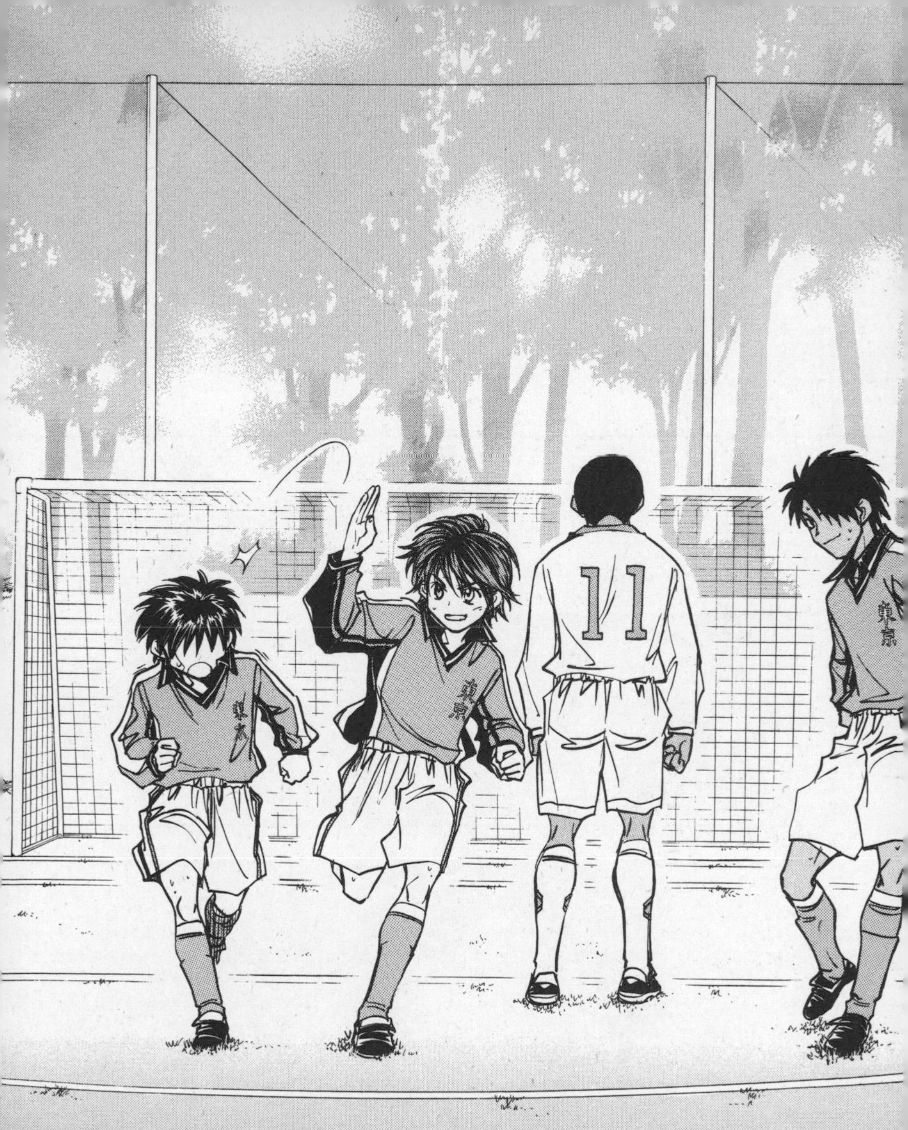

STAGE.185

From Gold General to Rook

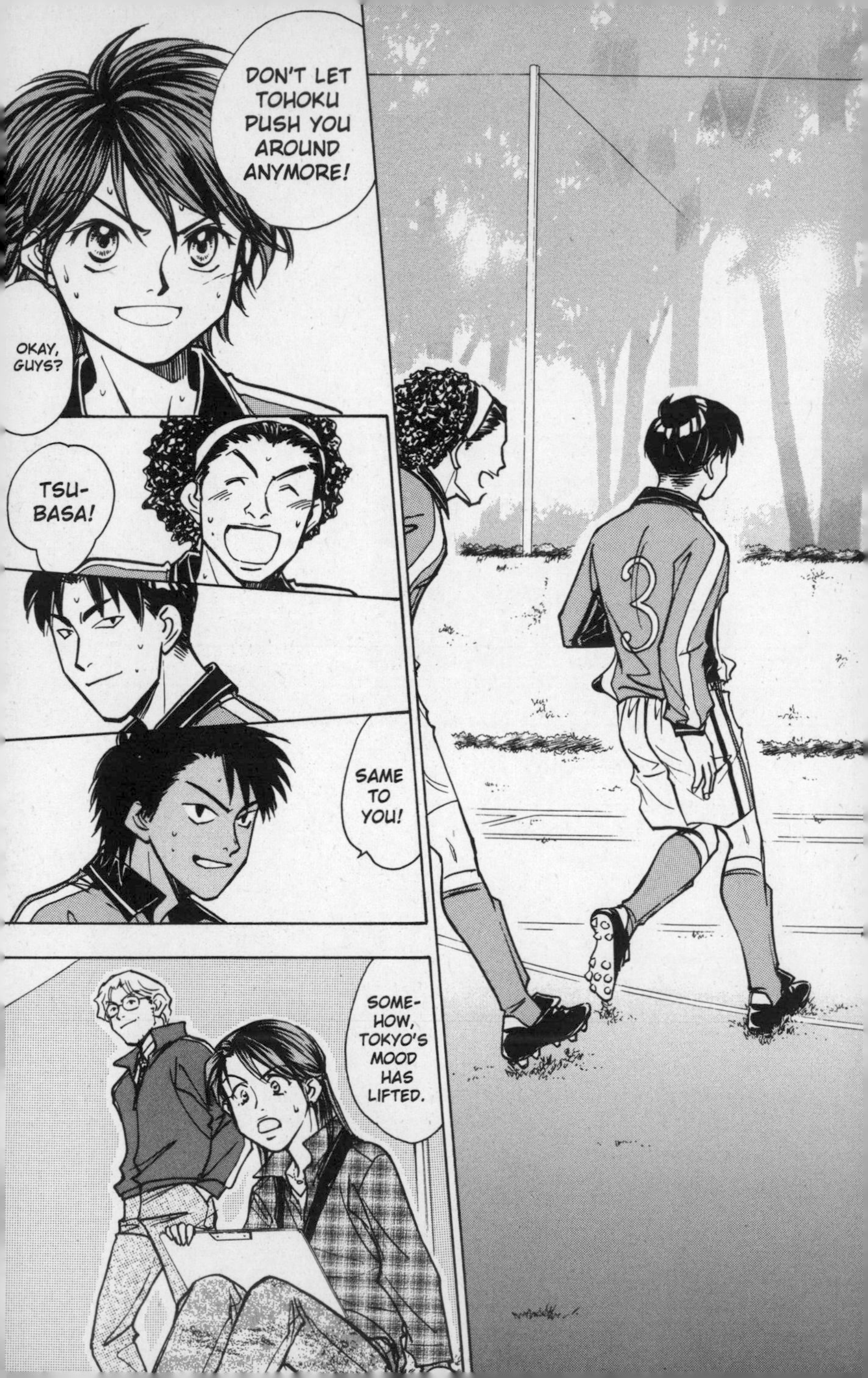
DON'T LET TOHOKU PUSH YOU AROUND ANYMORE!
OKAY, GUYS?
TSU-BASA!
SAME TO YOU!
SOME-HOW, TOKYO'S MOOD HAS LIFTED.

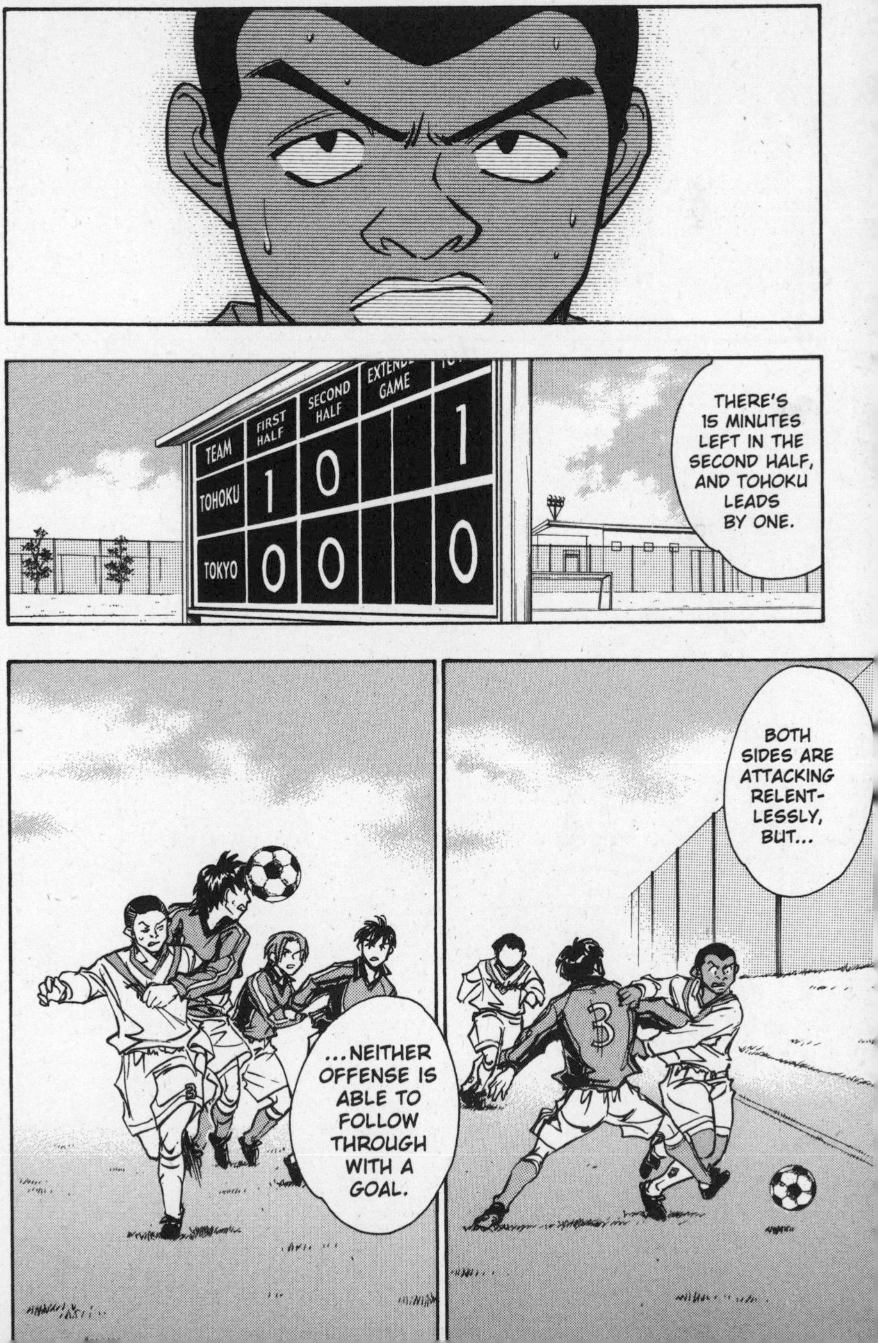
TEAM
FIRST HALF
SECOND HALF
TOHOKU
TOKYO
THERE'S 15 MINUTES LEFT IN THE SECOND HALF, AND TOHOKU LEADS BY ONE.
BOTH SIDES ARE ATTACKING RELENT-LESSLY, BUT...
...NEITHER OFFENSE IS ABLE TO FOLLOW THROUGH WITH A GOAL.

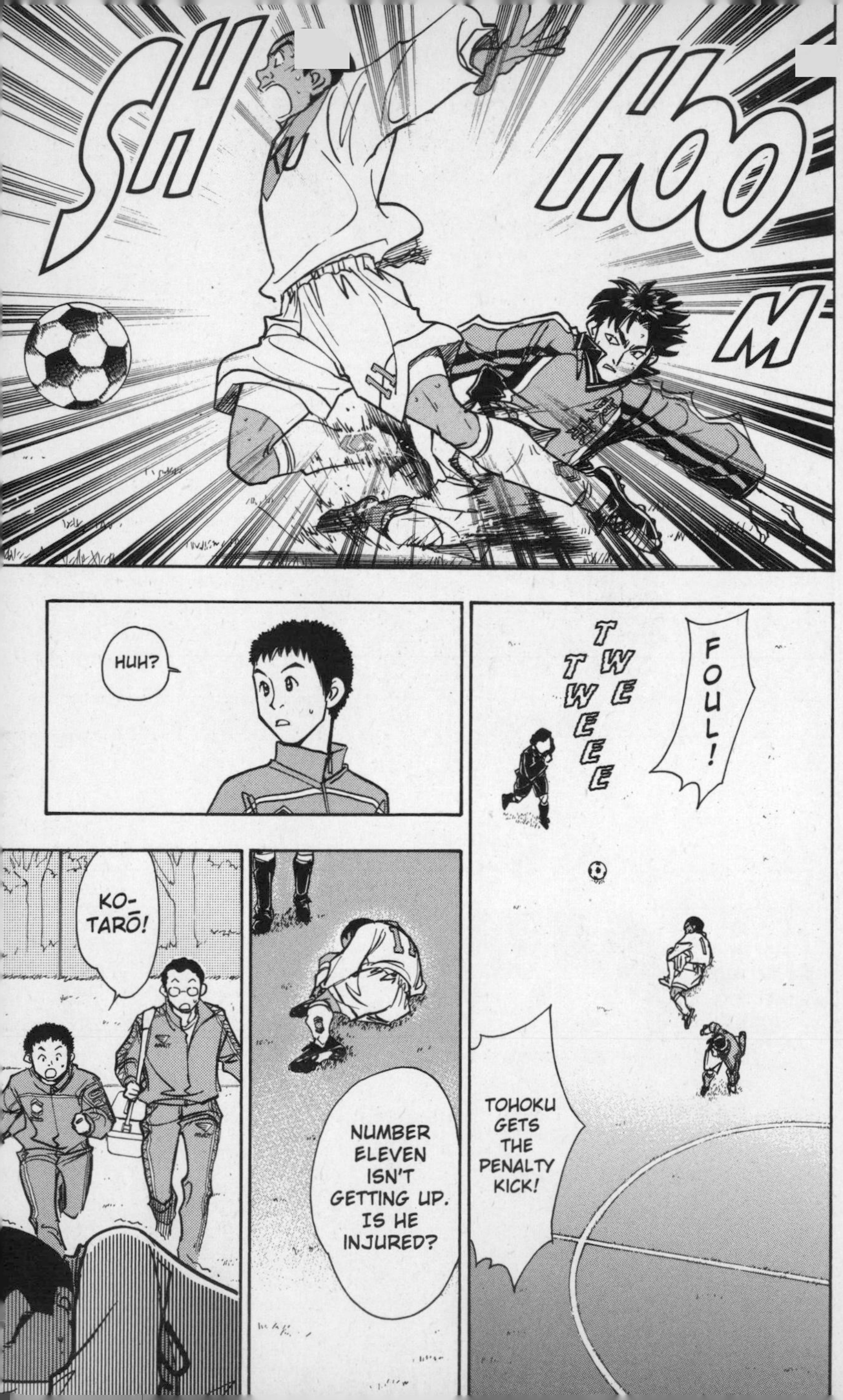
SHHOOM
FOUL!
TWEE
TWEEE
TOHOKU GETS THE PENALTY KICK!
HUH?
NUMBER ELEVEN ISN'T GETTING UP. IS HE INJURED?
KO-TARŌ!

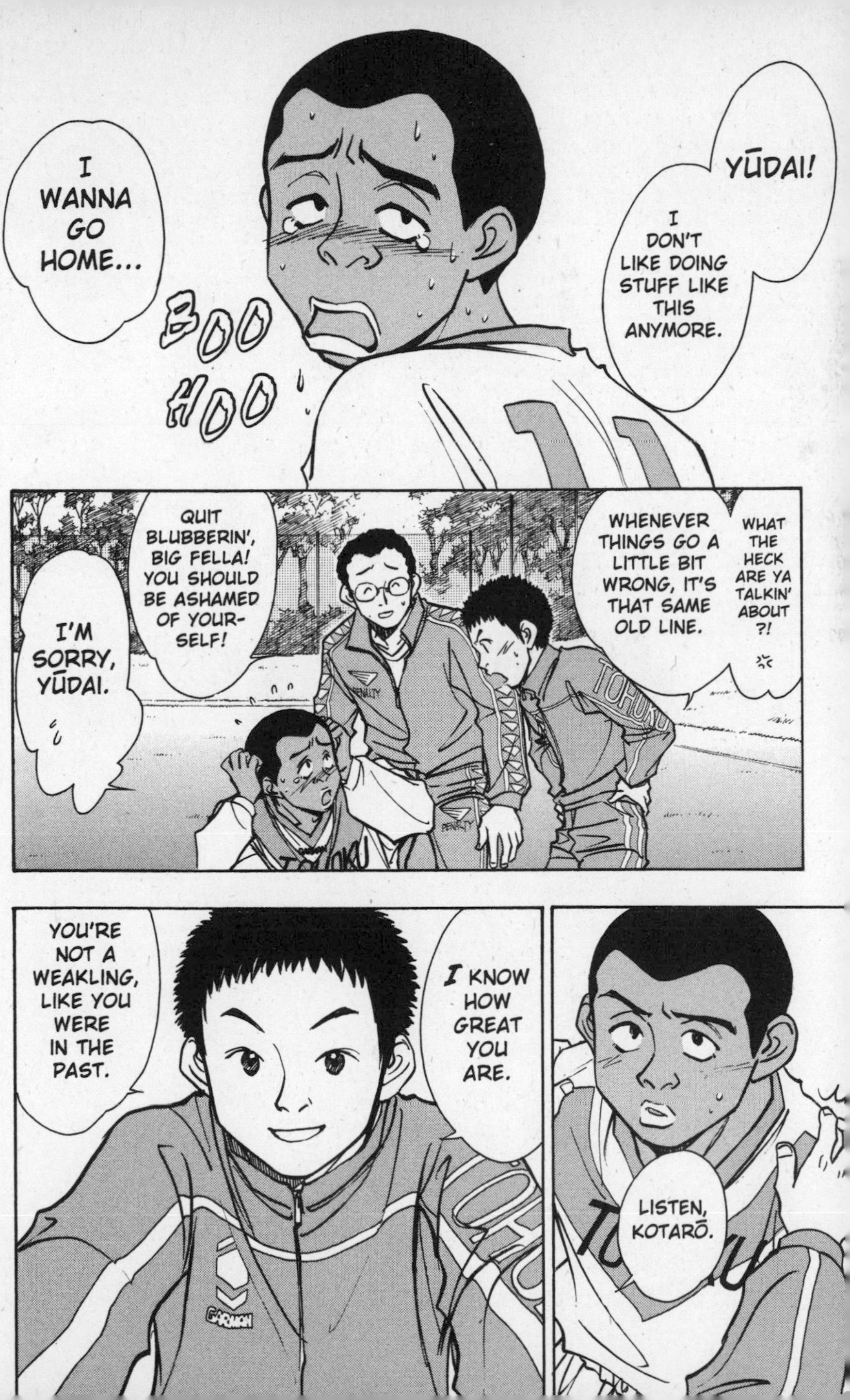
YŪDAI!
I DON'T LIKE DOING STUFF LIKE THIS ANYMORE.
BOO HOO
I WANNA GO HOME...
WHAT THE HECK ARE YA TALKIN' ABOUT?!
WHENEVER THINGS GO A LITTLE BIT WRONG, IT'S THAT SAME OLD LINE.
QUIT BLUBBERIN', BIG FELLA! YOU SHOULD BE ASHAMED OF YOUR-SELF!
I'M SORRY, YŪDAI.
LISTEN, KOTARŌ.
I KNOW HOW GREAT YOU ARE.
YOU'RE NOT A WEAKLING, LIKE YOU WERE IN THE PAST.

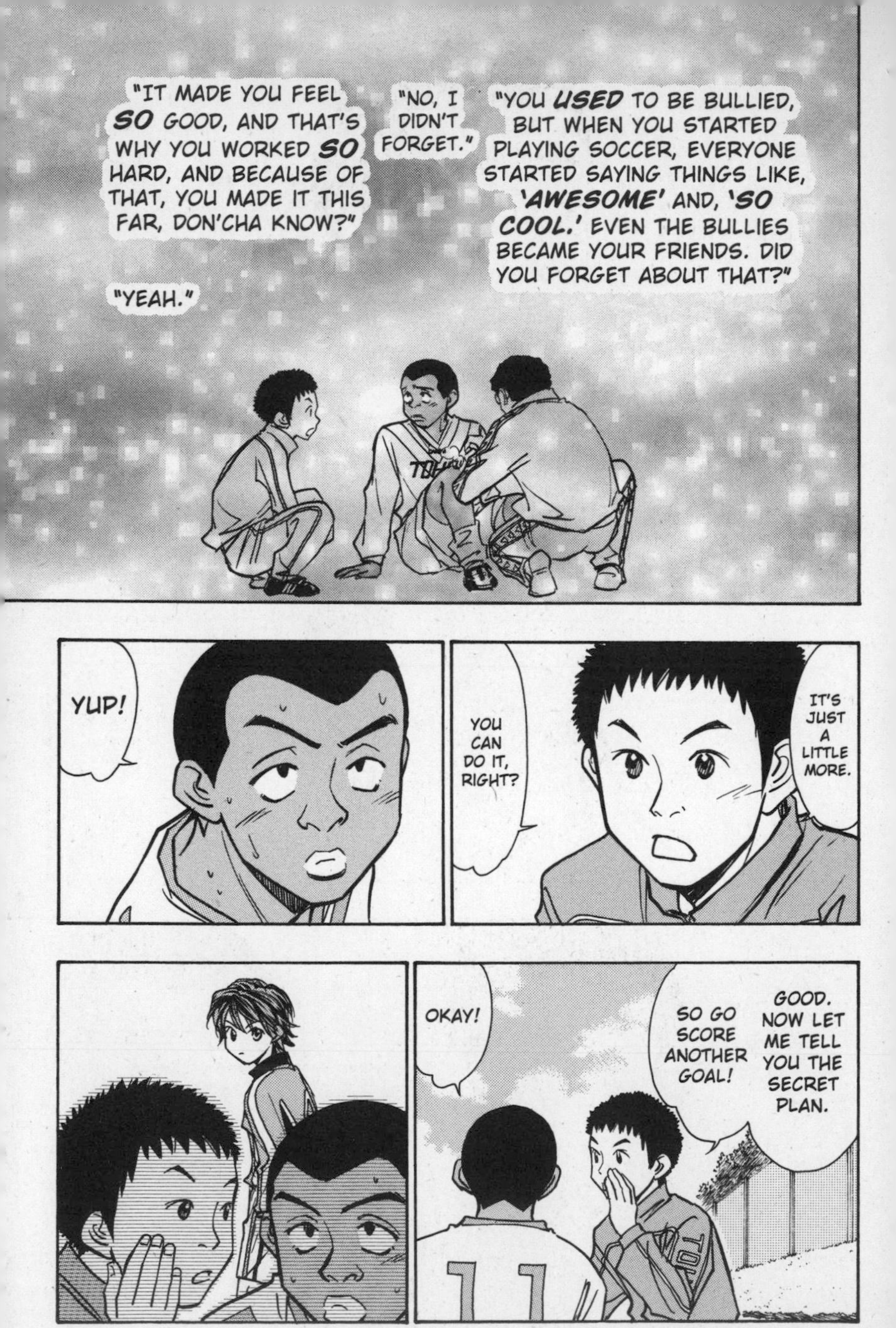
"YOU USED TO BE BULLIED, BUT WHEN YOU STARTED PLAYING SOCCER, EVERYONE STARTED SAYING THINGS LIKE, 'AWESOME' AND, 'SO COOL.' EVEN THE BULLIES BECAME YOUR FRIENDS. DID YOU FORGET ABOUT THAT?"
"NO, I DIDN'T FORGET."
"IT MADE YOU FEEL SO GOOD, AND THAT'S WHY YOU WORKED SO HARD, AND BECAUSE OF THAT, YOU MADE IT THIS FAR, DON'CHA KNOW?"
"YEAH."
IT'S JUST A LITTLE MORE.
YOU CAN DO IT, RIGHT?
YUP!
GOOD. NOW LET ME TELL YOU THE SECRET PLAN.
SO GO SCORE ANOTHER GOAL!
OKAY!

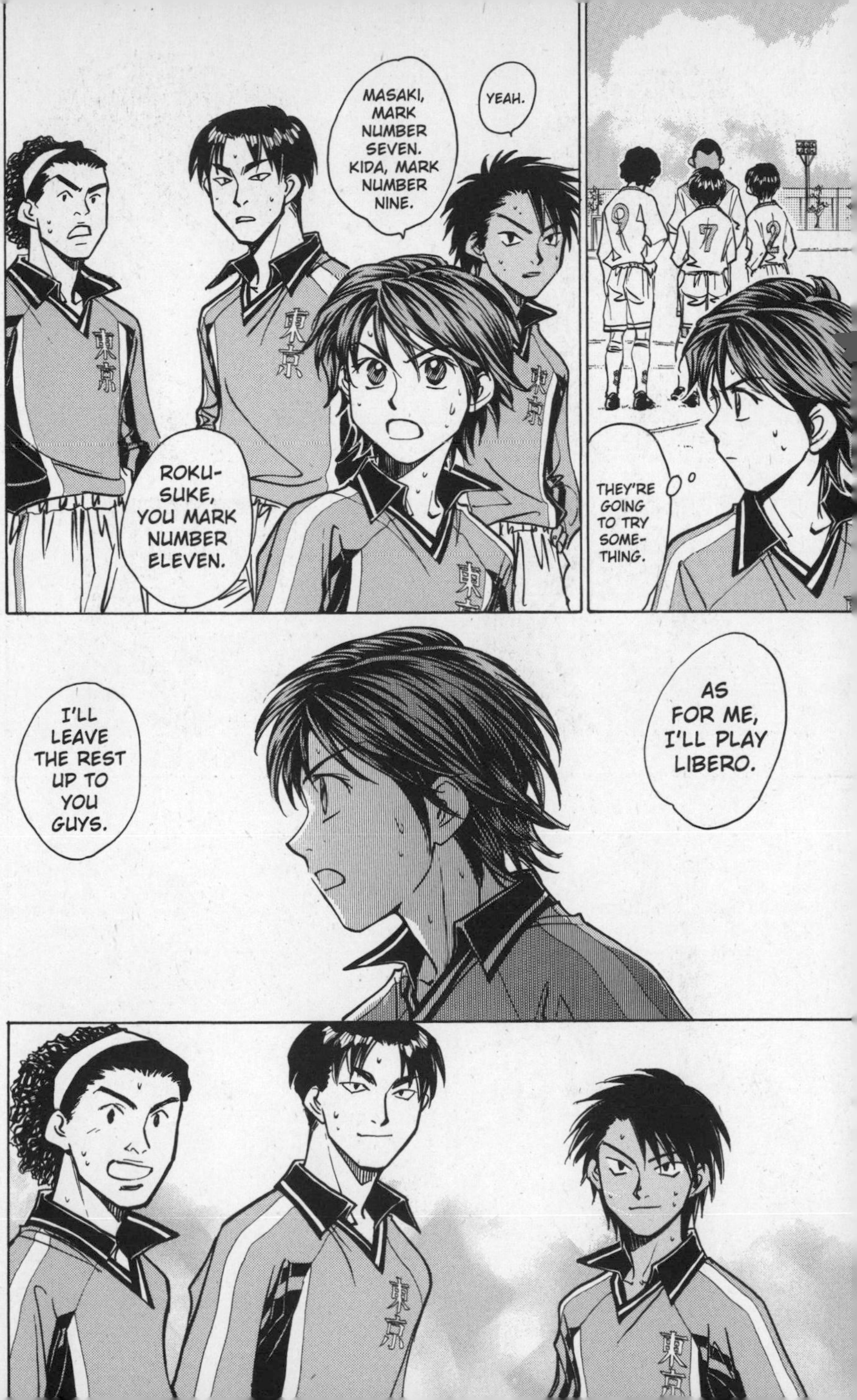
THEY'RE GOING TO TRY SOME-THING.
YEAH.
MASAKI, MARK NUMBER SEVEN. KIDA, MARK NUMBER NINE.
ROKU-SUKE, YOU MARK NUMBER ELEVEN.
AS FOR ME, I'LL PLAY LIBERO.
I'LL LEAVE THE REST UP TO YOU GUYS.

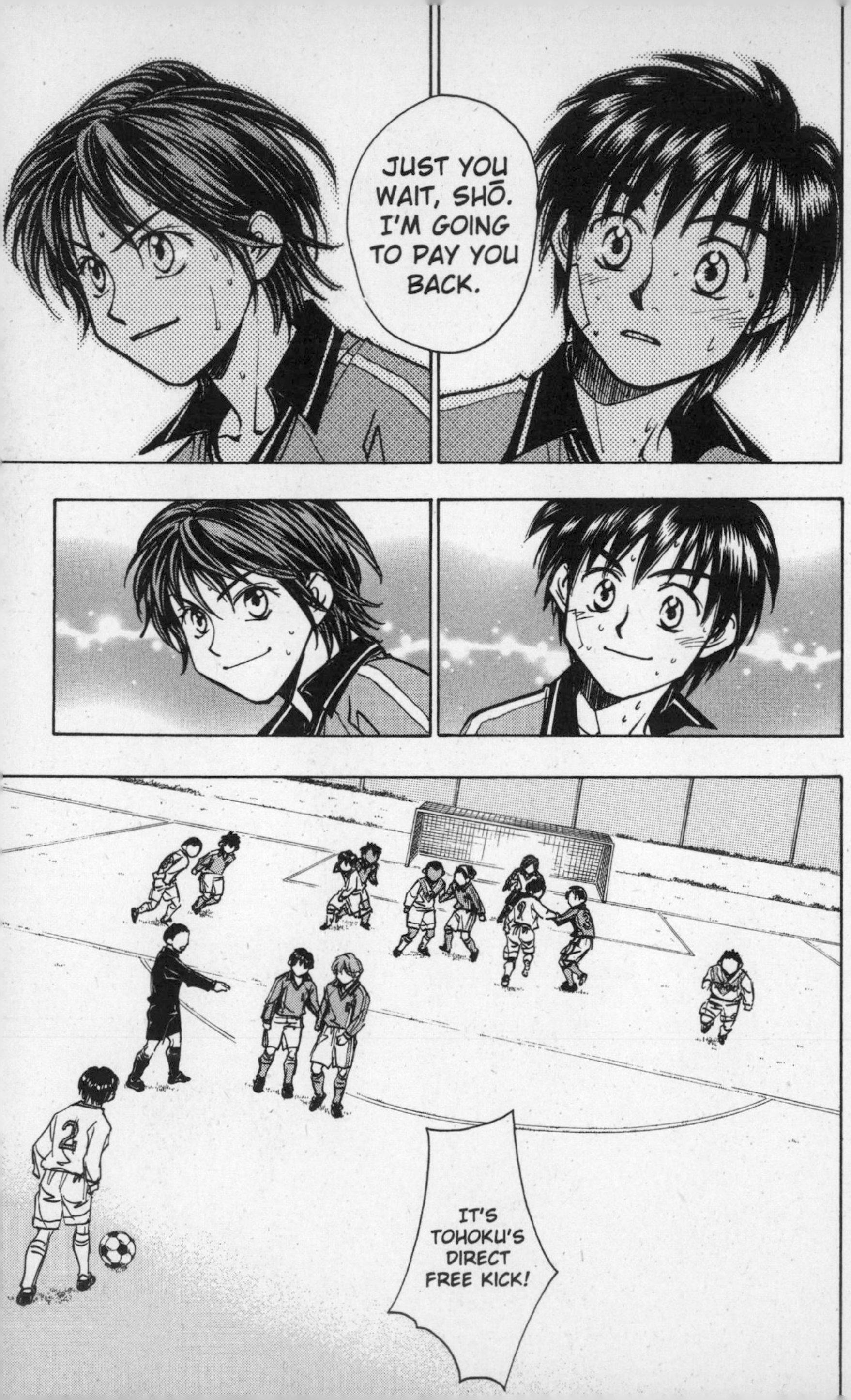
JUST YOU WAIT, SHŌ. I'M GOING TO PAY YOU BACK.
IT'S TOHOKU'S DIRECT FREE KICK!

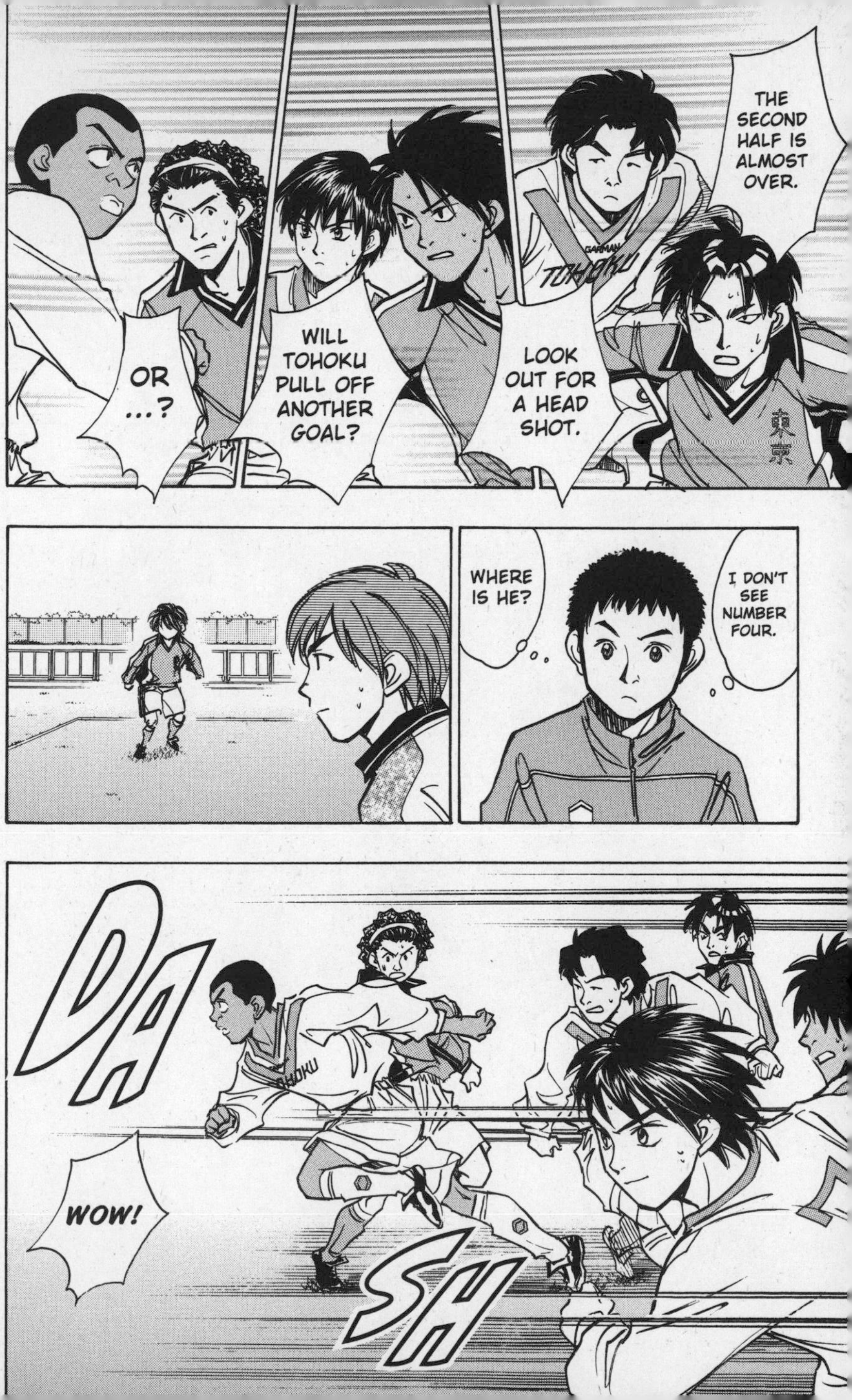
THE SECOND HALF IS ALMOST OVER.
LOOK OUT FOR A HEAD SHOT.
WILL TOHOKU PULL OFF ANOTHER GOAL?
OR ...?
I DON'T SEE NUMBER FOUR.
WHERE IS HE?
DA
SH
WOW!

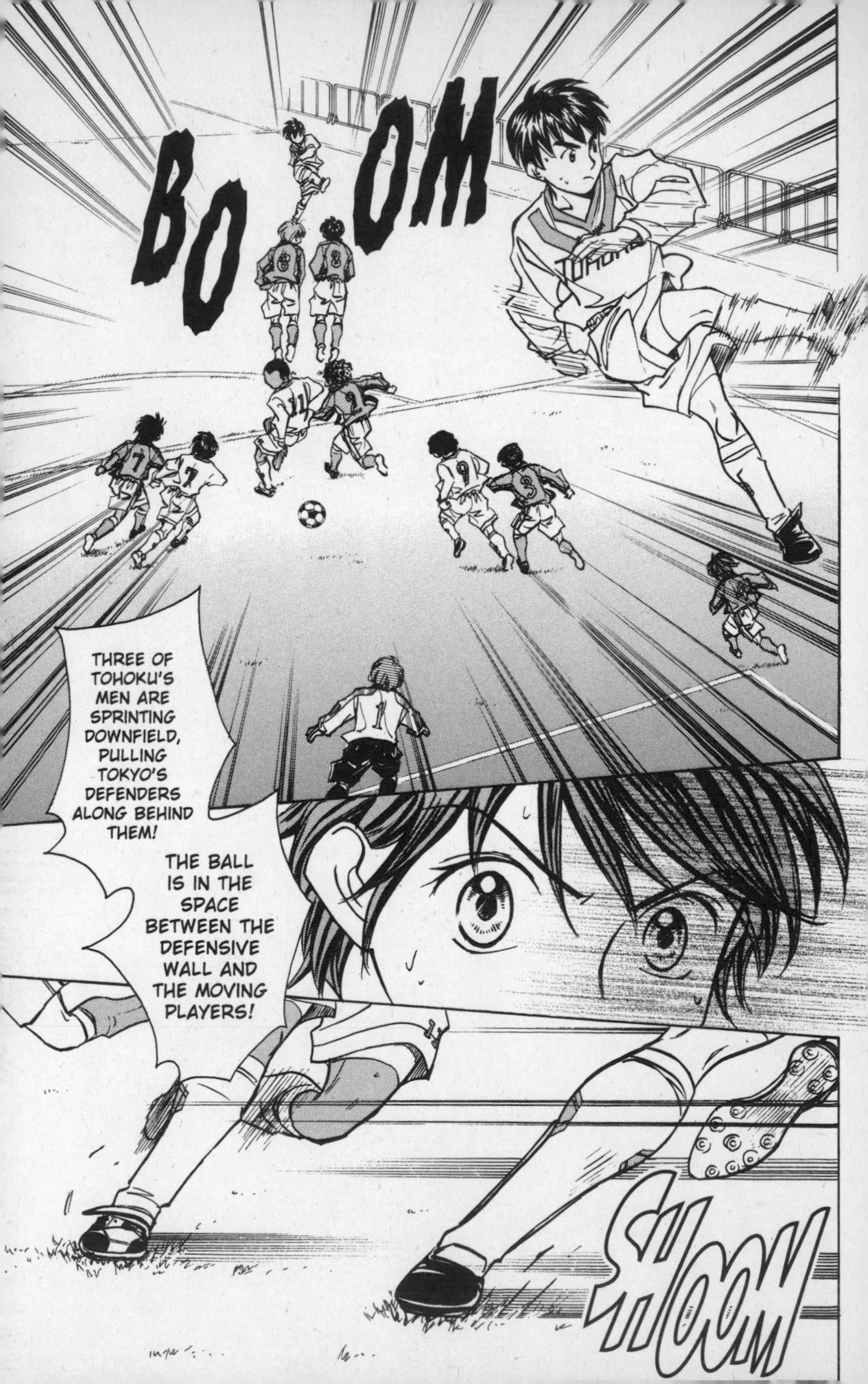
BOOM
THREE OF TOHOKU'S MEN ARE SPRINTING DOWNFIELD, PULLING TOKYO'S DEFENDERS ALONG BEHIND THEM!
THE BALL IS IN THE SPACE BETWEEN THE DEFENSIVE WALL AND THE MOVING PLAYERS!
SHOOM

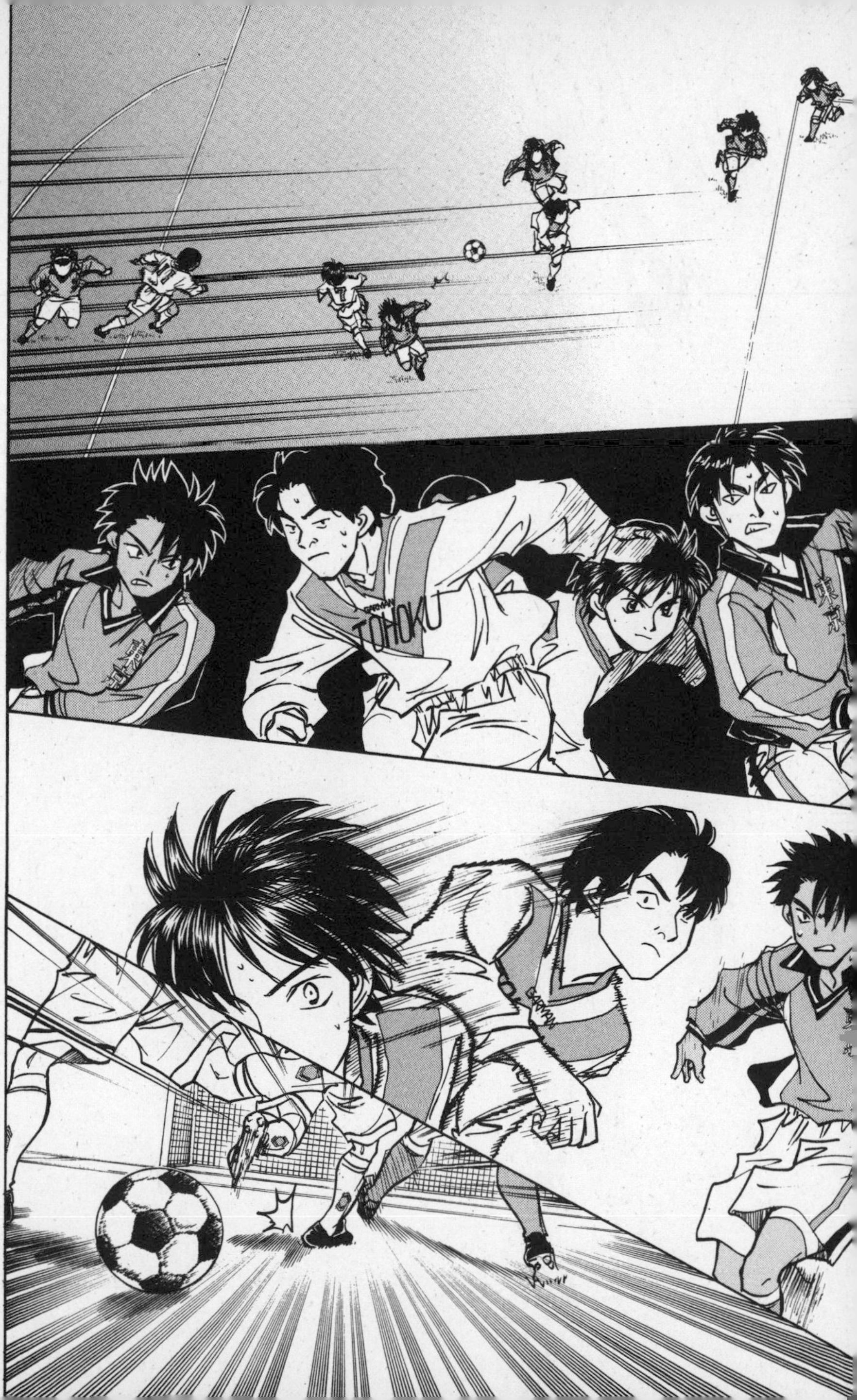
東京
TOHOKU

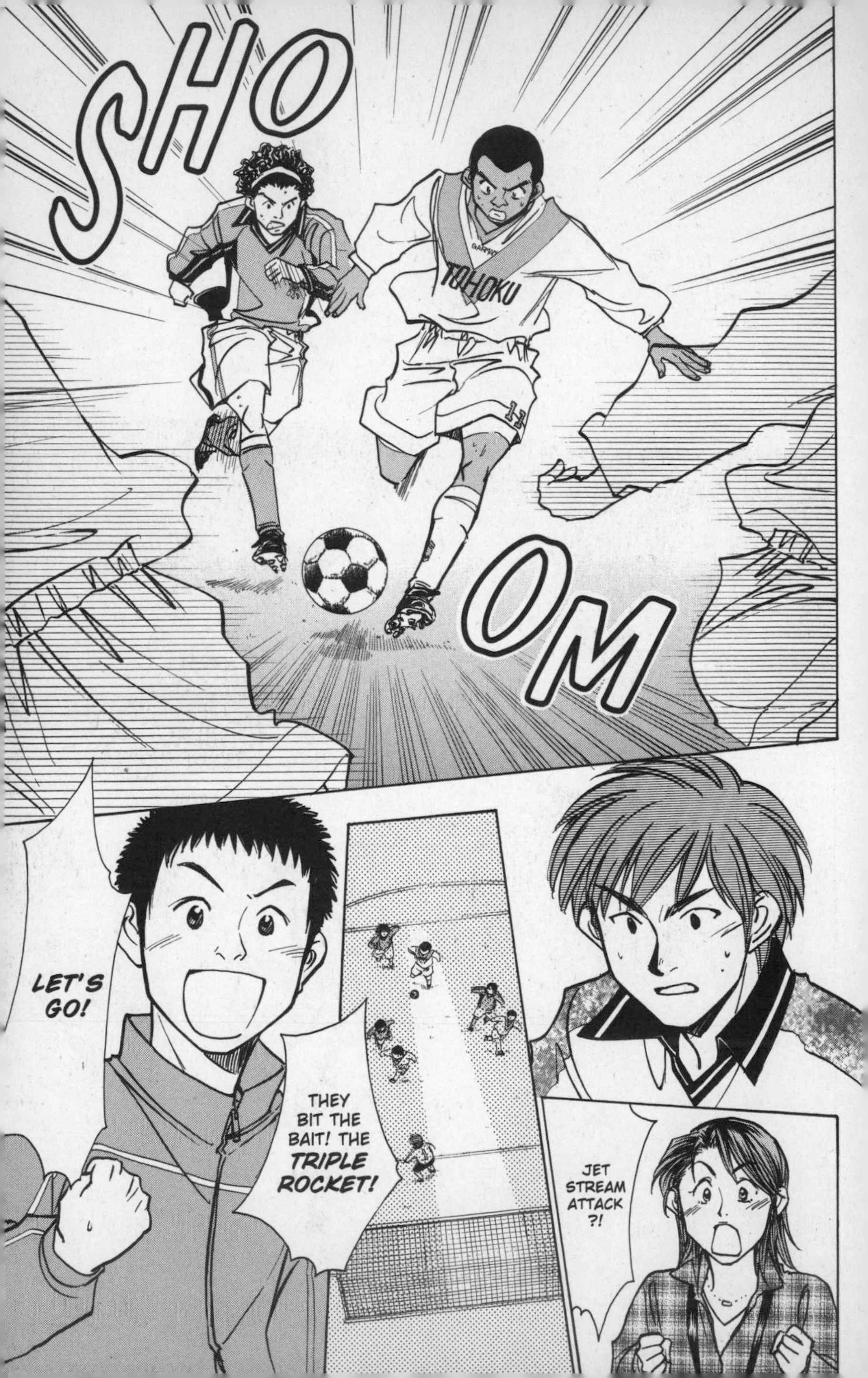
SHOOM
TOHOKU
JET STREAM ATTACK ?!
THEY BIT THE BAIT! THE TRIPLE ROCKET!
LET'S GO!

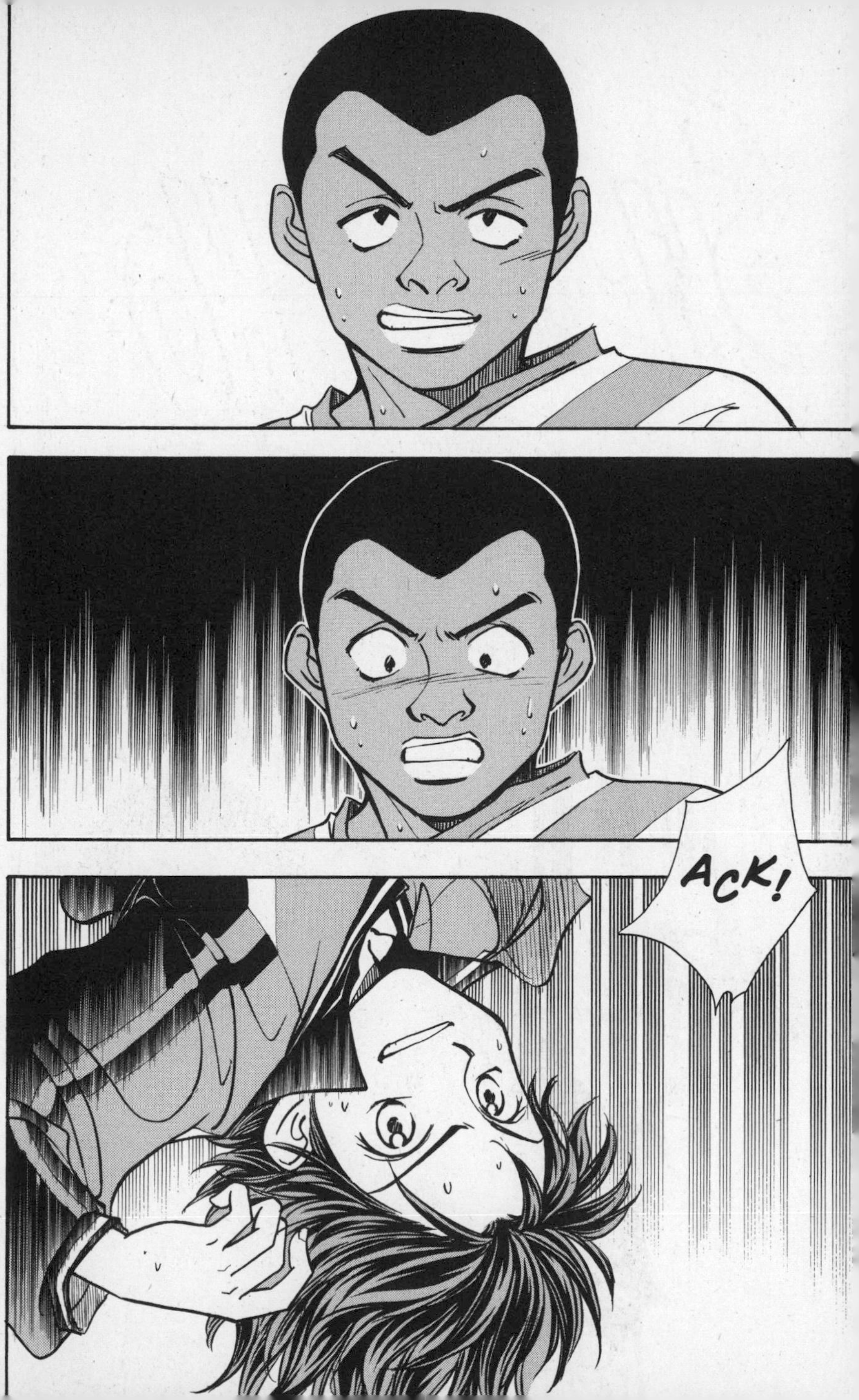
ACK!

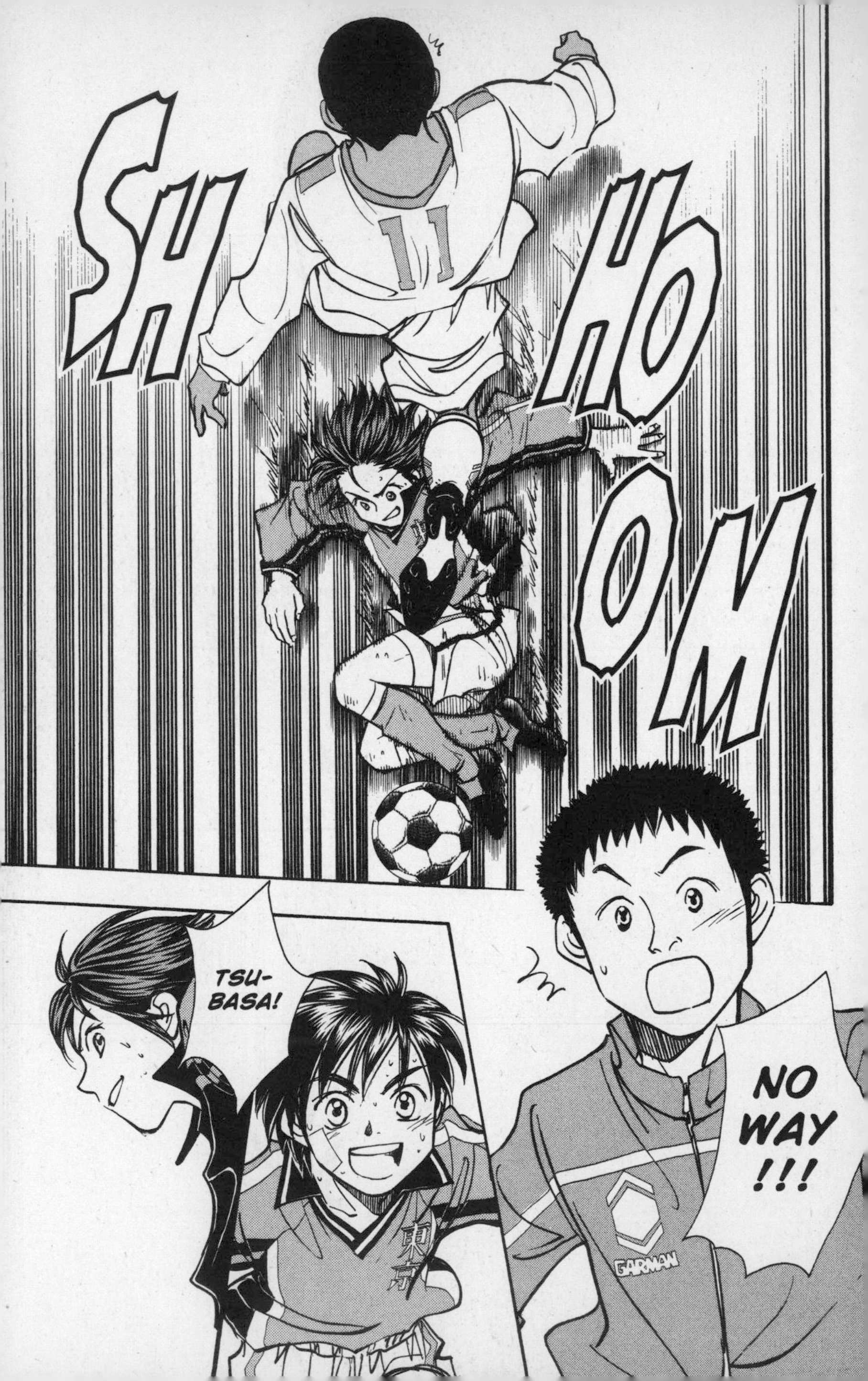
SHHOOM
NO WAY!!!
TSU-BASA!

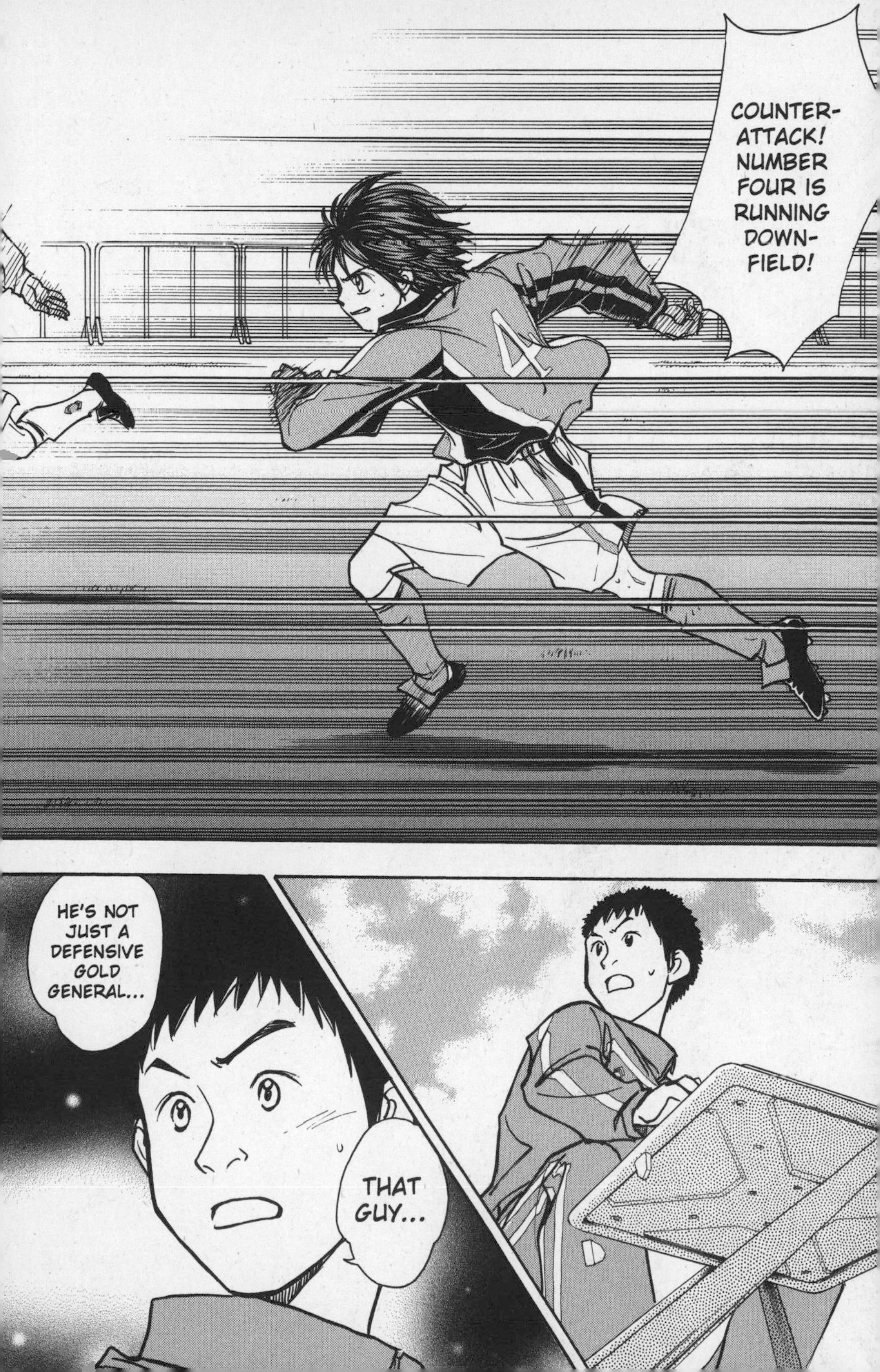
COUNTER-ATTACK! NUMBER FOUR IS RUNNING DOWN-FIELD!
THAT GUY...
HE'S NOT JUST A DEFENSIVE GOLD GENERAL...

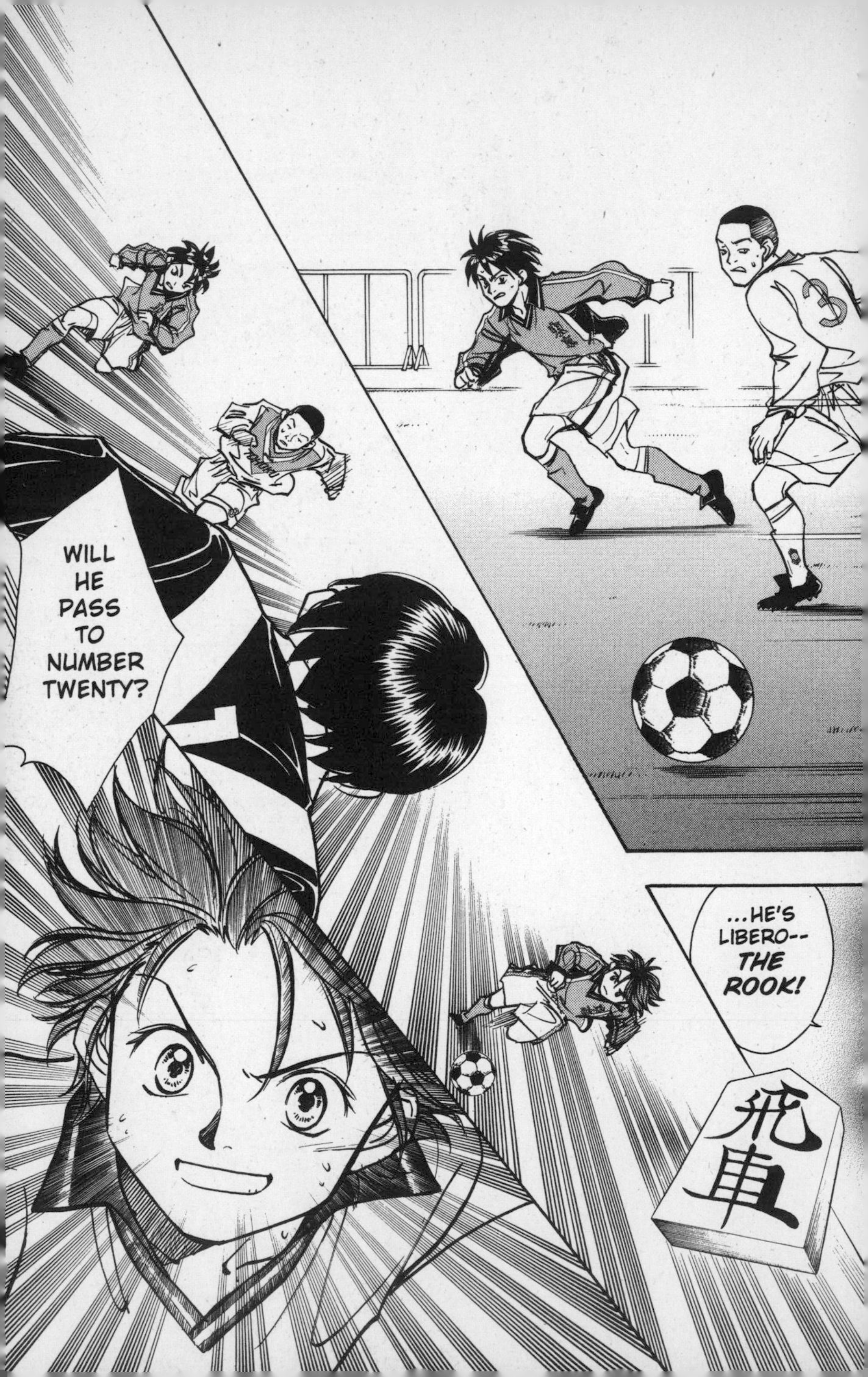
...HE'S LIBERO-- THE ROOK!
飛車
WILL HE PASS TO NUMBER TWENTY?

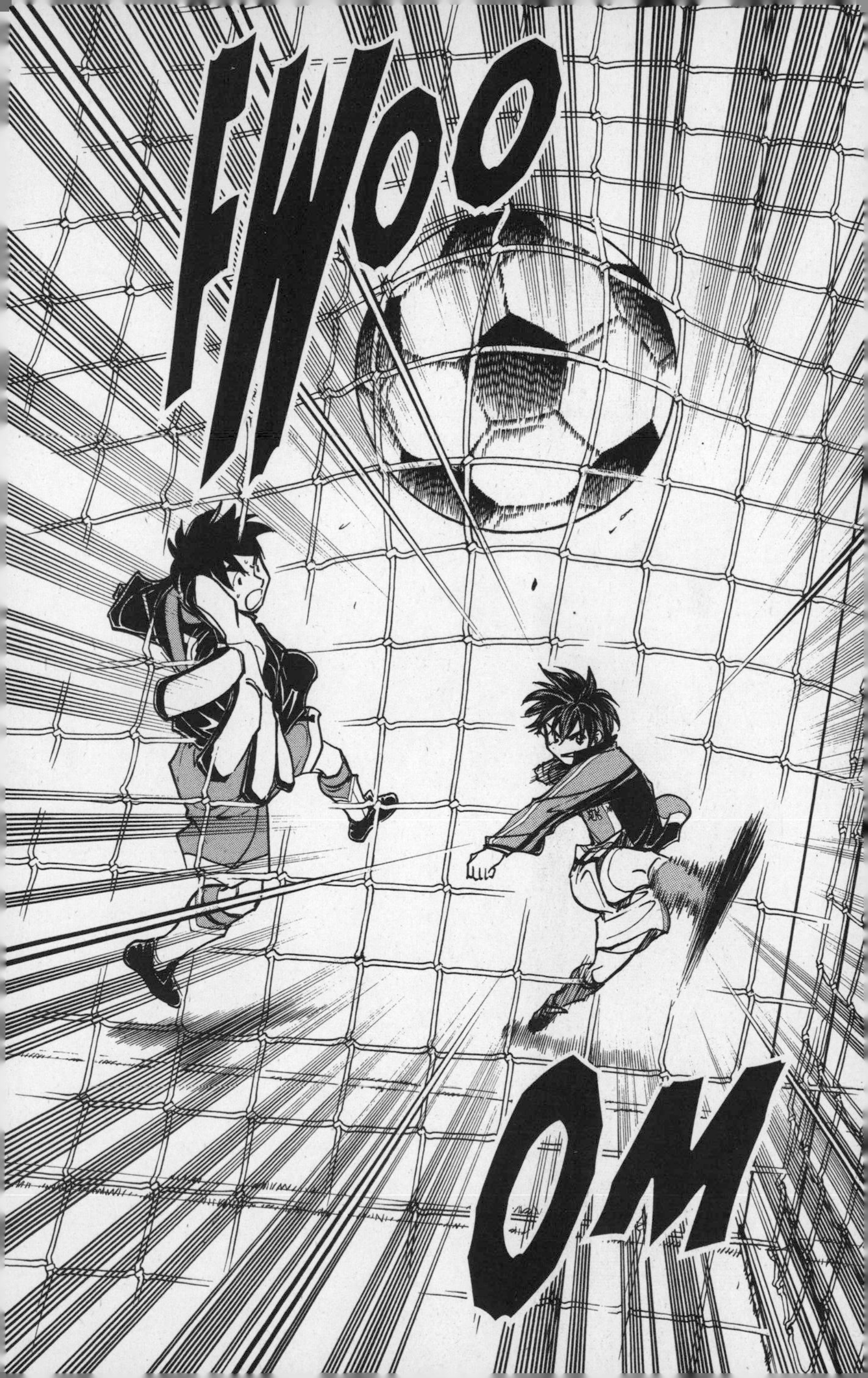
FWOO
OM

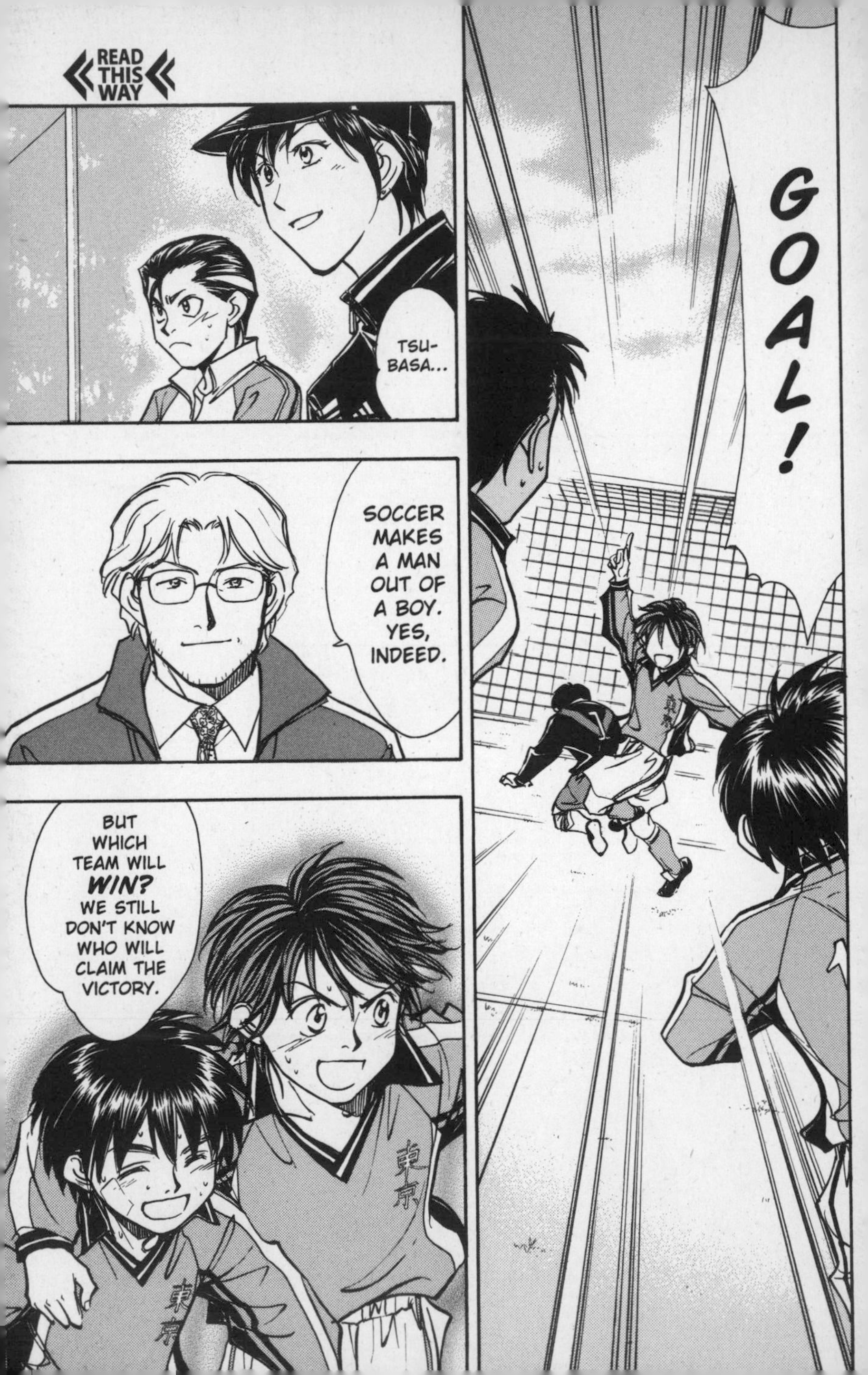
READ THIS WAY
GOAL!
TSU-BASA...
SOCCER MAKES A MAN OUT OF A BOY. YES, INDEED.
BUT WHICH TEAM WILL WIN? WE STILL DON'T KNOW WHO WILL CLAIM THE VICTORY.

STAGE.186 The Final Weapon's Willpower

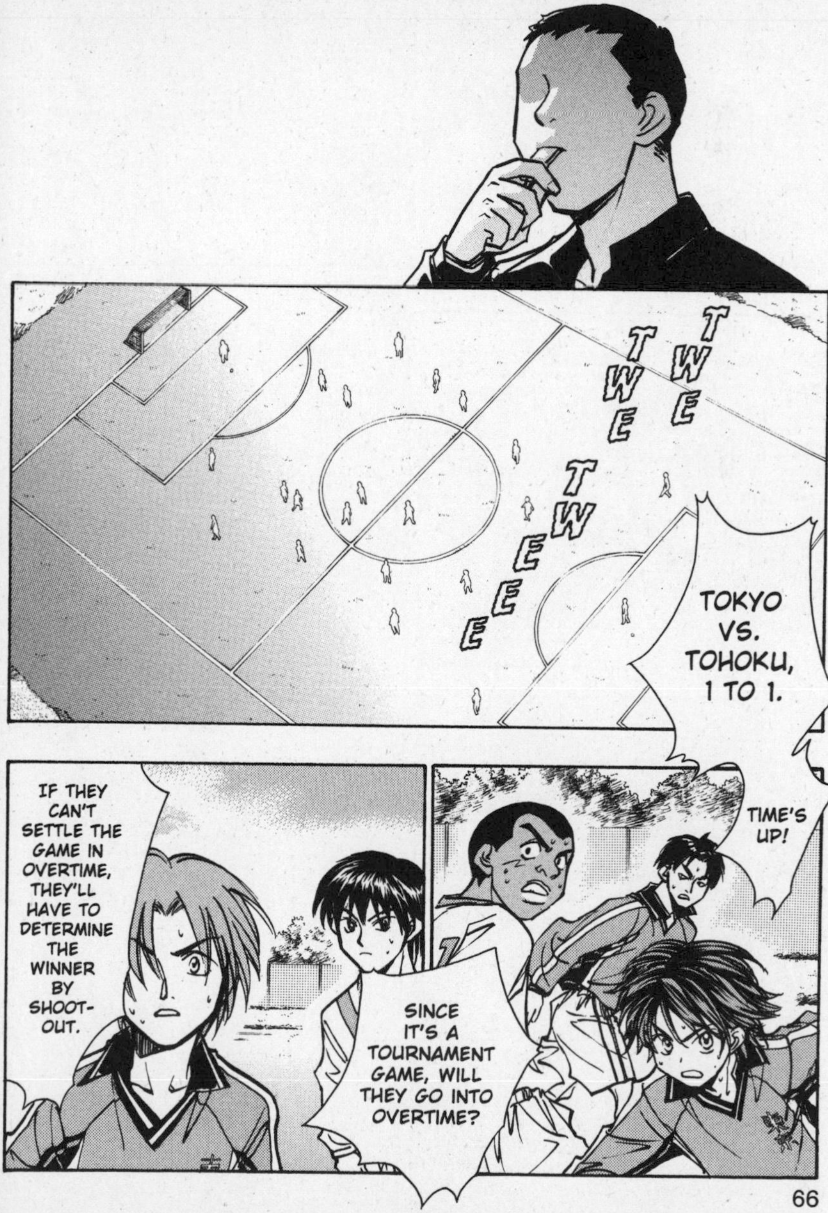
TWEE
TWEEEE
TOKYO VS. TOHOKU, 1 TO 1.
TIME'S UP!
SINCE IT'S A TOURNAMENT GAME, WILL THEY GO INTO OVERTIME?
IF THEY CAN'T SETTLE THE GAME IN OVERTIME, THEY'LL HAVE TO DETERMINE THE WINNER BY SHOOT-OUT.

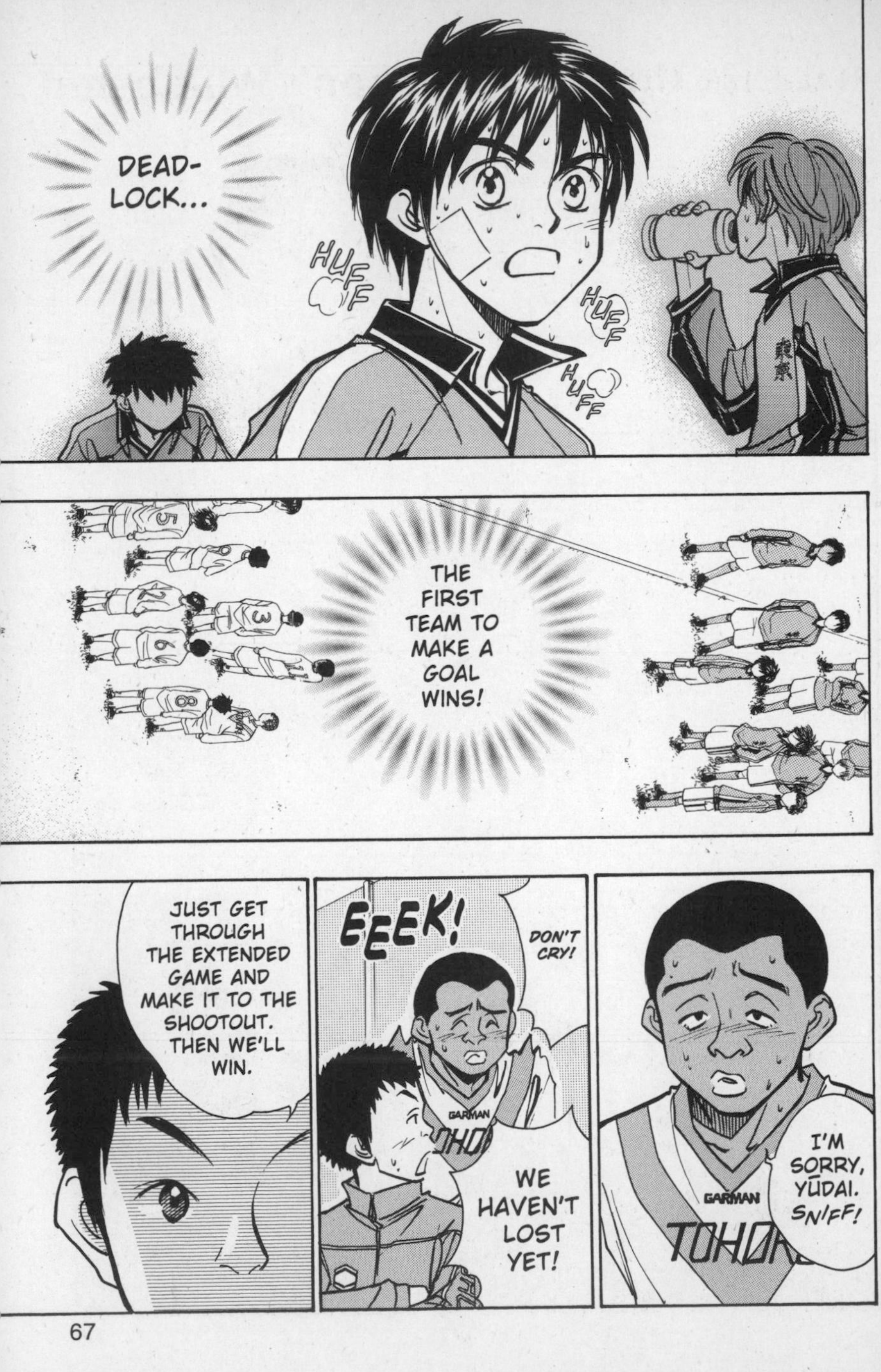
DEAD-LOCK...
HUFF
HUFF
HUFF
THE FIRST TEAM TO MAKE A GOAL WINS!
I'M SORRY, YŪDAI. SNIFF!
DON'T CRY!
EEEK!
WE HAVEN'T LOST YET!
JUST GET THROUGH THE EXTENDED GAME AND MAKE IT TO THE SHOOTOUT. THEN WE'LL WIN.

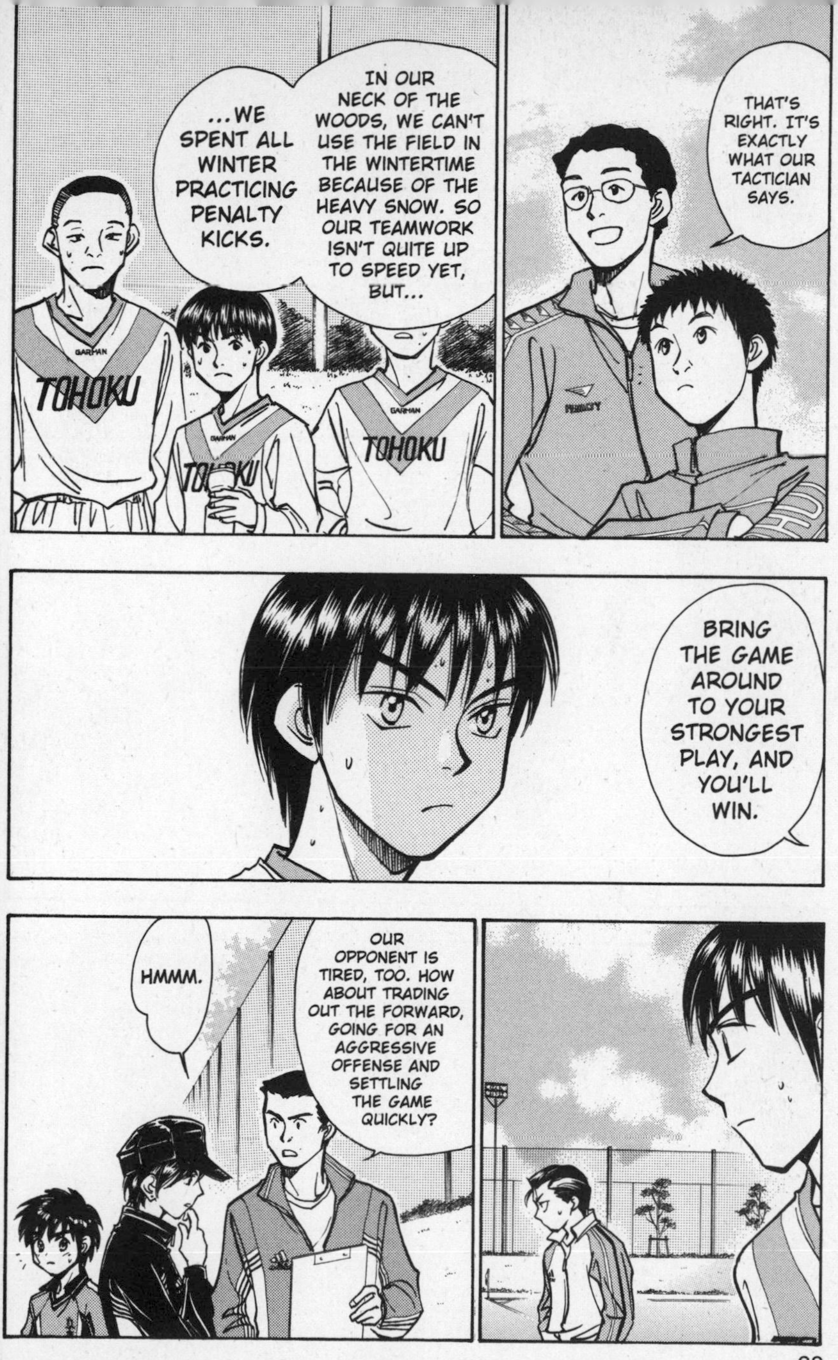
THAT'S RIGHT. IT'S EXACTLY WHAT OUR TACTICIAN SAYS.
IN OUR NECK OF THE WOODS, WE CAN'T USE THE FIELD IN THE WINTERTIME BECAUSE OF THE HEAVY SNOW. SO OUR TEAMWORK ISN'T QUITE UP TO SPEED YET, BUT...
...WE SPENT ALL WINTER PRACTICING PENALTY KICKS.
BRING THE GAME AROUND TO YOUR STRONGEST PLAY, AND YOU'LL WIN.
OUR OPPONENT IS TIRED, TOO. HOW ABOUT TRADING OUT THE FORWARD, GOING FOR AN AGGRESSIVE OFFENSE AND SETTLING THE GAME QUICKLY?
HMMM.

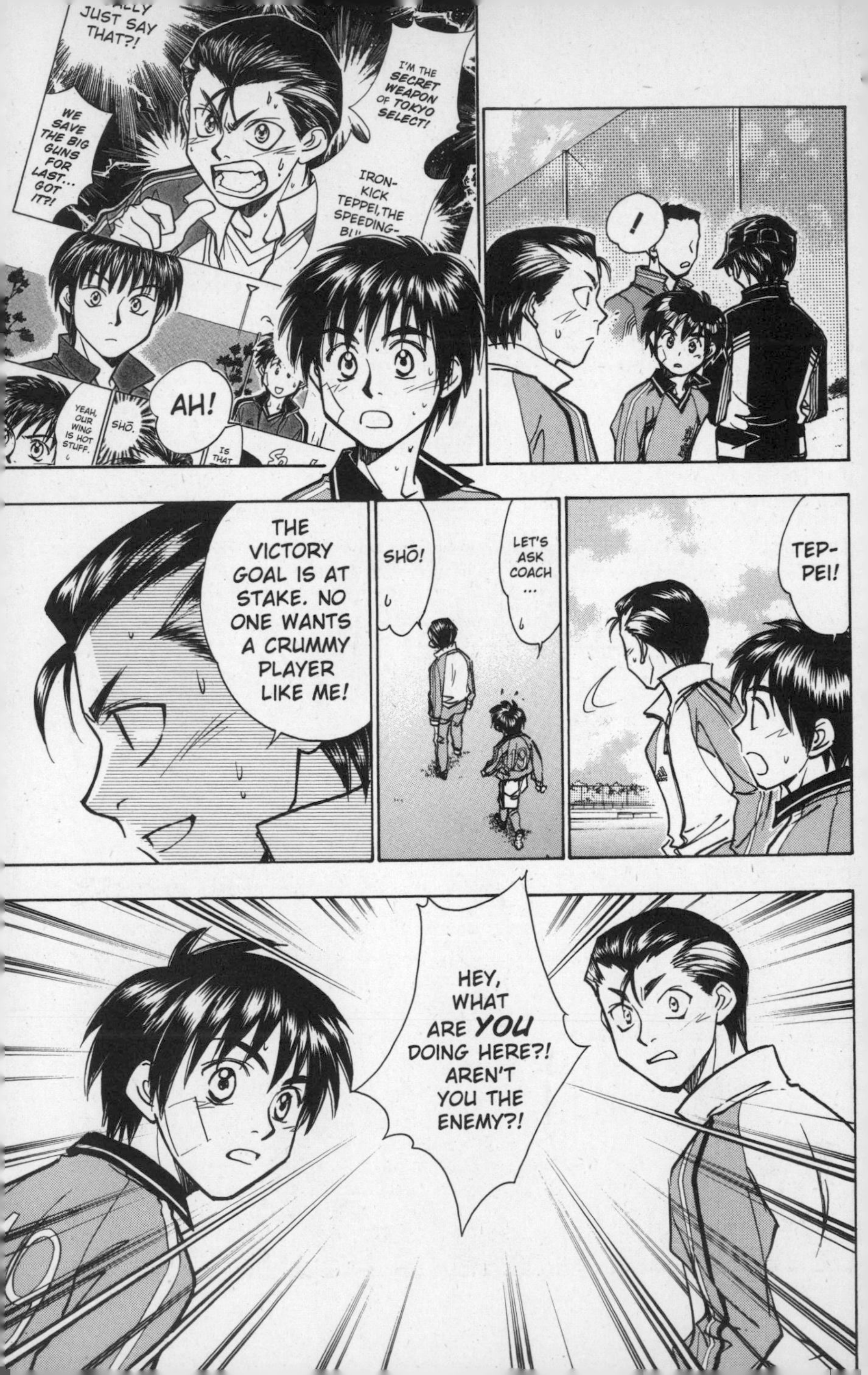
!
I'M THE SECRET WEAPON OF TOKYO SELECT!
IRON-KICK TEPPEI, THE SPEEDING-
JUST SAY THAT?!
WE SAVE THE BIG GUNS FOR LAST... GOT IT?!
AH!
IS THAT
SHŌ.
YEAH, OUR WING IS HOT STUFF.
TEP-PEI!
LET'S ASK COACH...
SHŌ!
THE VICTORY GOAL IS AT STAKE. NO ONE WANTS A CRUMMY PLAYER LIKE ME!
HEY, WHAT ARE *YOU* DOING HERE?! AREN'T YOU THE ENEMY?!

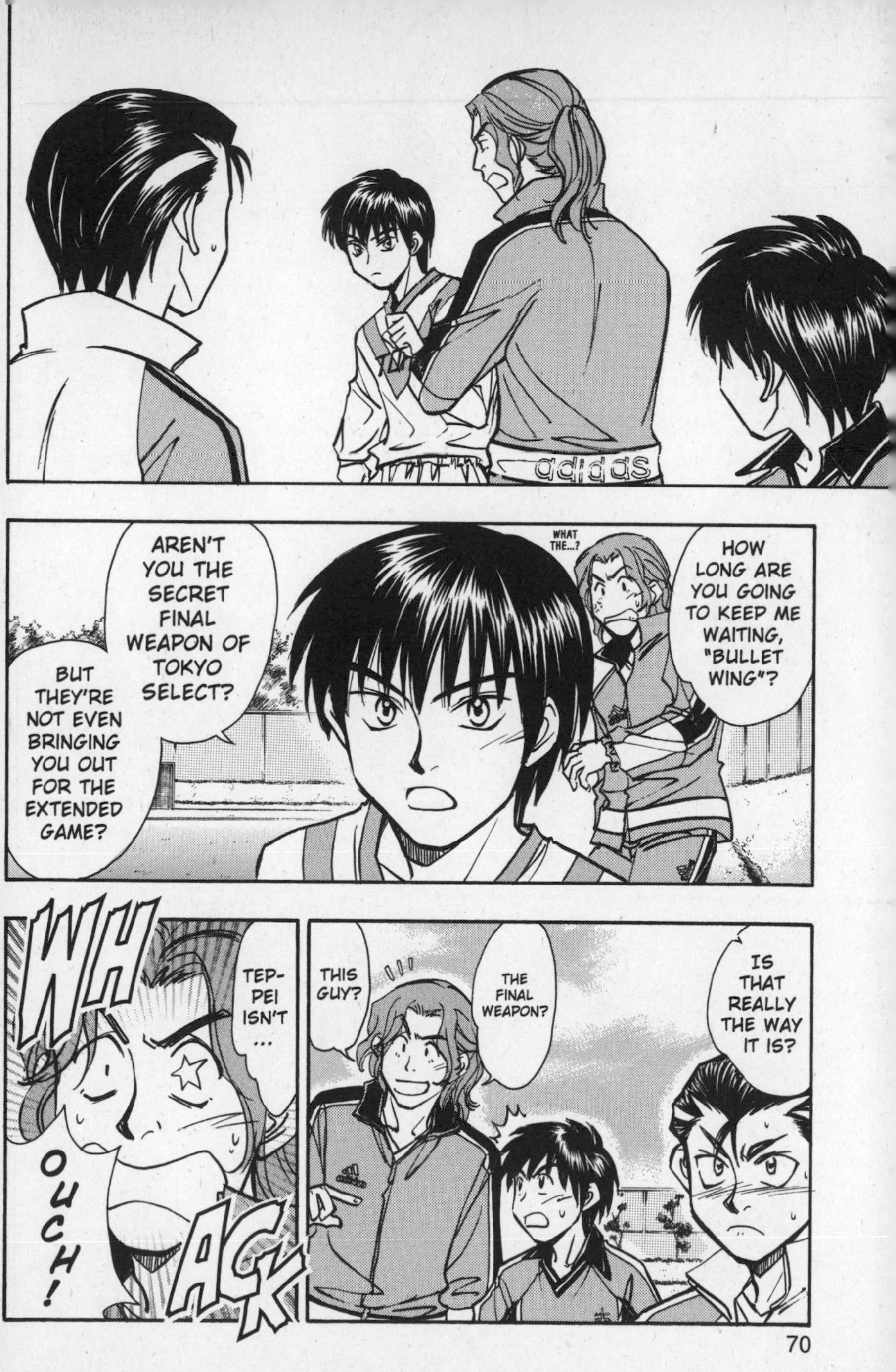
adidas
HOW LONG ARE YOU GOING TO KEEP ME WAITING, "BULLET WING"?
WHAT THE...?
AREN'T YOU THE SECRET FINAL WEAPON OF TOKYO SELECT?
BUT THEY'RE NOT EVEN BRINGING YOU OUT FOR THE EXTENDED GAME?
IS THAT REALLY THE WAY IT IS?
THE FINAL WEAPON?
THIS GUY?
TEP-PEI ISN'T ...
WHACK
OUCH!

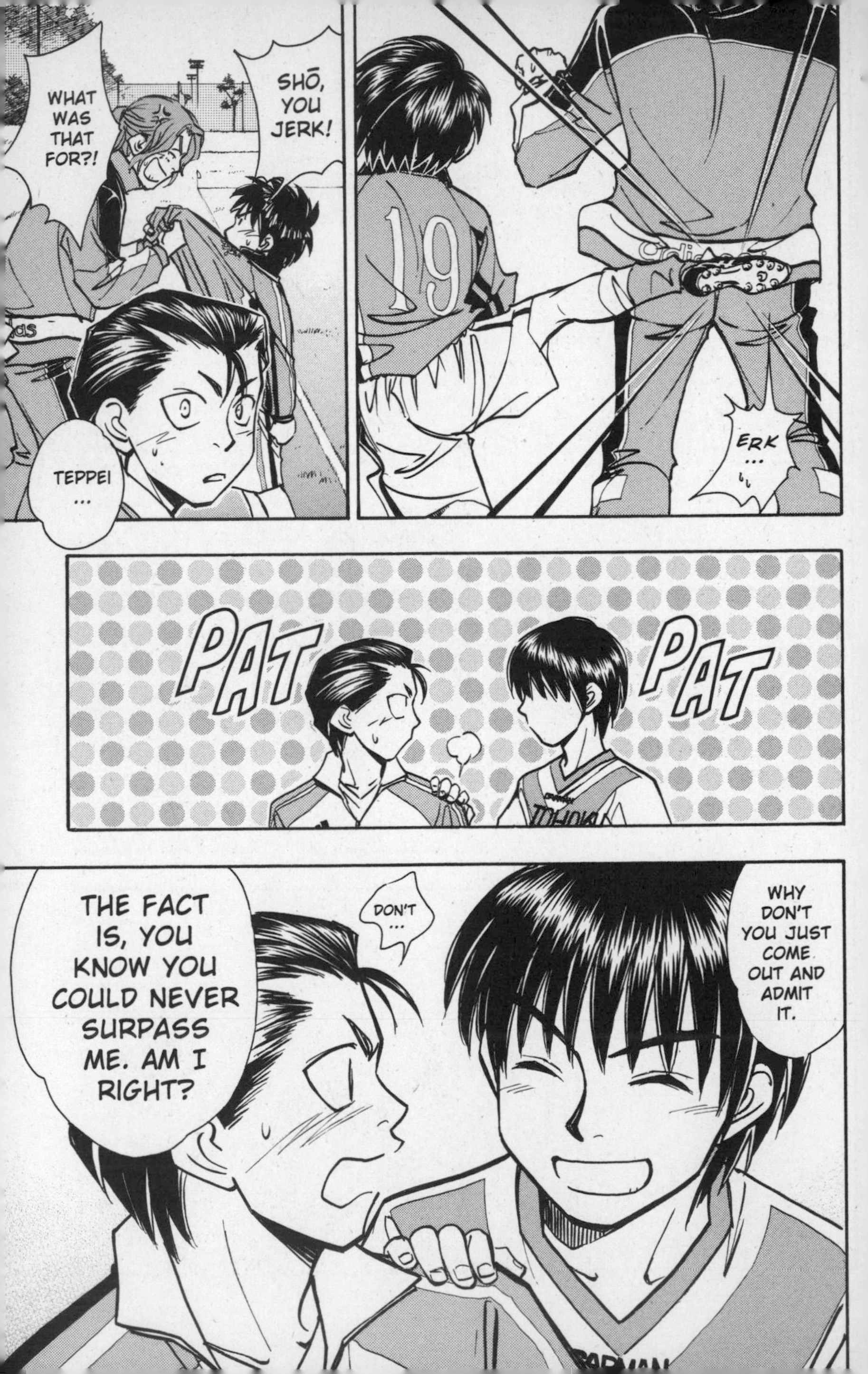
ERK ...
SHŌ, YOU JERK!
WHAT WAS THAT FOR?!
TEPPEI ...
PAT
PAT
WHY DON'T YOU JUST COME OUT AND ADMIT IT.
DON'T ...
THE FACT IS, YOU KNOW YOU COULD NEVER SURPASS ME. AM I RIGHT?

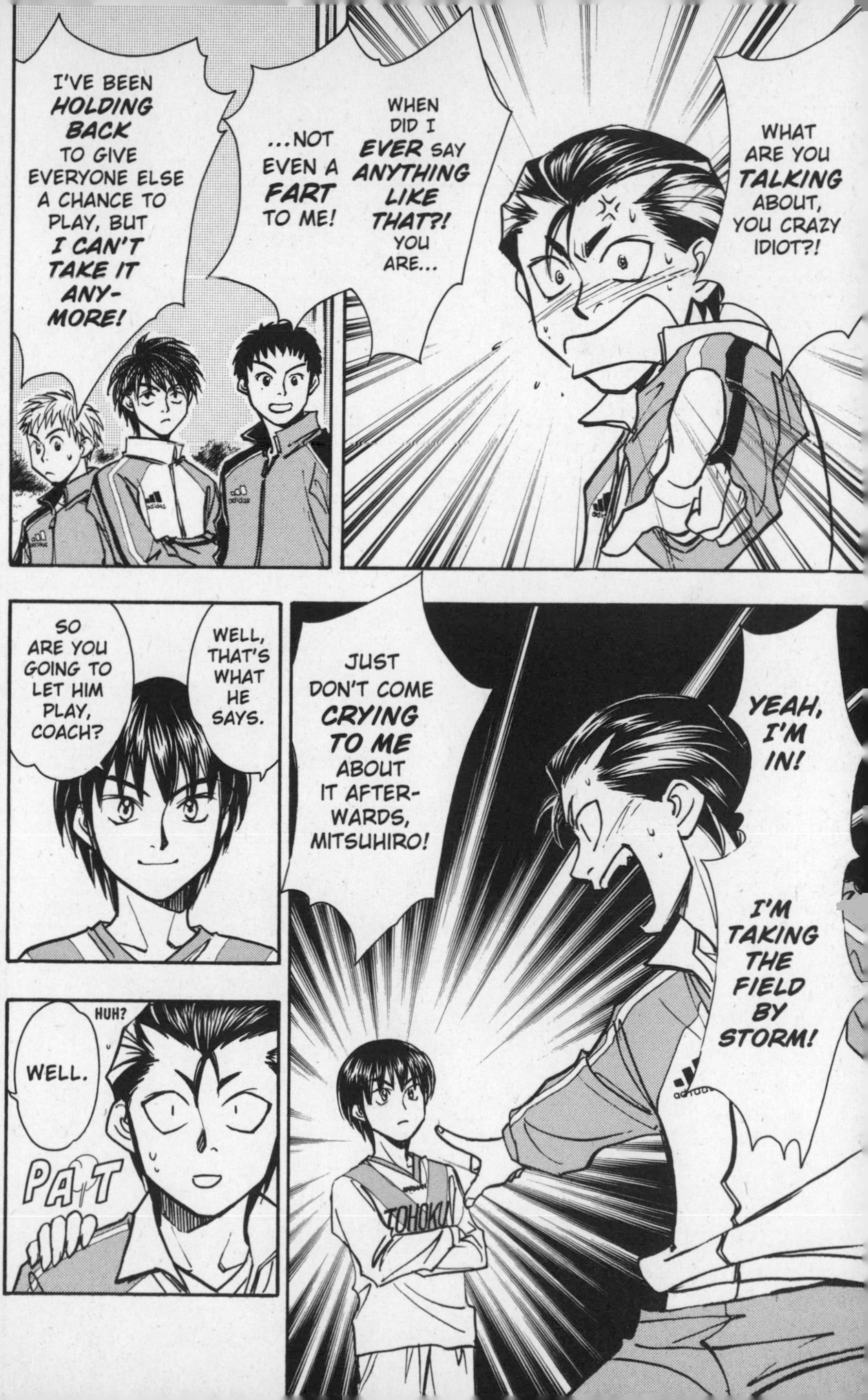
WHAT ARE YOU TALKING ABOUT, YOU CRAZY IDIOT?!
WHEN DID I EVER SAY ANYTHING LIKE THAT?! YOU ARE...
...NOT EVEN A FART TO ME!
I'VE BEEN HOLDING BACK TO GIVE EVERYONE ELSE A CHANCE TO PLAY, BUT I CAN'T TAKE IT ANY-MORE!
YEAH, I'M IN!
I'M TAKING THE FIELD BY STORM!
JUST DON'T COME CRYING TO ME ABOUT IT AFTER-WARDS, MITSUHIRO!
WELL, THAT'S WHAT HE SAYS.
SO ARE YOU GOING TO LET HIM PLAY, COACH?
HUH?
WELL.
PAT

READ THIS WAY

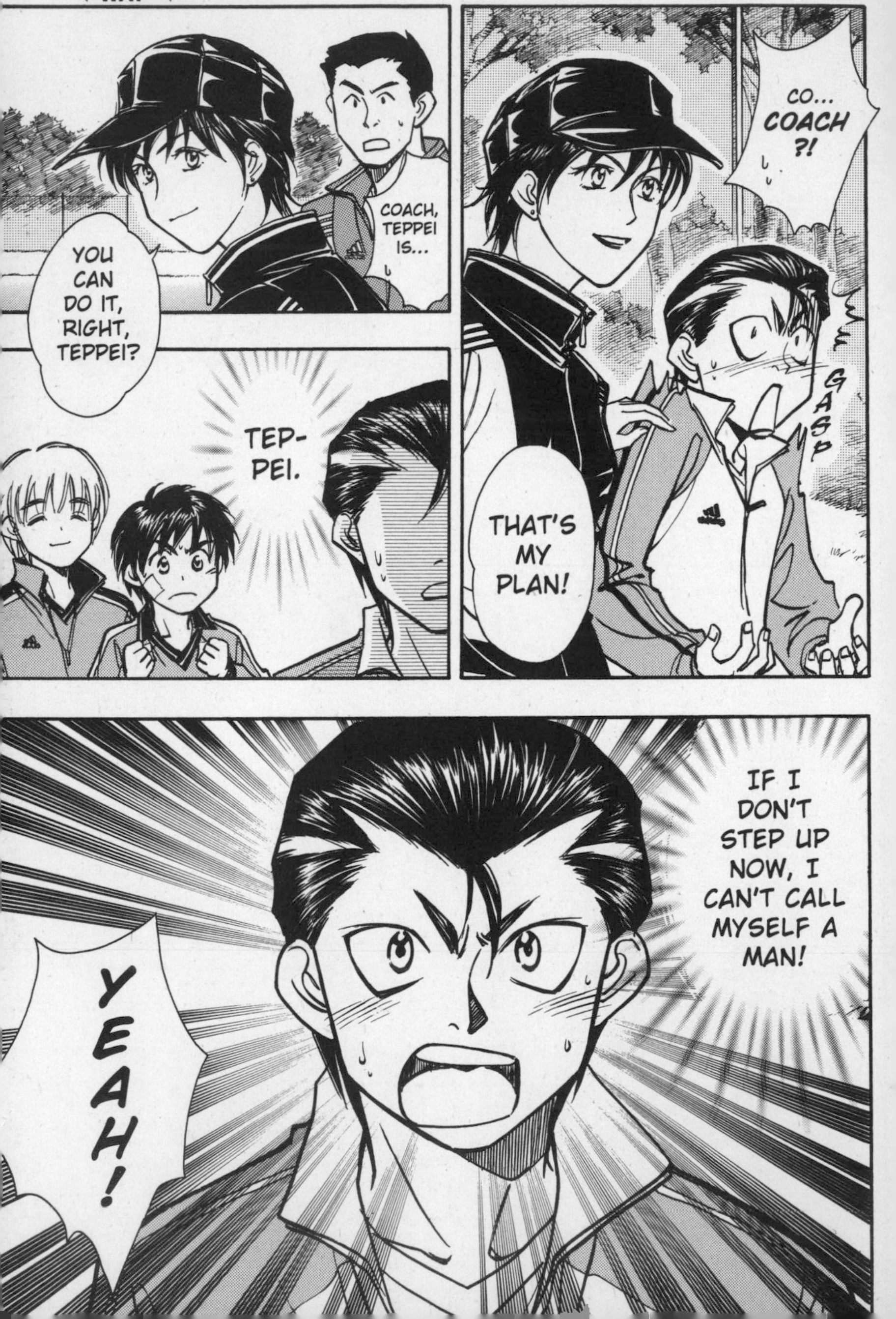
CO... COACH ?!
GASP
THAT'S MY PLAN!
COACH, TEPPEI IS...
YOU CAN DO IT, RIGHT, TEPPEI?
TEP-PEI.
IF I DON'T STEP UP NOW, I CAN'T CALL MYSELF A MAN!
YEAH!

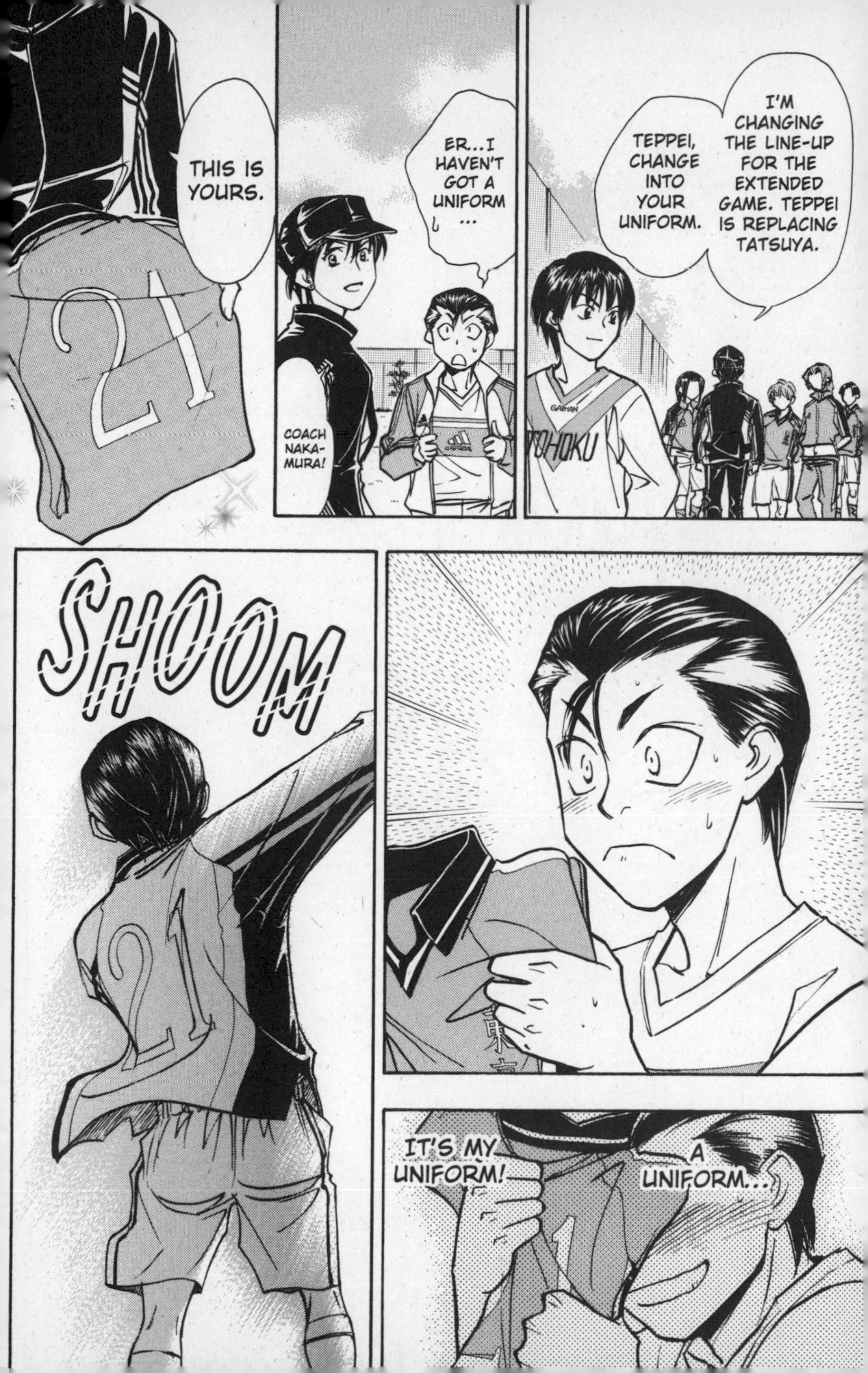
I'M CHANGING THE LINE-UP FOR THE EXTENDED GAME. TEPPEI IS REPLACING TATSUYA.
TEPPEI, CHANGE INTO YOUR UNIFORM.
TOHOKU
ER...I HAVEN'T GOT A UNIFORM ...
COACH NAKAMURA!
THIS IS YOURS.
A UNIFORM...
IT'S MY UNIFORM!
SHOOM

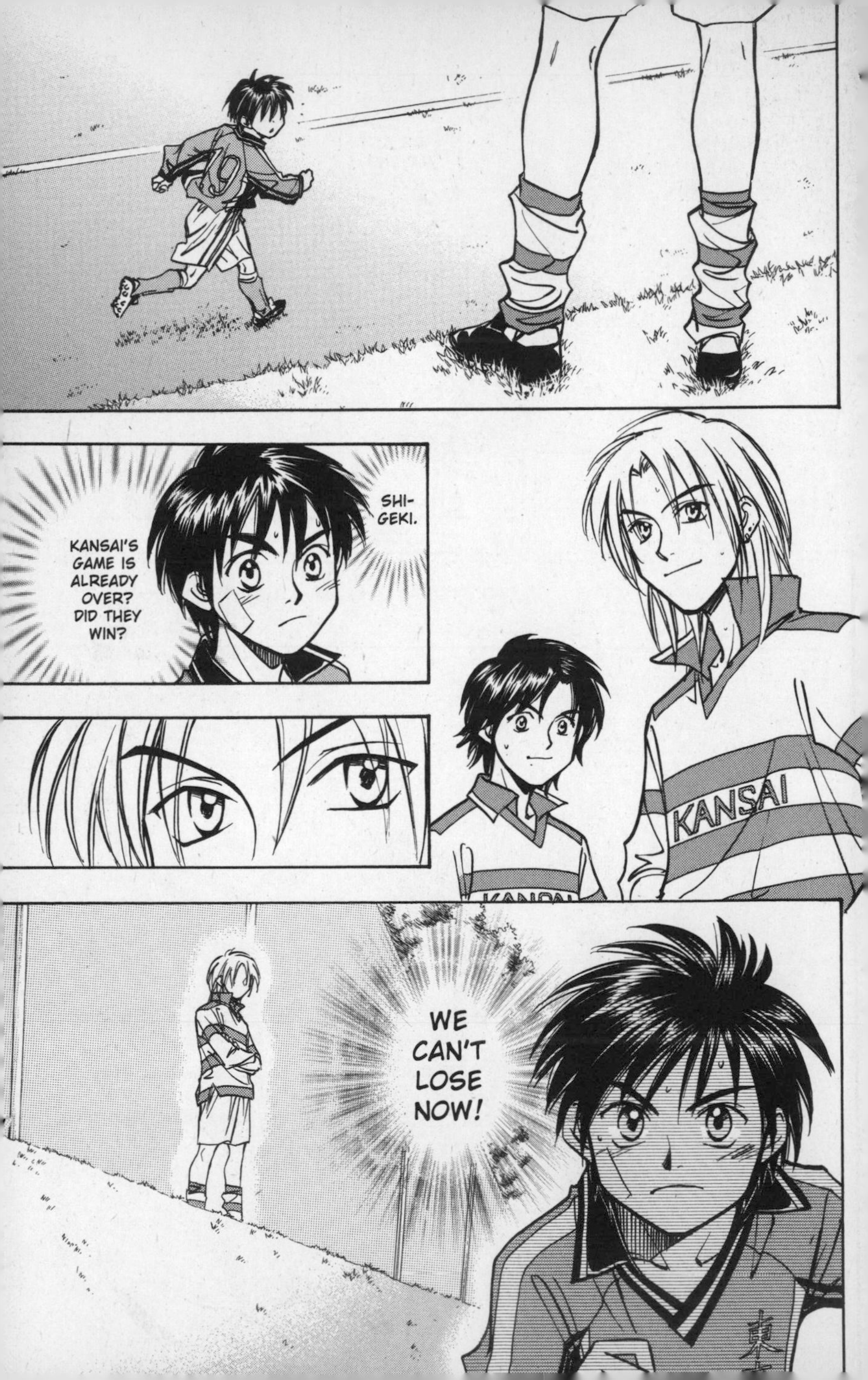
KANSAI
SHI-GEKI.
KANSAI'S GAME IS ALREADY OVER? DID THEY WIN?
WE CAN'T LOSE NOW!

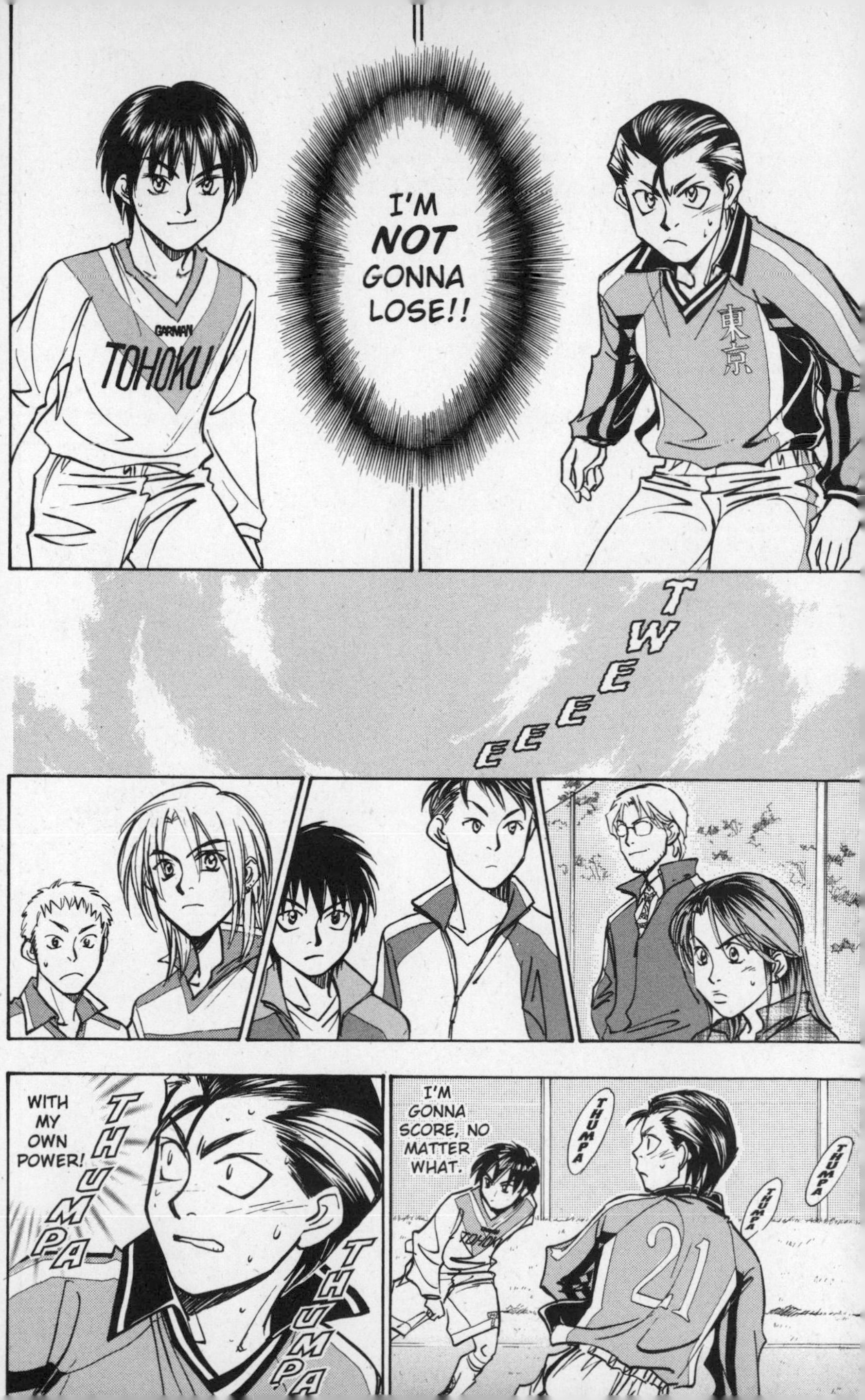
東京
I'M NOT GONNA LOSE!!
GARMAN
TOHOKU
TWEEEE
I'M GONNA SCORE, NO MATTER WHAT.
THUMPA
THUMPA
THUMPA
21
WITH MY OWN POWER!
THUMPA
THUMPA

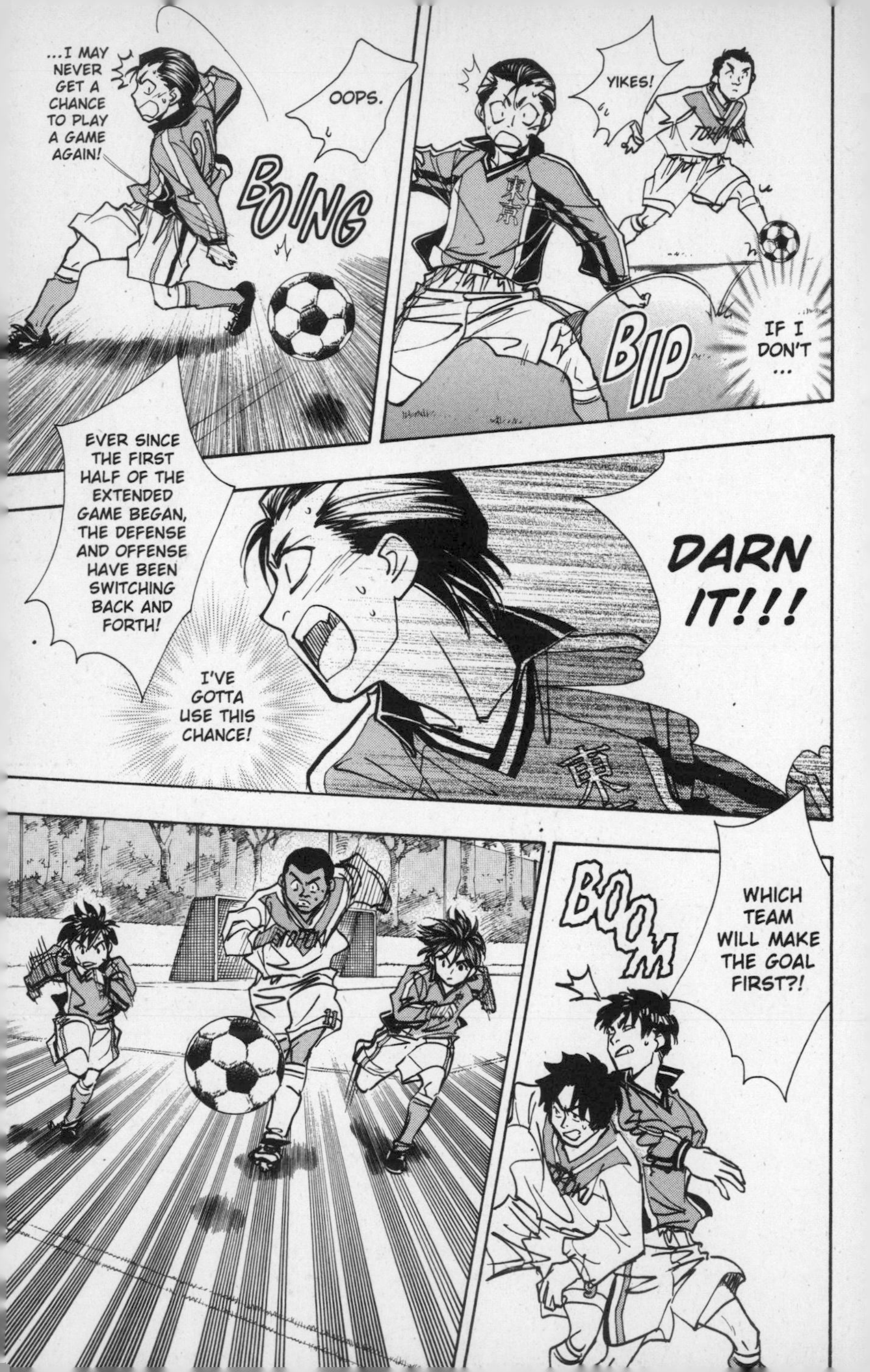
YIKES!
IF I DON'T ...
BIP
OOPS.
...I MAY NEVER GET A CHANCE TO PLAY A GAME AGAIN!
BOING
DARN IT!!!
EVER SINCE THE FIRST HALF OF THE EXTENDED GAME BEGAN, THE DEFENSE AND OFFENSE HAVE BEEN SWITCHING BACK AND FORTH!
I'VE GOTTA USE THIS CHANCE!
WHICH TEAM WILL MAKE THE GOAL FIRST?!
BOOM

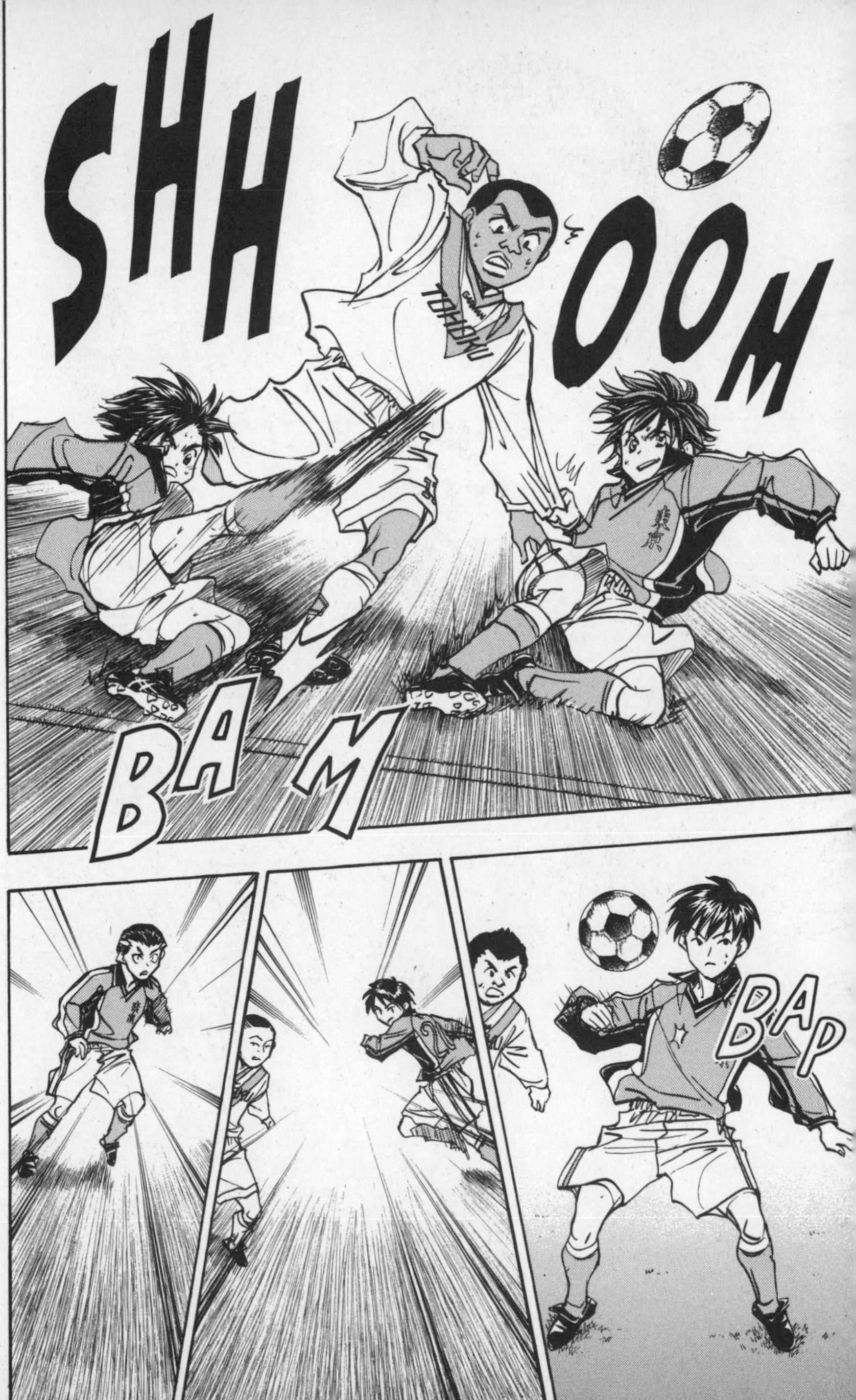
SHH OOM
TOHOKU
BAM
BAP

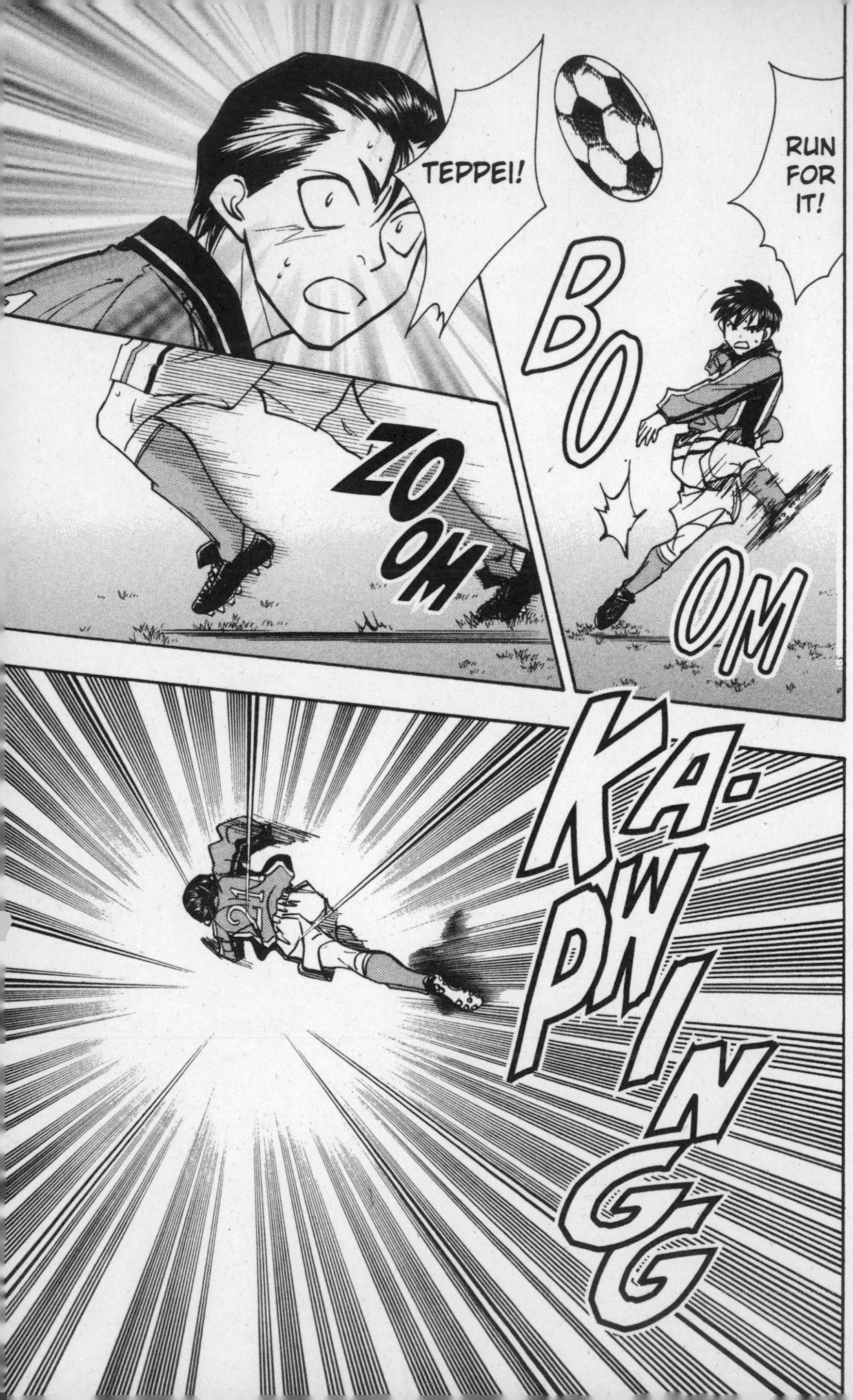
RUN FOR IT!
BOOOM
TEPPEI!
ZOOM
KA-PWINGG

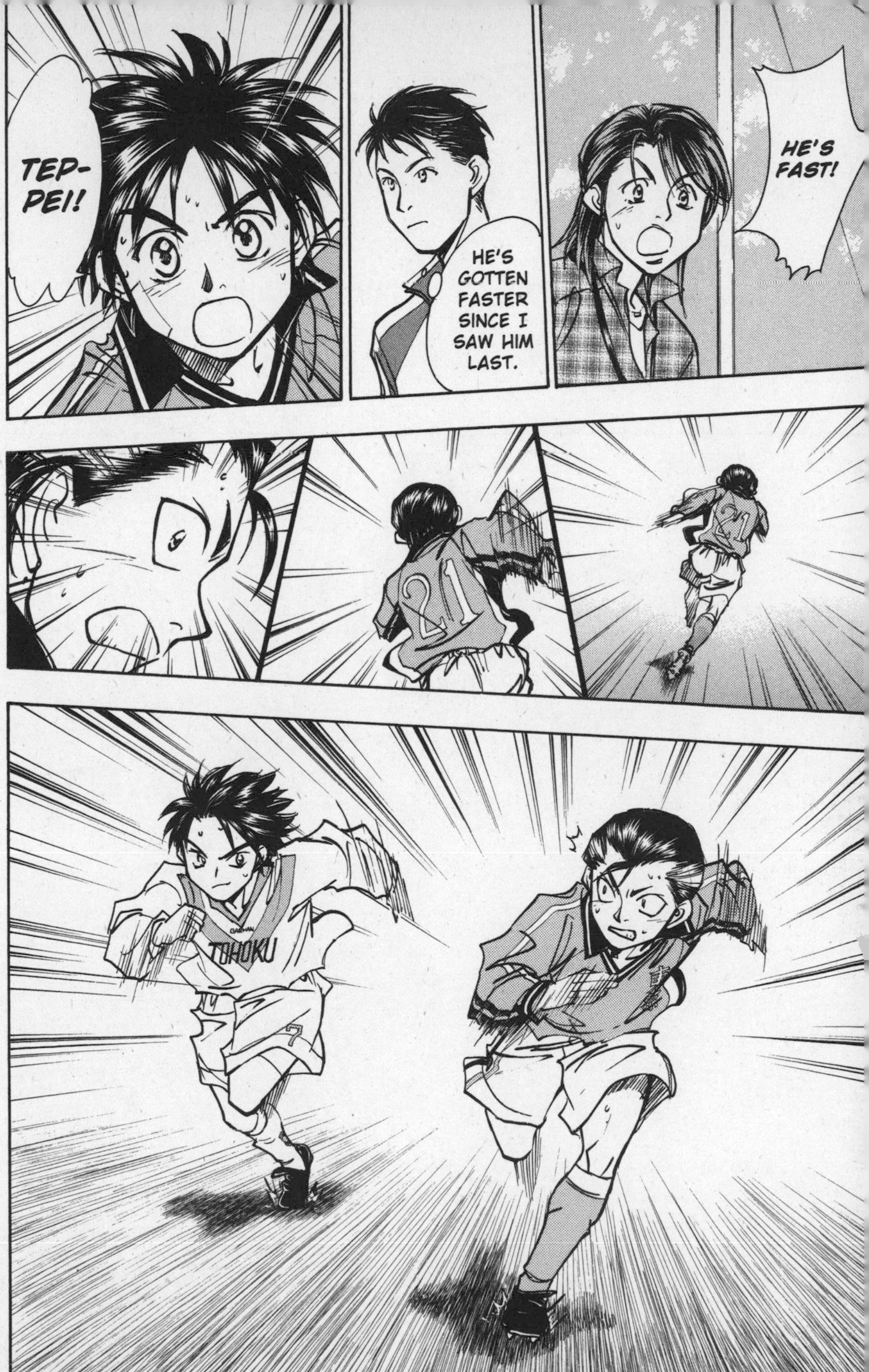
HE'S FAST!
HE'S GOTTEN FASTER SINCE I SAW HIM LAST.
TEP-PEI!
TOHOKU

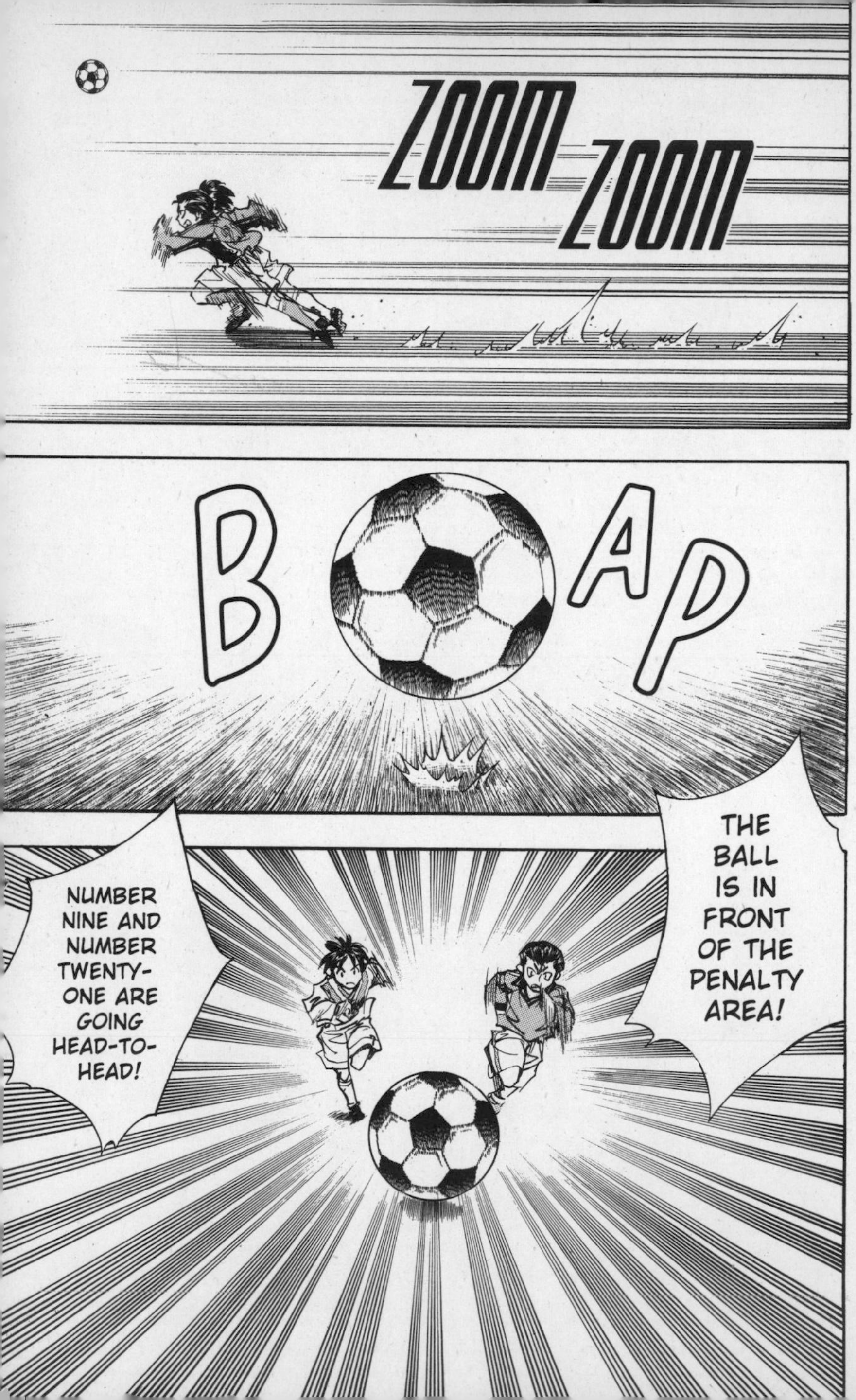
ZOOM ZOOM
BOAP
THE BALL IS IN FRONT OF THE PENALTY AREA!
NUMBER NINE AND NUMBER TWENTY-ONE ARE GOING HEAD-TO-HEAD!

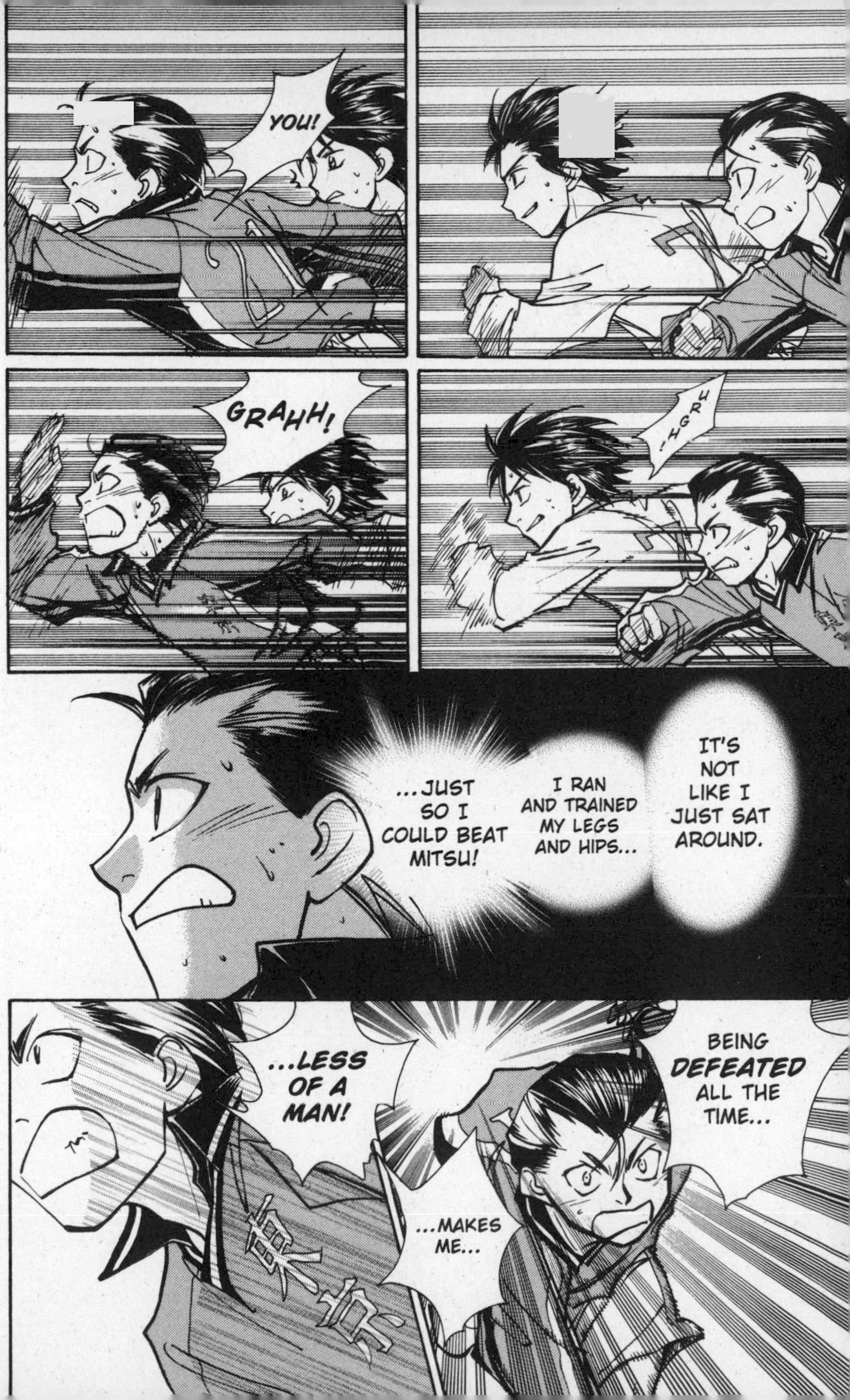
YOU!
URGH!
GRAHH!
IT'S NOT LIKE I JUST SAT AROUND.
I RAN AND TRAINED MY LEGS AND HIPS...
...JUST SO I COULD BEAT MITSU!
BEING DEFEATED ALL THE TIME...
...MAKES ME...
...LESS OF A MAN!

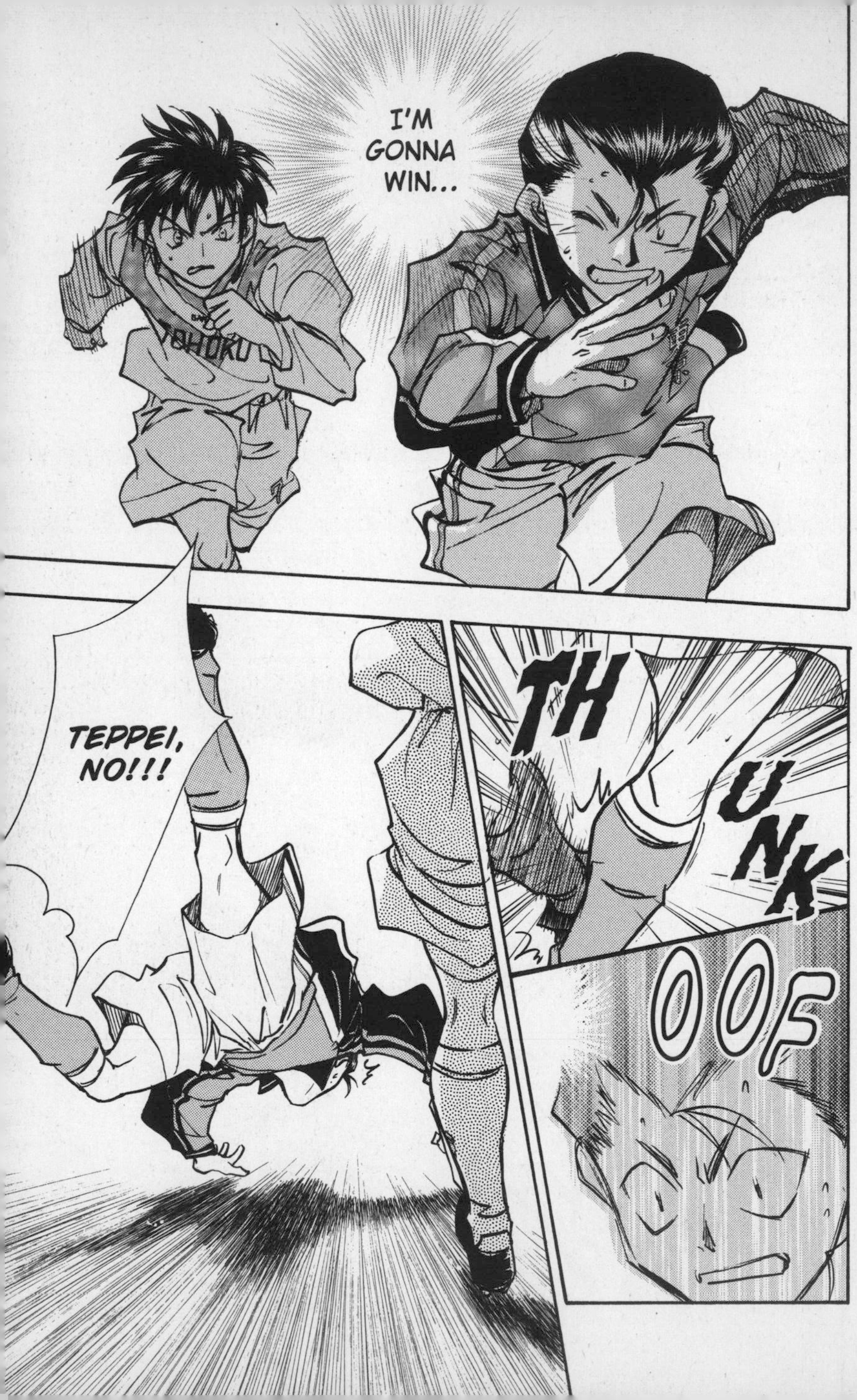
I'M GONNA WIN...
THUNK
OOF
TEPPEI, NO!!!

GARMAN

WHISTLE!

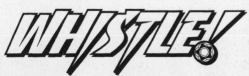

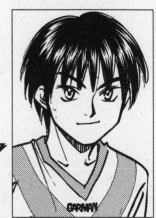

STAGE.187

Not Gonna Quit Soccer

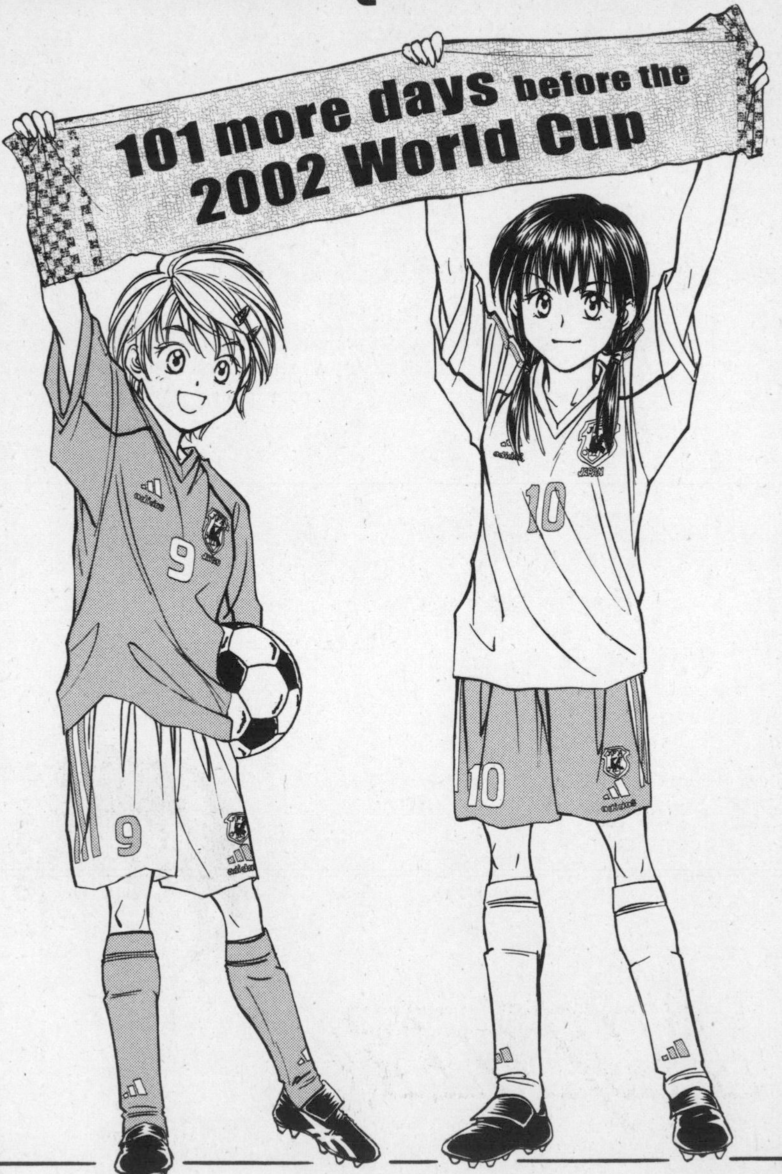
101 more days before the
2002 World Cup

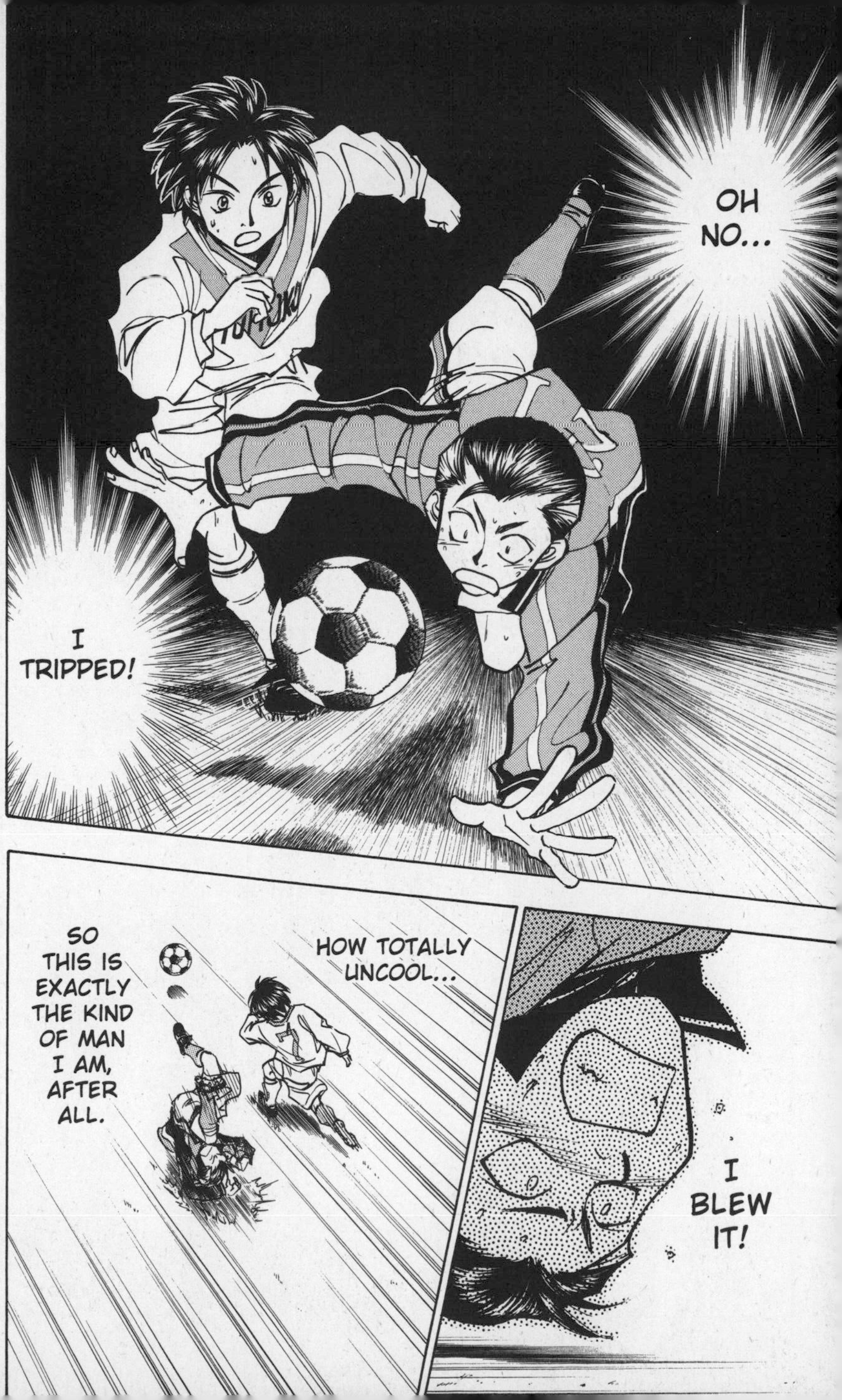
OH NO...
I TRIPPED!
I BLEW IT!
HOW TOTALLY UNCOOL...
SO THIS IS EXACTLY THE KIND OF MAN I AM, AFTER ALL.

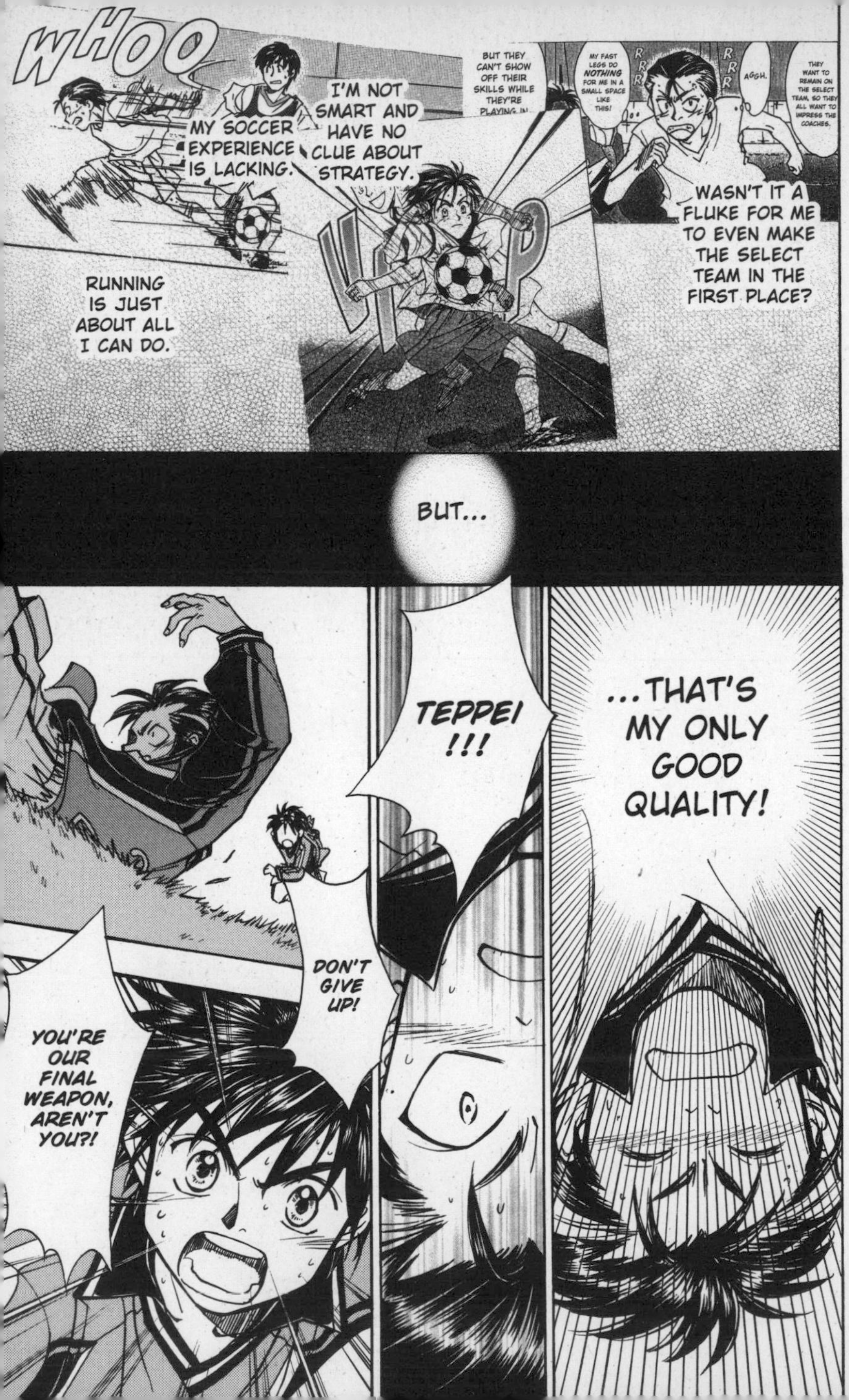
THEY WANT TO REMAIN ON THE SELECT TEAM, SO THEY ALL WANT TO IMPRESS THE COACHES.
AGGH.
RRR
RRR
MY FAST LEGS DO NOTHING FOR ME IN A SMALL SPACE LIKE THIS!
BUT THEY CAN'T SHOW OFF THEIR SKILLS WHILE THEY'RE PLAYING IN
WASN'T IT A FLUKE FOR ME TO EVEN MAKE THE SELECT TEAM IN THE FIRST PLACE?
I'M NOT SMART AND HAVE NO CLUE ABOUT STRATEGY.
WHOO
MY SOCCER EXPERIENCE IS LACKING.
RUNNING IS JUST ABOUT ALL I CAN DO.
BUT...
...THAT'S MY ONLY GOOD QUALITY!
TEPPEI!!!
DON'T GIVE UP!
YOU'RE OUR FINAL WEAPON, AREN'T YOU?!

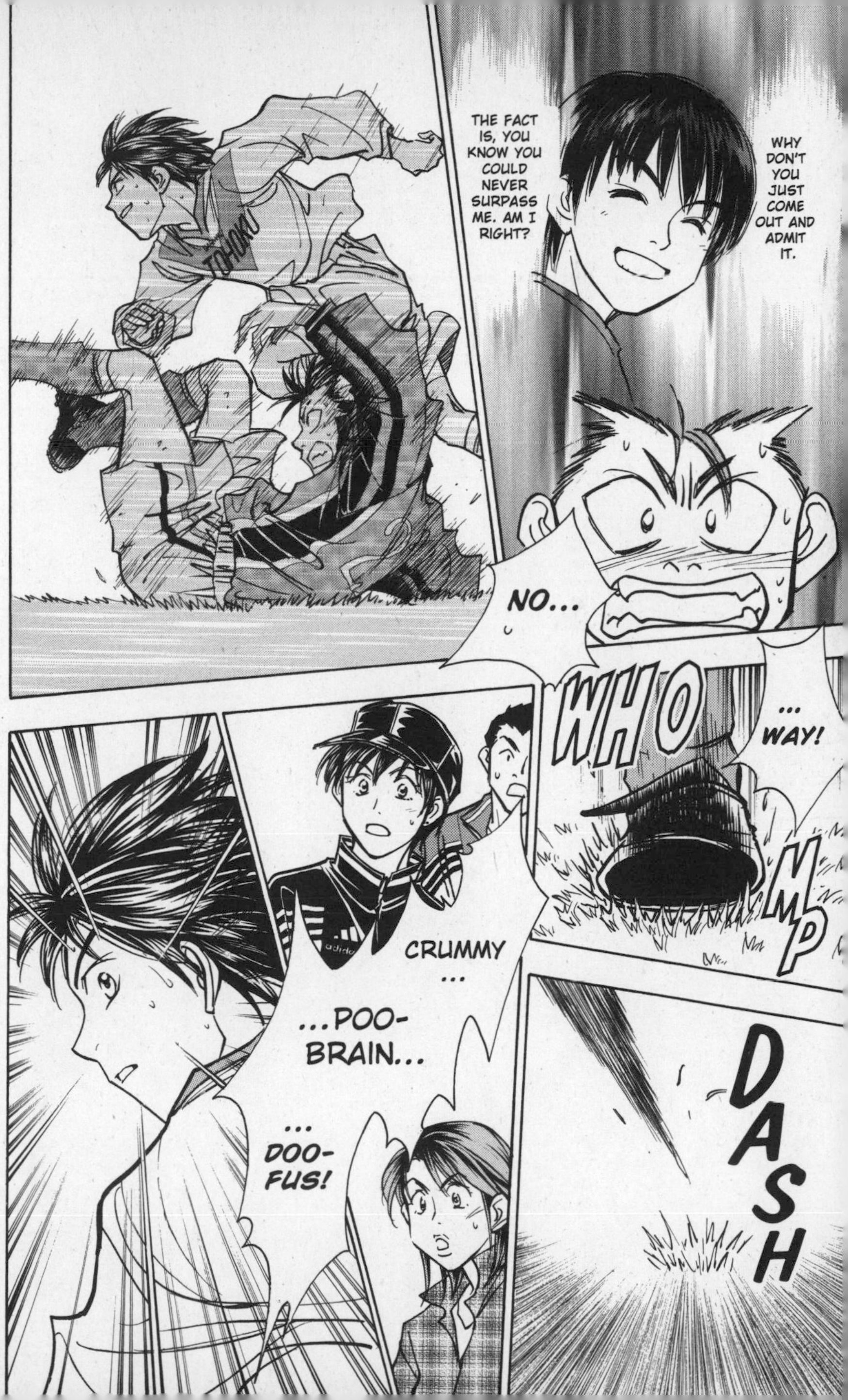

WHY DON'T YOU JUST COME OUT AND ADMIT IT.
THE FACT IS, YOU KNOW YOU COULD NEVER SURPASS ME. AM I RIGHT?
NO...
TOHOKU
... WAY!
WHOMP
DASH
CRUMMY ...
...POO-BRAIN...
... DOO-FUS!

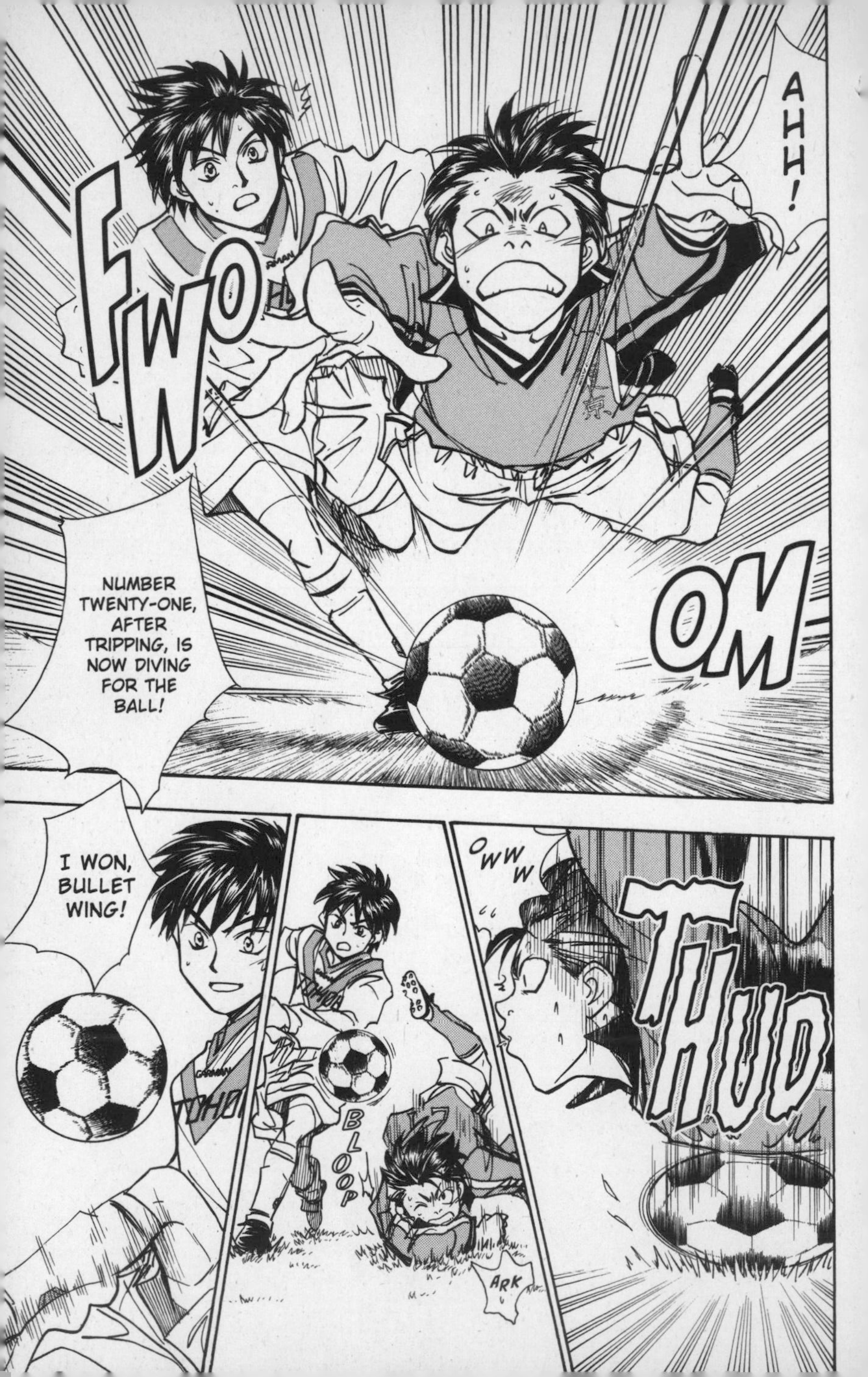
AHH!
FWOOM
NUMBER TWENTY-ONE, AFTER TRIPPING, IS NOW DIVING FOR THE BALL!
OWWW
THUD
BLOOP
ARK
I WON, BULLET WING!

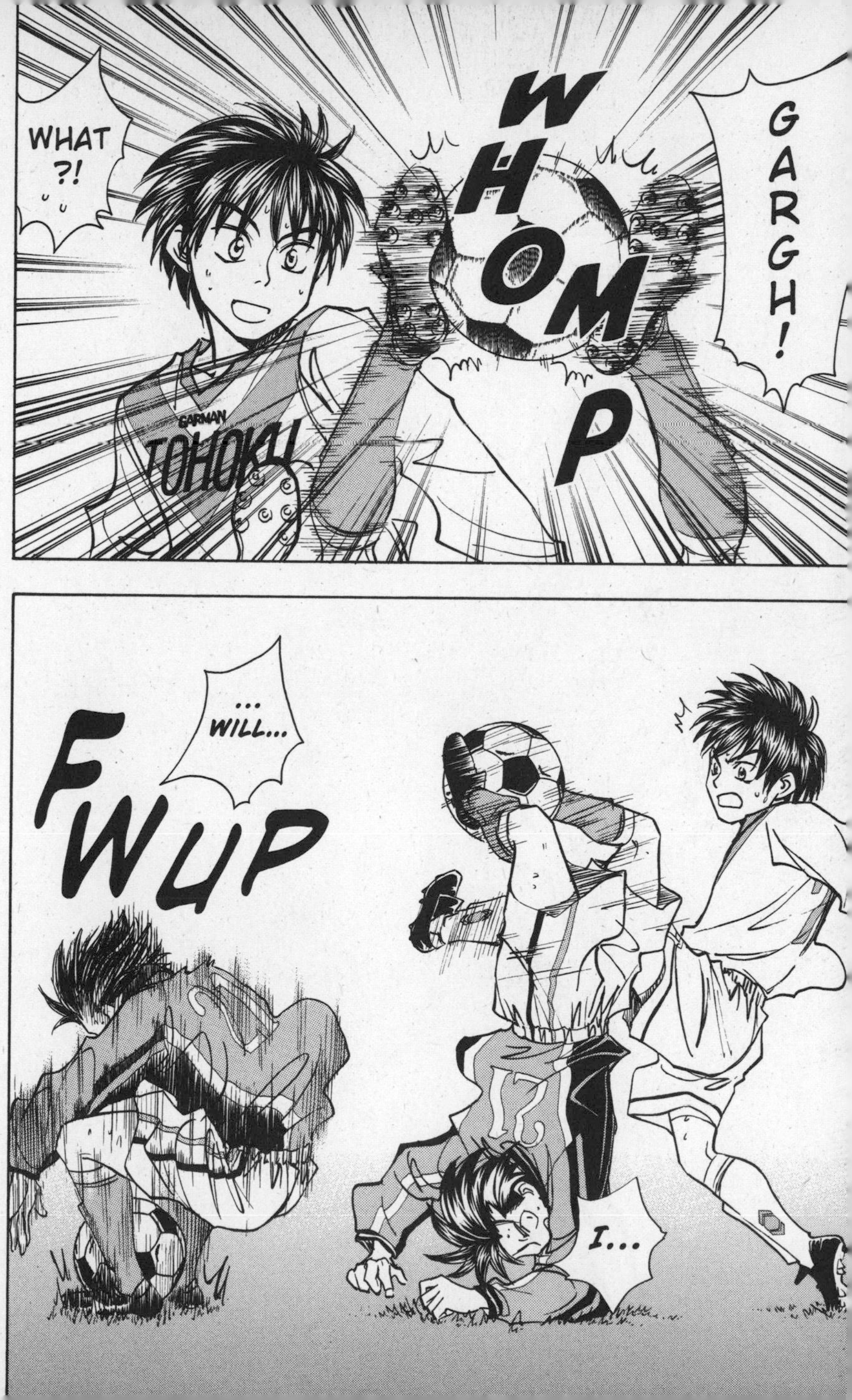
GARGH!
WHOMP
WHAT ?!
GARMAN
TOHOKU
... WILL...
I...
FWUP

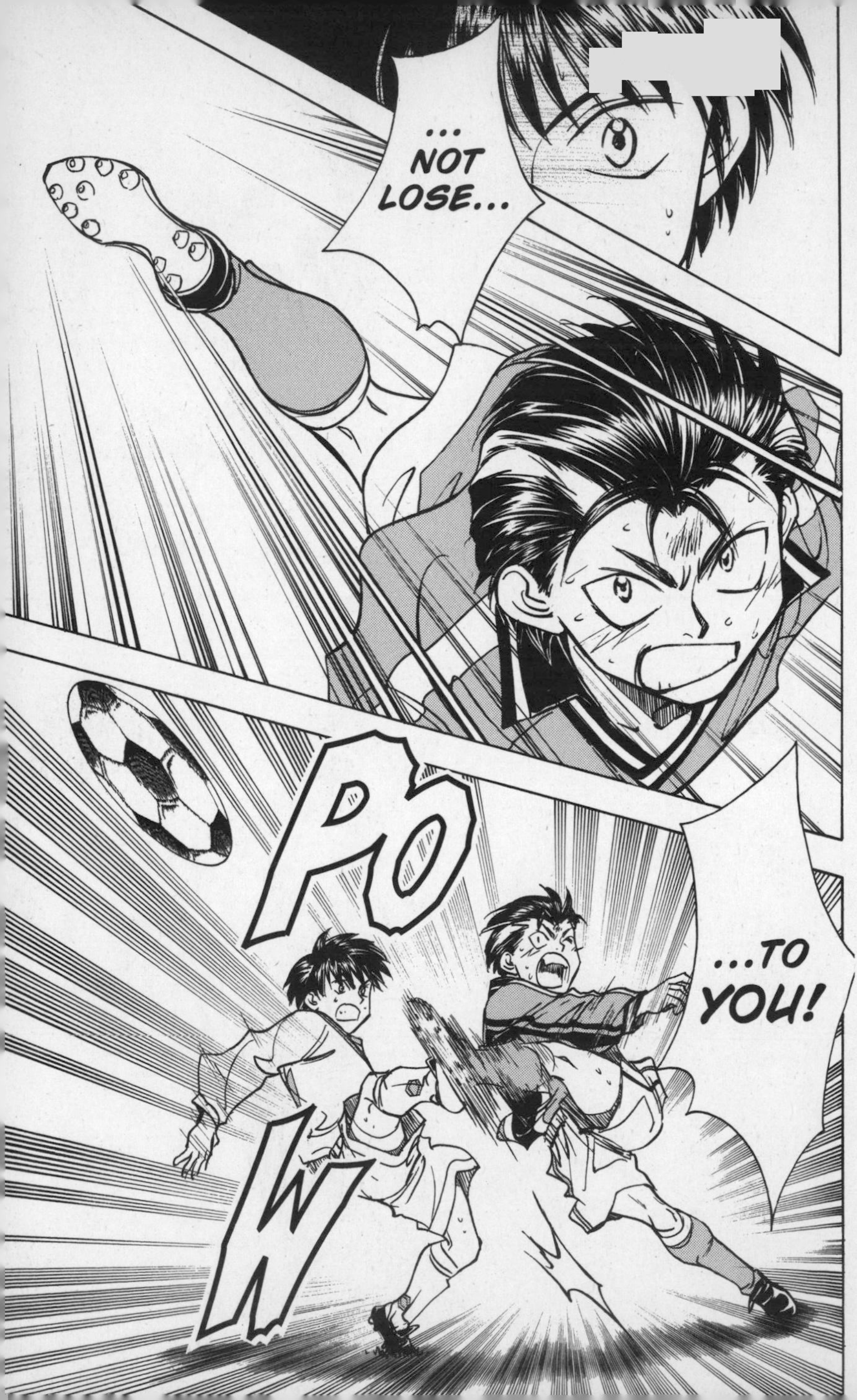
... NOT LOSE...
...TO YOU!
POW

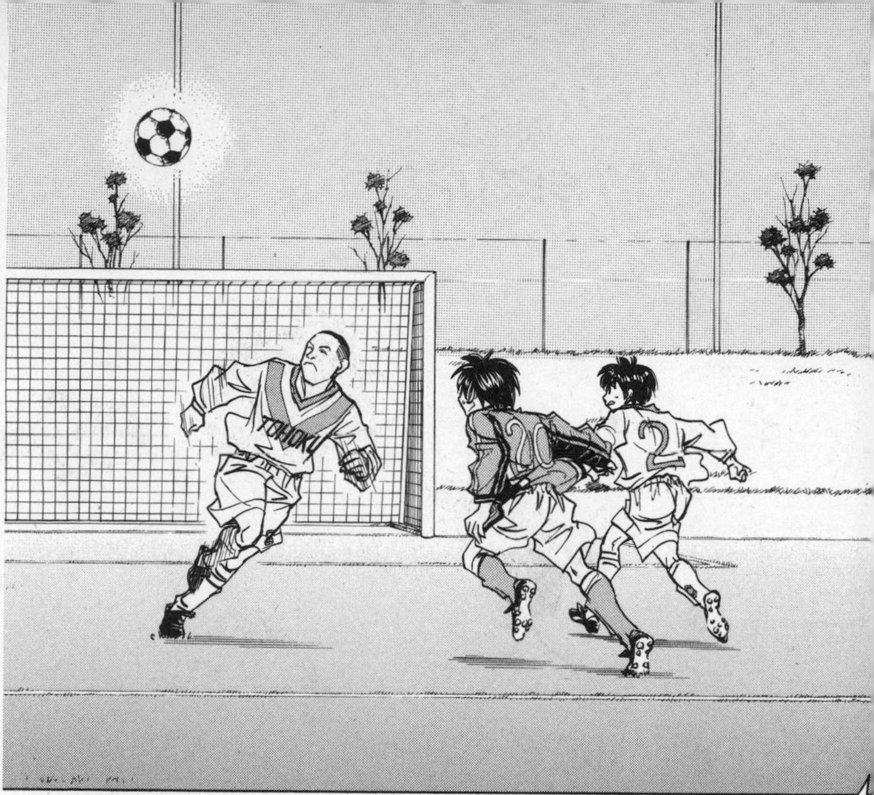

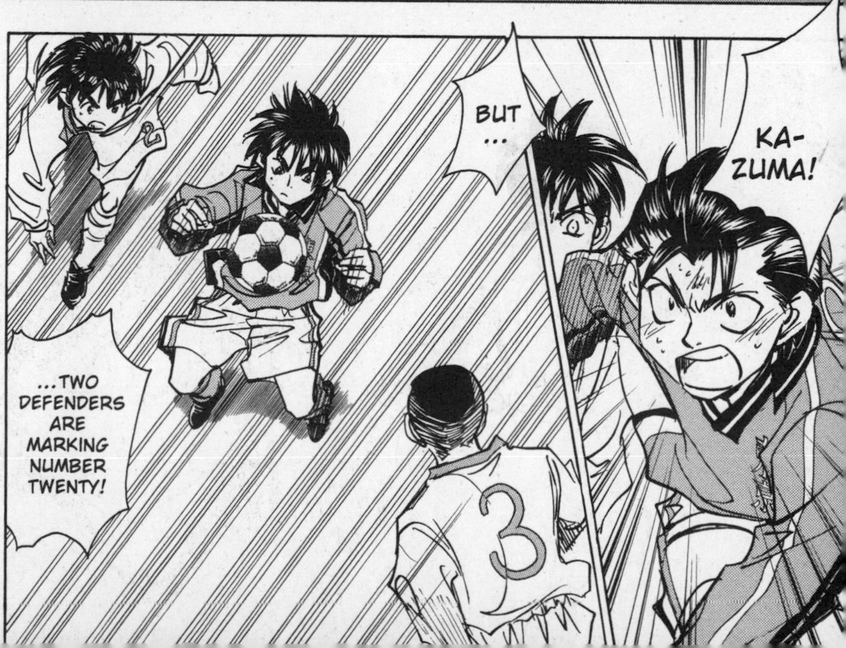
KA-ZUMA!
BUT ...
...TWO DEFENDERS ARE MARKING NUMBER TWENTY!

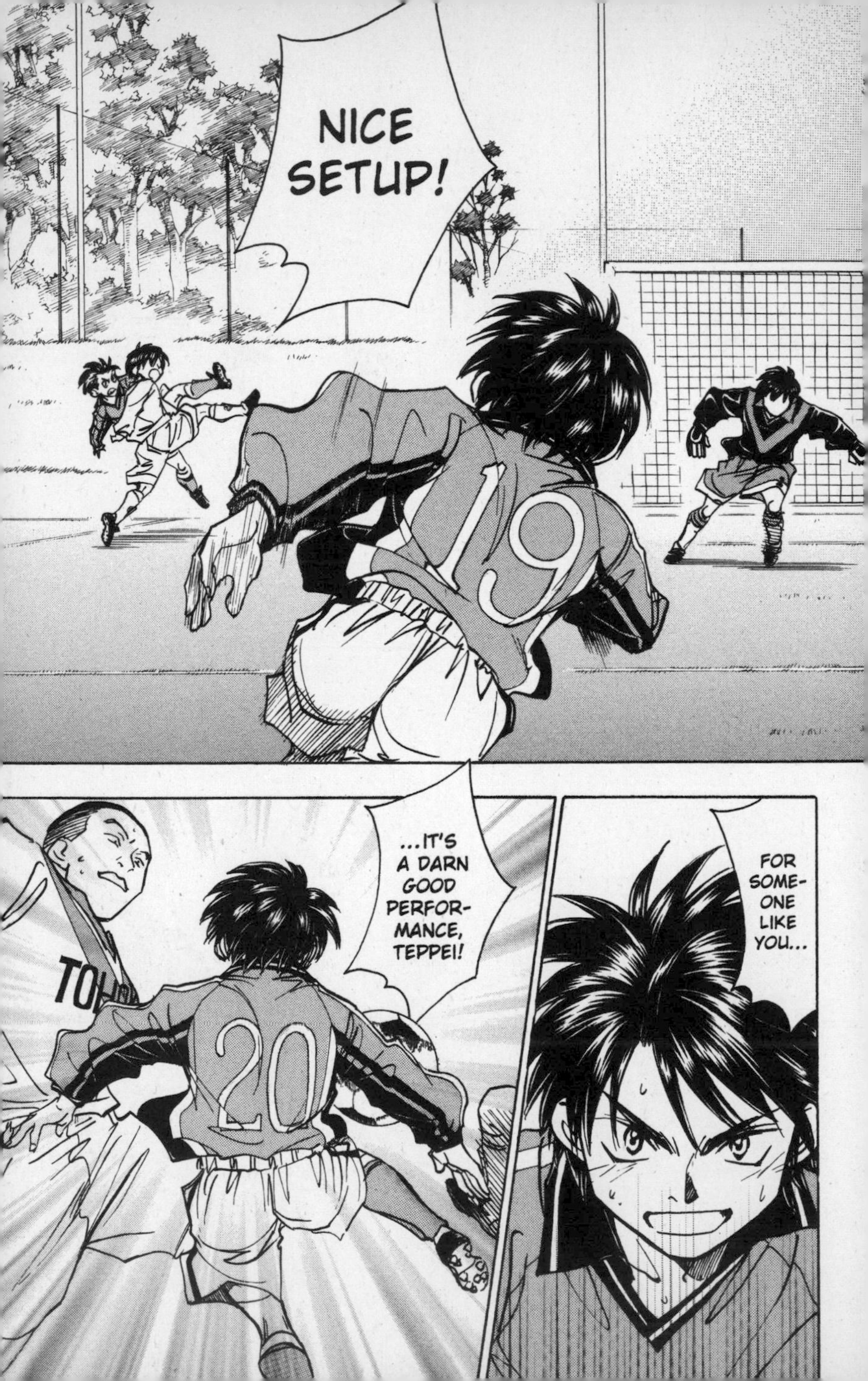
NICE SETUP!
FOR SOME-ONE LIKE YOU...
...IT'S A DARN GOOD PERFOR-MANCE, TEPPEI!

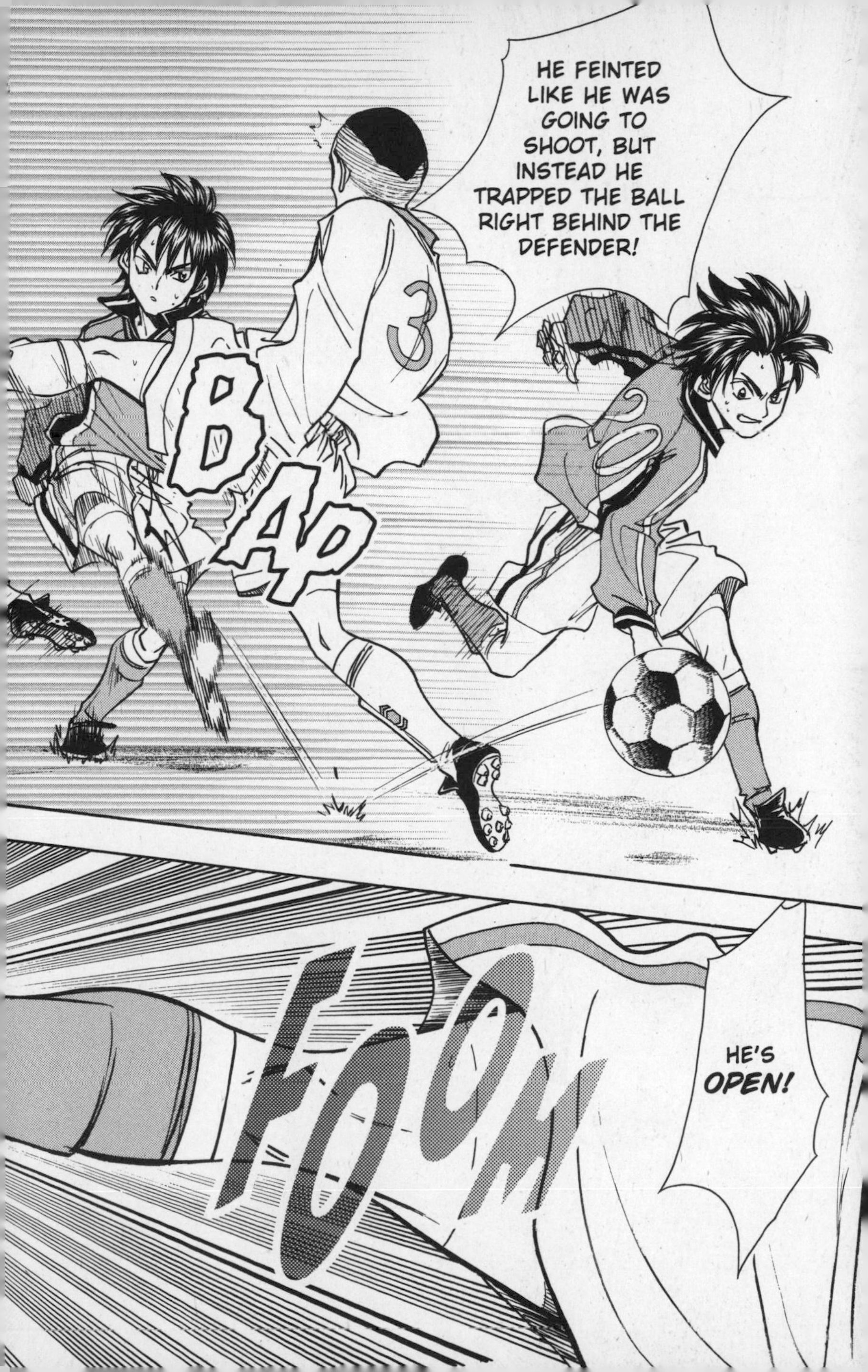
HE FEINTED LIKE HE WAS GOING TO SHOOT, BUT INSTEAD HE TRAPPED THE BALL RIGHT BEHIND THE DEFENDER!
BAP
HE'S OPEN!
FOOM

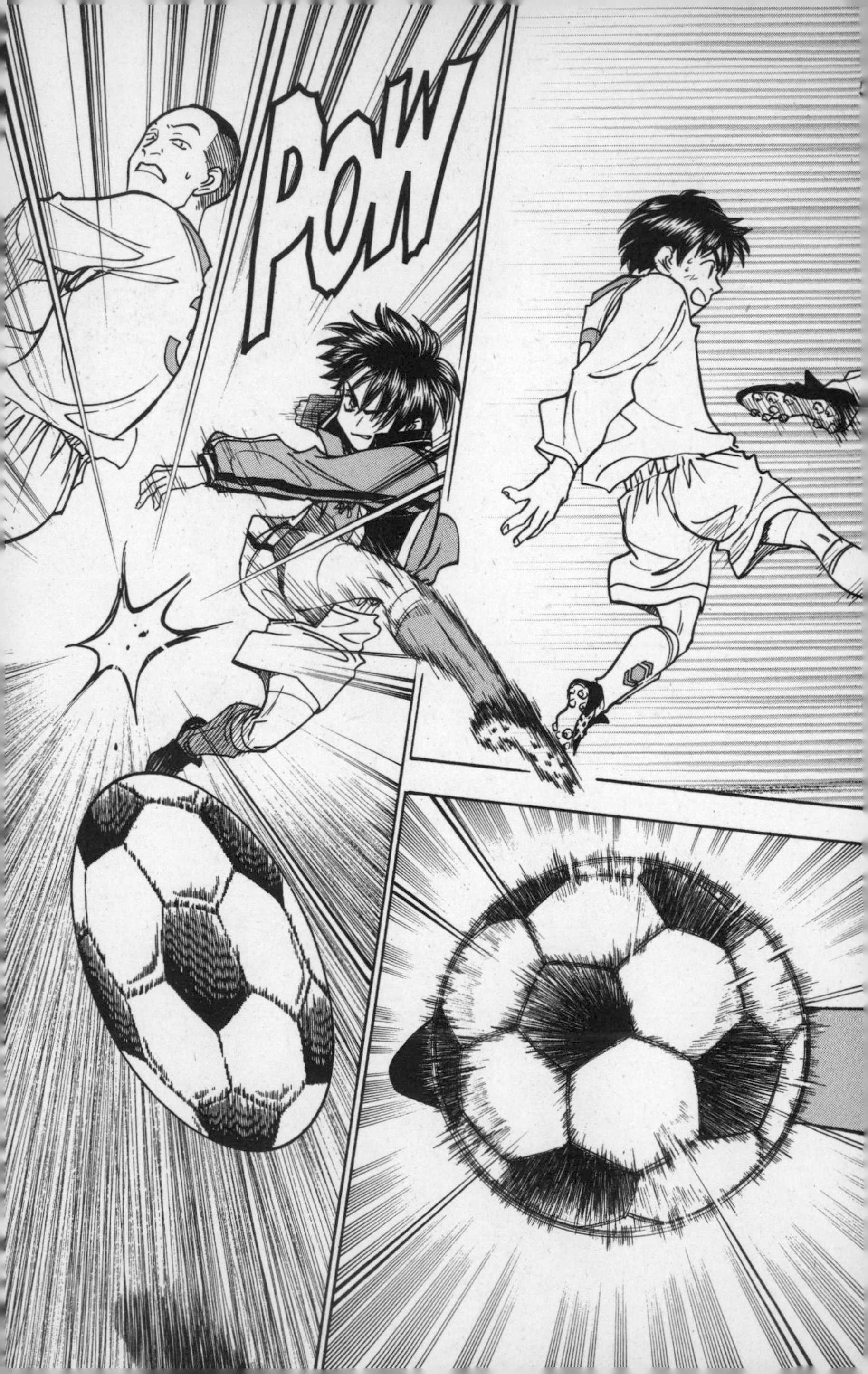
POW

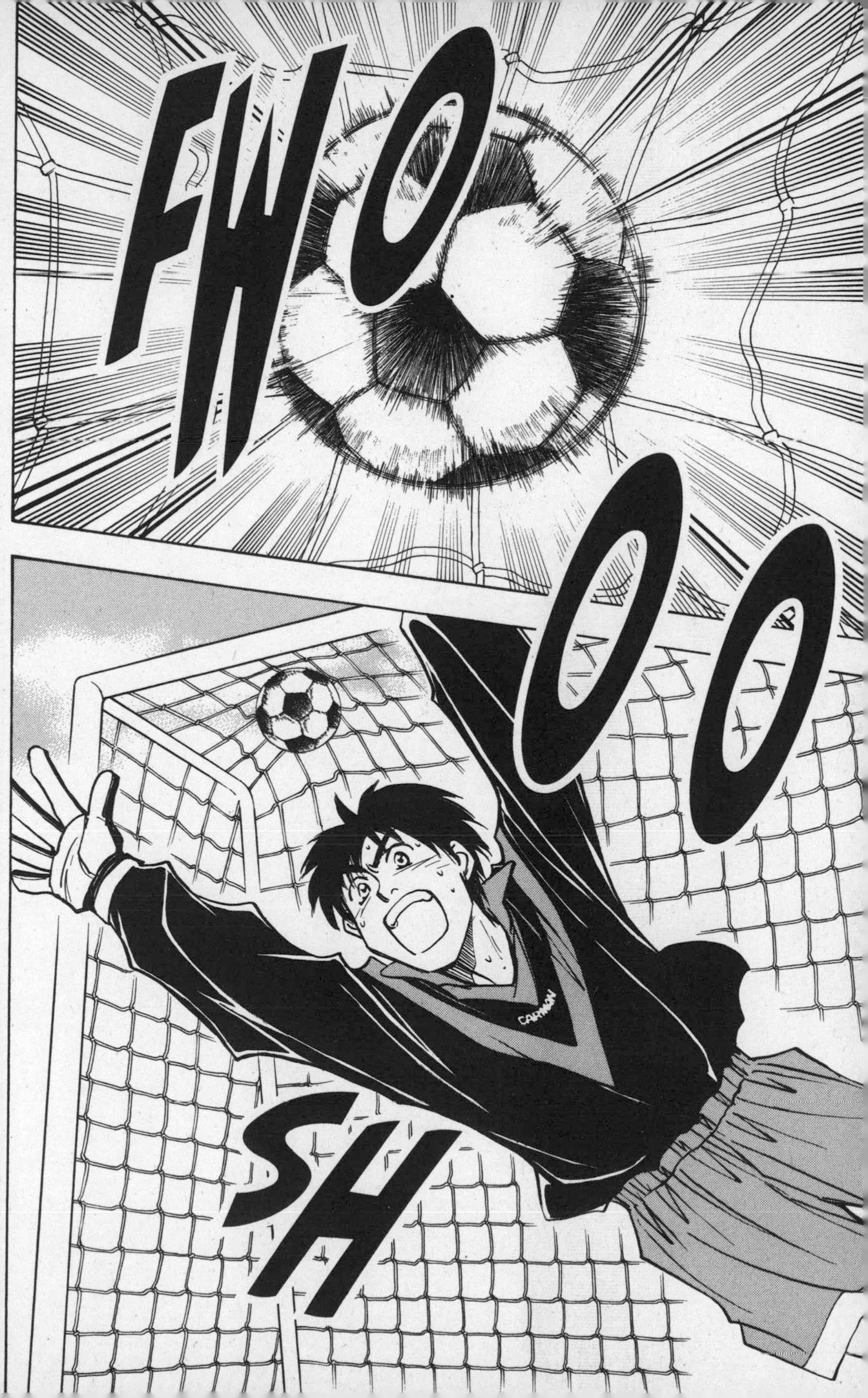
FWOOOOSH

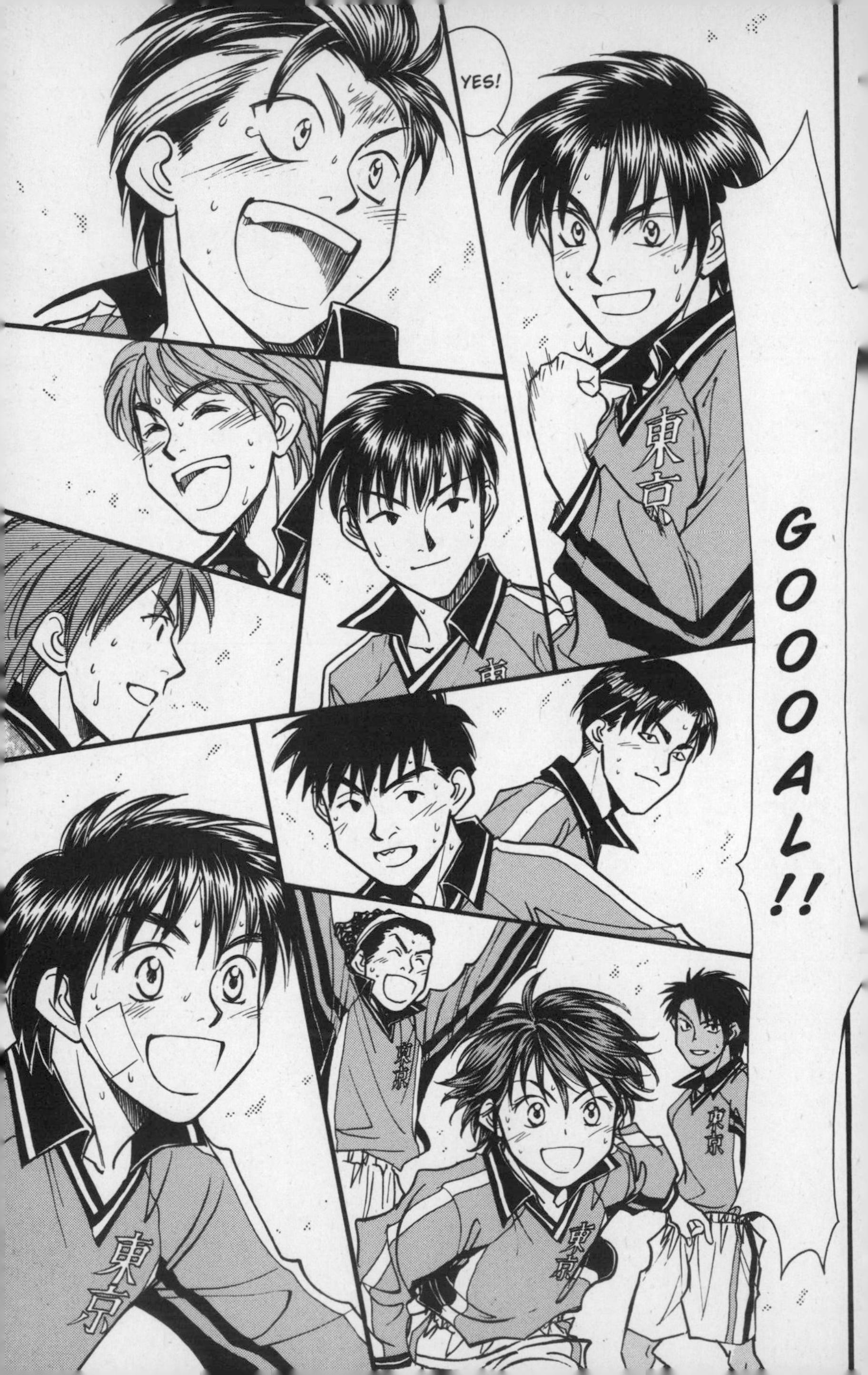

GOOOAL!!
YES!

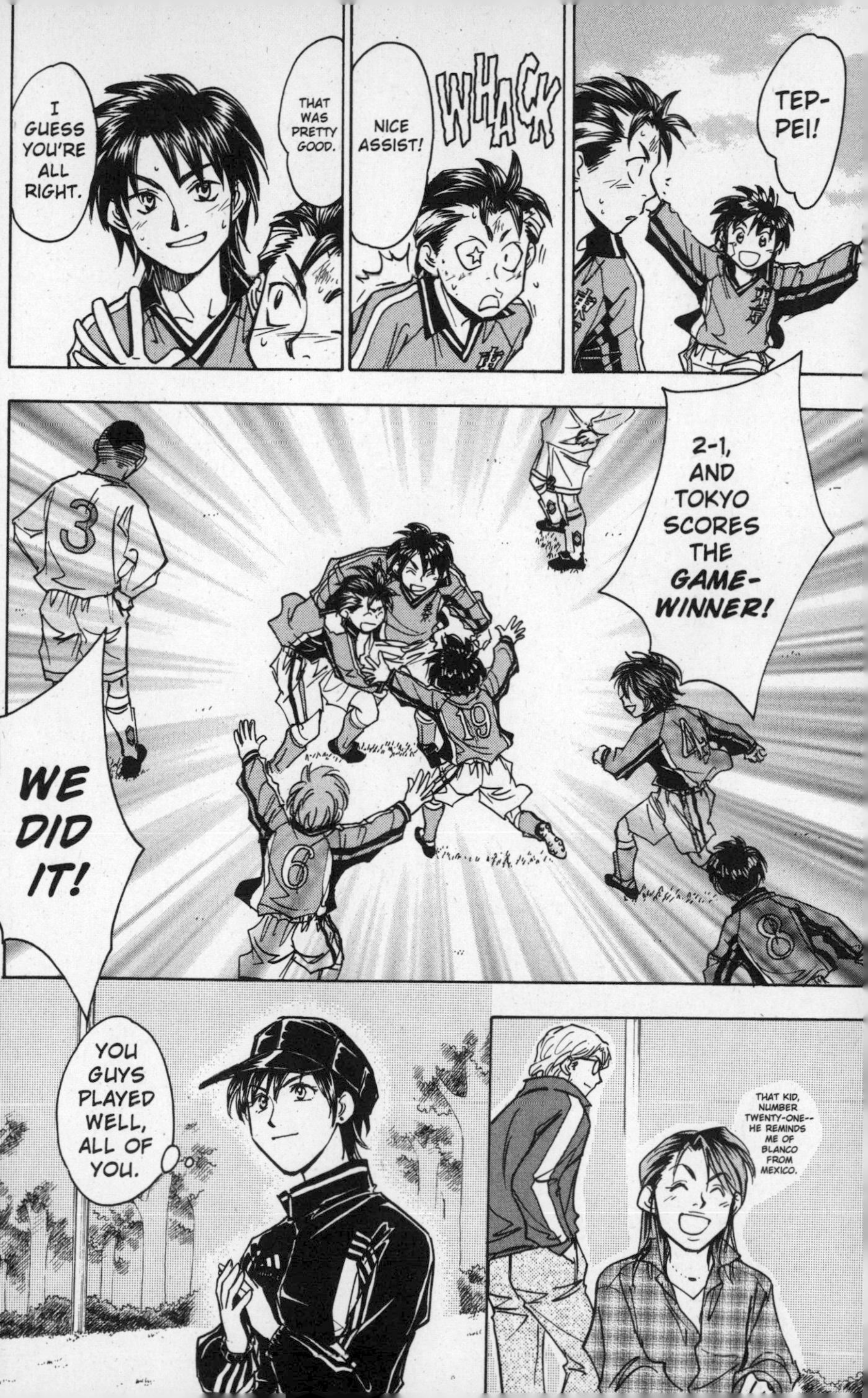
TEP-PEI!
WHACK
NICE ASSIST!
THAT WAS PRETTY GOOD.
I GUESS YOU'RE ALL RIGHT.
2-1, AND TOKYO SCORES THE GAME-WINNER!
WE DID IT!
THAT KID, NUMBER TWENTY-ONE-- HE REMINDS ME OF BLANCO FROM MEXICO.
YOU GUYS PLAYED WELL, ALL OF YOU.

READ THIS WAY

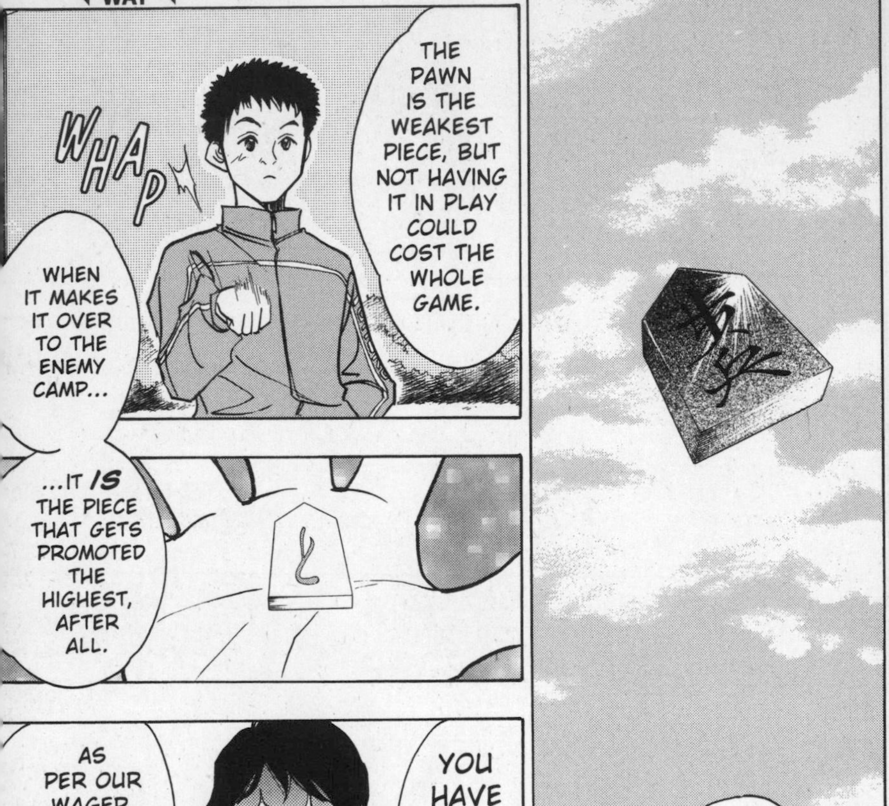
A PAWN BEAT US IN THE END, AFTER ALL.
THE PAWN IS THE WEAKEST PIECE, BUT NOT HAVING IT IN PLAY COULD COST THE WHOLE GAME.
WHAP
WHEN IT MAKES IT OVER TO THE ENEMY CAMP...
...IT IS THE PIECE THAT GETS PROMOTED THE HIGHEST, AFTER ALL.
YOU HAVE LOST, YŪDAI.
AS PER OUR WAGER, YOU MUST NOW JOIN THE SHOGI CLUB.
OH NO!

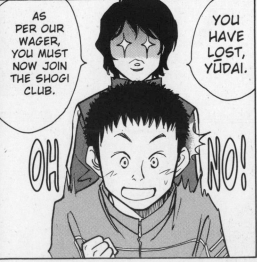

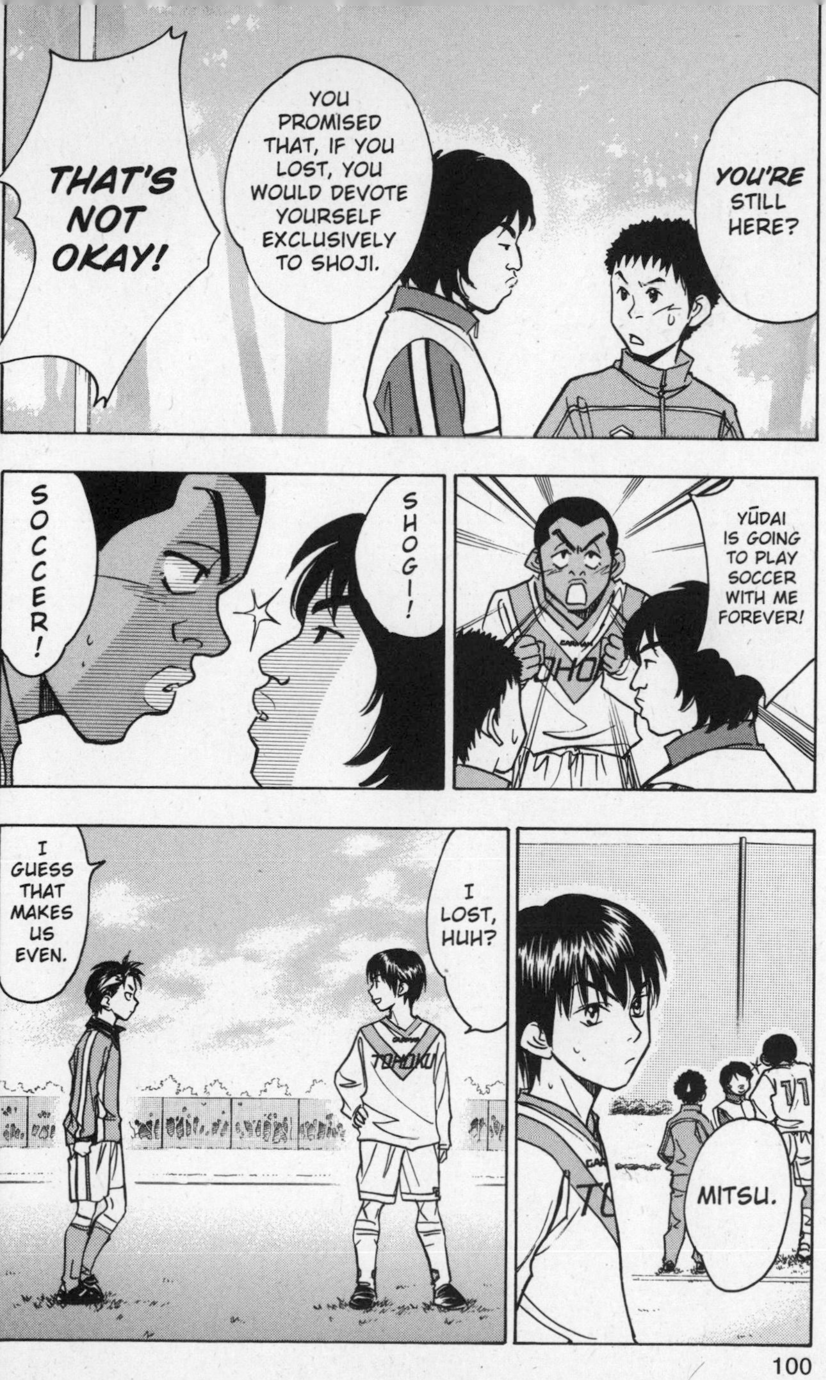
YOU'RE STILL HERE?
YOU PROMISED THAT, IF YOU LOST, YOU WOULD DEVOTE YOURSELF EXCLUSIVELY TO SHOJI.
THAT'S NOT OKAY!
YŪDAI IS GOING TO PLAY SOCCER WITH ME FOREVER!
SHOGI!
SOCCER!
MITSU.
I LOST, HUH?
I GUESS THAT MAKES US EVEN.

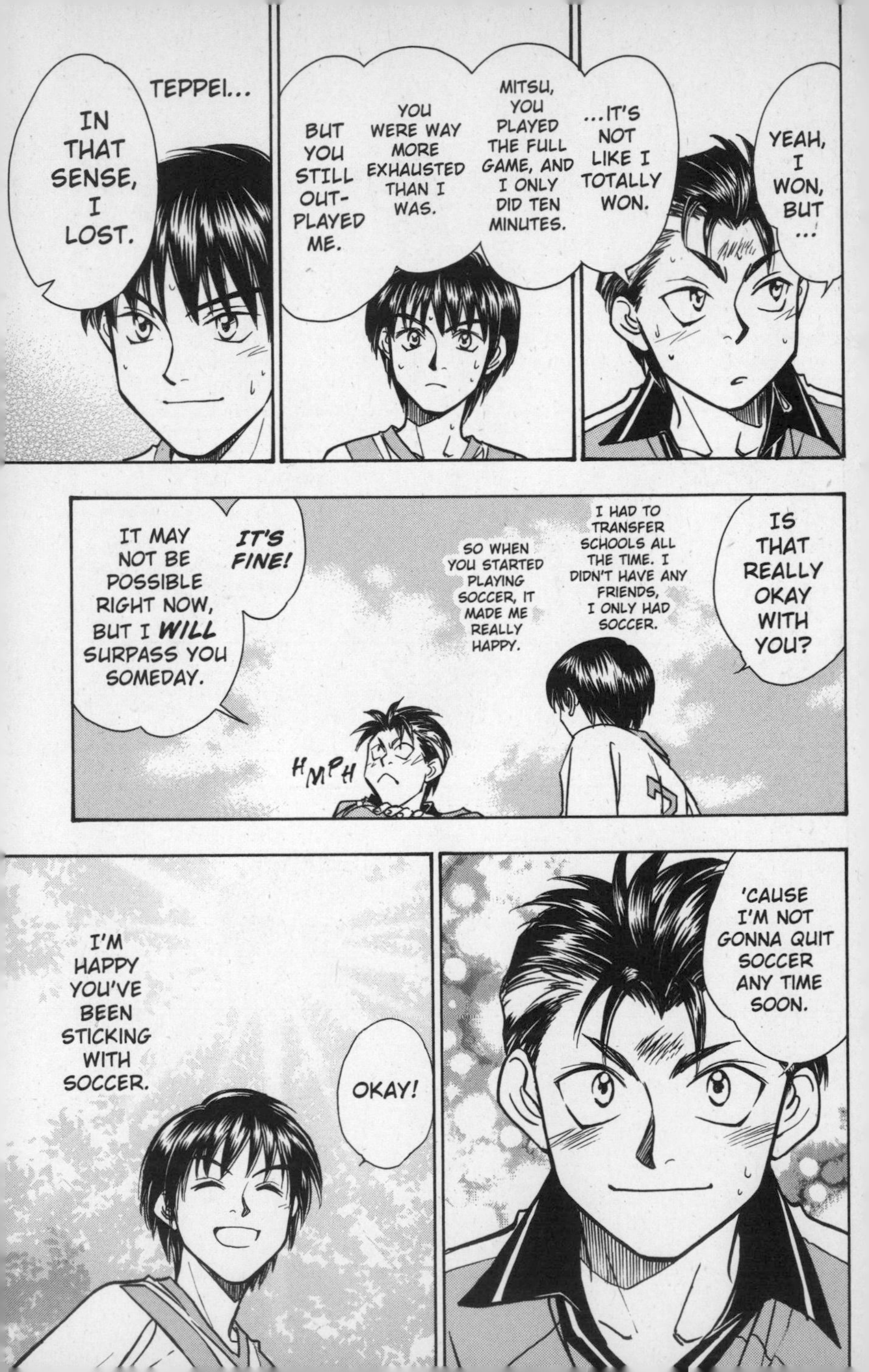
YEAH, I WON, BUT ...
...IT'S NOT LIKE I TOTALLY WON.
MITSU, YOU PLAYED THE FULL GAME, AND I ONLY DID TEN MINUTES.
YOU WERE WAY MORE EXHAUSTED THAN I WAS.
BUT YOU STILL OUT-PLAYED ME.
TEPPEI...
IN THAT SENSE, I LOST.
IS THAT REALLY OKAY WITH YOU?
I HAD TO TRANSFER SCHOOLS ALL THE TIME. I DIDN'T HAVE ANY FRIENDS, I ONLY HAD SOCCER.
SO WHEN YOU STARTED PLAYING SOCCER, IT MADE ME REALLY HAPPY.
IT'S FINE!
IT MAY NOT BE POSSIBLE RIGHT NOW, BUT I **WILL** SURPASS YOU SOMEDAY.
HMPH
'CAUSE I'M NOT GONNA QUIT SOCCER ANY TIME SOON.
I'M HAPPY YOU'VE BEEN STICKING WITH SOCCER.
OKAY!

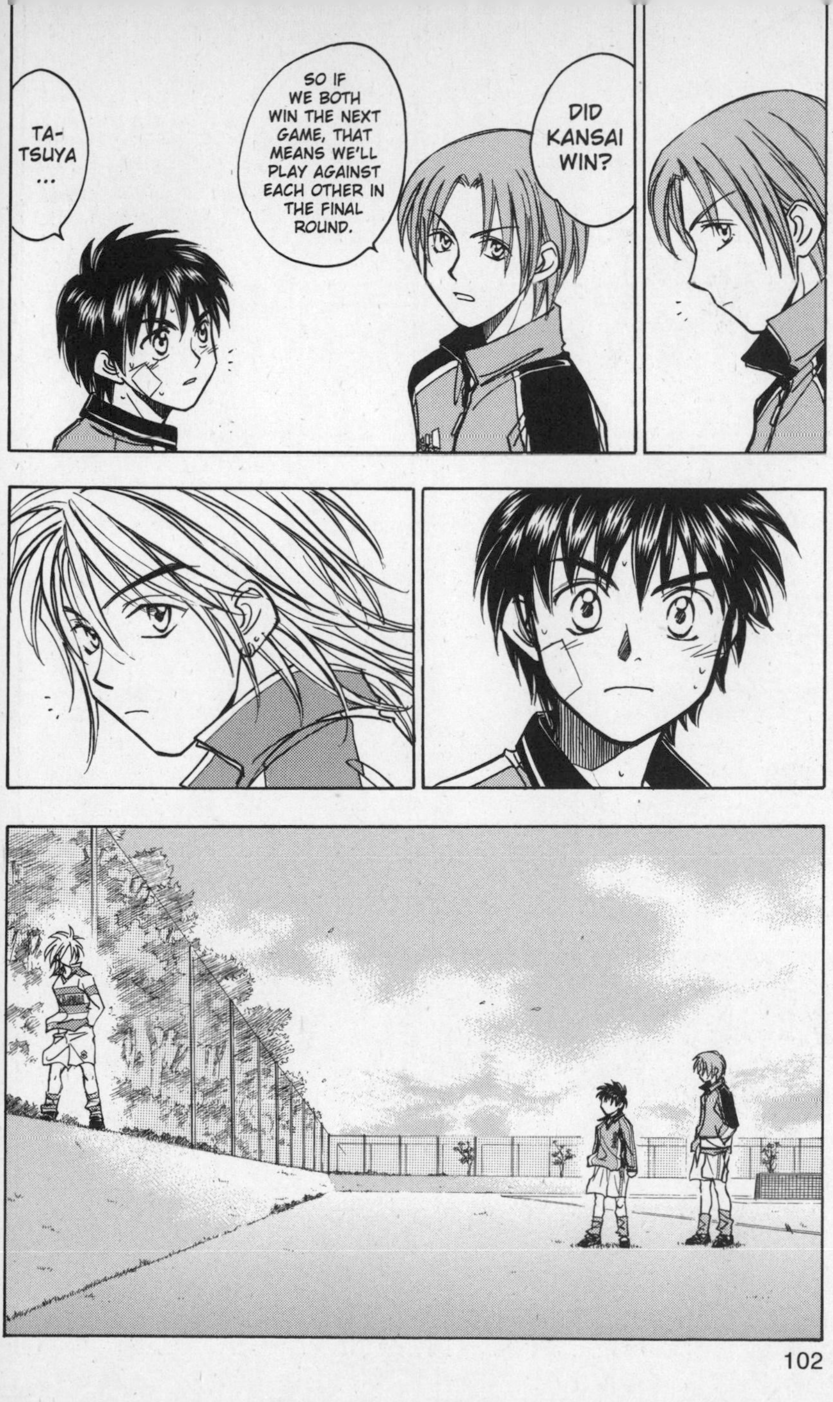
DID KANSAI WIN?
SO IF WE BOTH WIN THE NEXT GAME, THAT MEANS WE'LL PLAY AGAINST EACH OTHER IN THE FINAL ROUND.
TA-TSUYA ...

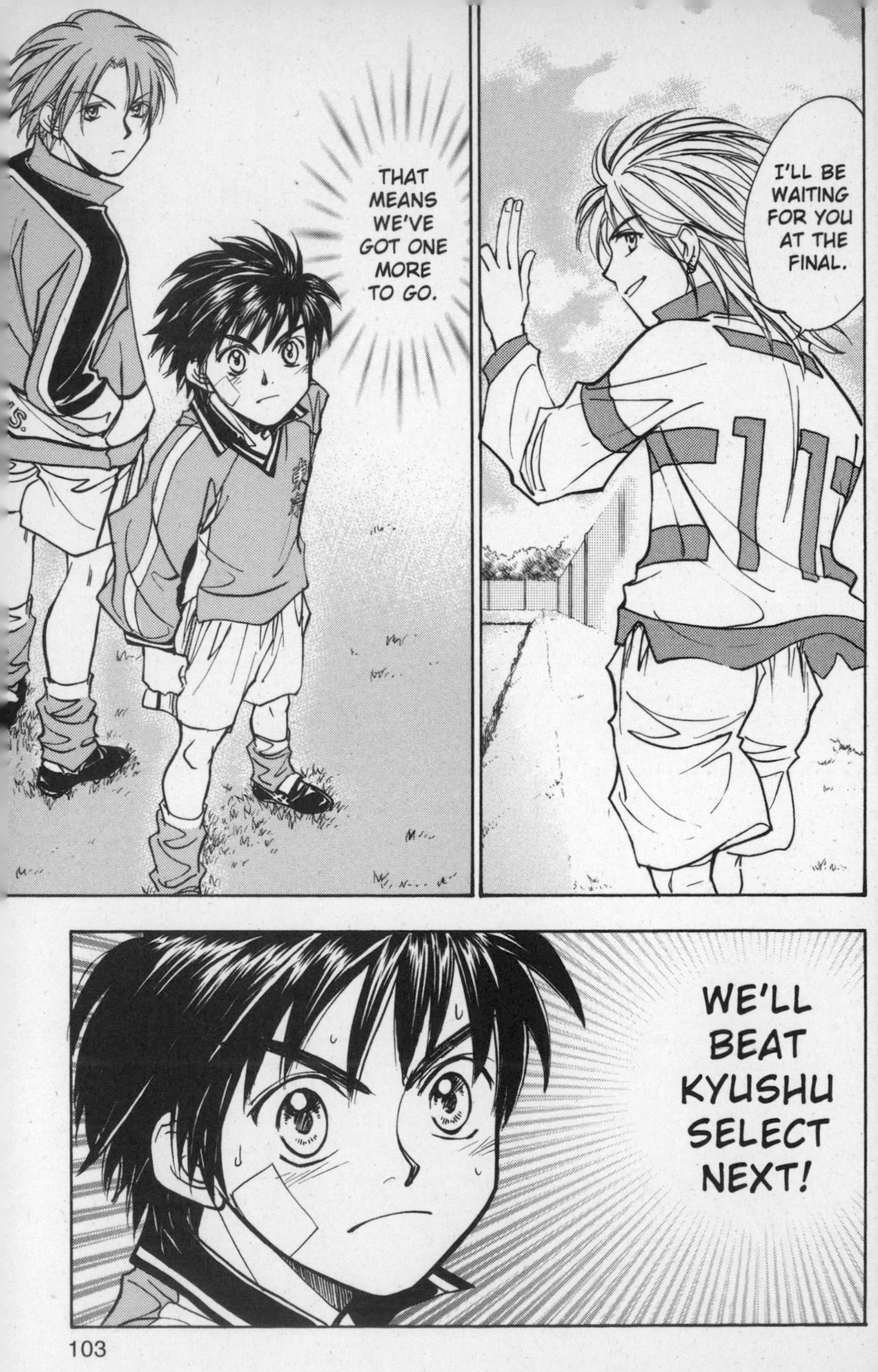
I'LL BE WAITING FOR YOU AT THE FINAL.
THAT MEANS WE'VE GOT ONE MORE TO GO.
WE'LL BEAT KYUSHU SELECT NEXT!

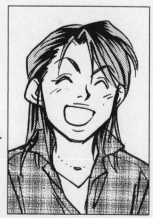

WHISTLE!

STAGE.188 The Night Before the Play-off

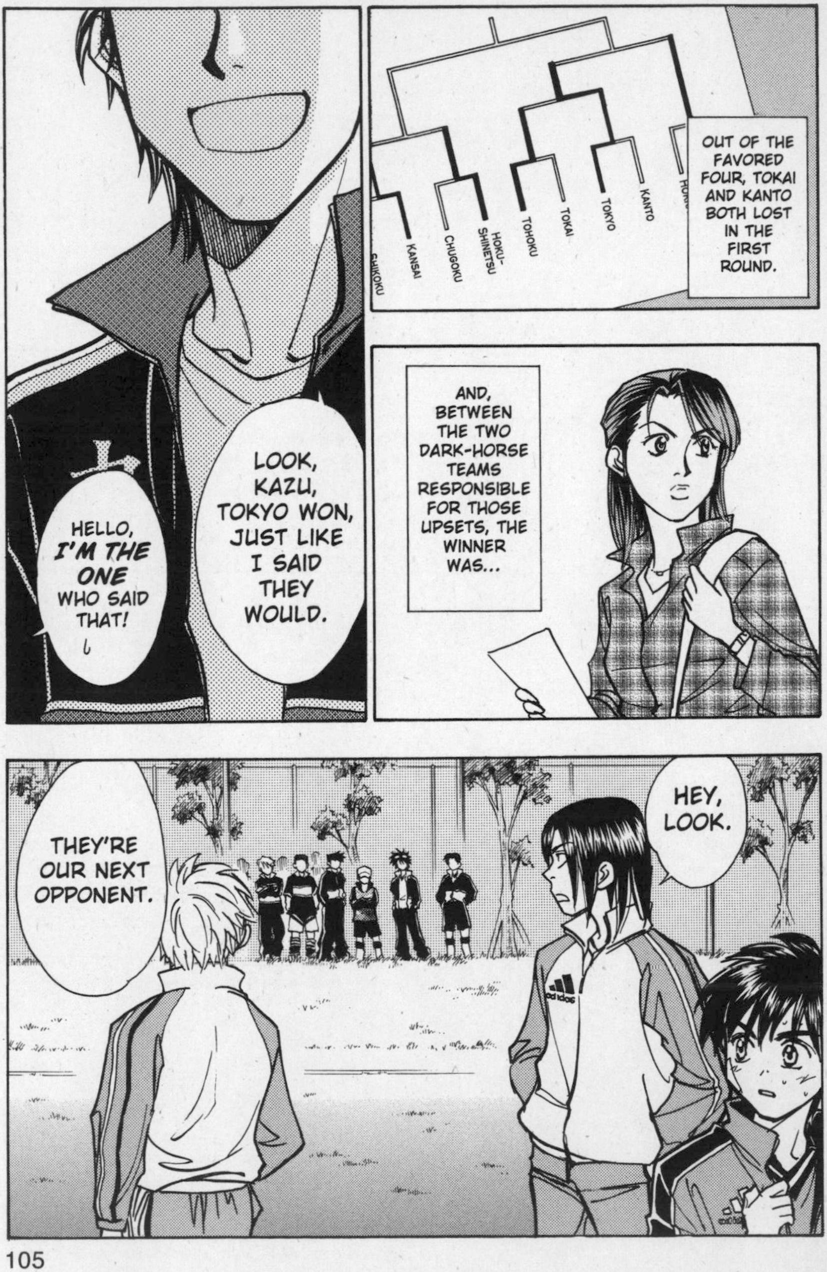
OUT OF THE FAVORED FOUR, TOKAI AND KANTO BOTH LOST IN THE FIRST ROUND.
KANTO
TOKYO
TOKAI
TOHOKU
HOKU-SHINETSU
CHUGOKU
KANSAI
SHIKOKU
AND, BETWEEN THE TWO DARK-HORSE TEAMS RESPONSIBLE FOR THOSE UPSETS, THE WINNER WAS...
LOOK, KAZU, TOKYO WON, JUST LIKE I SAID THEY WOULD.
HELLO, *I'M THE ONE* WHO SAID THAT!
HEY, LOOK.
THEY'RE OUR NEXT OPPONENT.

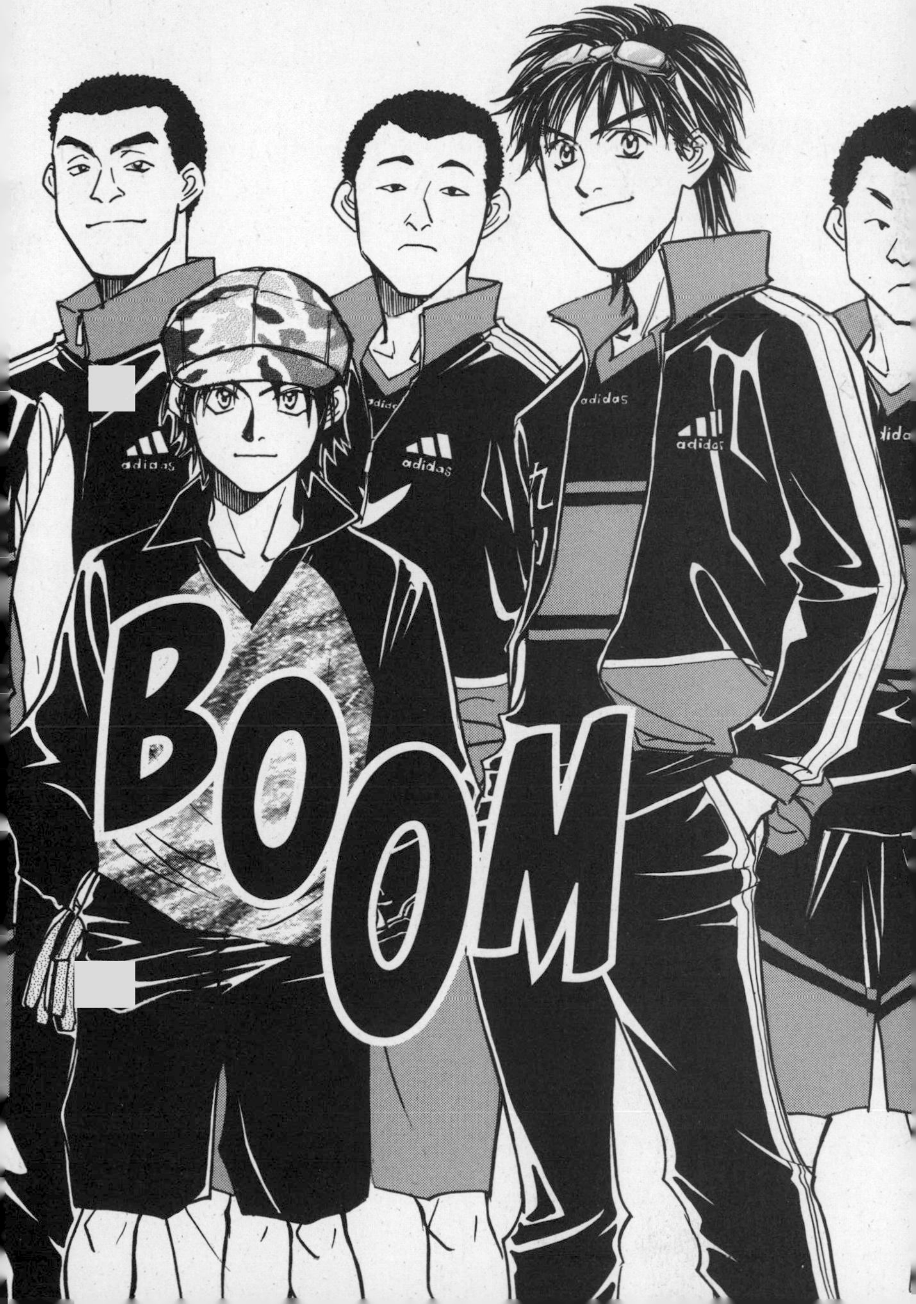
BOOM

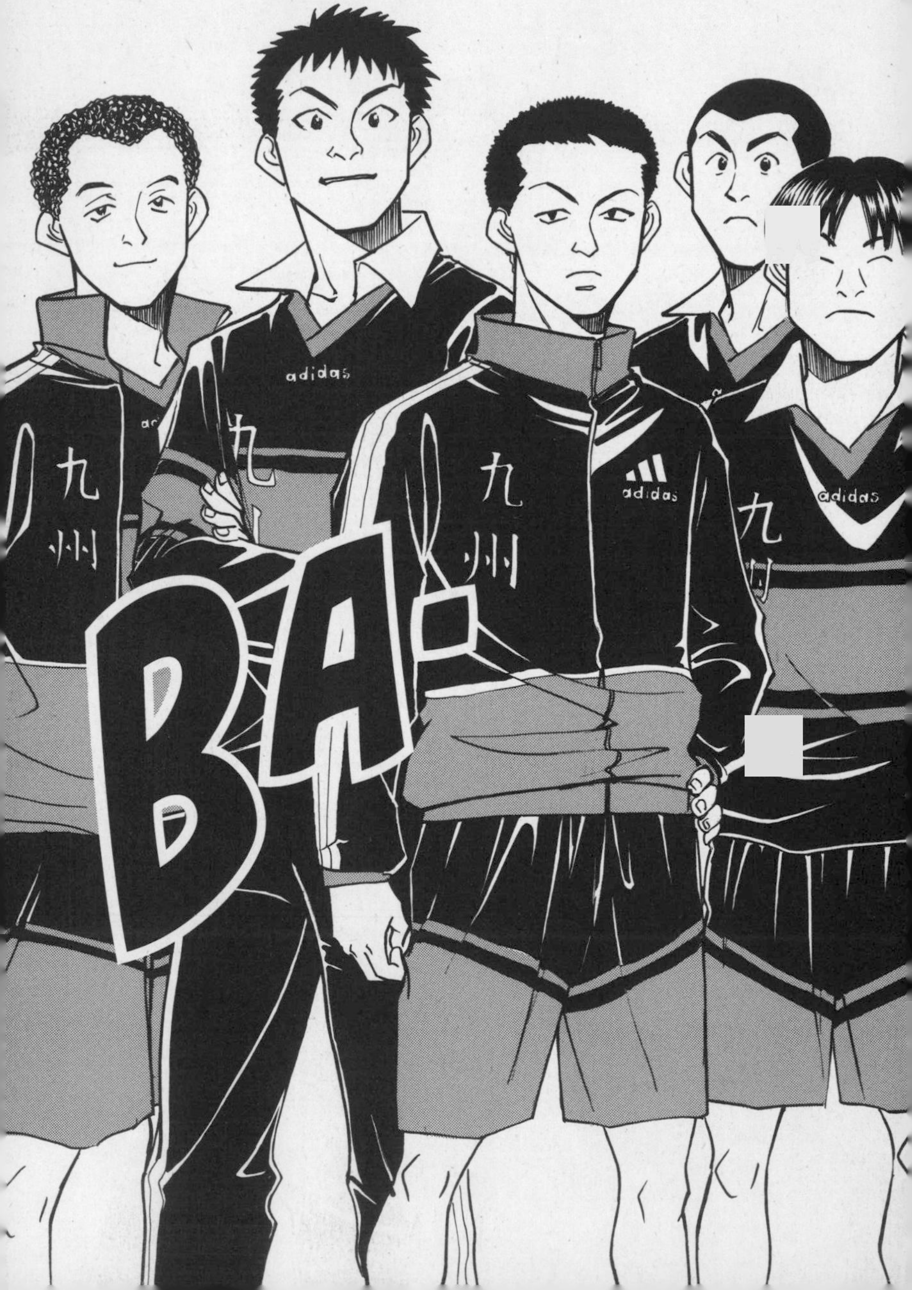
BA-
adidas
九州
adidas
九州
adidas
九州
adidas
九州

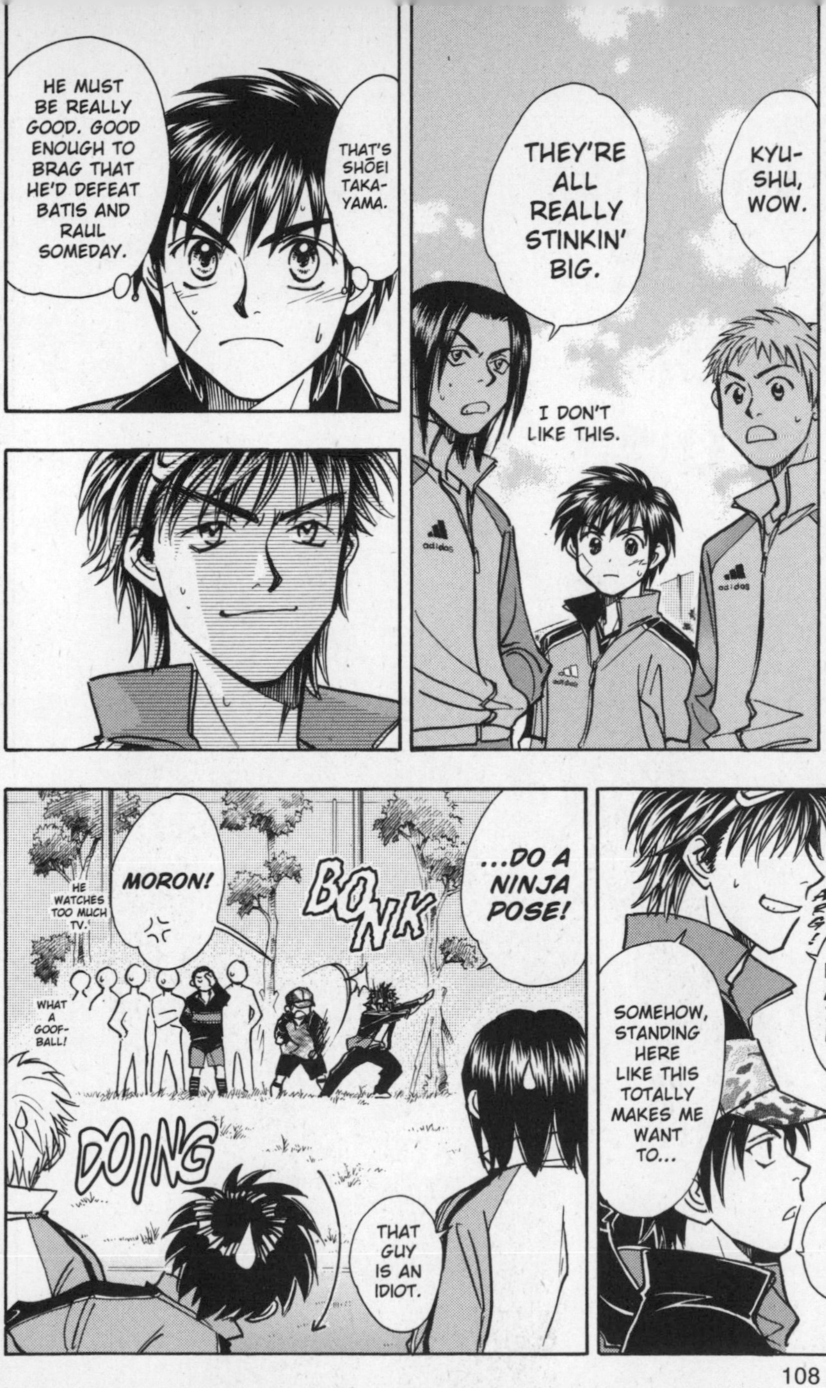
KYU-SHU, WOW.
THEY'RE ALL REALLY STINKIN' BIG.
I DON'T LIKE THIS.
THAT'S SHŌEI TAKA-YAMA.
HE MUST BE REALLY GOOD. GOOD ENOUGH TO BRAG THAT HE'D DEFEAT BATIS AND RAUL SOMEDAY.
ACK! ARG!
KAZU.
SOMEHOW, STANDING HERE LIKE THIS TOTALLY MAKES ME WANT TO...
HUH?
...DO A NINJA POSE!
BONK
MORON!
HE WATCHES TOO MUCH TV.
WHAT A GOOF-BALL!
DOING
THAT GUY IS AN IDIOT.

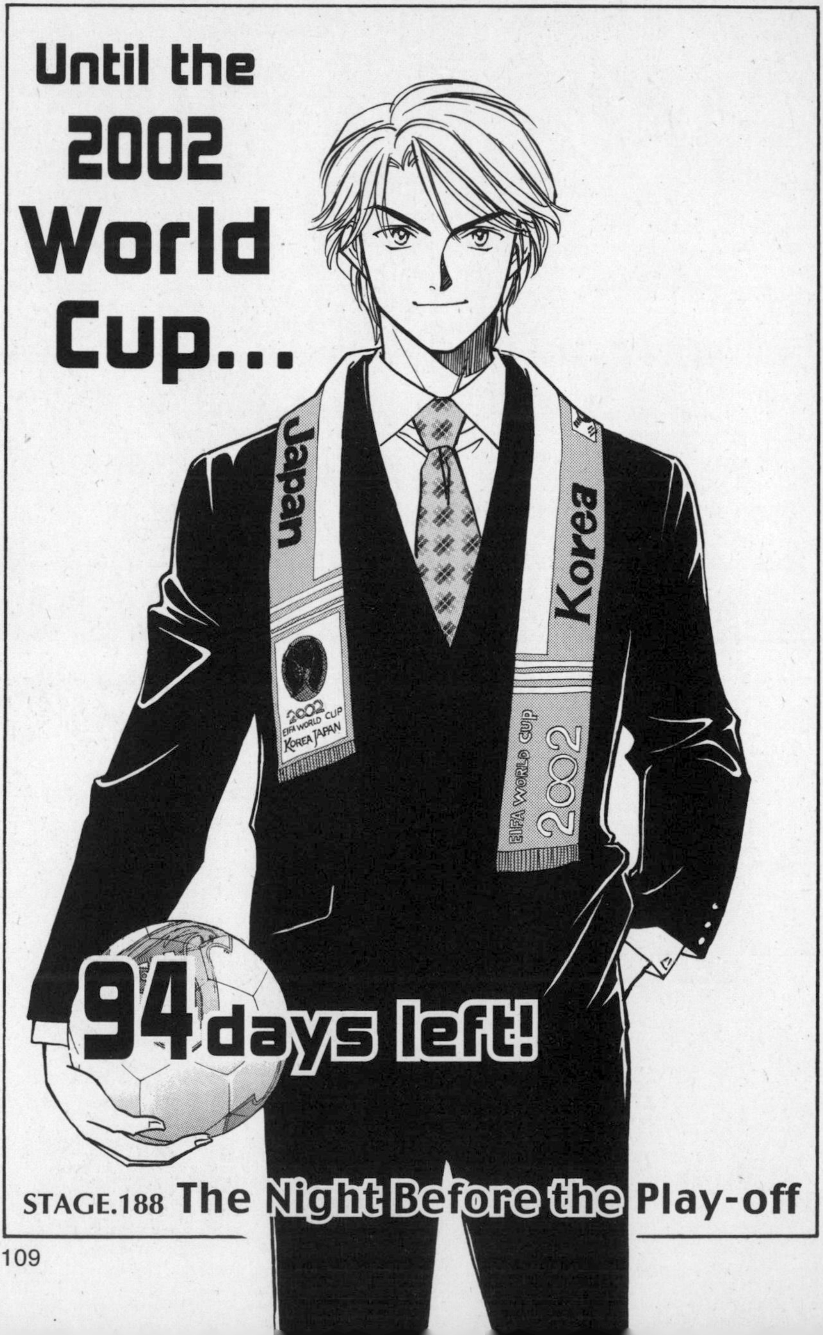
Until the 2002 World Cup...
94 days left!
Japan
Korea
2002 FIFA WORLD CUP KOREA JAPAN
FIFA WORLD CUP 2002
STAGE.188 The Night Before the Play-off

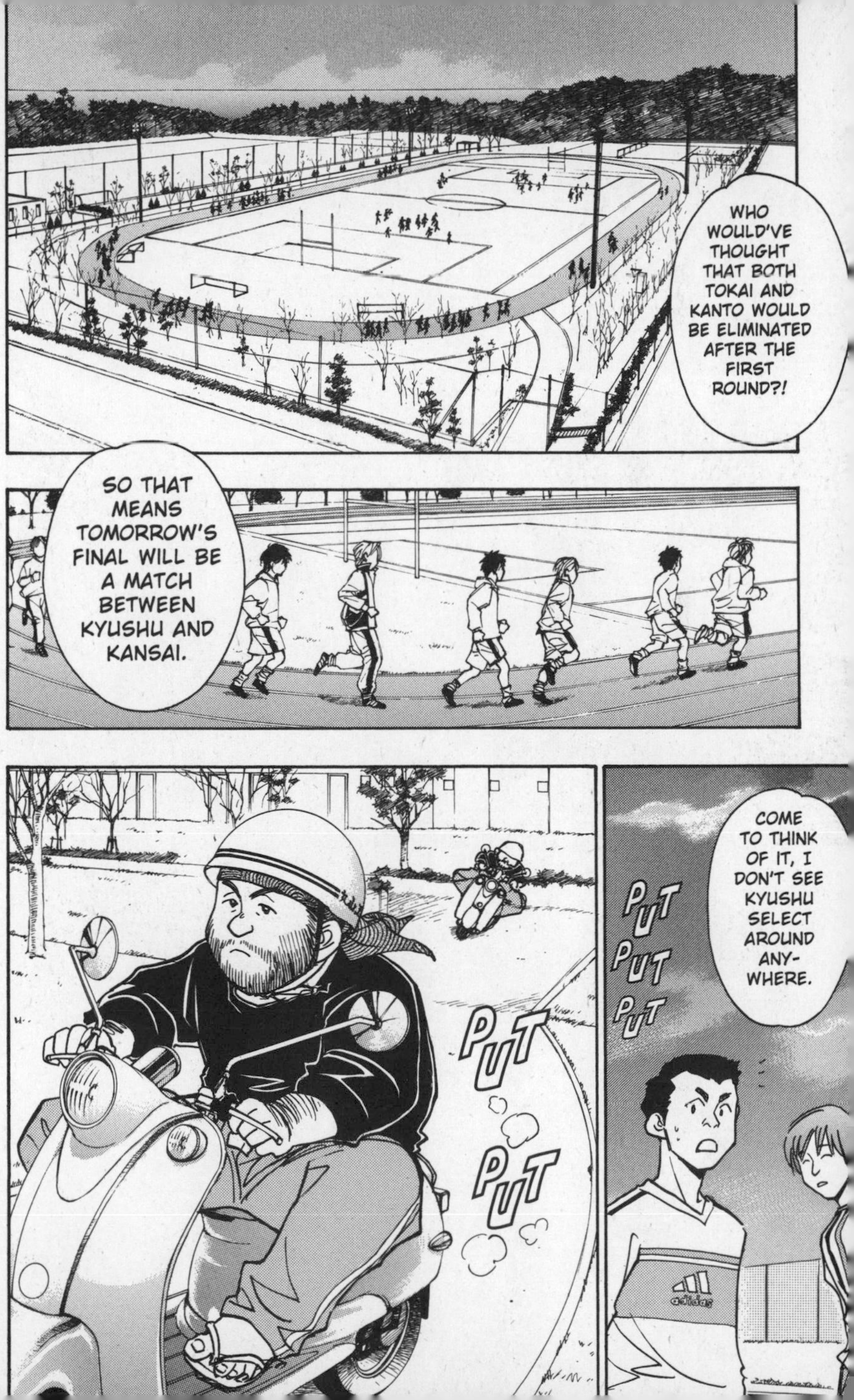
WHO WOULD'VE THOUGHT THAT BOTH TOKAI AND KANTO WOULD BE ELIMINATED AFTER THE FIRST ROUND?!
SO THAT MEANS TOMORROW'S FINAL WILL BE A MATCH BETWEEN KYUSHU AND KANSAI.
COME TO THINK OF IT, I DON'T SEE KYUSHU SELECT AROUND ANY-WHERE.
PUT PUT PUT
PUT
PUT

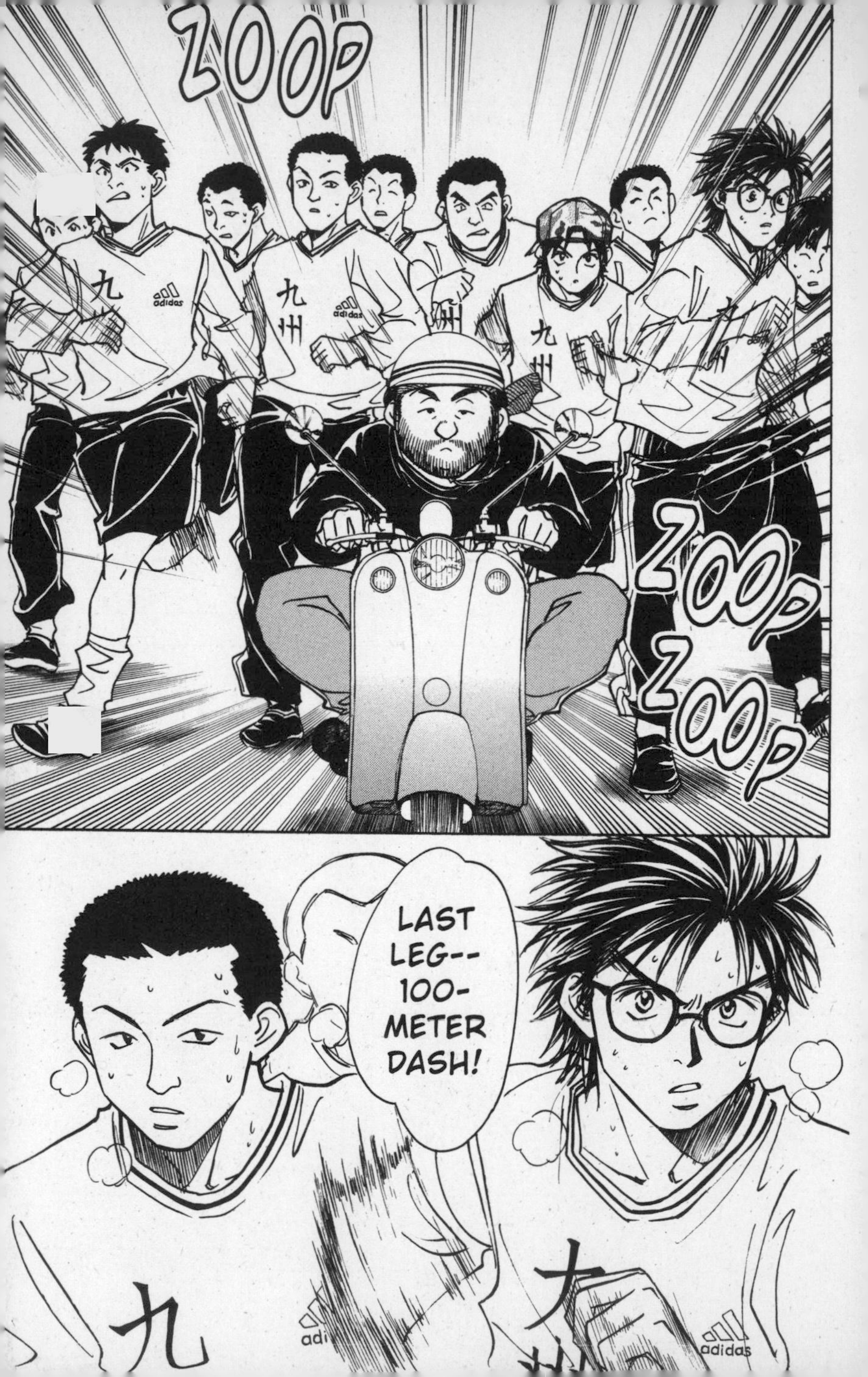
ZOOP
ZOOP ZOOP
LAST LEG-- 100-METER DASH!

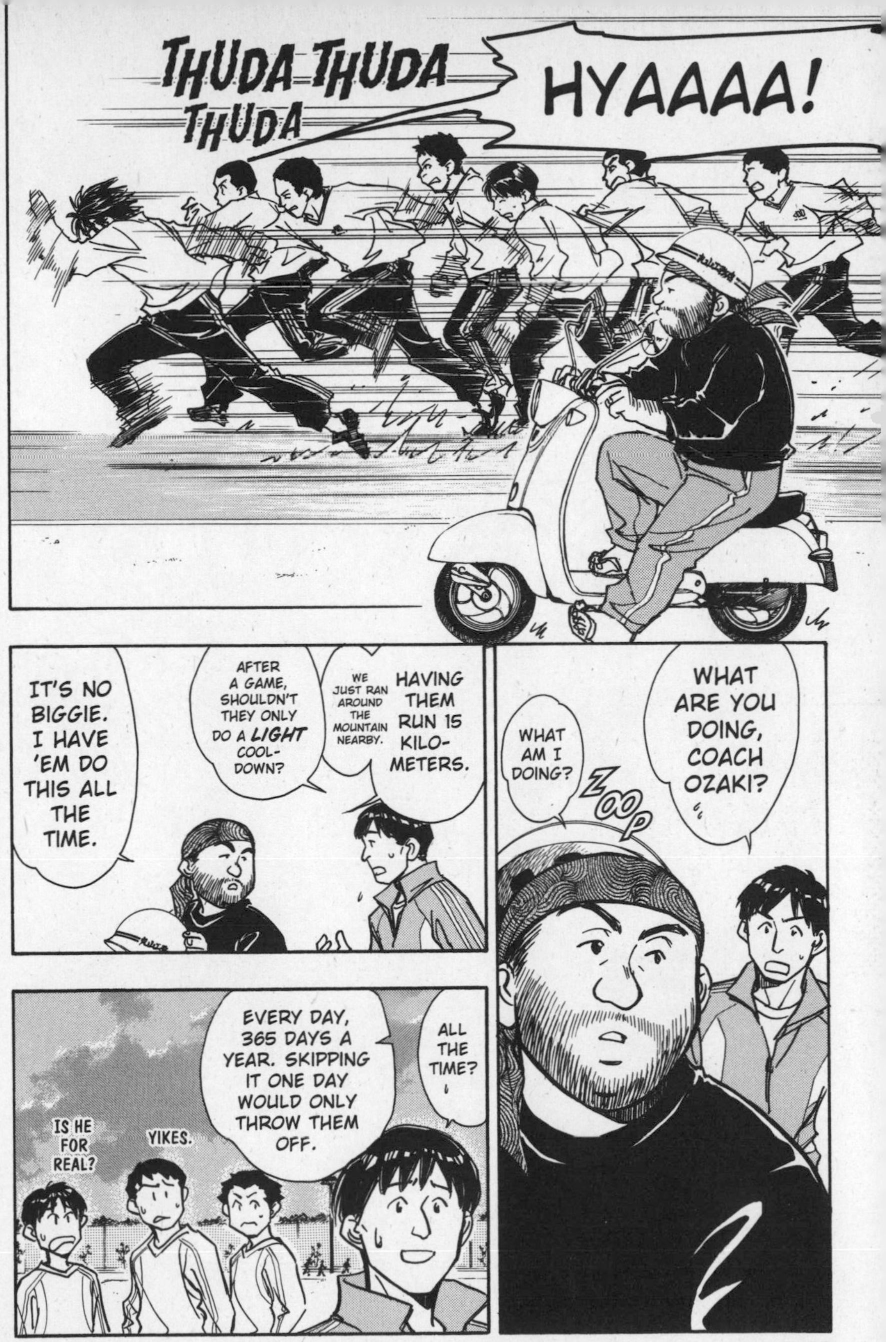
HYAAAA!
THUDA THUDA THUDA
WHAT ARE YOU DOING, COACH OZAKI?
WHAT AM I DOING?
ZOOP
HAVING THEM RUN 15 KILOMETERS.
WE JUST RAN AROUND THE MOUNTAIN NEARBY.
AFTER A GAME, SHOULDN'T THEY ONLY DO A LIGHT COOL-DOWN?
IT'S NO BIGGIE. I HAVE 'EM DO THIS ALL THE TIME.
ALL THE TIME?
EVERY DAY, 365 DAYS A YEAR. SKIPPING IT ONE DAY WOULD ONLY THROW THEM OFF.
YIKES.
IS HE FOR REAL?

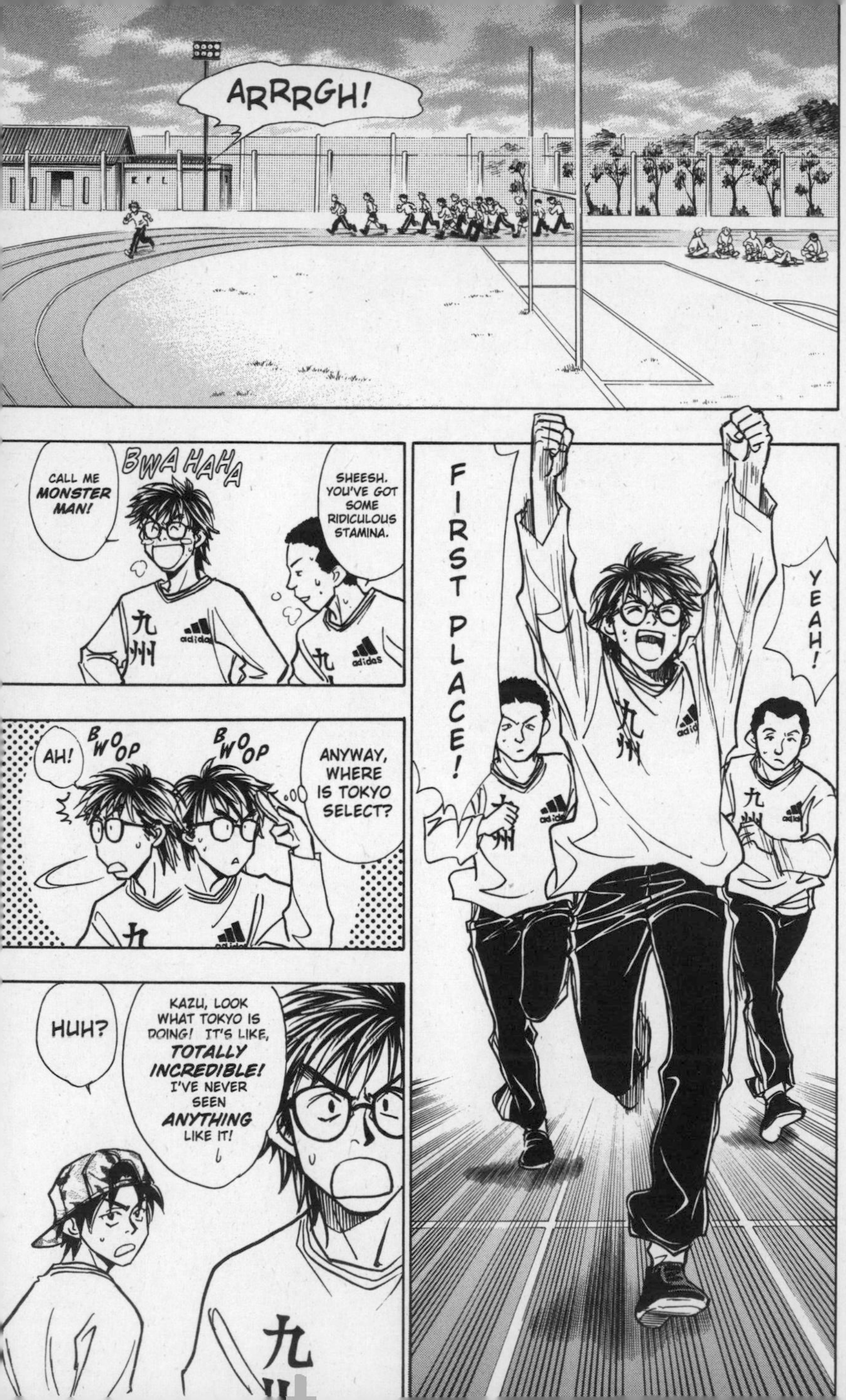
ARRRGH!
FIRST PLACE!
YEAH!
SHEESH. YOU'VE GOT SOME RIDICULOUS STAMINA.
BWA HAHA
CALL ME MONSTER MAN!
ANYWAY, WHERE IS TOKYO SELECT?
BWOOP
BWOOP
AH!
KAZU, LOOK WHAT TOKYO IS DOING! IT'S LIKE, TOTALLY INCREDIBLE! I'VE NEVER SEEN ANYTHING LIKE IT!
HUH?

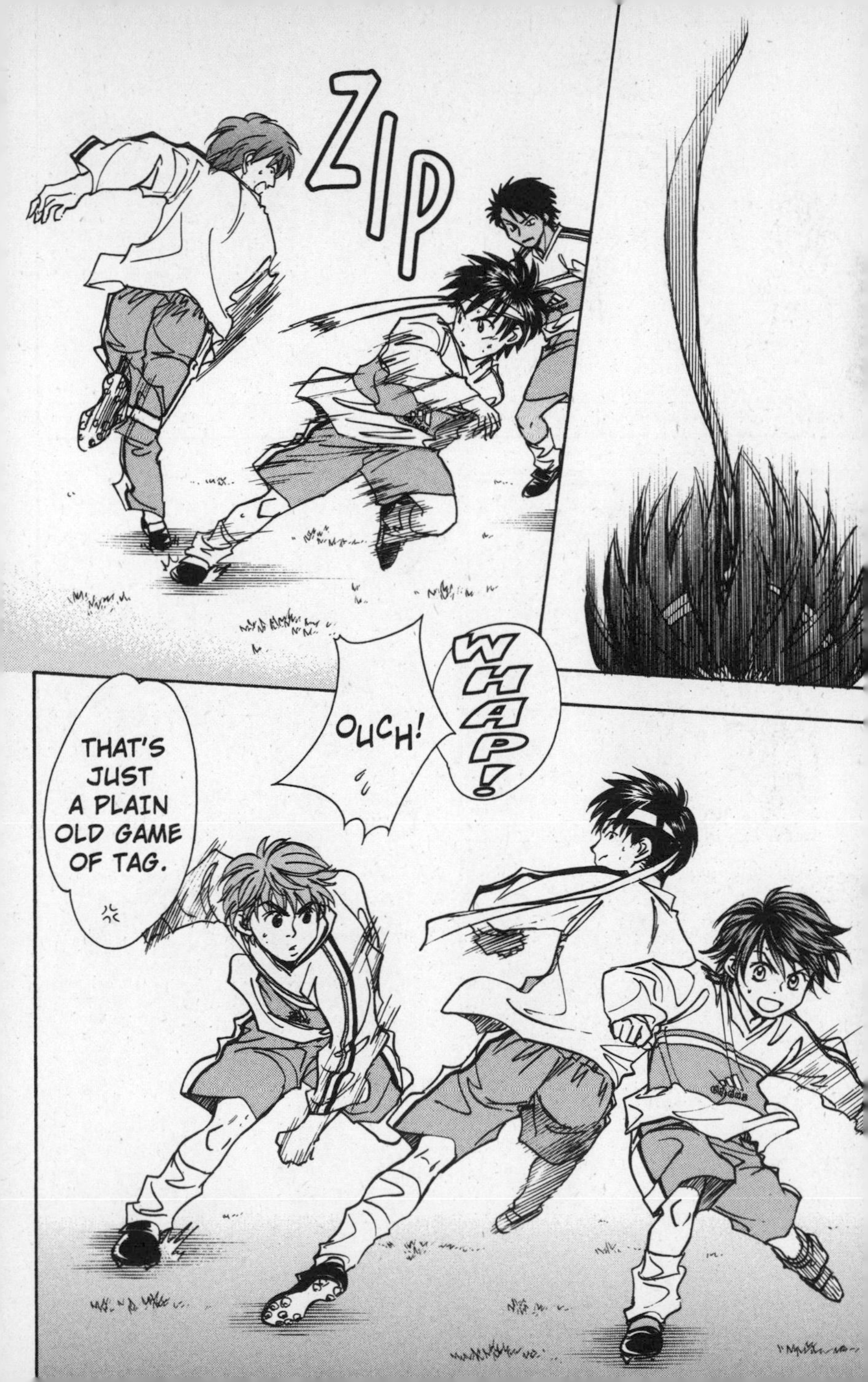
ZIP
WHAP!
OUCH!
THAT'S JUST A PLAIN OLD GAME OF TAG.

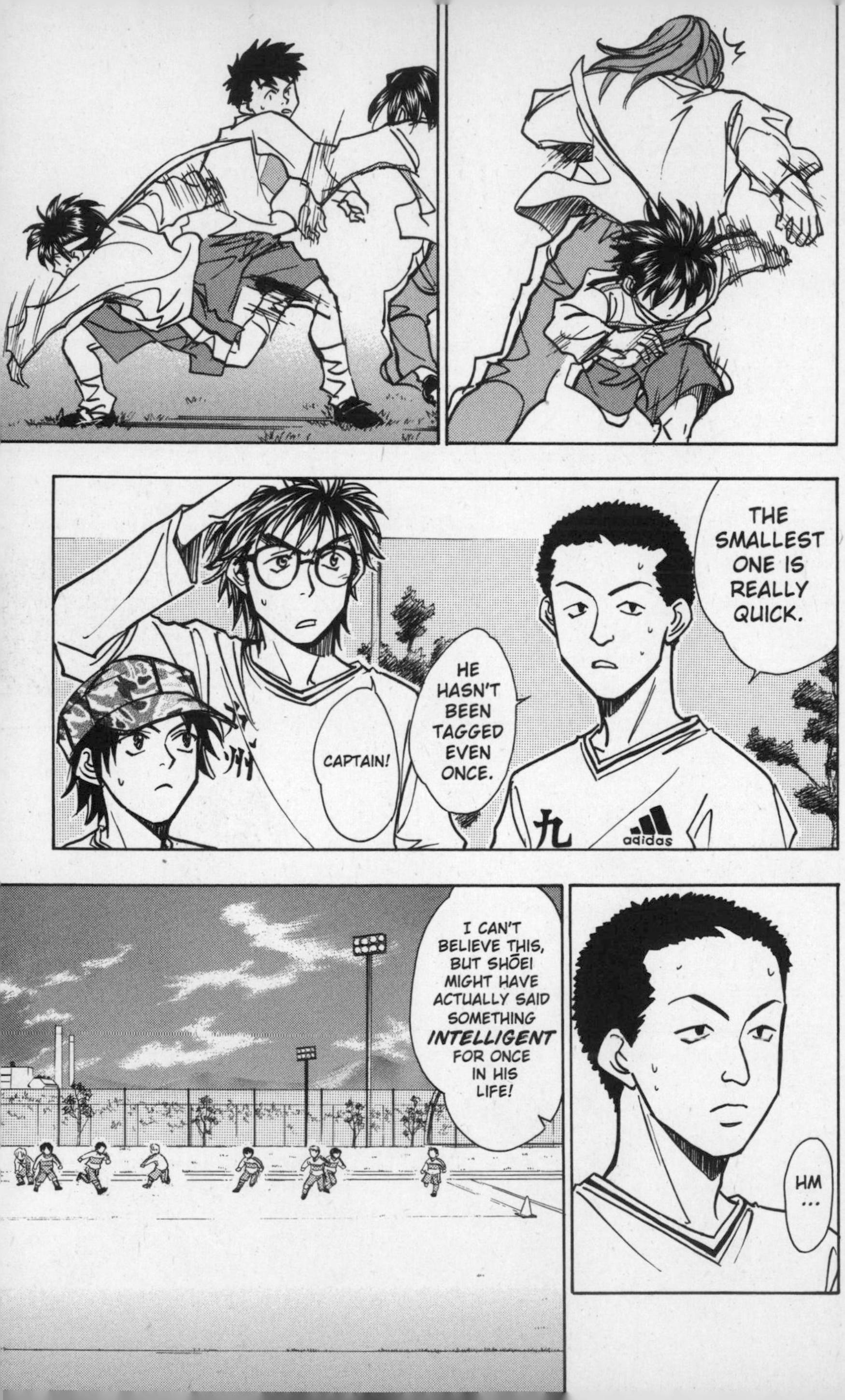
THE SMALLEST ONE IS REALLY QUICK.
HE HASN'T BEEN TAGGED EVEN ONCE.
CAPTAIN!
I CAN'T BELIEVE THIS, BUT SHŌEI MIGHT HAVE ACTUALLY SAID SOMETHING ***INTELLIGENT*** FOR ONCE IN HIS LIFE!
HM ...

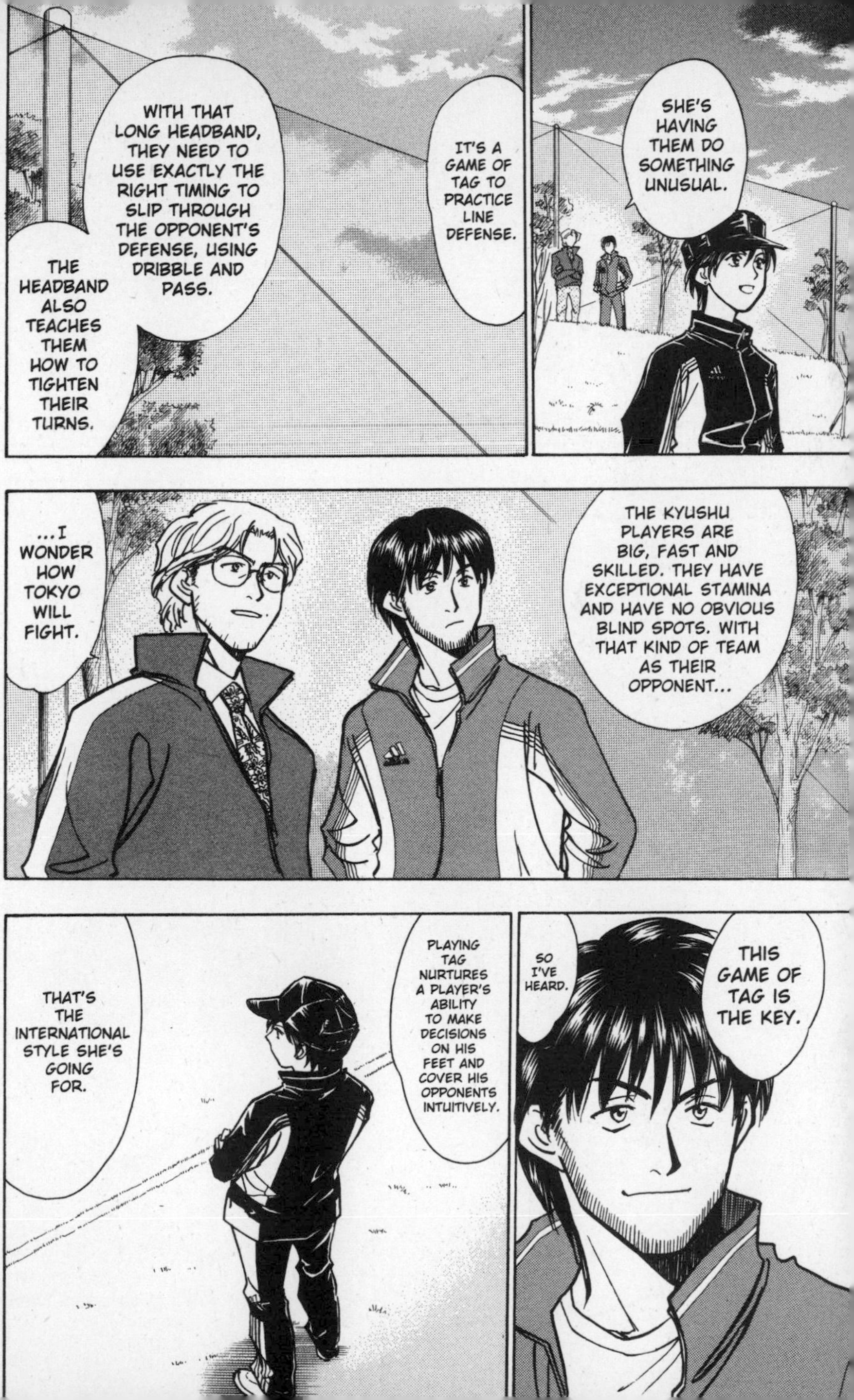
SHE'S HAVING THEM DO SOMETHING UNUSUAL.
IT'S A GAME OF TAG TO PRACTICE LINE DEFENSE.
WITH THAT LONG HEADBAND, THEY NEED TO USE EXACTLY THE RIGHT TIMING TO SLIP THROUGH THE OPPONENT'S DEFENSE, USING DRIBBLE AND PASS.
THE HEADBAND ALSO TEACHES THEM HOW TO TIGHTEN THEIR TURNS.
THE KYUSHU PLAYERS ARE BIG, FAST AND SKILLED. THEY HAVE EXCEPTIONAL STAMINA AND HAVE NO OBVIOUS BLIND SPOTS. WITH THAT KIND OF TEAM AS THEIR OPPONENT...
...I WONDER HOW TOKYO WILL FIGHT.
THIS GAME OF TAG IS THE KEY.
SO I'VE HEARD.
PLAYING TAG NURTURES A PLAYER'S ABILITY TO MAKE DECISIONS ON HIS FEET AND COVER HIS OPPONENTS INTUITIVELY.
THAT'S THE INTERNATIONAL STYLE SHE'S GOING FOR.

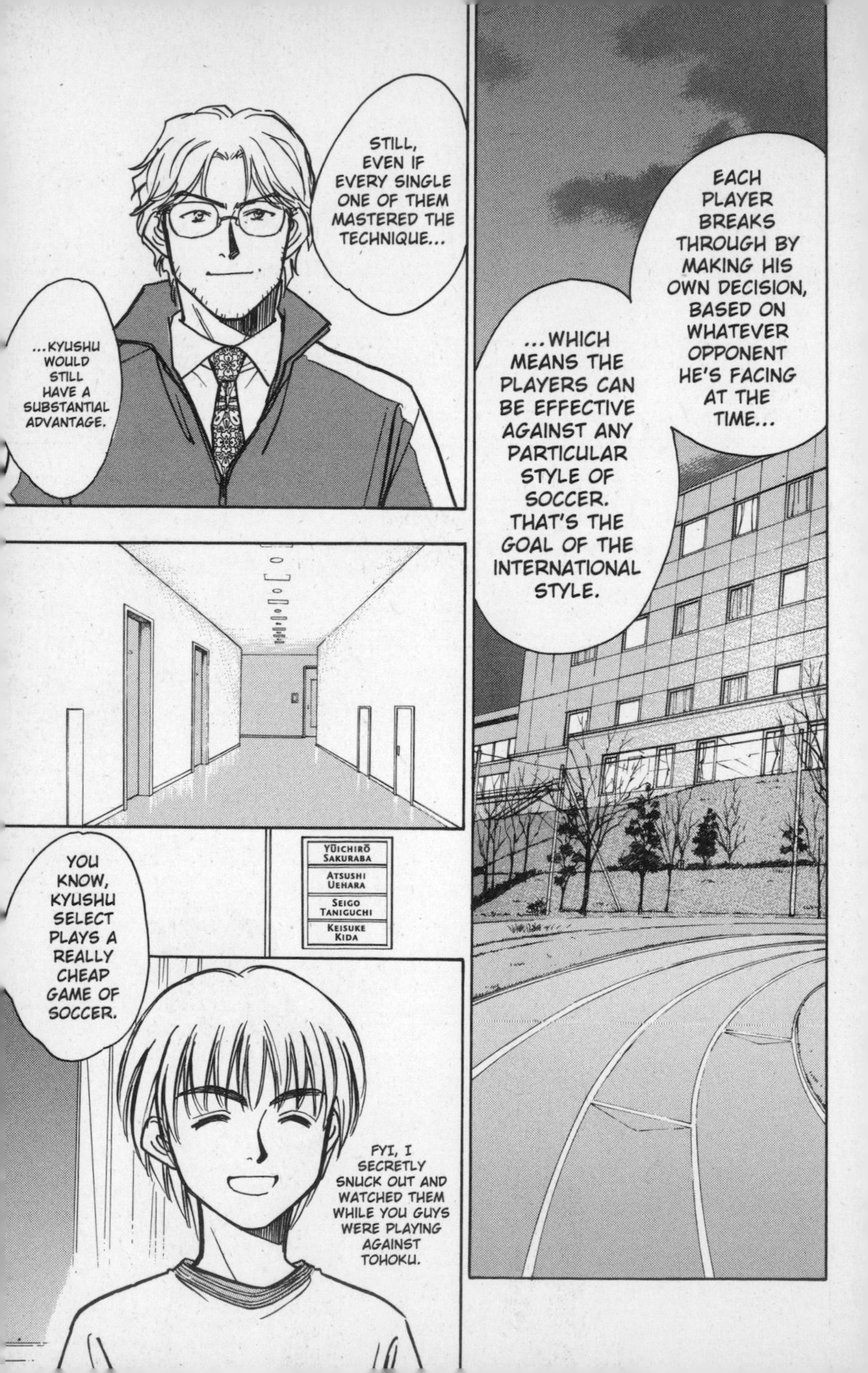
EACH PLAYER BREAKS THROUGH BY MAKING HIS OWN DECISION, BASED ON WHATEVER OPPONENT HE'S FACING AT THE TIME...
...WHICH MEANS THE PLAYERS CAN BE EFFECTIVE AGAINST ANY PARTICULAR STYLE OF SOCCER. THAT'S THE GOAL OF THE INTERNATIONAL STYLE.
STILL, EVEN IF EVERY SINGLE ONE OF THEM MASTERED THE TECHNIQUE...
...KYUSHU WOULD STILL HAVE A SUBSTANTIAL ADVANTAGE.
YŪICHIRŌ SAKURABA
ATSUSHI UEHARA
SEIGO TANIGUCHI
KEISUKE KIDA
YOU KNOW, KYUSHU SELECT PLAYS A REALLY CHEAP GAME OF SOCCER.
FYI, I SECRETLY SNUCK OUT AND WATCHED THEM WHILE YOU GUYS WERE PLAYING AGAINST TOHOKU.

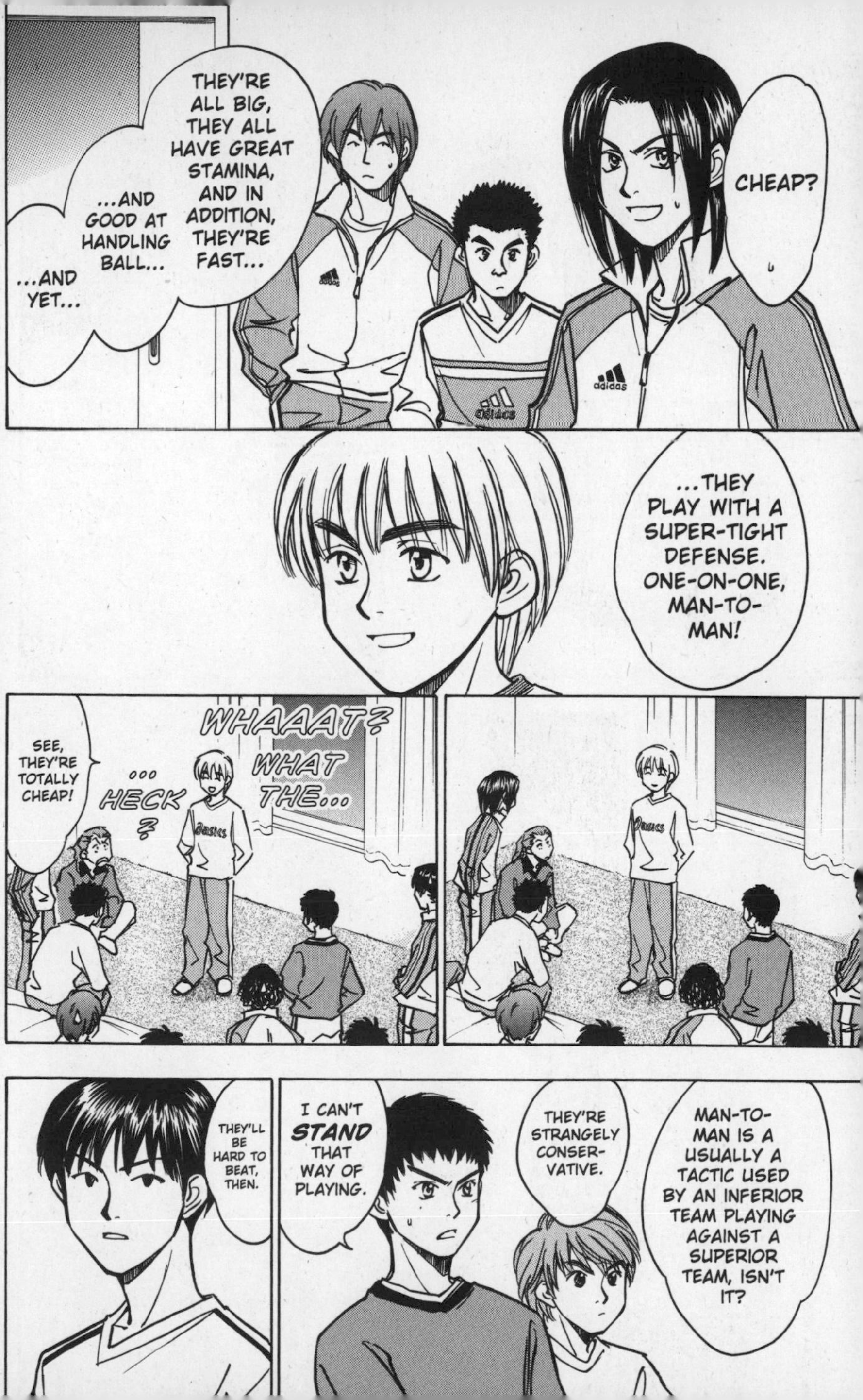
CHEAP?
THEY'RE ALL BIG, THEY ALL HAVE GREAT STAMINA, AND IN ADDITION, THEY'RE FAST...
...AND GOOD AT HANDLING BALL...
...AND YET...
...THEY PLAY WITH A SUPER-TIGHT DEFENSE. ONE-ON-ONE, MAN-TO-MAN!
WHAAAT?
WHAT THE...
...HECK?
SEE, THEY'RE TOTALLY CHEAP!
MAN-TO-MAN IS A USUALLY A TACTIC USED BY AN INFERIOR TEAM PLAYING AGAINST A SUPERIOR TEAM, ISN'T IT?
THEY'RE STRANGELY CONSERVATIVE.
I CAN'T ***STAND*** THAT WAY OF PLAYING.
THEY'LL BE HARD TO BEAT, THEN.

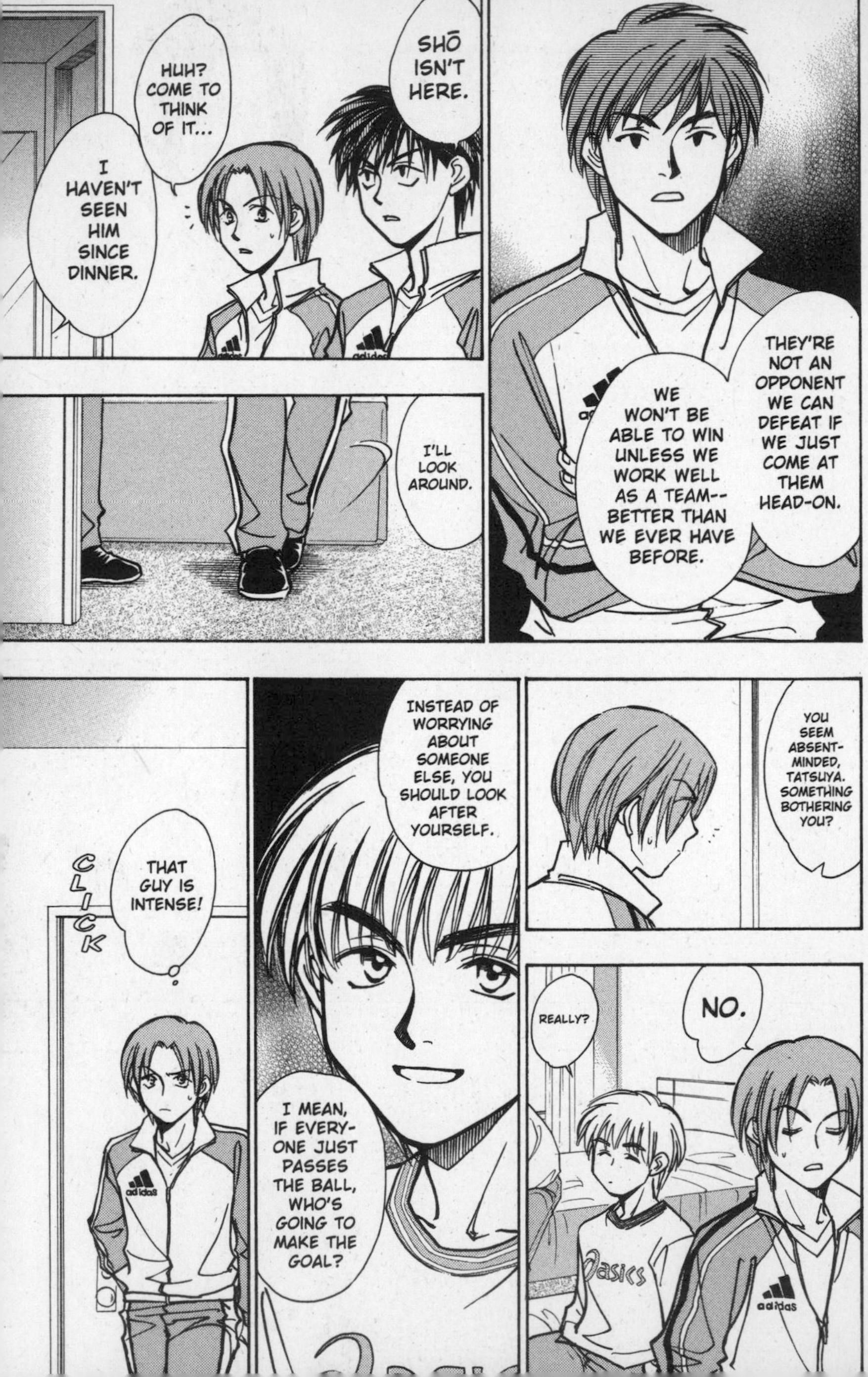
THEY'RE NOT AN OPPONENT WE CAN DEFEAT IF WE JUST COME AT THEM HEAD-ON.
WE WON'T BE ABLE TO WIN UNLESS WE WORK WELL AS A TEAM--BETTER THAN WE EVER HAVE BEFORE.
SHŌ ISN'T HERE.
HUH? COME TO THINK OF IT...
I HAVEN'T SEEN HIM SINCE DINNER.
I'LL LOOK AROUND.
YOU SEEM ABSENT-MINDED, TATSUYA. SOMETHING BOTHERING YOU?
NO.
REALLY?
INSTEAD OF WORRYING ABOUT SOMEONE ELSE, YOU SHOULD LOOK AFTER YOURSELF.
I MEAN, IF EVERYONE JUST PASSES THE BALL, WHO'S GOING TO MAKE THE GOAL?
CLICK
THAT GUY IS INTENSE!

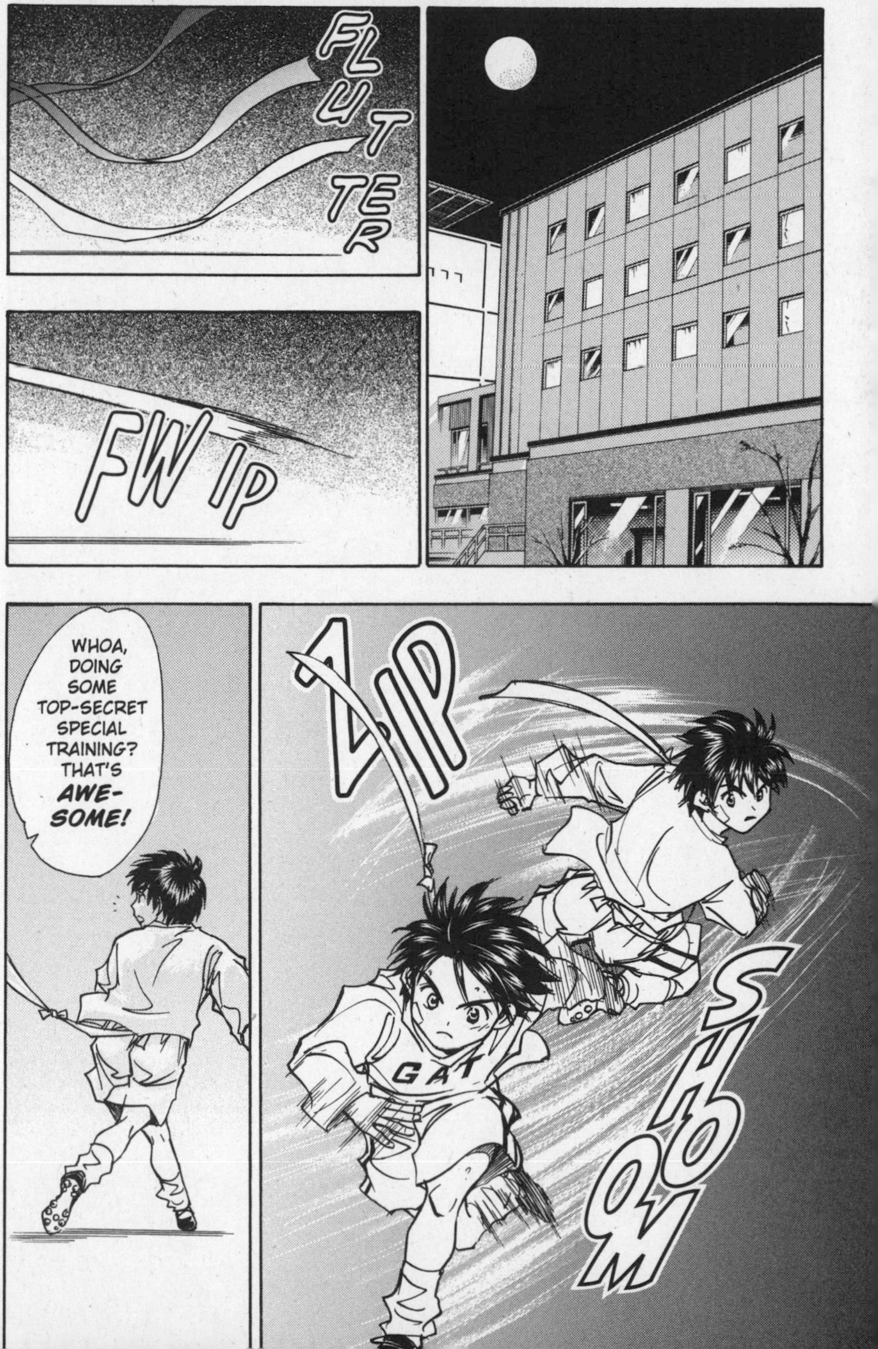
FLUTTER
FWIP
ZIP
SHOOOM
WHOA, DOING SOME TOP-SECRET SPECIAL TRAINING? THAT'S **AWESOME!**

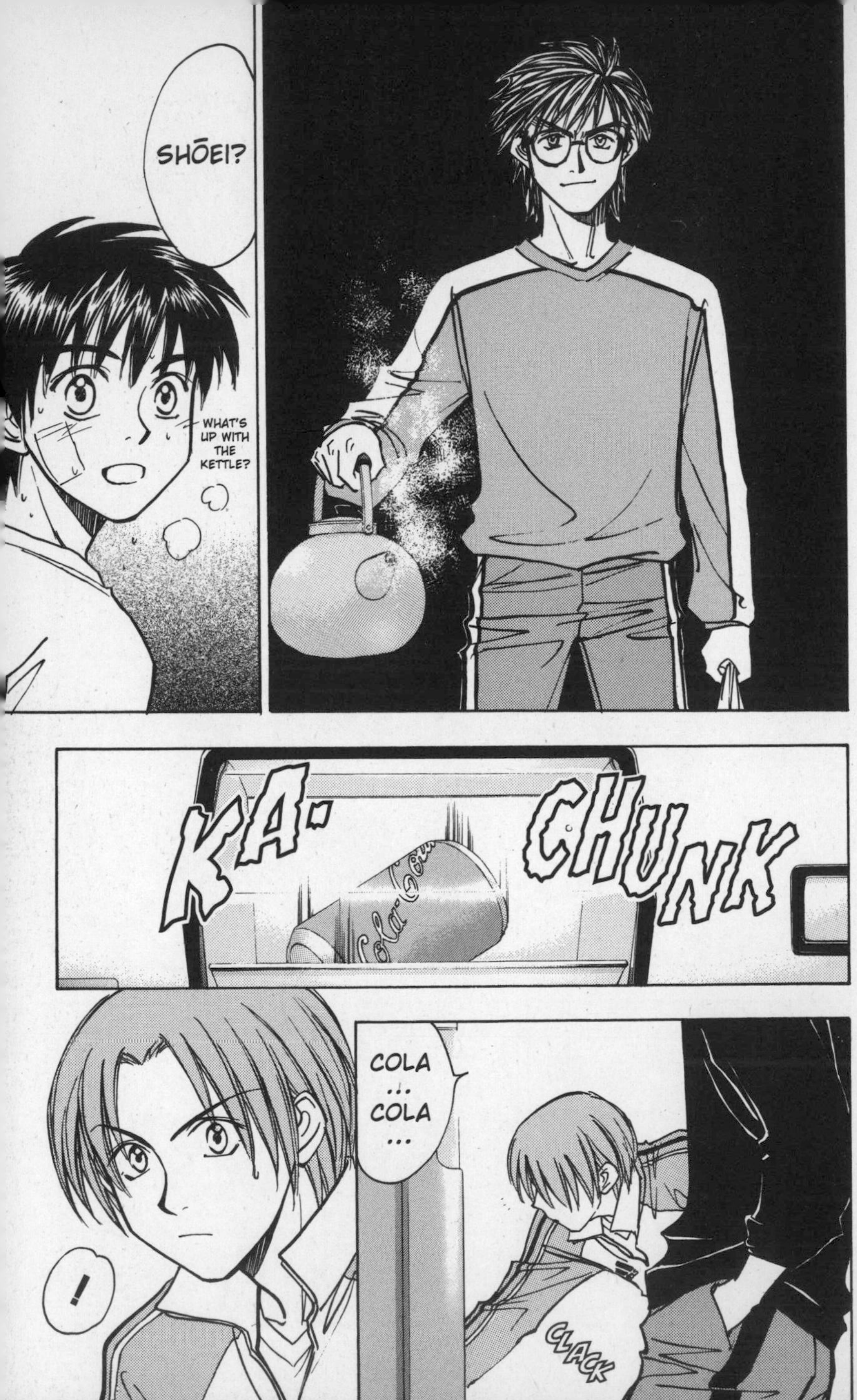
SHŌEI?
WHAT'S UP WITH THE KETTLE?
KA-CHUNK
COLA ... COLA ...
CLACK
!

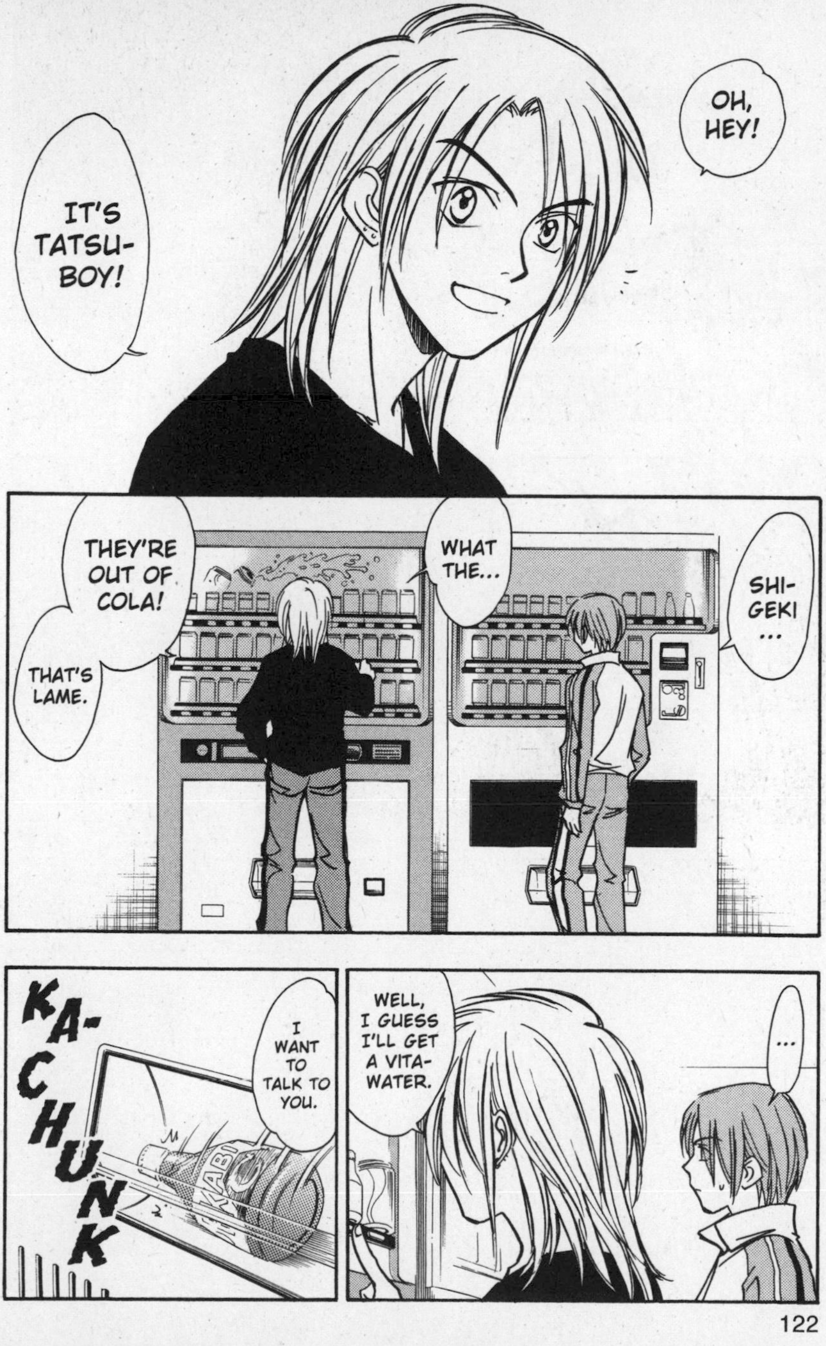
OH, HEY!
IT'S TATSU-BOY!
SHI-GEKI...
WHAT THE...
THEY'RE OUT OF COLA!
THAT'S LAME.
...
WELL, I GUESS I'LL GET A VITA-WATER.
I WANT TO TALK TO YOU.
KA-CHUNK

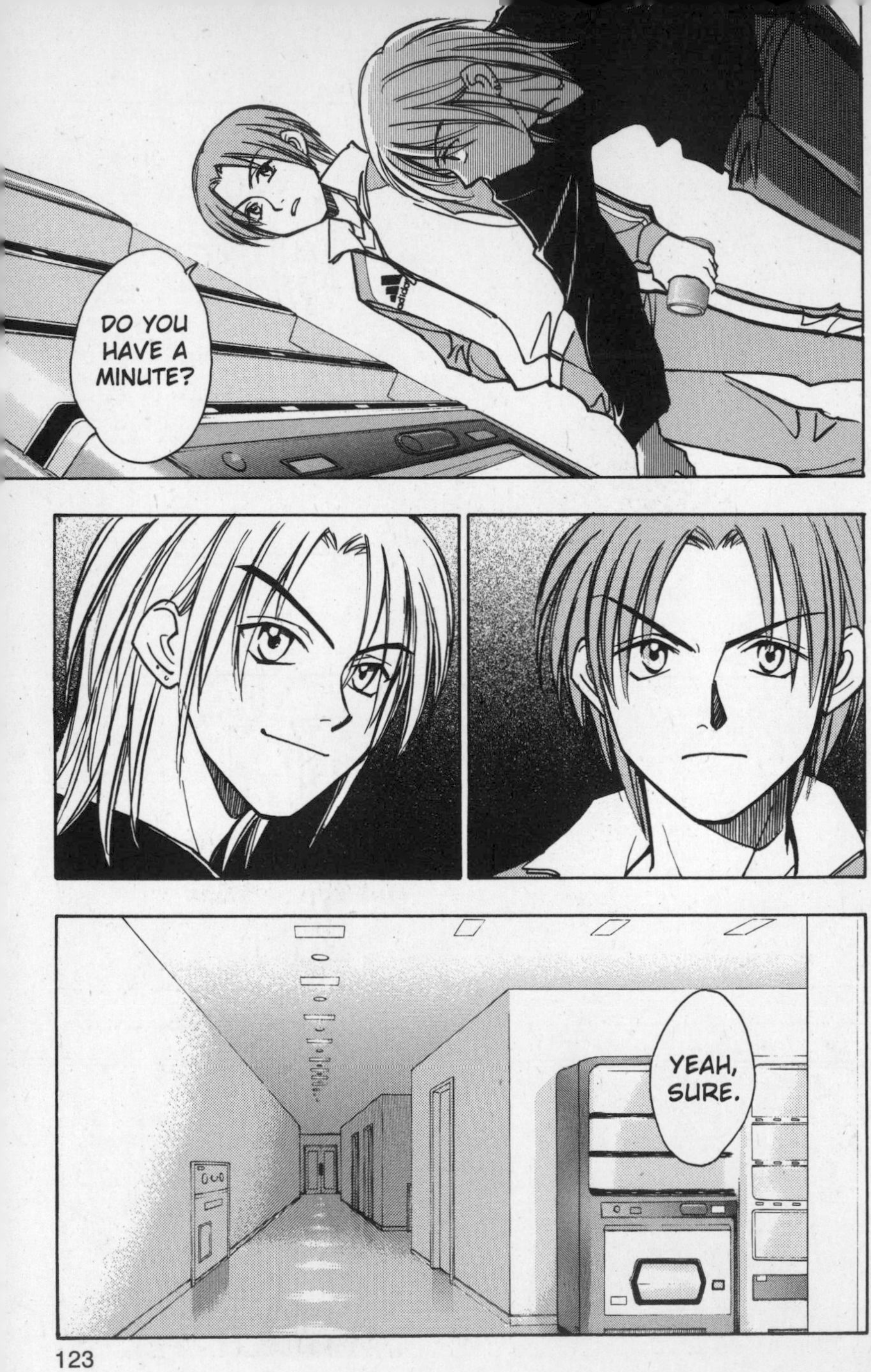
DO YOU HAVE A MINUTE?
YEAH, SURE.

WHISTLE!

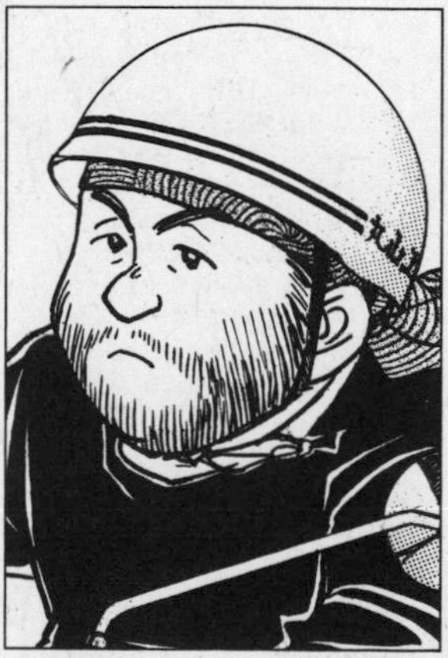

STAGE.189 He Scares Me

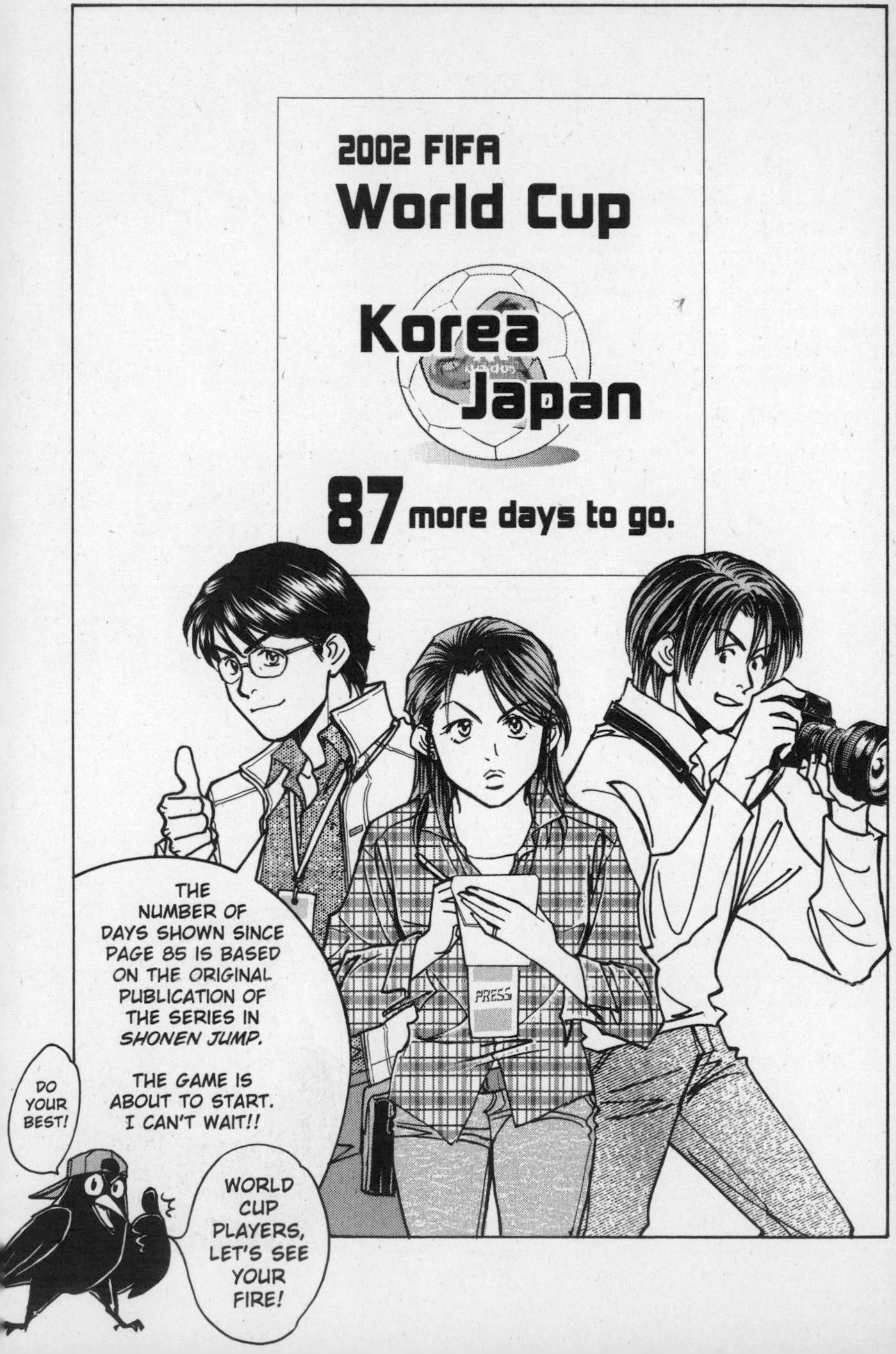
2002 FIFA
World Cup
Korea
Japan
87 more days to go.
PRESS
THE NUMBER OF DAYS SHOWN SINCE PAGE 85 IS BASED ON THE ORIGINAL PUBLICATION OF THE SERIES IN *SHONEN JUMP*.
THE GAME IS ABOUT TO START. I CAN'T WAIT!!
WORLD CUP PLAYERS, LET'S SEE YOUR FIRE!
DO YOUR BEST!

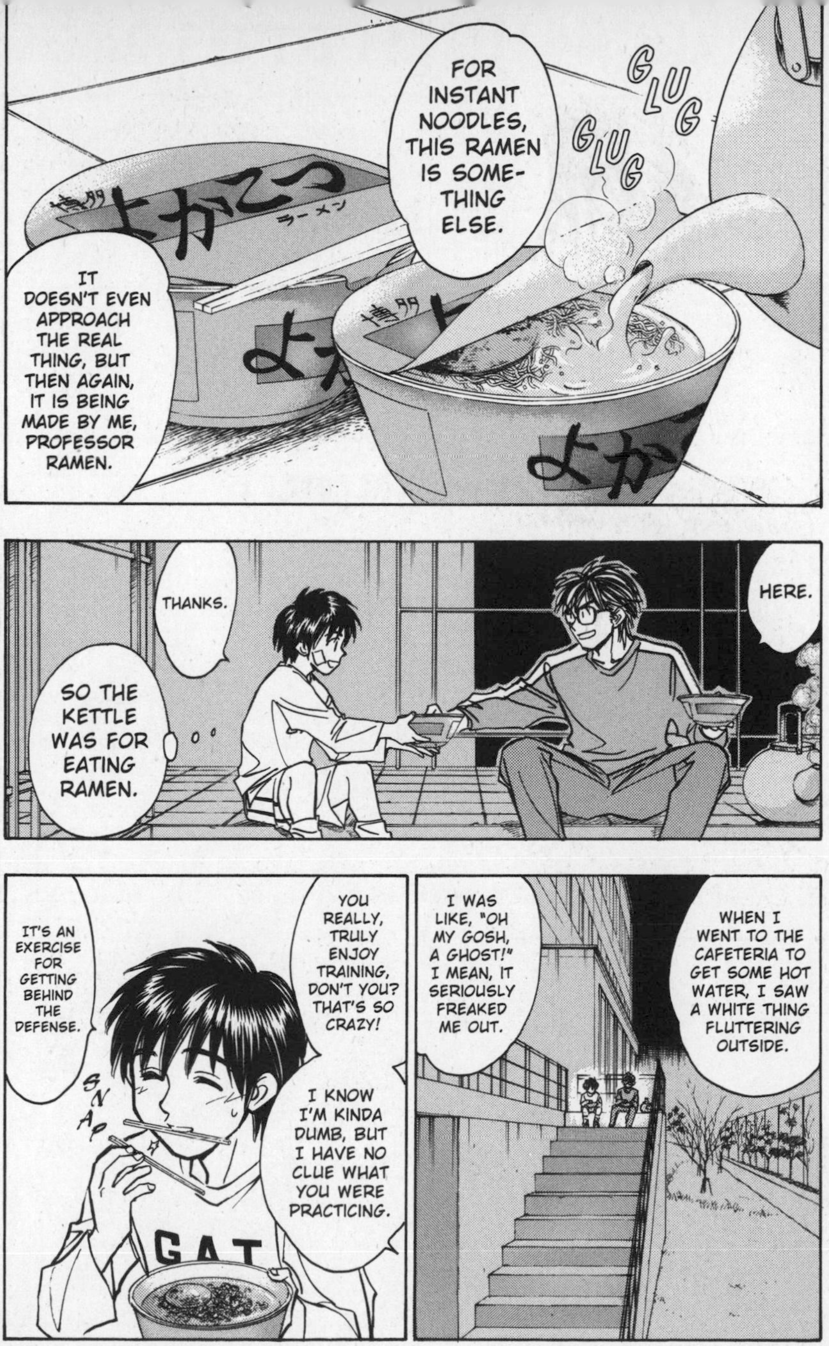
GLUG GLUG
FOR INSTANT NOODLES, THIS RAMEN IS SOME-THING ELSE.
よかこつ
ラーメン
IT DOESN'T EVEN APPROACH THE REAL THING, BUT THEN AGAIN, IT IS BEING MADE BY ME, PROFESSOR RAMEN.
HERE.
THANKS.
SO THE KETTLE WAS FOR EATING RAMEN.
...
WHEN I WENT TO THE CAFETERIA TO GET SOME HOT WATER, I SAW A WHITE THING FLUTTERING OUTSIDE.
I WAS LIKE, "OH MY GOSH, A GHOST!" I MEAN, IT SERIOUSLY FREAKED ME OUT.
YOU REALLY, TRULY ENJOY TRAINING, DON'T YOU? THAT'S SO CRAZY!
I KNOW I'M KINDA DUMB, BUT I HAVE NO CLUE WHAT YOU WERE PRACTICING.
IT'S AN EXERCISE FOR GETTING BEHIND THE DEFENSE.
SNAP
GAT

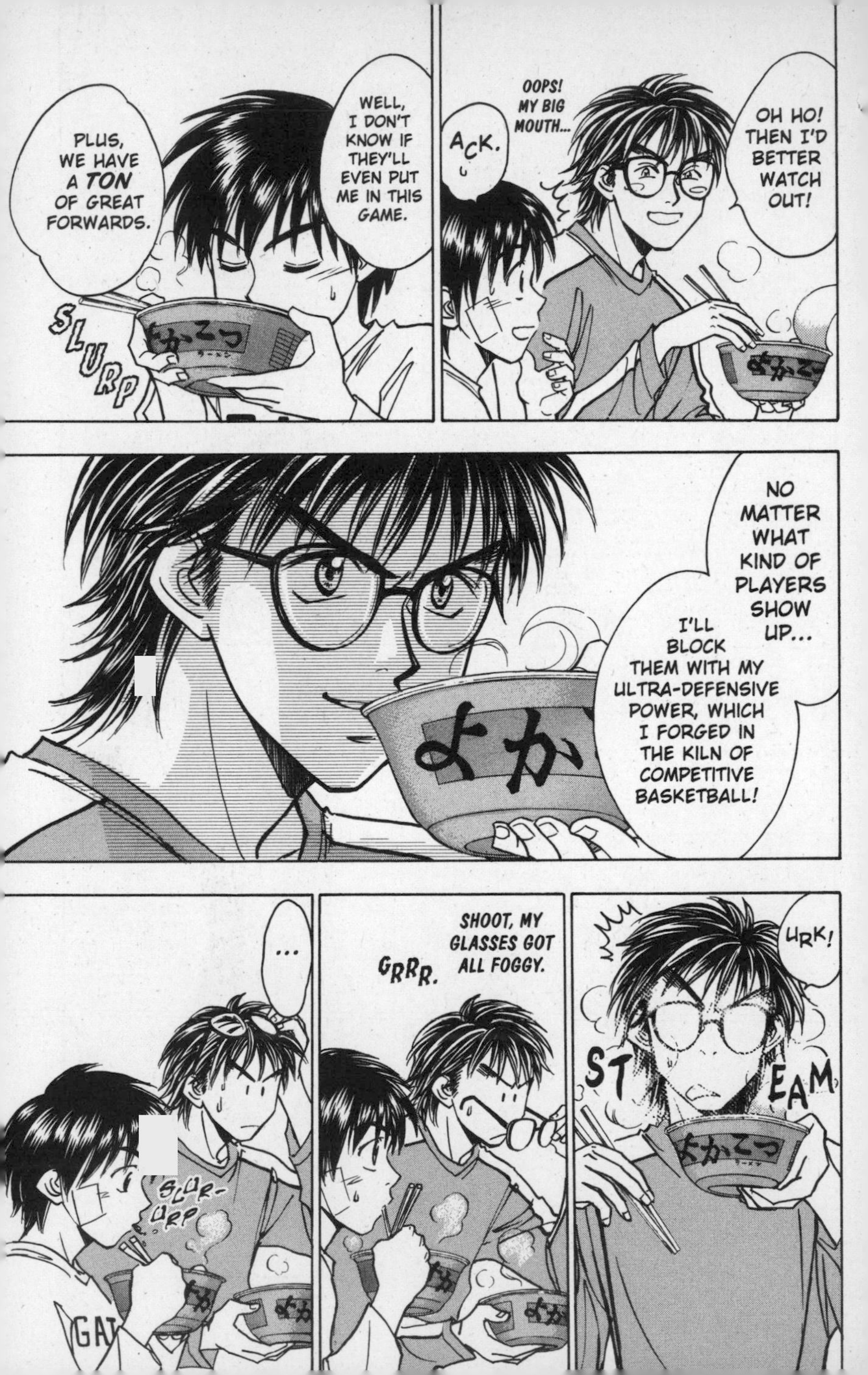
OH HO! THEN I'D BETTER WATCH OUT!
OOPS! MY BIG MOUTH...
ACK.
WELL, I DON'T KNOW IF THEY'LL EVEN PUT ME IN THIS GAME.
PLUS, WE HAVE A TON OF GREAT FORWARDS.
SLURP
NO MATTER WHAT KIND OF PLAYERS SHOW UP...
I'LL BLOCK THEM WITH MY ULTRA-DEFENSIVE POWER, WHICH I FORGED IN THE KILN OF COMPETITIVE BASKETBALL!
URK!
STEAM
SHOOT, MY GLASSES GOT ALL FOGGY.
GRRR.
...
SLUR-URP

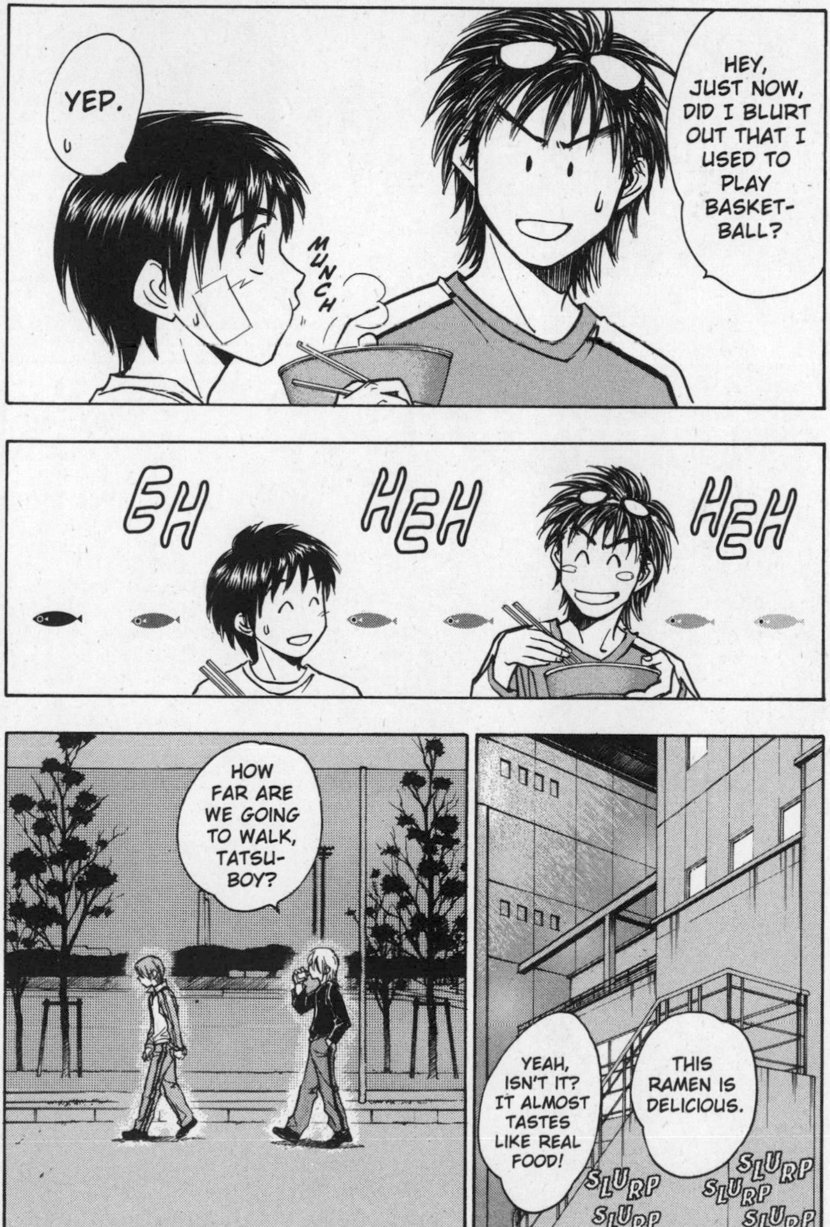
HEY, JUST NOW, DID I BLURT OUT THAT I USED TO PLAY BASKET-BALL?
YEP.
MUNCH
EH
HEH
HEH
THIS RAMEN IS DELICIOUS.
YEAH, ISN'T IT? IT ALMOST TASTES LIKE REAL FOOD!
SLURP SLURP SLURP SLURP
SLURP SLURP
HOW FAR ARE WE GOING TO WALK, TATSU-BOY?

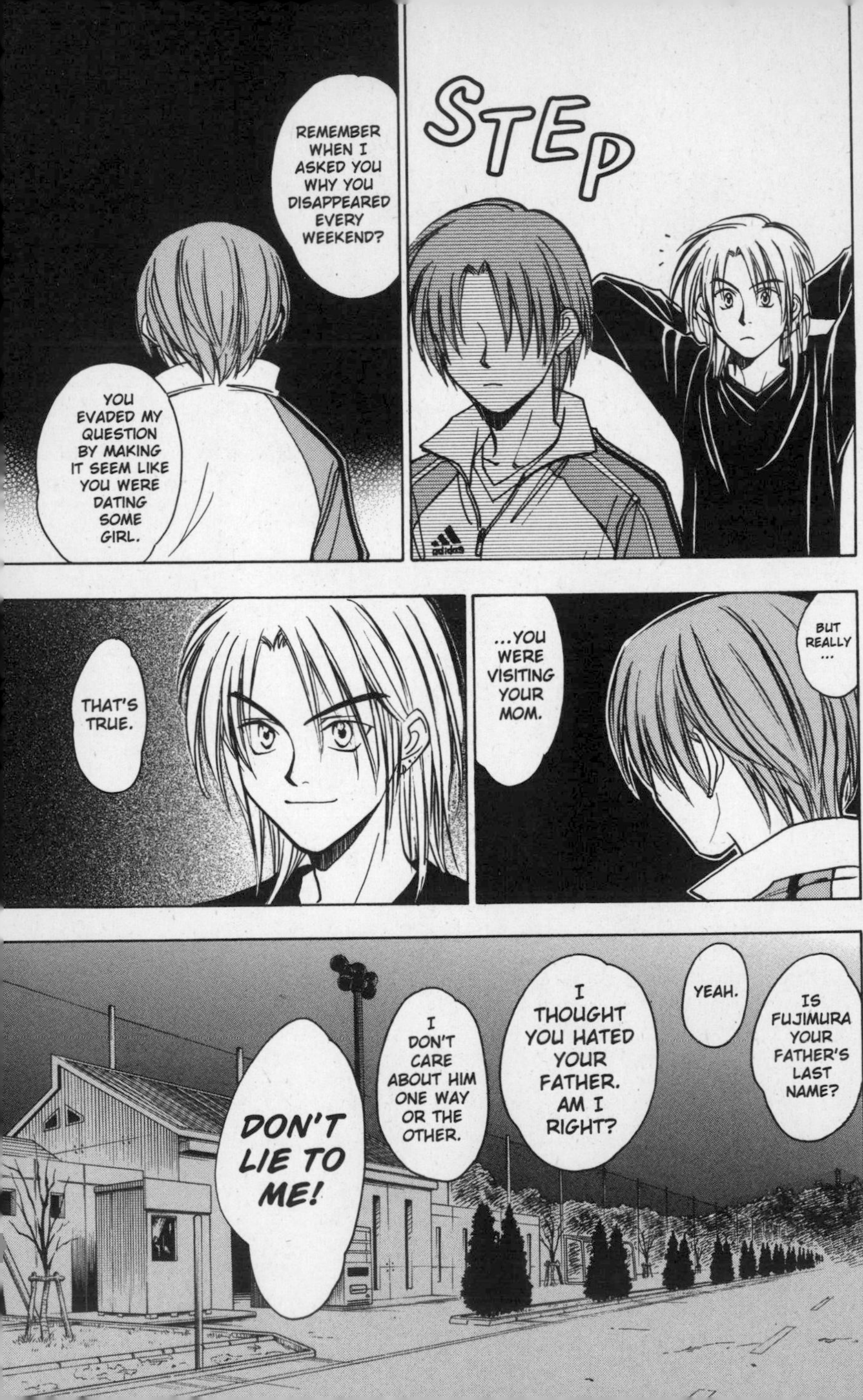
STEP
REMEMBER WHEN I ASKED YOU WHY YOU DISAPPEARED EVERY WEEKEND?
YOU EVADED MY QUESTION BY MAKING IT SEEM LIKE YOU WERE DATING SOME GIRL.
BUT REALLY...
...YOU WERE VISITING YOUR MOM.
THAT'S TRUE.
IS FUJIMURA YOUR FATHER'S LAST NAME?
YEAH.
I THOUGHT YOU HATED YOUR FATHER. AM I RIGHT?
I DON'T CARE ABOUT HIM ONE WAY OR THE OTHER.
DON'T LIE TO ME!

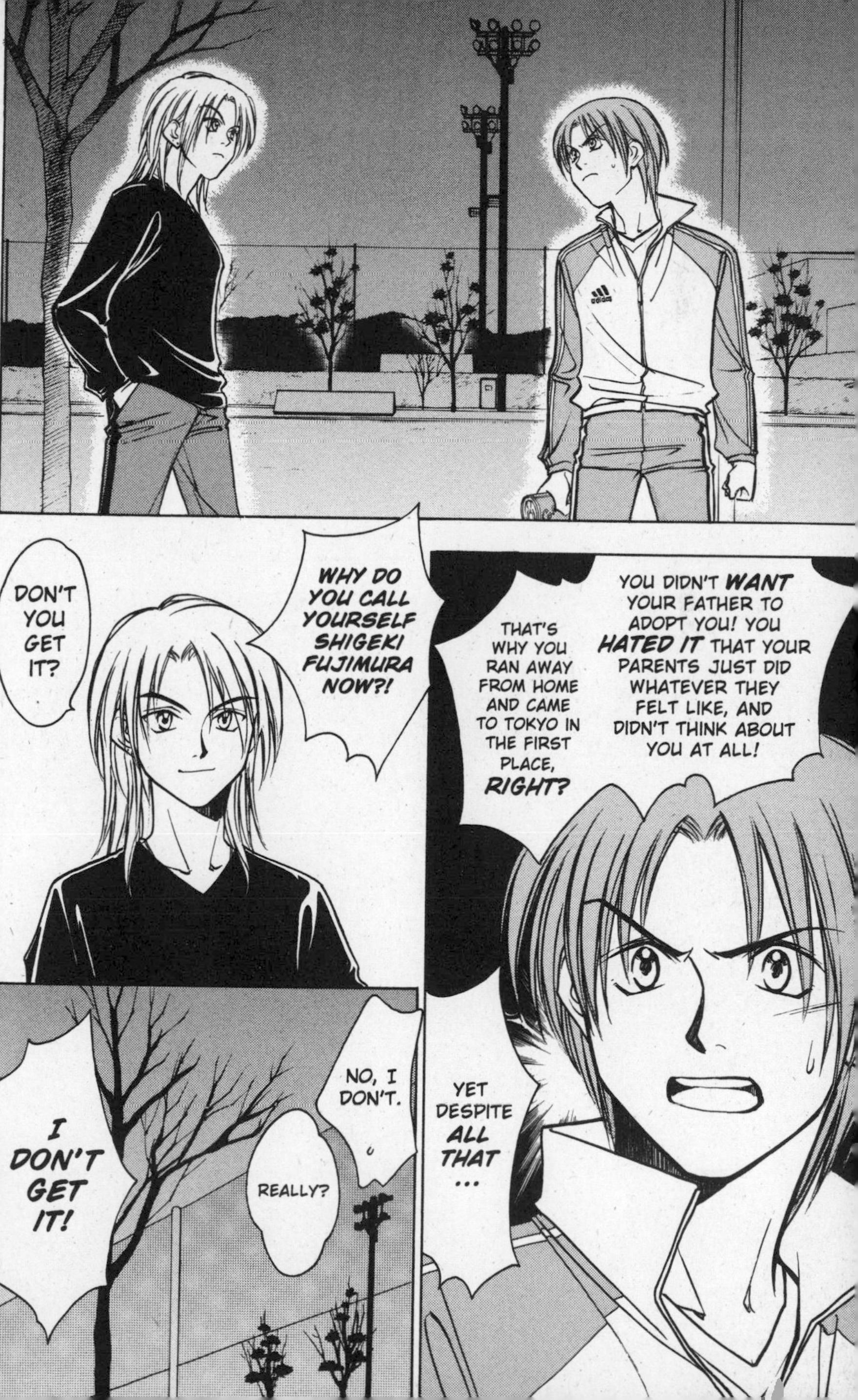
YOU DIDN'T WANT YOUR FATHER TO ADOPT YOU! YOU HATED IT THAT YOUR PARENTS JUST DID WHATEVER THEY FELT LIKE, AND DIDN'T THINK ABOUT YOU AT ALL!
THAT'S WHY YOU RAN AWAY FROM HOME AND CAME TO TOKYO IN THE FIRST PLACE, RIGHT?
YET DESPITE ALL THAT...
WHY DO YOU CALL YOURSELF SHIGEKI FUJIMURA NOW?!
DON'T YOU GET IT?
NO, I DON'T.
REALLY?
I DON'T GET IT!

READ THIS WAY

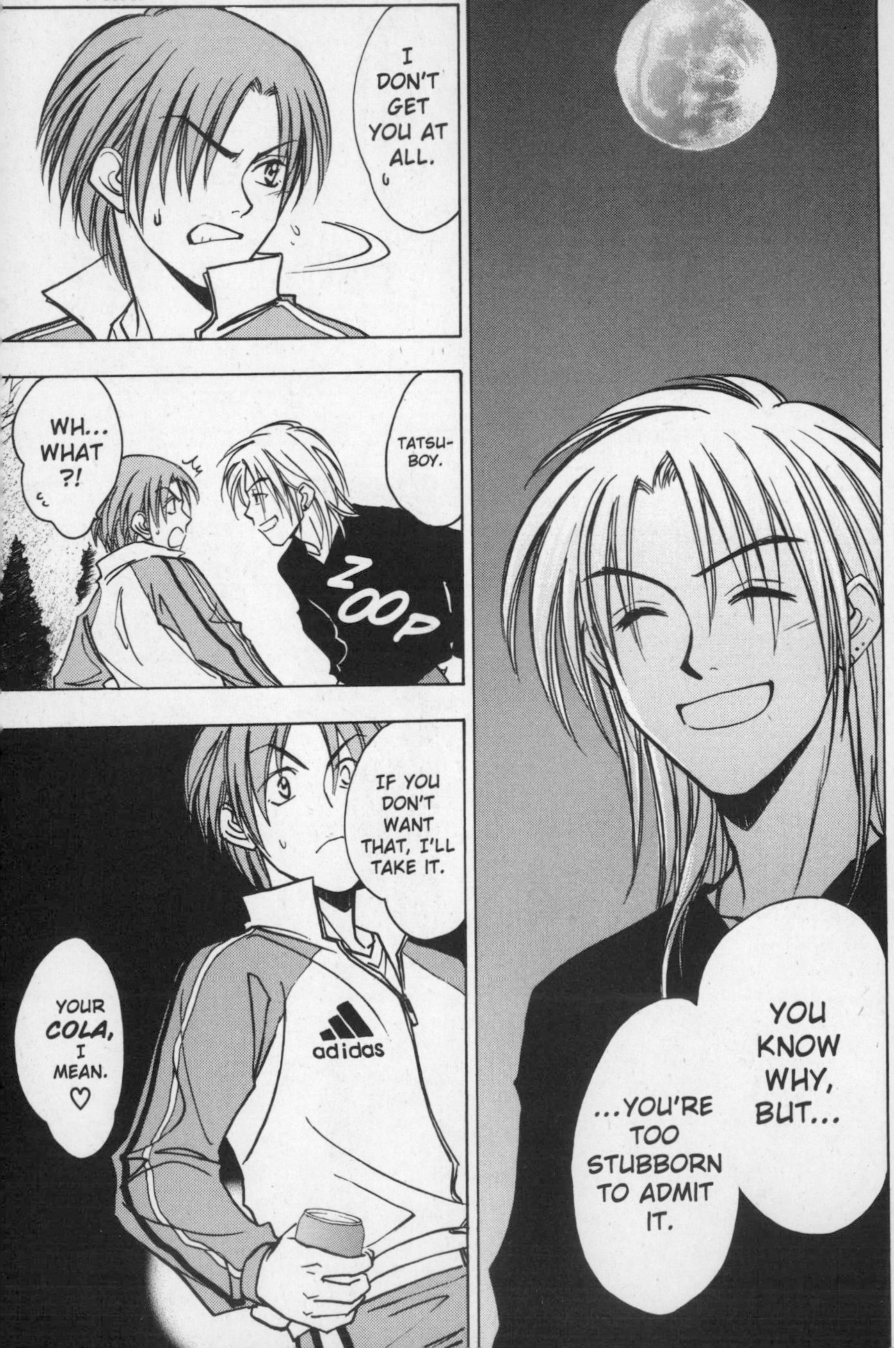
YOU KNOW WHY, BUT...
...YOU'RE TOO STUBBORN TO ADMIT IT.
I DON'T GET YOU AT ALL.
TATSU-BOY.
ZOOP
WH... WHAT ?!
IF YOU DON'T WANT THAT, I'LL TAKE IT.
YOUR COLA, I MEAN. ♡
adidas

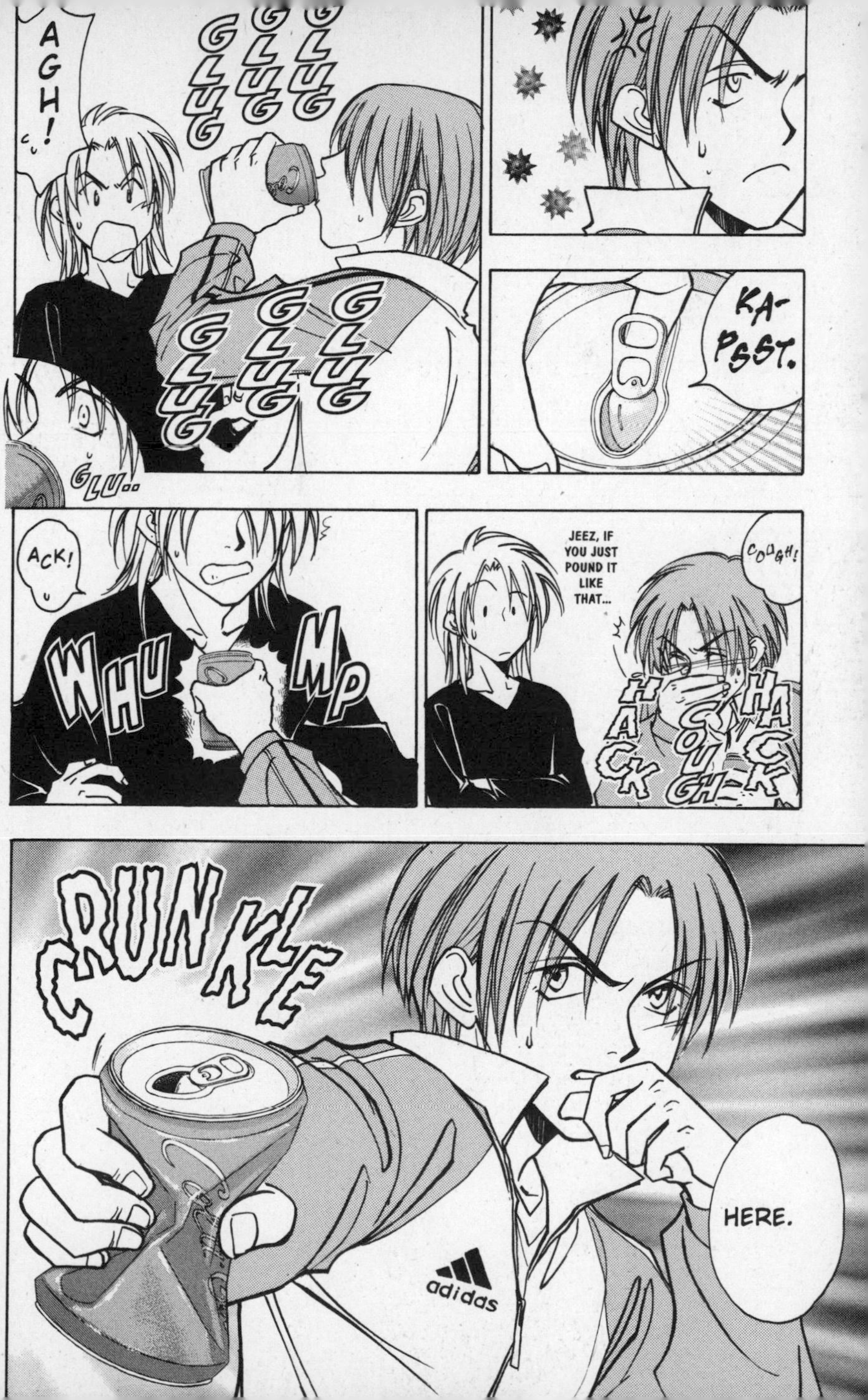
KA-PSST.
GLUG GLUG GLUG
AGH!
GLUG GLUG GLUG
GLU..
COUGH!
JEEZ, IF YOU JUST POUND IT LIKE THAT...
HACK COUGH HACK
ACK!
WHUMP
HERE.
CRUNKLE

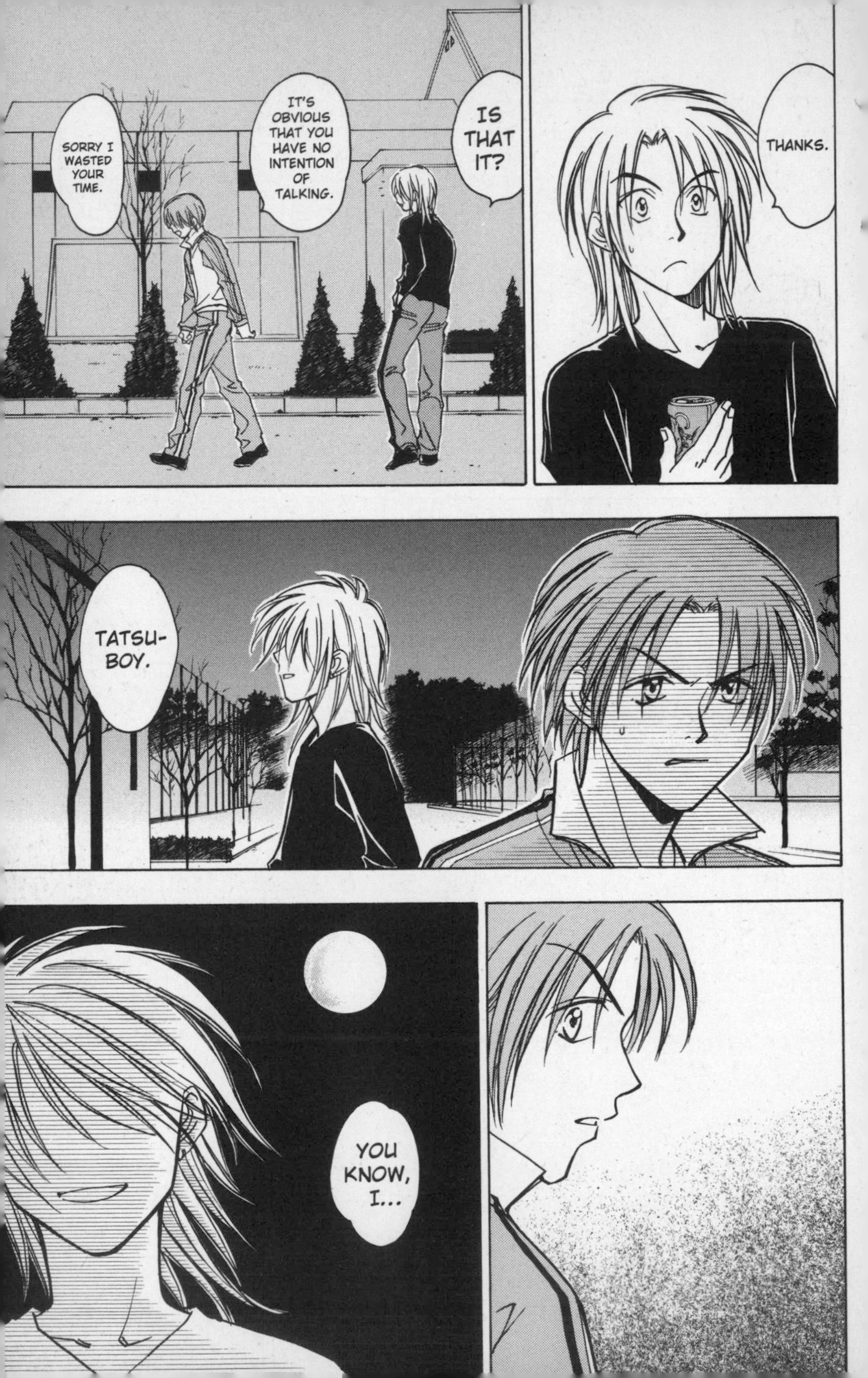
THANKS.
IS THAT IT?
IT'S OBVIOUS THAT YOU HAVE NO INTENTION OF TALKING.
SORRY I WASTED YOUR TIME.
TATSU-BOY.
YOU KNOW, I...

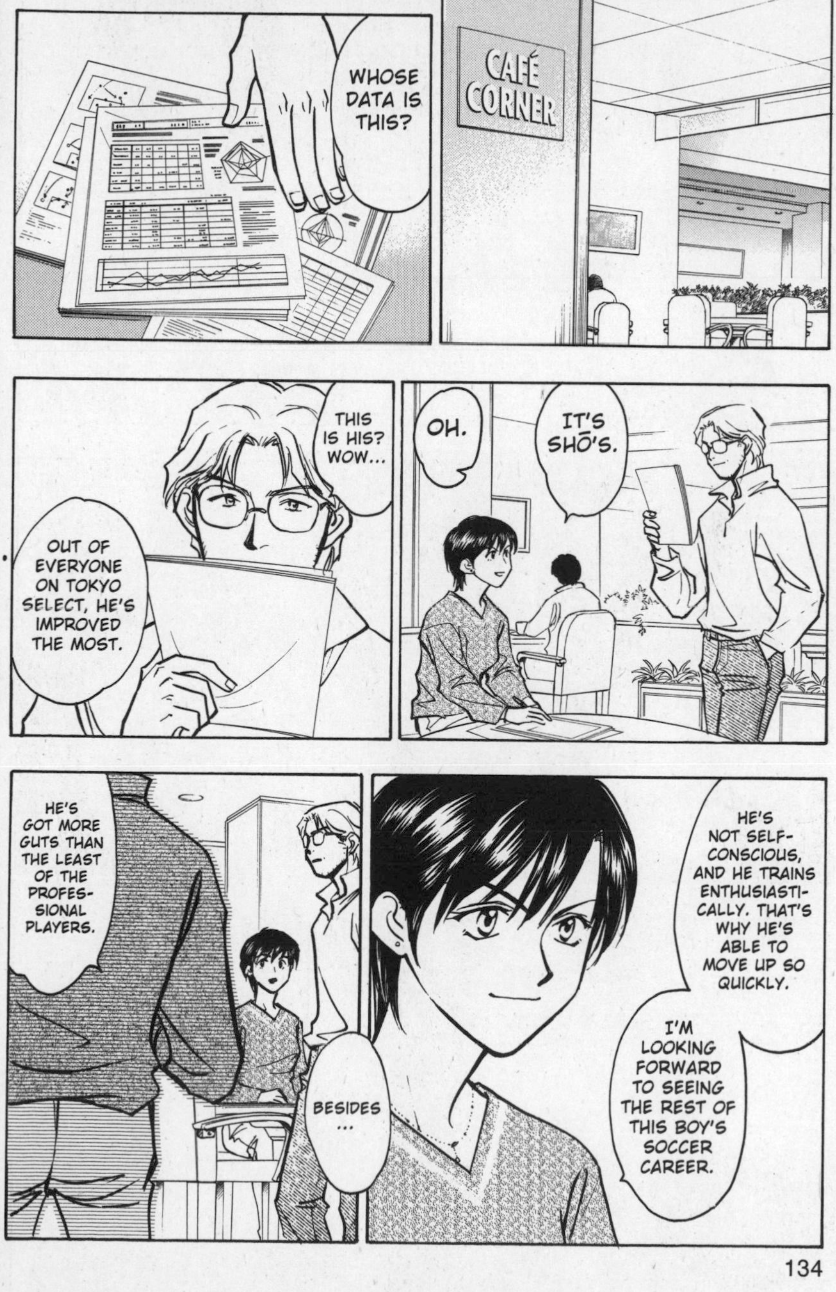
CAFÉ CORNER
WHOSE DATA IS THIS?
IT'S SHŌ'S.
OH.
THIS IS HIS? WOW...
OUT OF EVERYONE ON TOKYO SELECT, HE'S IMPROVED THE MOST.
HE'S NOT SELF-CONSCIOUS, AND HE TRAINS ENTHUSIASTI-CALLY. THAT'S WHY HE'S ABLE TO MOVE UP SO QUICKLY.
I'M LOOKING FORWARD TO SEEING THE REST OF THIS BOY'S SOCCER CAREER.
HE'S GOT MORE GUTS THAN THE LEAST OF THE PROFES-SIONAL PLAYERS.
BESIDES...

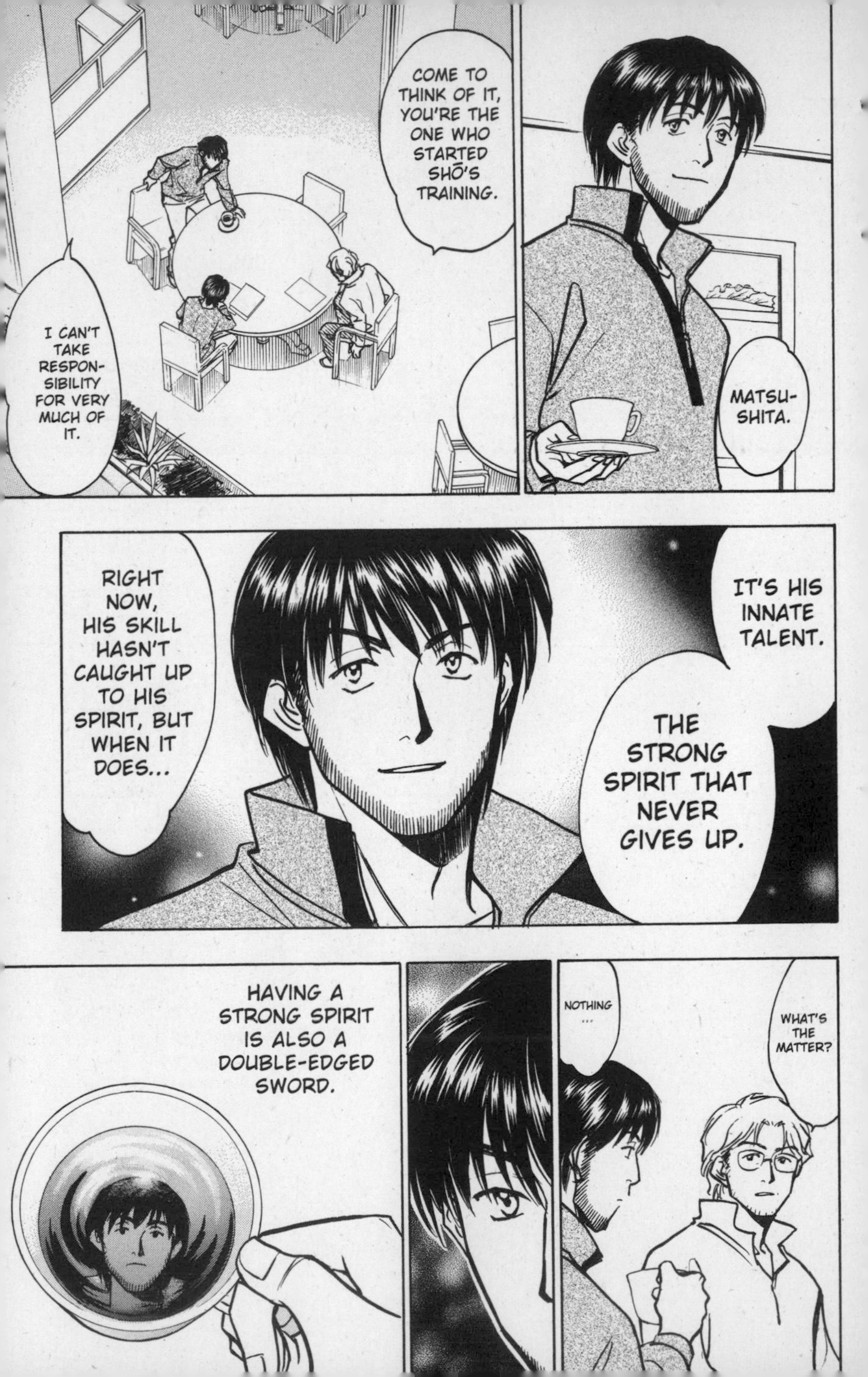
MATSU-SHITA.
COME TO THINK OF IT, YOU'RE THE ONE WHO STARTED SHŌ'S TRAINING.
I CAN'T TAKE RESPON-SIBILITY FOR VERY MUCH OF IT.
IT'S HIS INNATE TALENT.
THE STRONG SPIRIT THAT NEVER GIVES UP.
RIGHT NOW, HIS SKILL HASN'T CAUGHT UP TO HIS SPIRIT, BUT WHEN IT DOES...
WHAT'S THE MATTER?
NOTHING...
HAVING A STRONG SPIRIT IS ALSO A DOUBLE-EDGED SWORD.

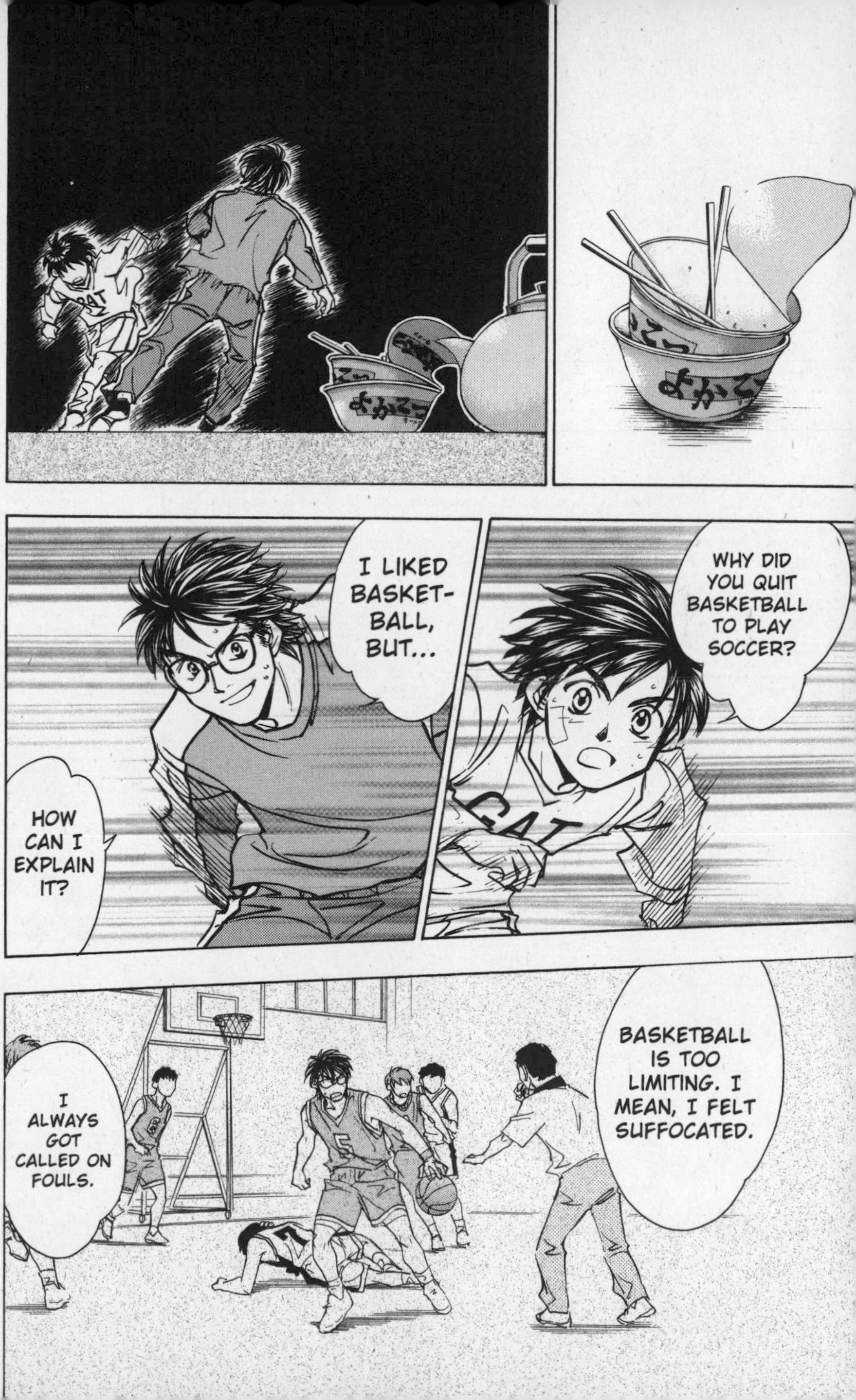
WHY DID YOU QUIT BASKETBALL TO PLAY SOCCER?
I LIKED BASKET-BALL, BUT...
HOW CAN I EXPLAIN IT?
BASKETBALL IS TOO LIMITING. I MEAN, I FELT SUFFOCATED.
I ALWAYS GOT CALLED ON FOULS.

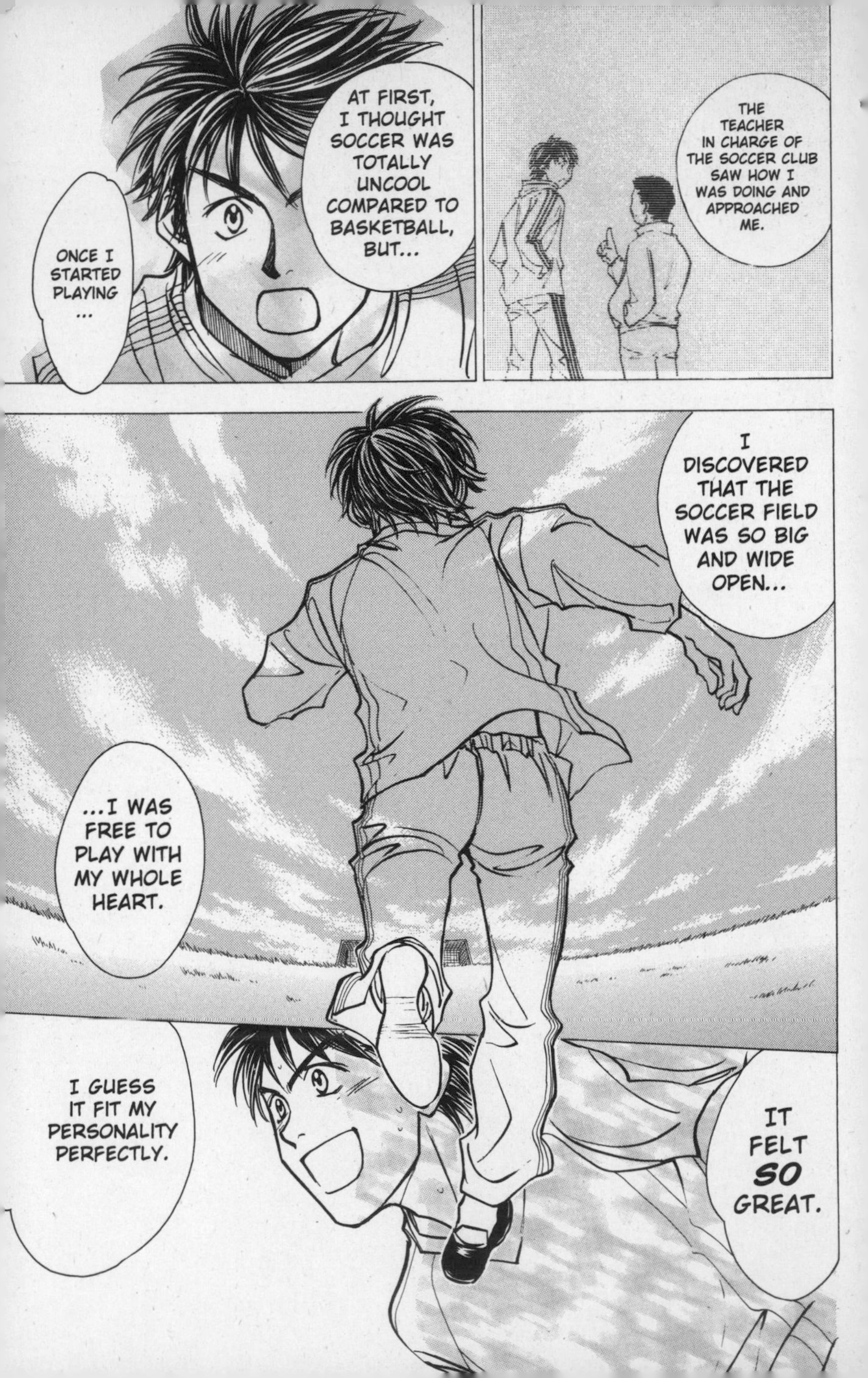
THE TEACHER IN CHARGE OF THE SOCCER CLUB SAW HOW I WAS DOING AND APPROACHED ME.
AT FIRST, I THOUGHT SOCCER WAS TOTALLY UNCOOL COMPARED TO BASKETBALL, BUT...
ONCE I STARTED PLAYING...
I DISCOVERED THAT THE SOCCER FIELD WAS SO BIG AND WIDE OPEN...
...I WAS FREE TO PLAY WITH MY WHOLE HEART.
IT FELT *SO* GREAT.
I GUESS IT FIT MY PERSONALITY PERFECTLY.

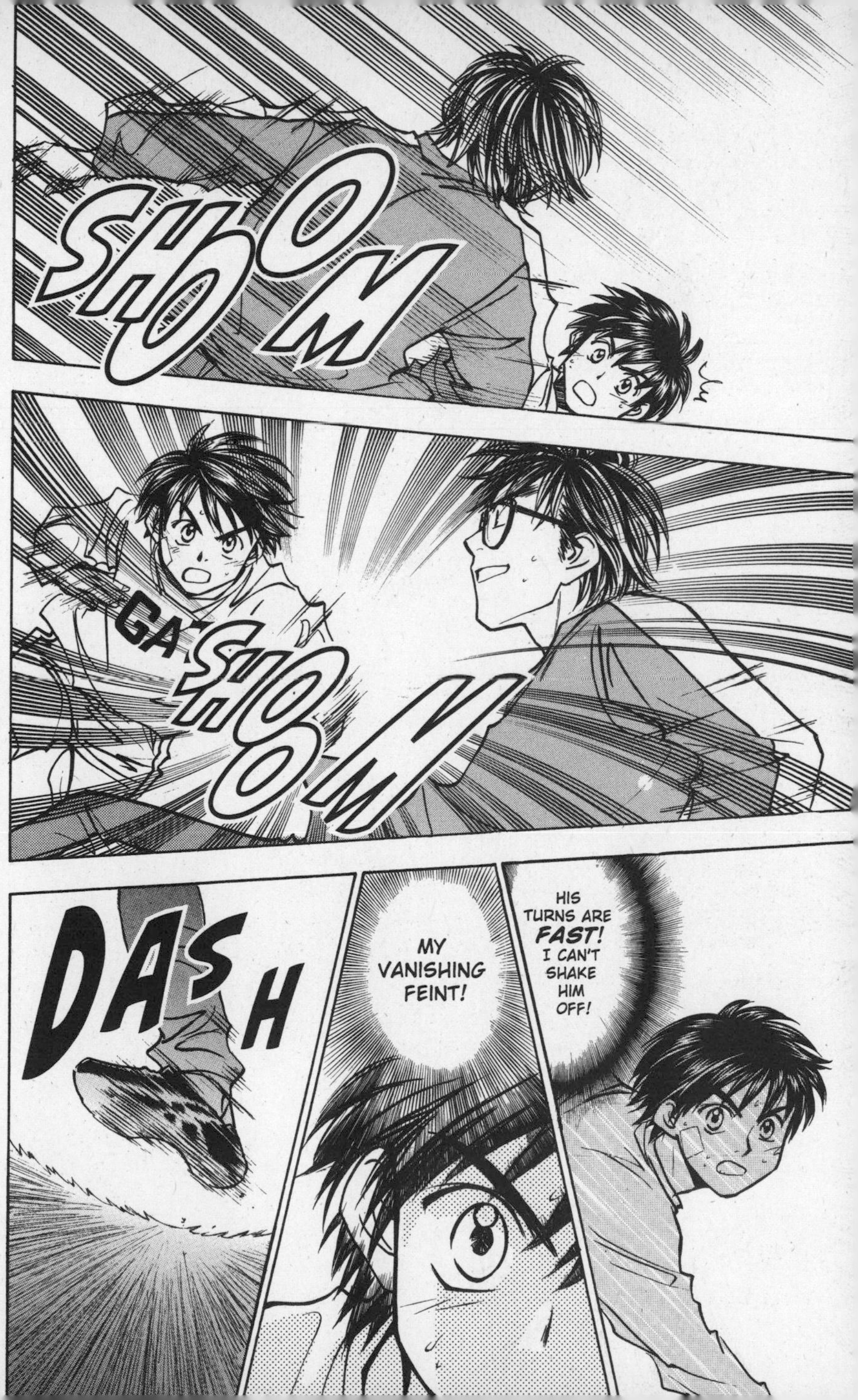
SHOOM
GASHOOM
HIS TURNS ARE FAST! I CAN'T SHAKE HIM OFF!
MY VANISHING FEINT!
DASH

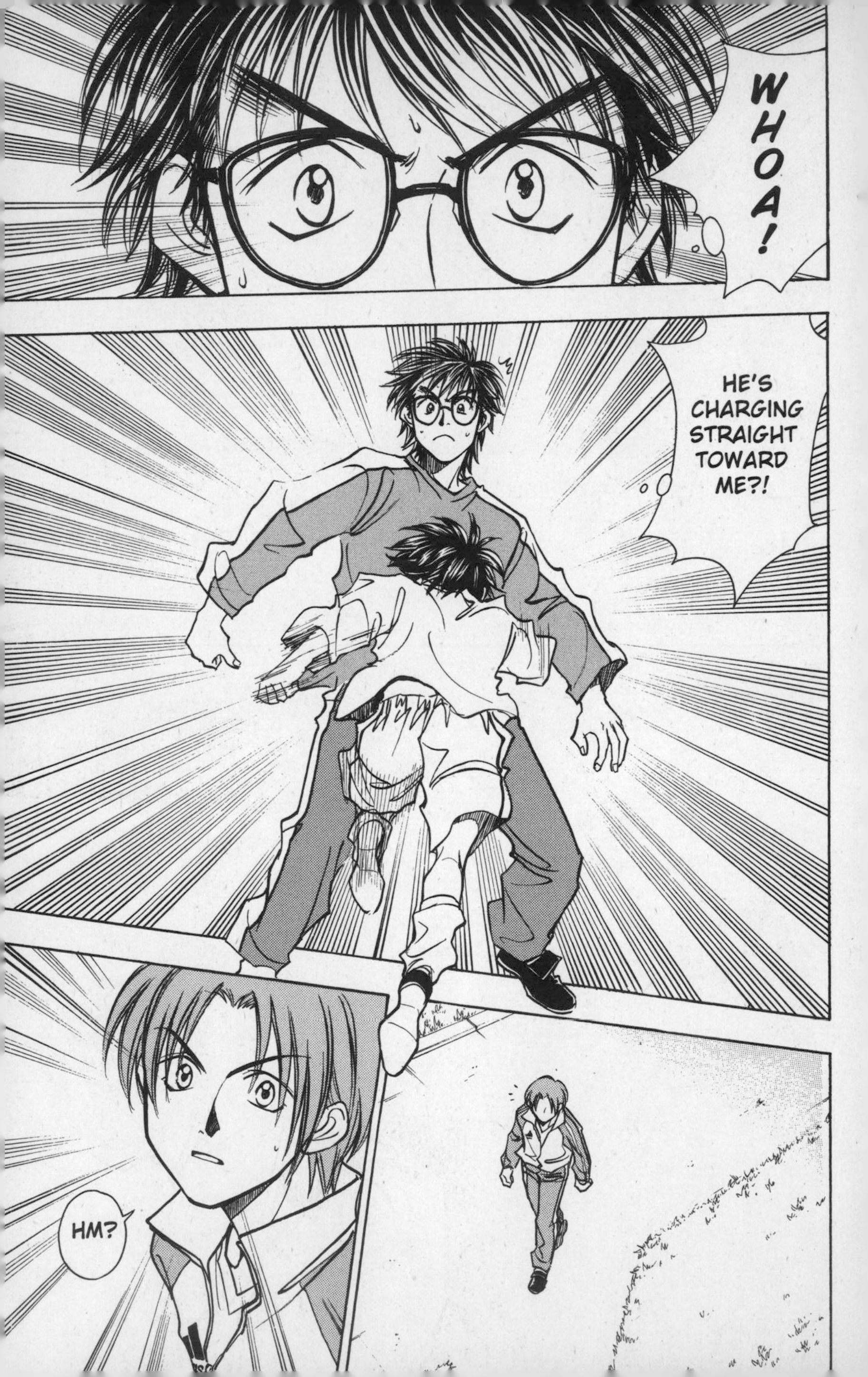
WHOA!
HE'S CHARGING STRAIGHT TOWARD ME?!
HM?

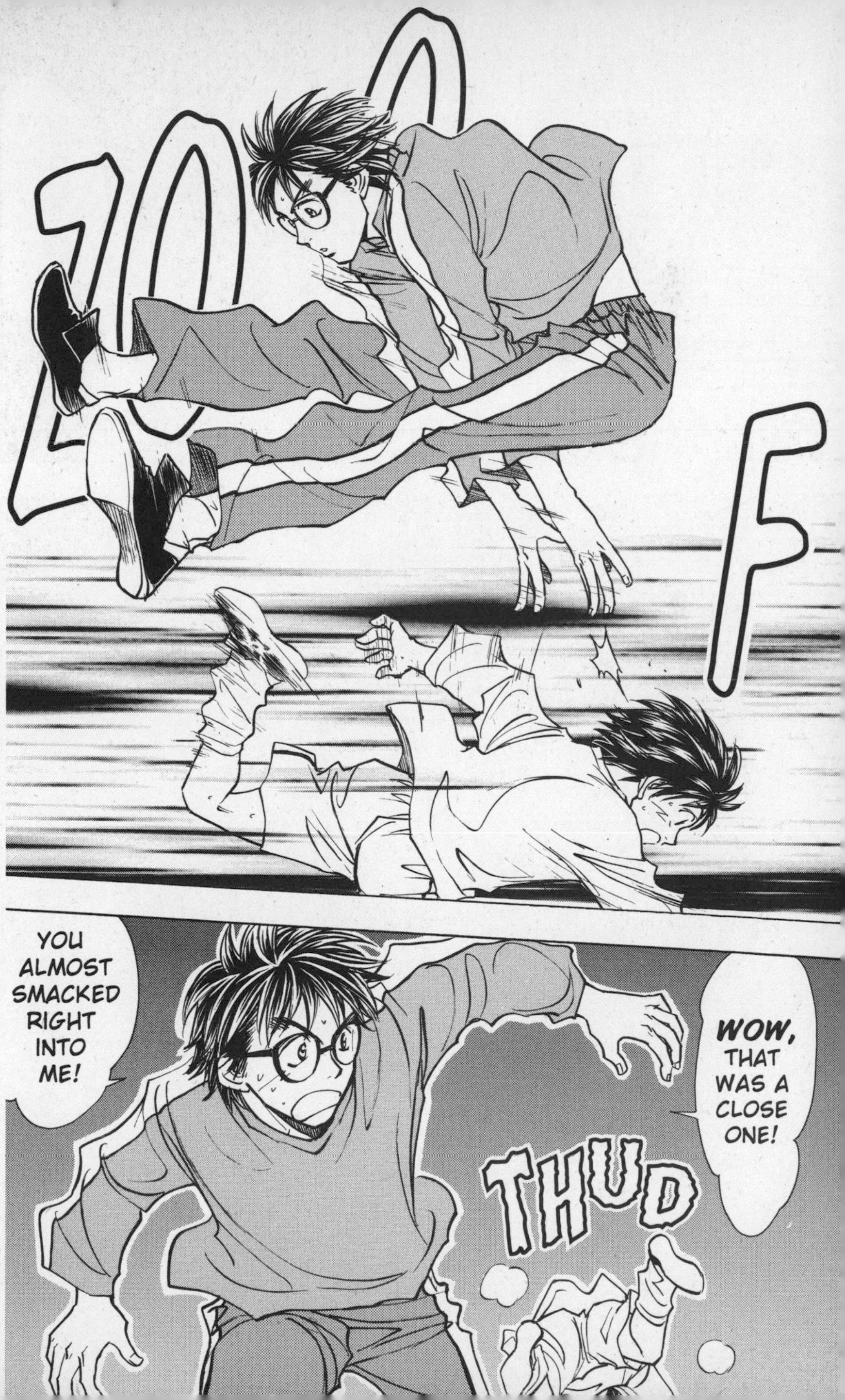
ZOOF
WOW, THAT WAS A CLOSE ONE!
YOU ALMOST SMACKED RIGHT INTO ME!
THUD

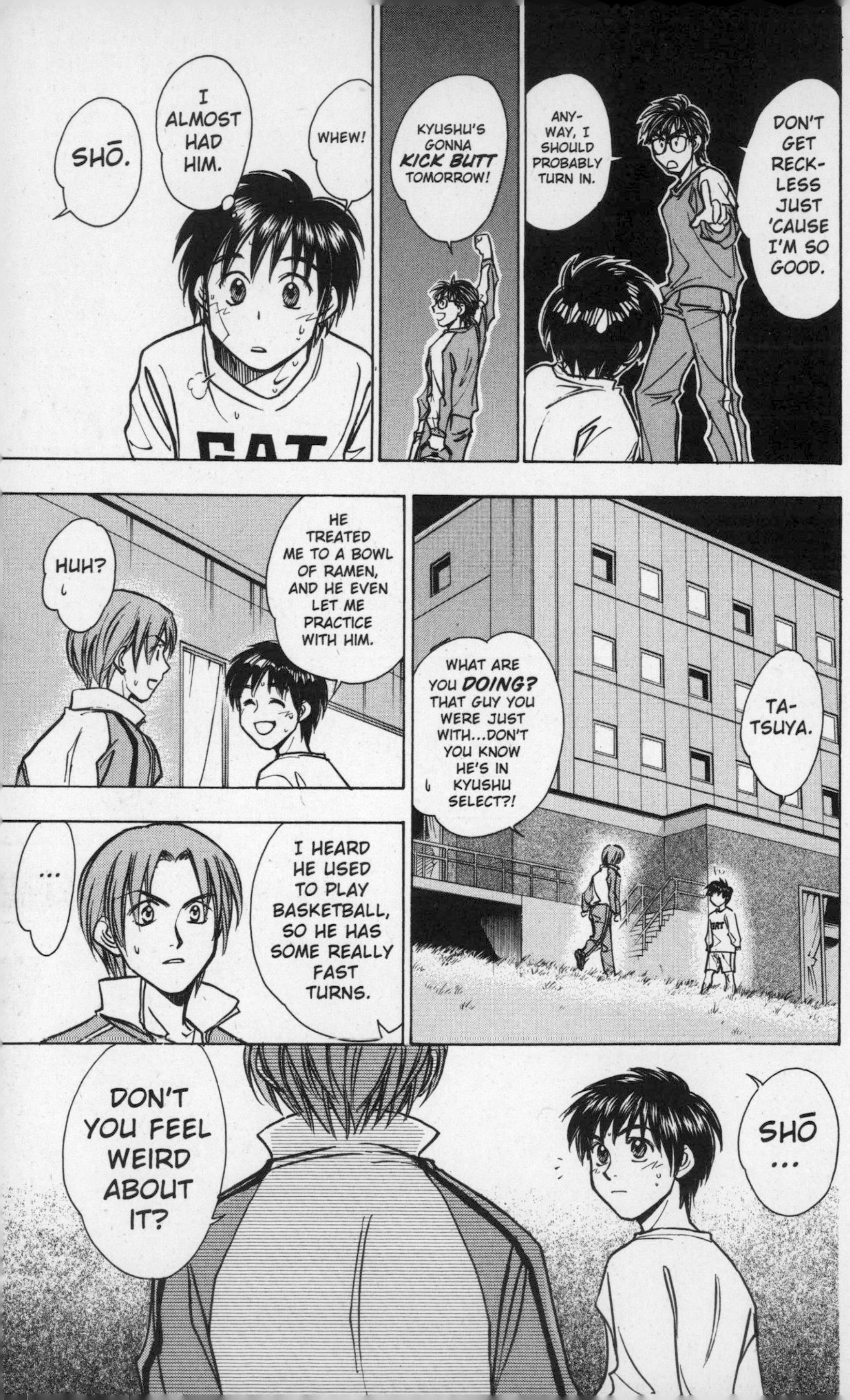
DON'T GET RECKLESS JUST 'CAUSE I'M SO GOOD.
ANYWAY, I SHOULD PROBABLY TURN IN.
KYUSHU'S GONNA KICK BUTT TOMORROW!
WHEW!
I ALMOST HAD HIM.
SHŌ.
TATSUYA.
WHAT ARE YOU DOING? THAT GUY YOU WERE JUST WITH...DON'T YOU KNOW HE'S IN KYUSHU SELECT?!
HE TREATED ME TO A BOWL OF RAMEN, AND HE EVEN LET ME PRACTICE WITH HIM.
HUH?
I HEARD HE USED TO PLAY BASKETBALL, SO HE HAS SOME REALLY FAST TURNS.
...
SHŌ...
DON'T YOU FEEL WEIRD ABOUT IT?

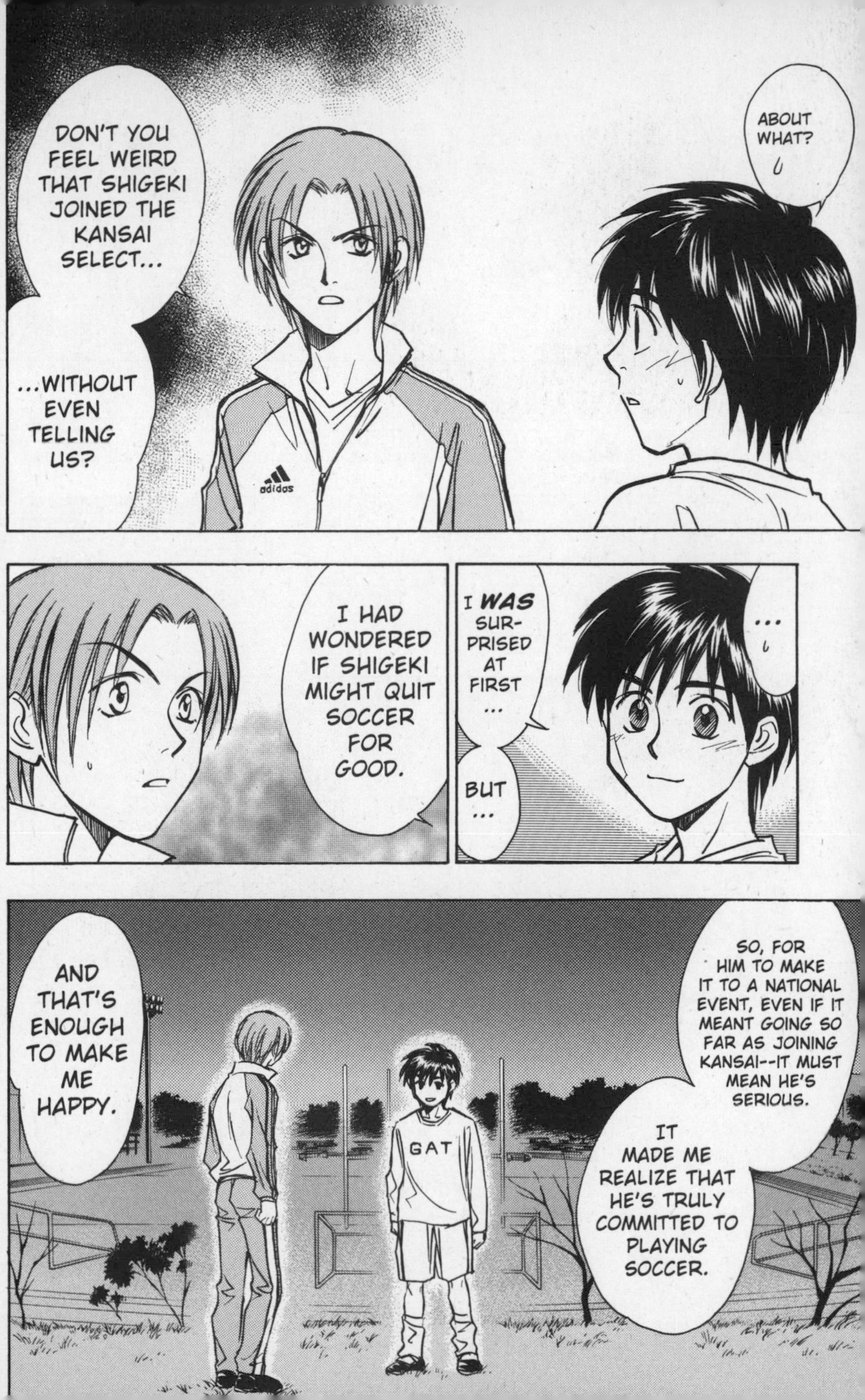
ABOUT WHAT?
DON'T YOU FEEL WEIRD THAT SHIGEKI JOINED THE KANSAI SELECT...
...WITHOUT EVEN TELLING US?
adidas
...
I *WAS* SUR-PRISED AT FIRST...
BUT...
I HAD WONDERED IF SHIGEKI MIGHT QUIT SOCCER FOR GOOD.
SO, FOR HIM TO MAKE IT TO A NATIONAL EVENT, EVEN IF IT MEANT GOING SO FAR AS JOINING KANSAI--IT MUST MEAN HE'S SERIOUS.
IT MADE ME REALIZE THAT HE'S TRULY COMMITTED TO PLAYING SOCCER.
GAT
AND THAT'S ENOUGH TO MAKE ME HAPPY.

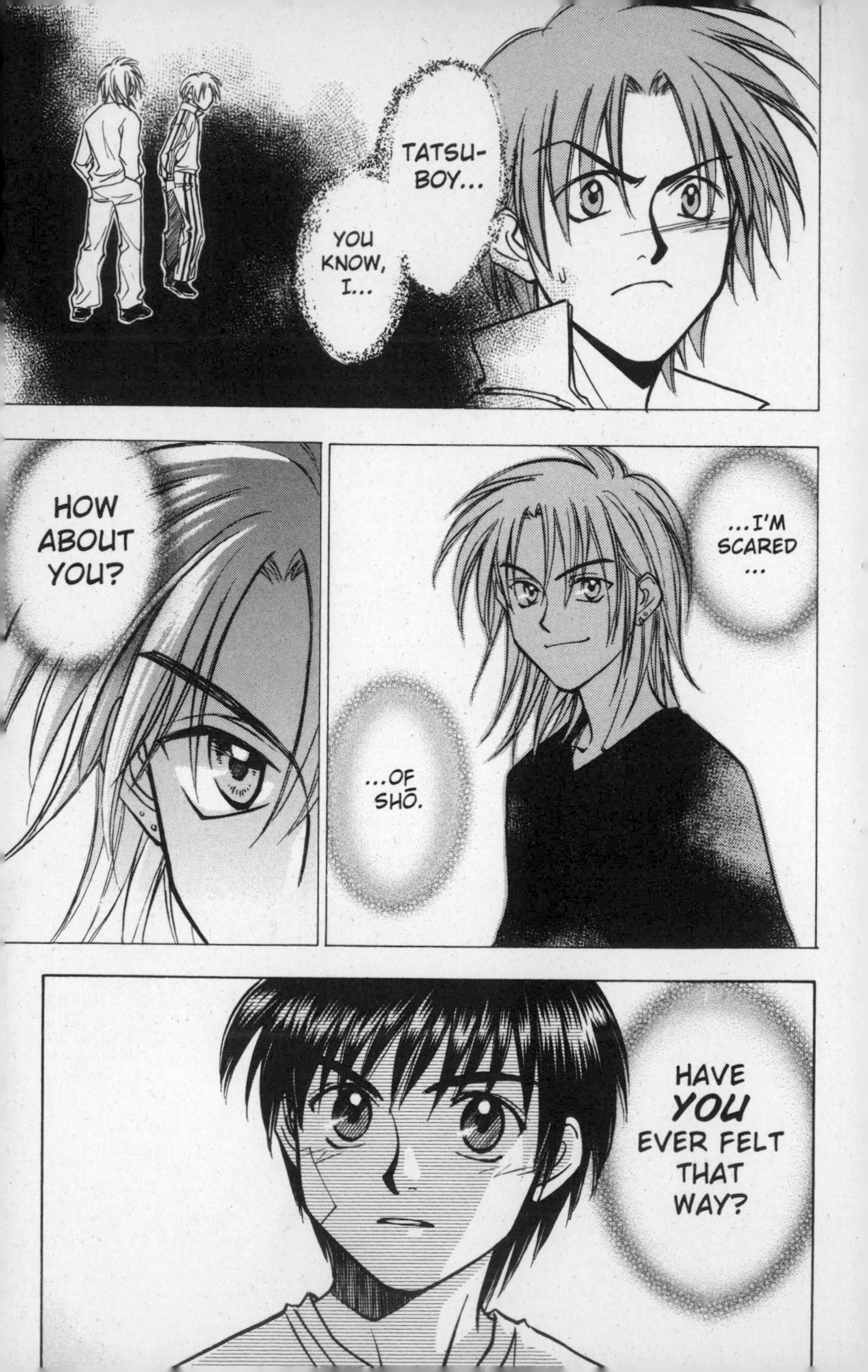
TATSU-BOY...
YOU KNOW, I...
...I'M SCARED...
...OF SHŌ.
HOW ABOUT YOU?
HAVE *YOU* EVER FELT THAT WAY?

WHISTLE!

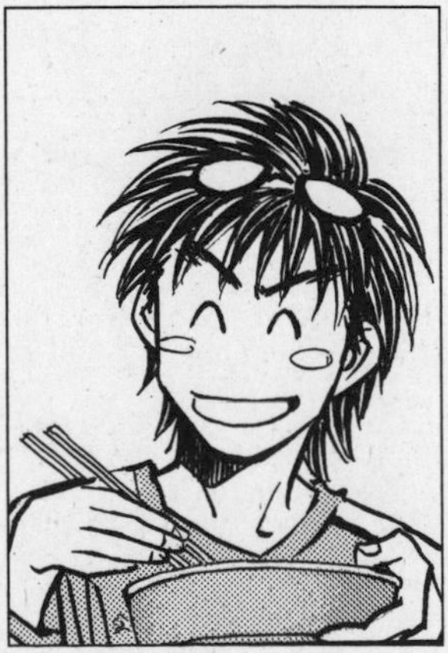

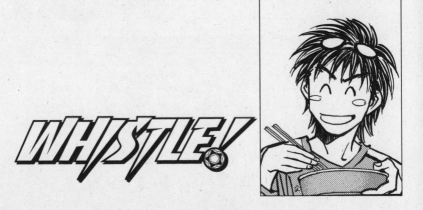

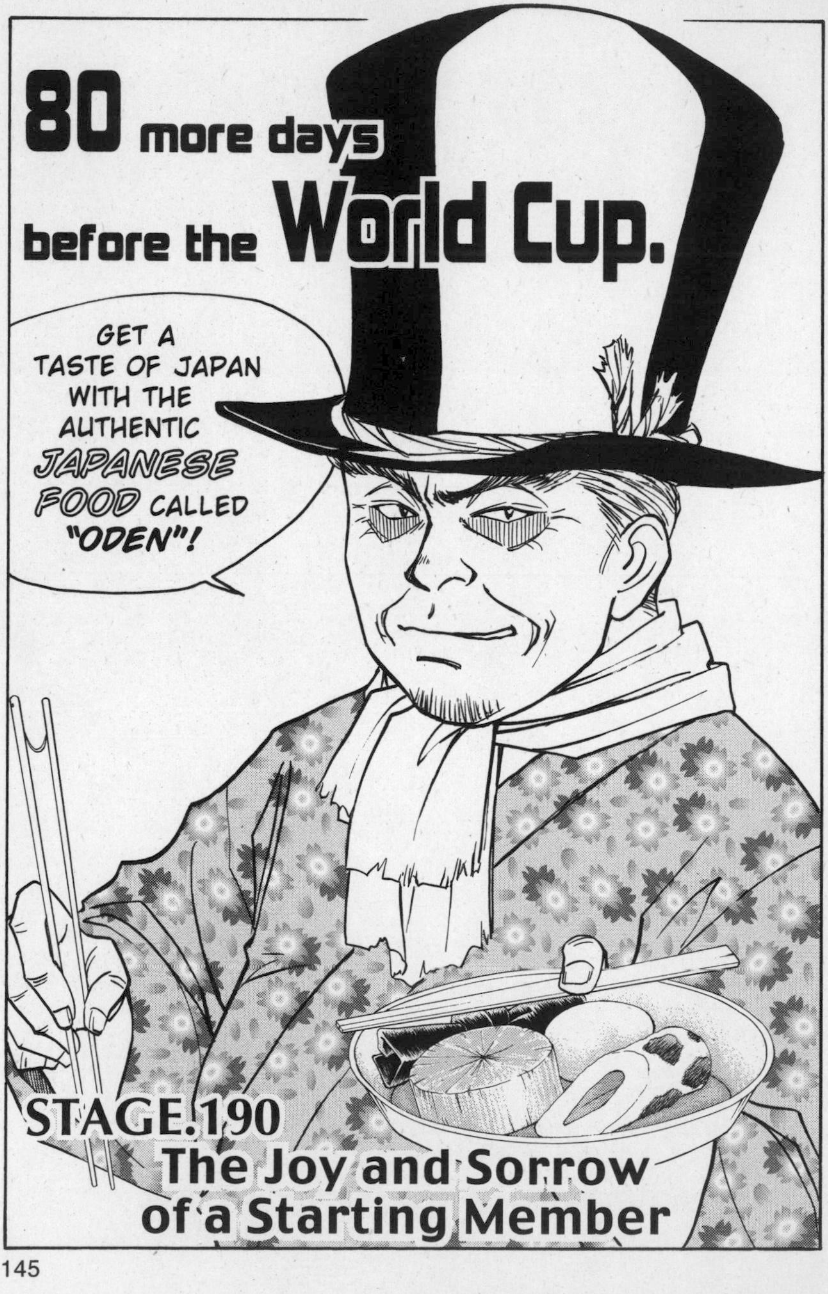
80 more days before the World Cup.
GET A TASTE OF JAPAN WITH THE AUTHENTIC JAPANESE FOOD CALLED "ODEN"!
STAGE.190
The Joy and Sorrow of a Starting Member

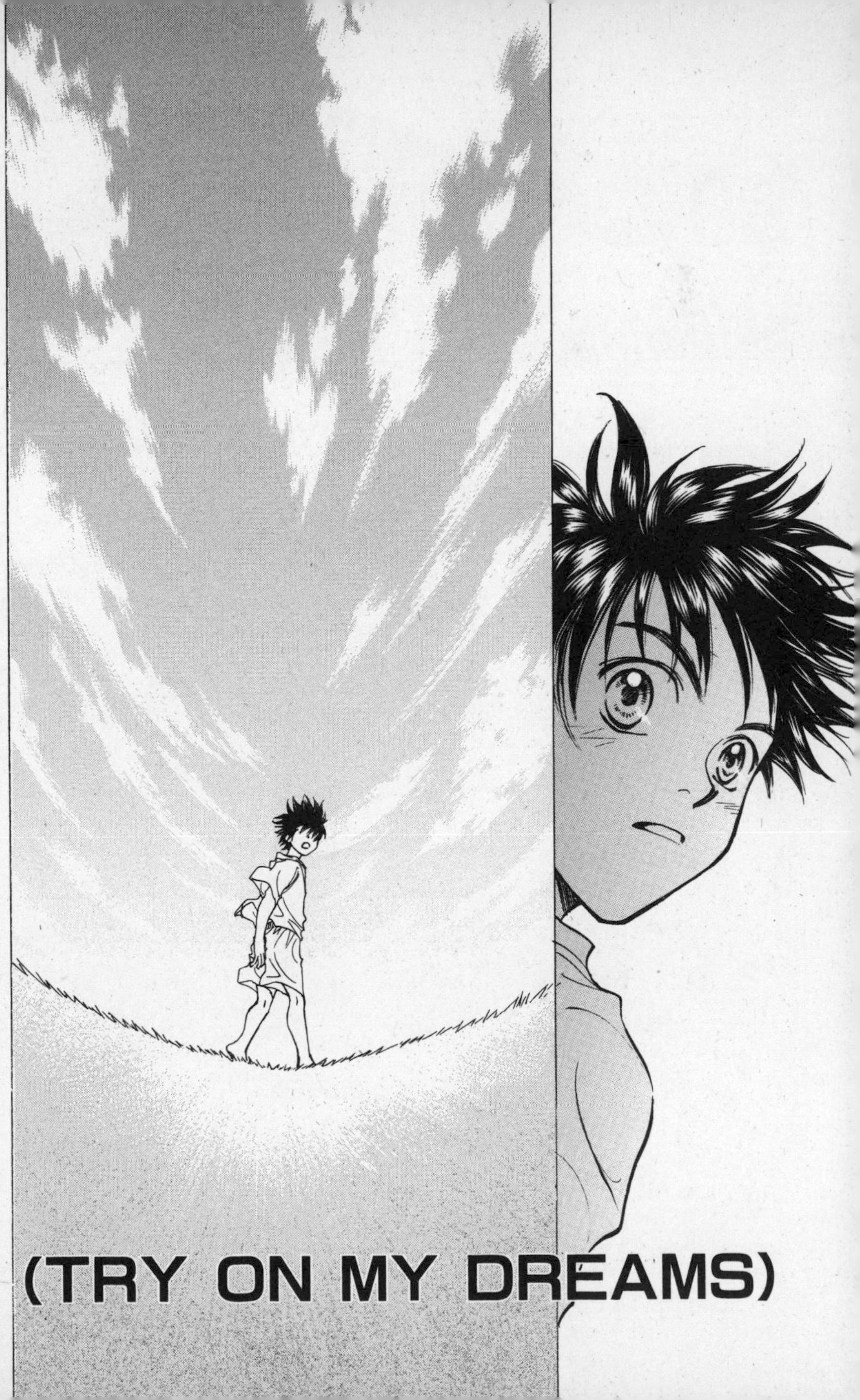
(TRY ON MY DREAMS)

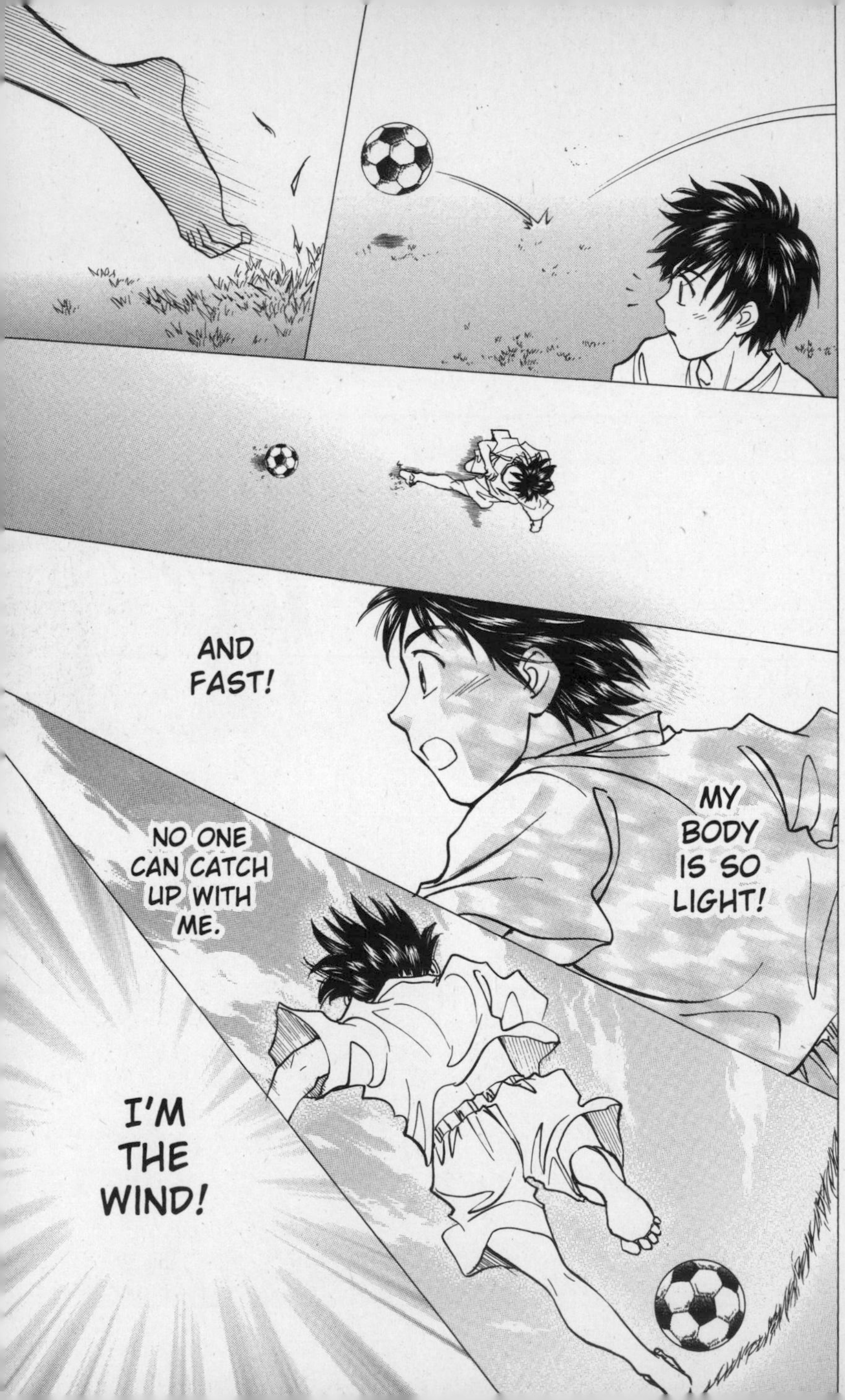
MY BODY IS SO LIGHT!
AND FAST!
NO ONE CAN CATCH UP WITH ME.
I'M THE WIND!

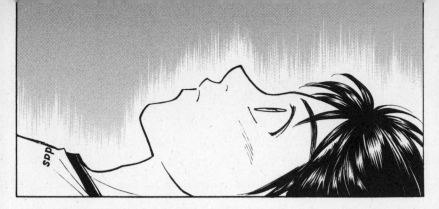

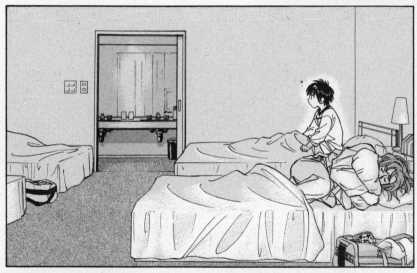

I FEEL LIKE I WAS DREAMING, BUT I CAN'T REMEMBER WHAT IT WAS ABOUT.

A DREAM?

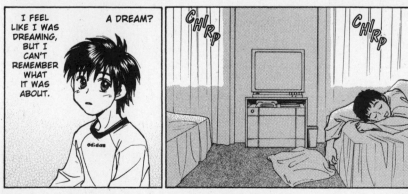

CHIRP

CHIRP

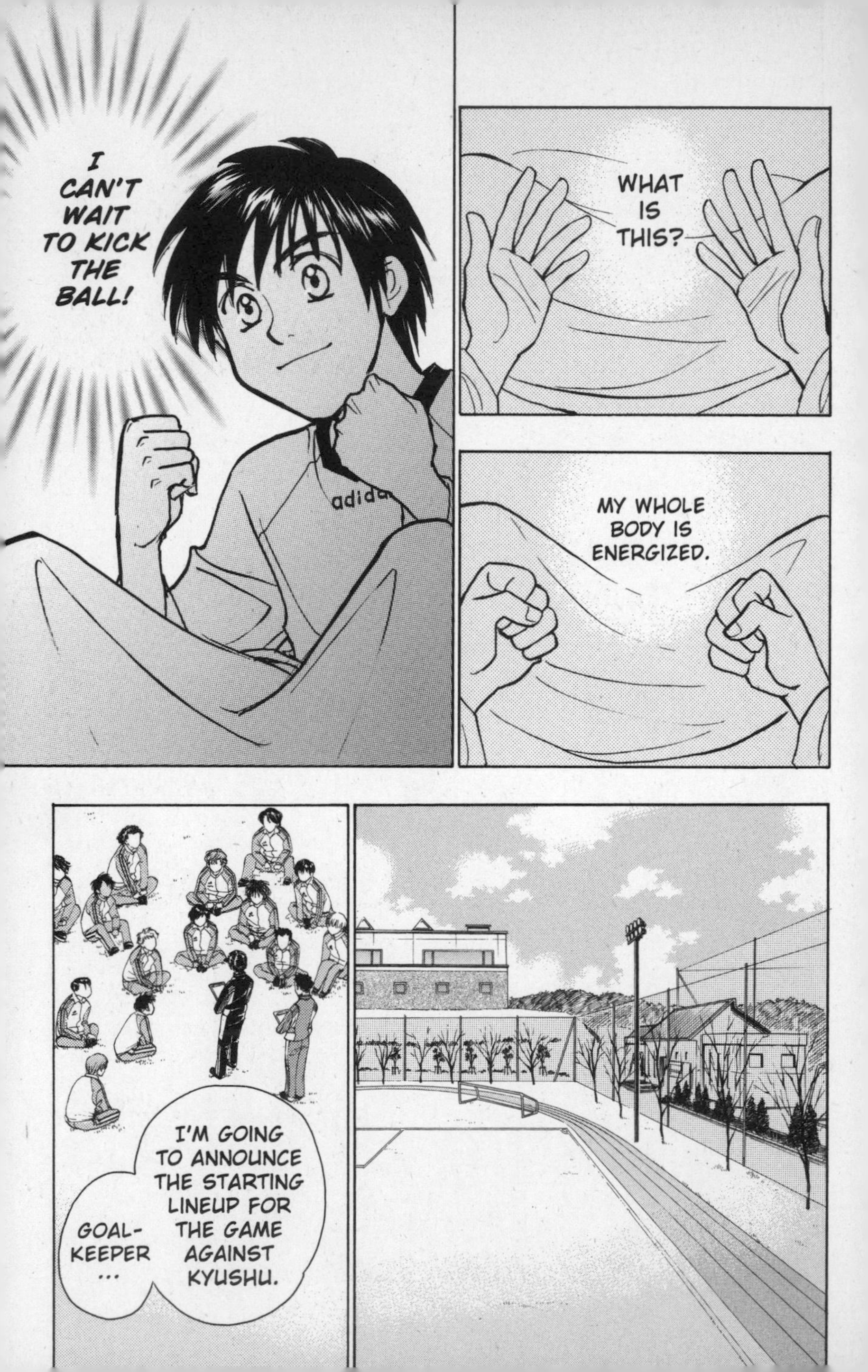
WHAT IS THIS?
MY WHOLE BODY IS ENERGIZED.
I CAN'T WAIT TO KICK THE BALL!
I'M GOING TO ANNOUNCE THE STARTING LINEUP FOR THE GAME AGAINST KYUSHU.
GOAL-KEEPER ...

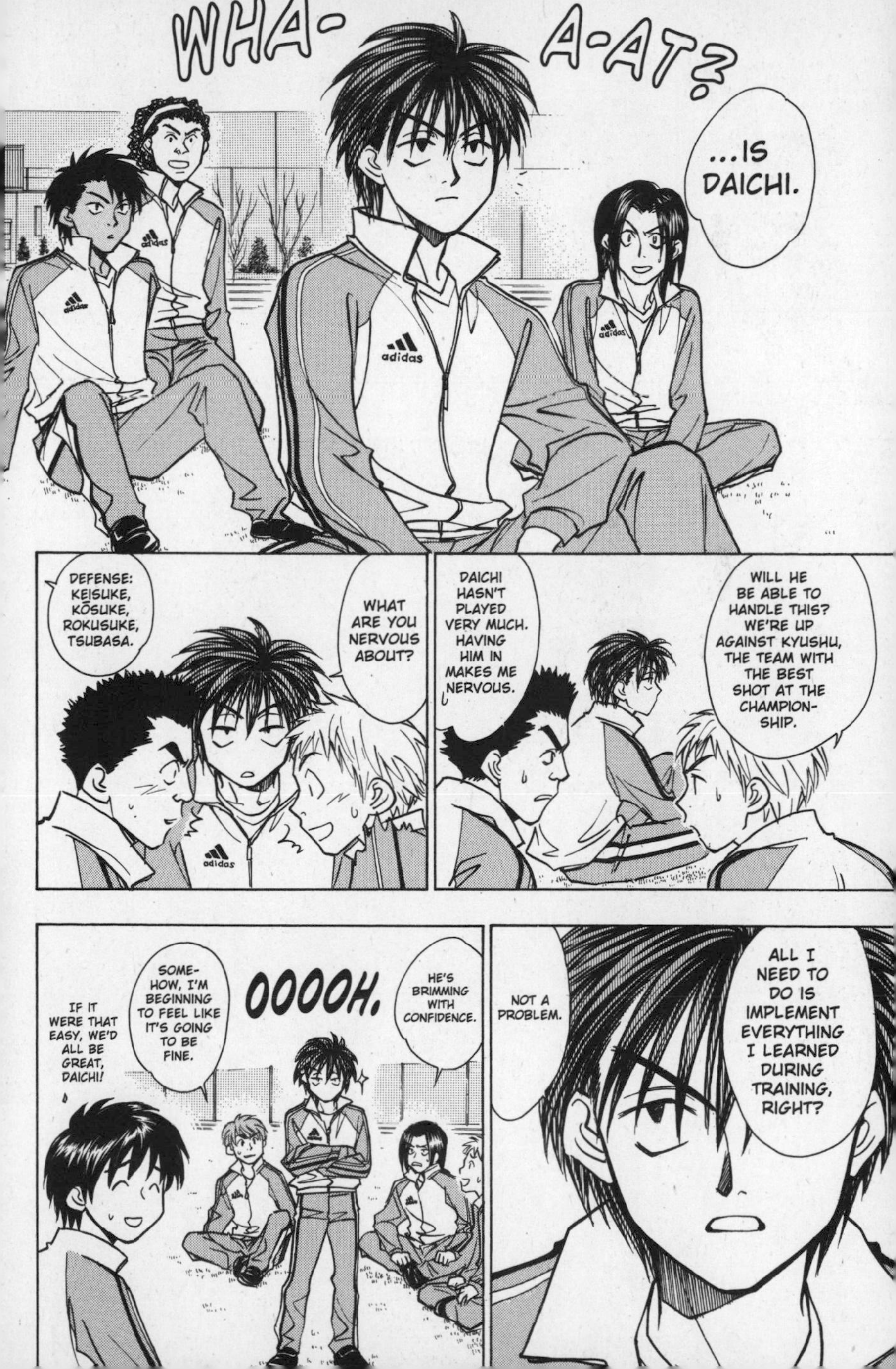
...IS DAICHI.
WHA- A-AT?
WILL HE BE ABLE TO HANDLE THIS? WE'RE UP AGAINST KYUSHU, THE TEAM WITH THE BEST SHOT AT THE CHAMPION-SHIP.
DAICHI HASN'T PLAYED VERY MUCH. HAVING HIM IN MAKES ME NERVOUS.
WHAT ARE YOU NERVOUS ABOUT?
DEFENSE: KEISUKE, KŌSUKE, ROKUSUKE, TSUBASA.
ALL I NEED TO DO IS IMPLEMENT EVERYTHING I LEARNED DURING TRAINING, RIGHT?
NOT A PROBLEM.
HE'S BRIMMING WITH CONFIDENCE.
OOOOH.
SOME-HOW, I'M BEGINNING TO FEEL LIKE IT'S GOING TO BE FINE.
IF IT WERE THAT EASY, WE'D ALL BE GREAT, DAICHI!

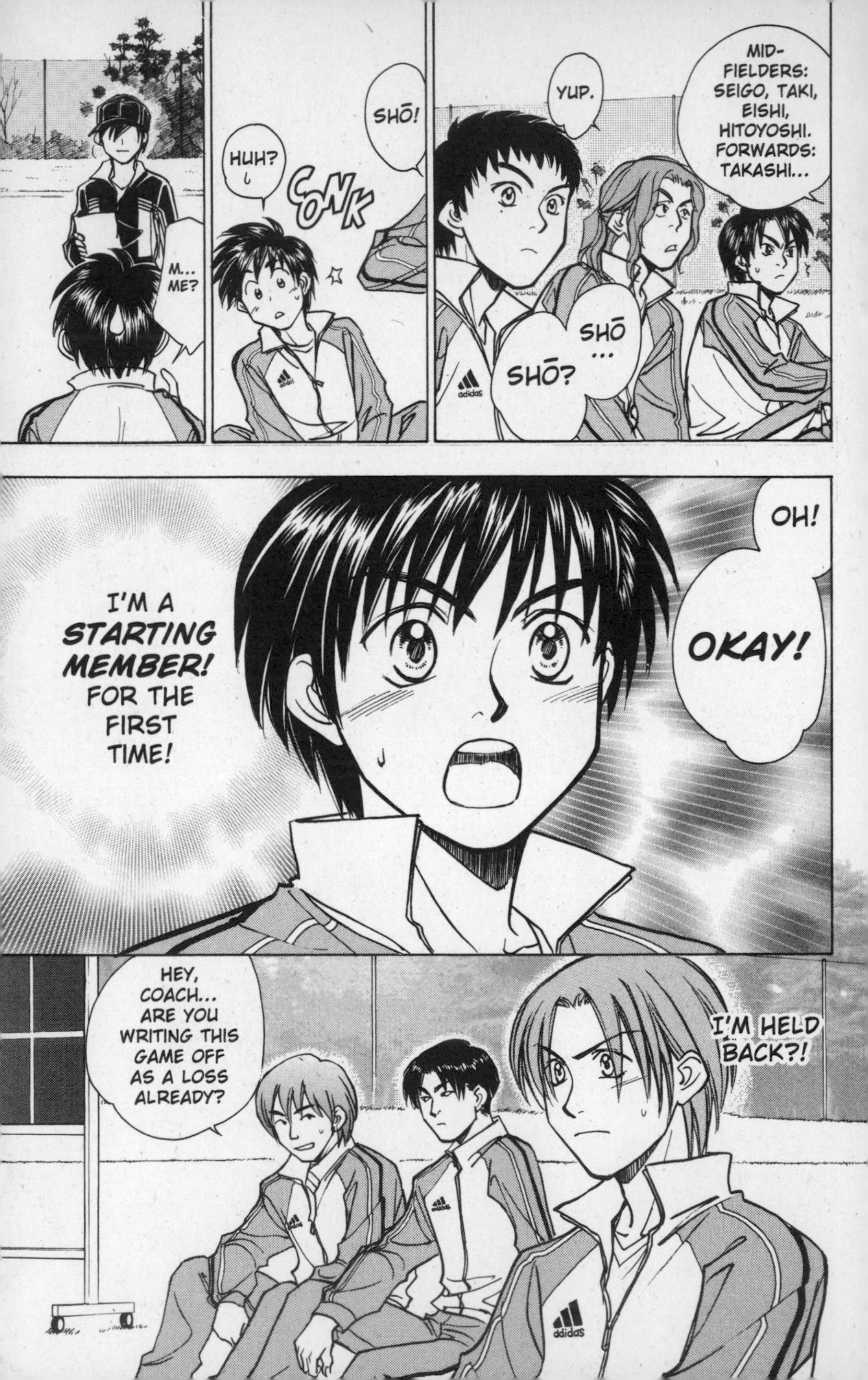
MID-FIELDERS: SEIGO, TAKI, EISHI, HITOYOSHI. FORWARDS: TAKASHI...
YUP.
SHŌ...
SHŌ?
SHŌ!
CONK
HUH?
M... ME?
OH!
OKAY!
I'M A STARTING MEMBER! FOR THE FIRST TIME!
I'M HELD BACK?!
HEY, COACH... ARE YOU WRITING THIS GAME OFF AS A LOSS ALREADY?

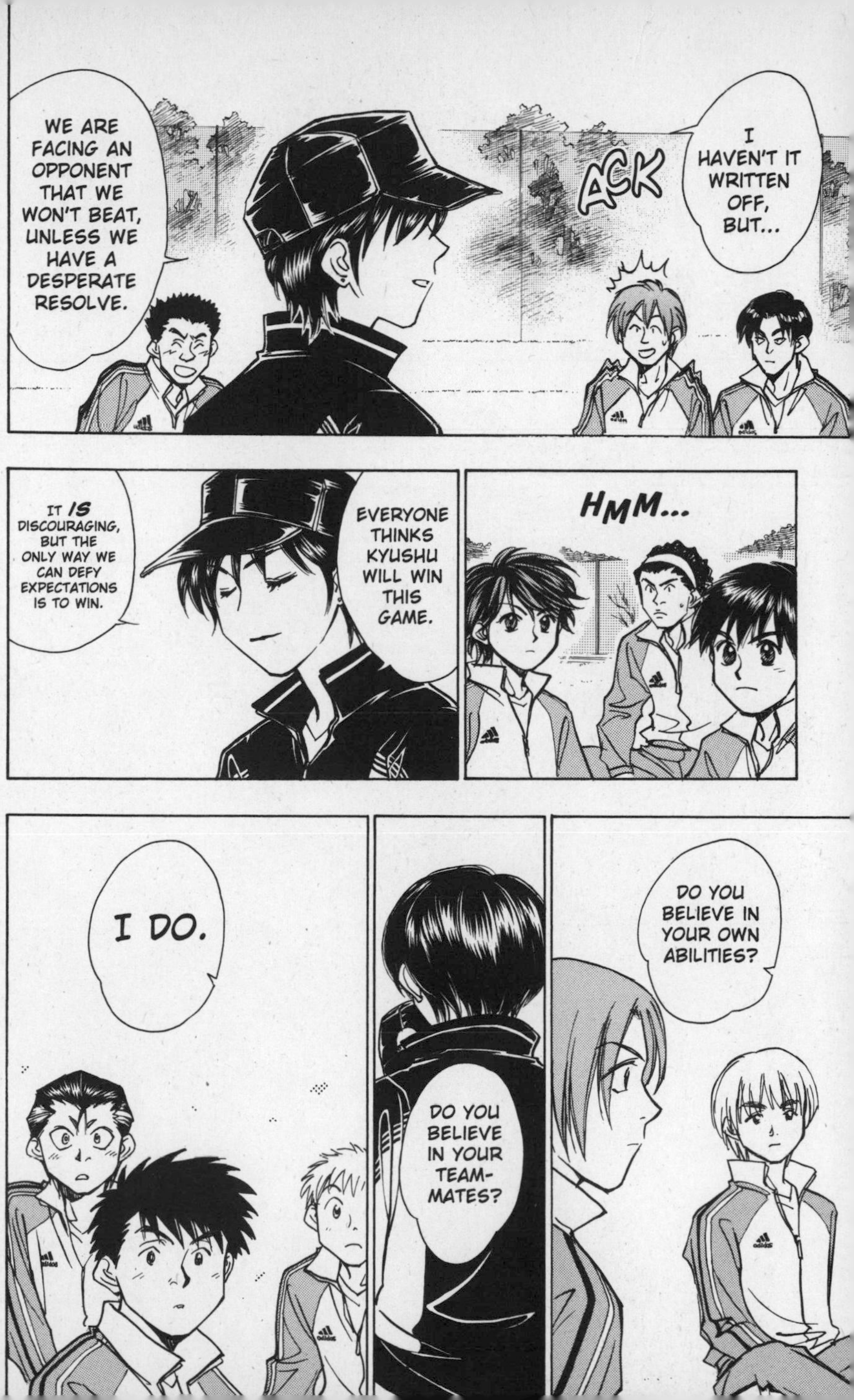
I HAVEN'T IT WRITTEN OFF, BUT...
ACK
WE ARE FACING AN OPPONENT THAT WE WON'T BEAT, UNLESS WE HAVE A DESPERATE RESOLVE.
HMM...
EVERYONE THINKS KYUSHU WILL WIN THIS GAME.
IT *IS* DISCOURAGING, BUT THE ONLY WAY WE CAN DEFY EXPECTATIONS IS TO WIN.
DO YOU BELIEVE IN YOUR OWN ABILITIES?
DO YOU BELIEVE IN YOUR TEAM-MATES?
I DO.

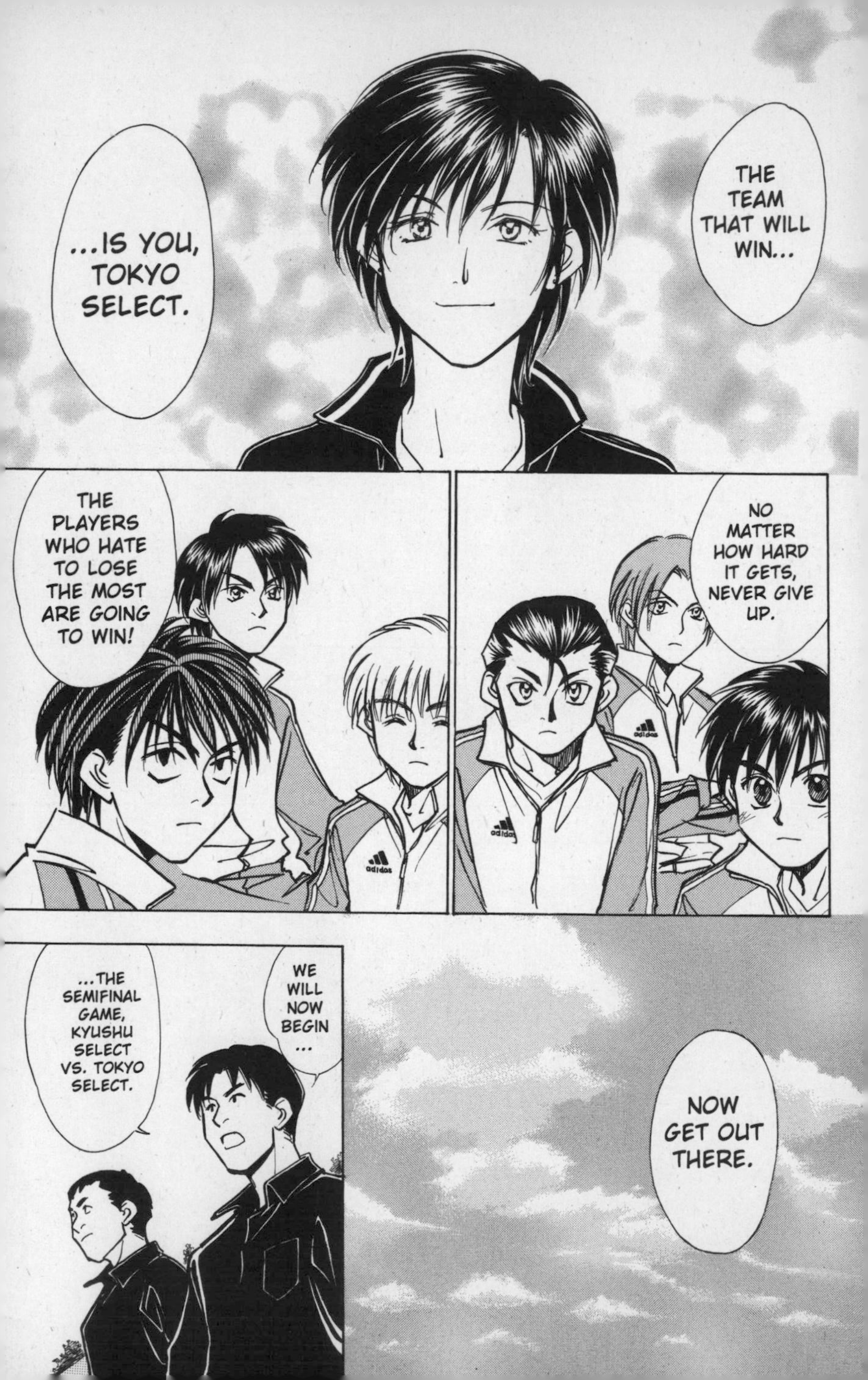
THE TEAM THAT WILL WIN...
...IS YOU, TOKYO SELECT.
NO MATTER HOW HARD IT GETS, NEVER GIVE UP.
THE PLAYERS WHO HATE TO LOSE THE MOST ARE GOING TO WIN!
NOW GET OUT THERE.
WE WILL NOW BEGIN...
...THE SEMIFINAL GAME, KYUSHU SELECT VS. TOKYO SELECT.

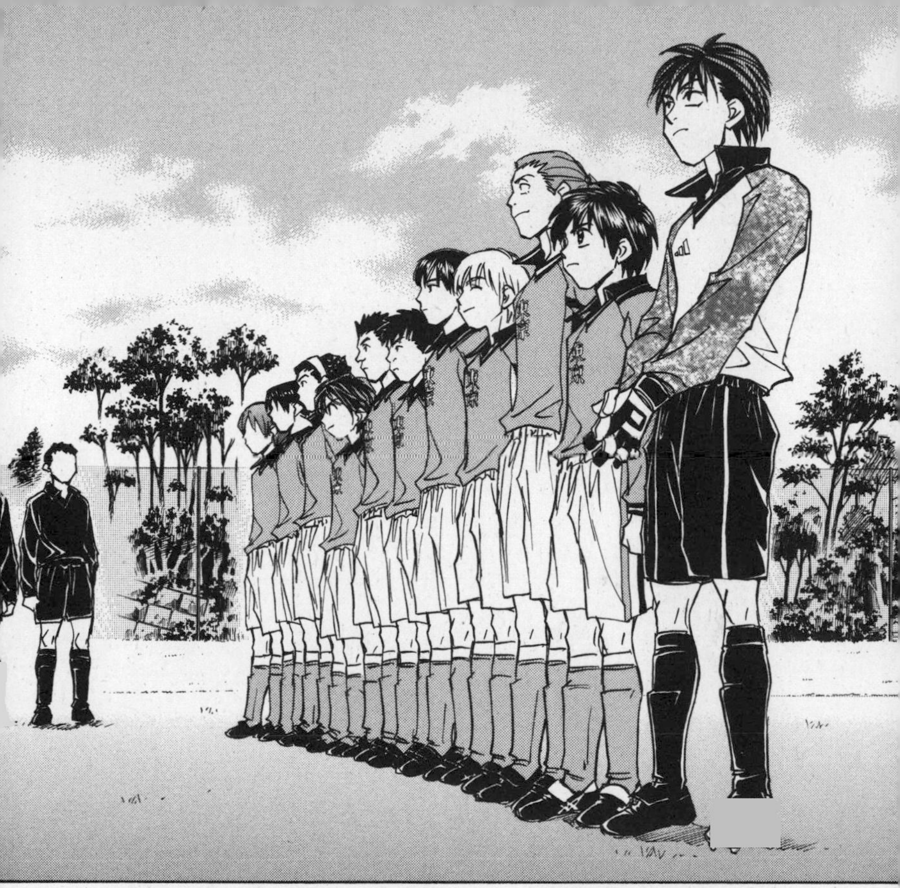

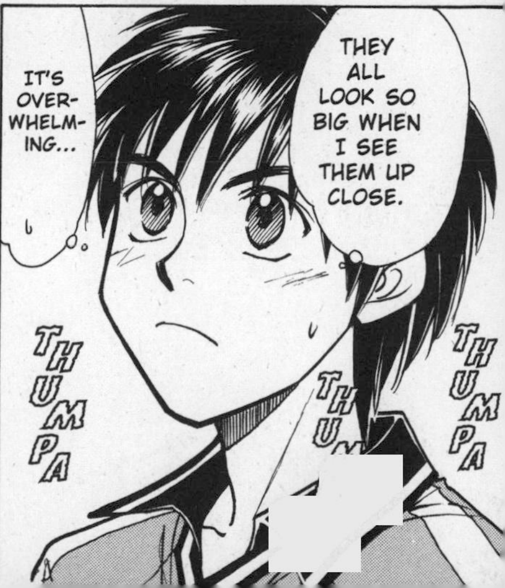
THEY ALL LOOK SO BIG WHEN I SEE THEM UP CLOSE.
IT'S OVER-WHELM-ING...
THUMPA
THUM
THUMPA

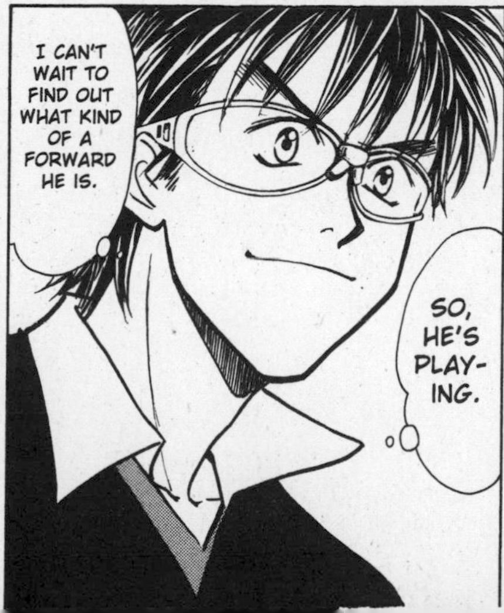
SO, HE'S PLAY-ING.
I CAN'T WAIT TO FIND OUT WHAT KIND OF A FORWARD HE IS.

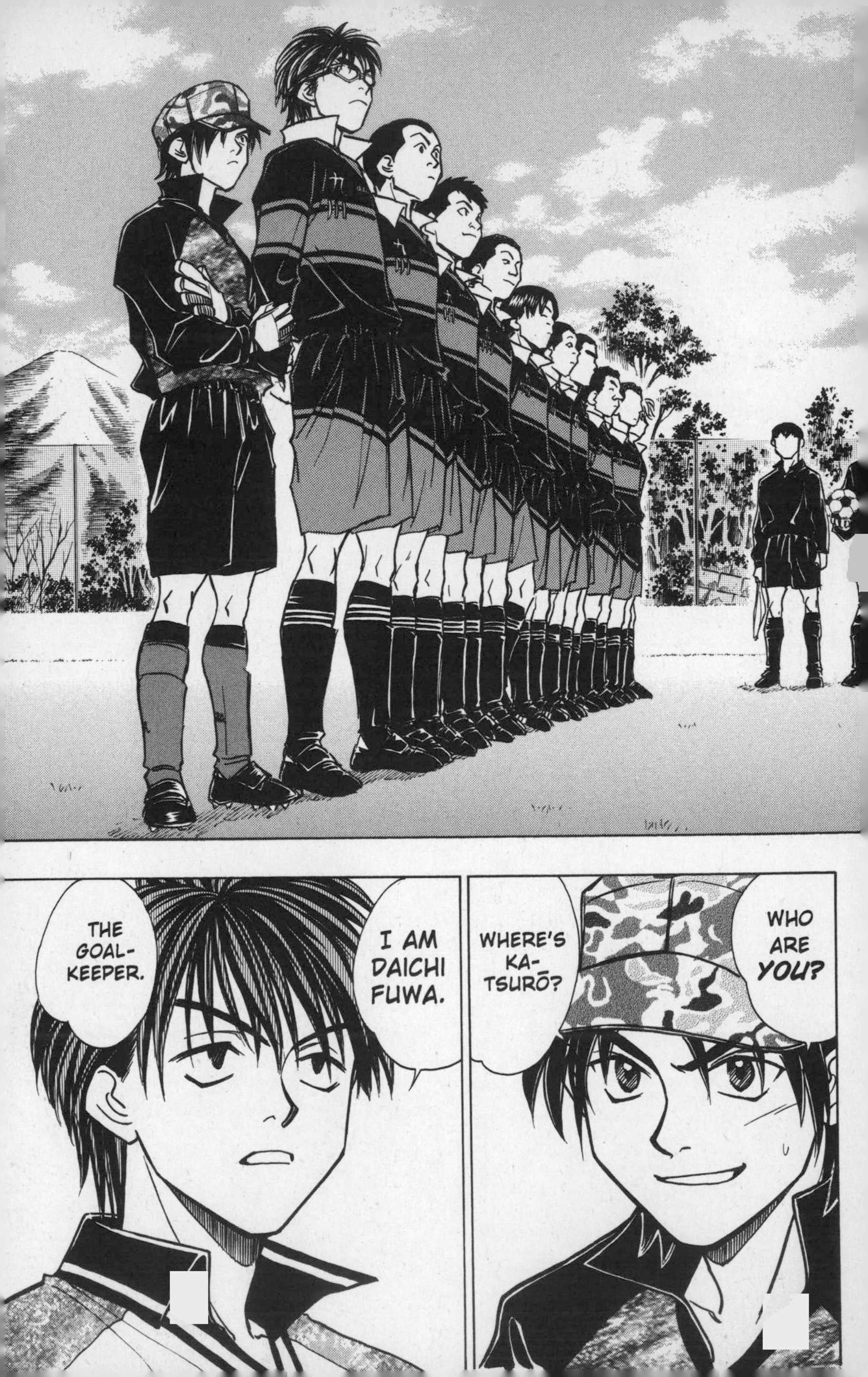
WHO ARE *YOU*?
WHERE'S KA-TSURŌ?
I AM DAICHI FUWA.
THE GOAL-KEEPER.

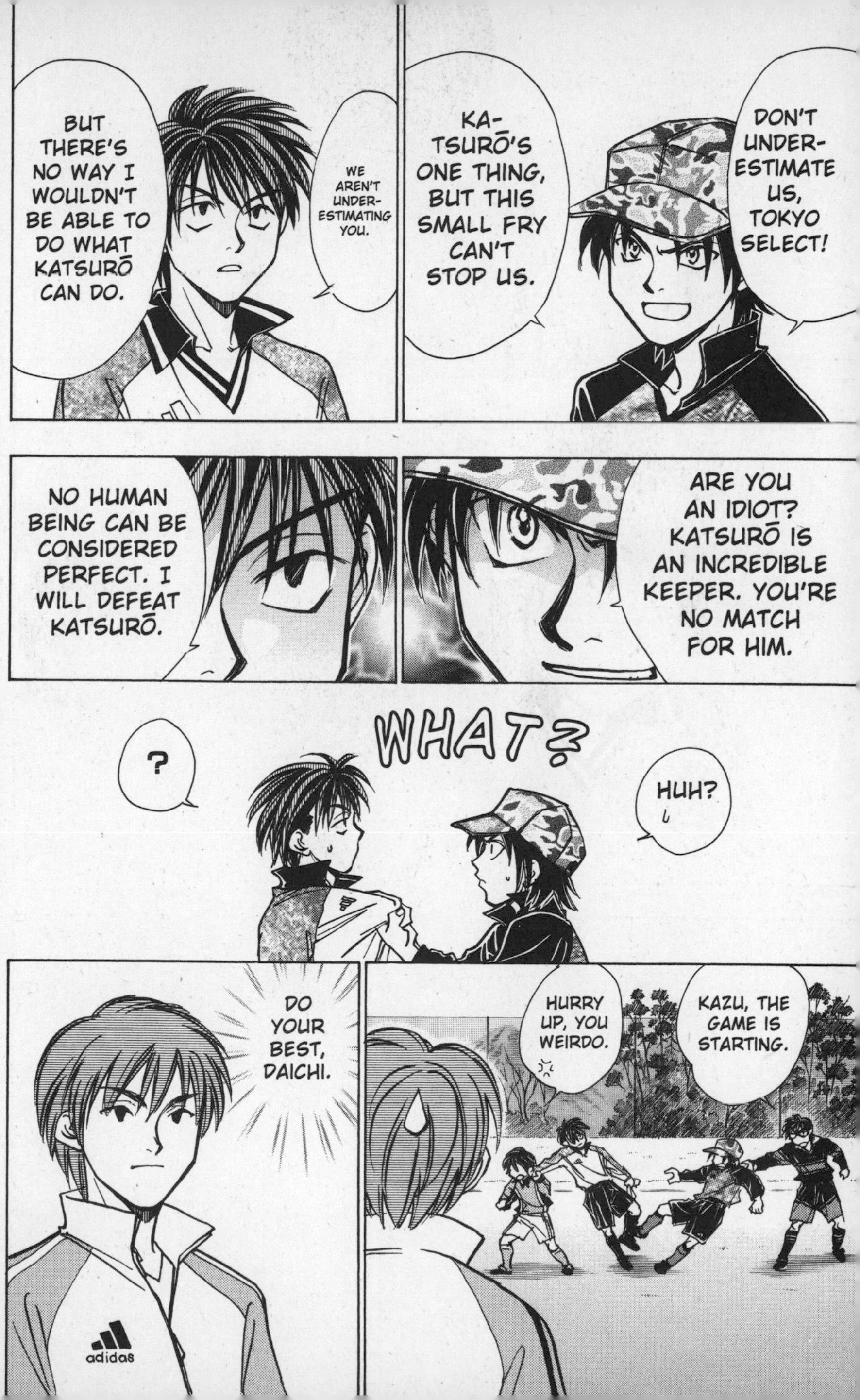
DON'T UNDER-ESTIMATE US, TOKYO SELECT!
KA-TSURŌ'S ONE THING, BUT THIS SMALL FRY CAN'T STOP US.
WE AREN'T UNDER-ESTIMATING YOU.
BUT THERE'S NO WAY I WOULDN'T BE ABLE TO DO WHAT KATSURŌ CAN DO.
ARE YOU AN IDIOT? KATSURŌ IS AN INCREDIBLE KEEPER. YOU'RE NO MATCH FOR HIM.
NO HUMAN BEING CAN BE CONSIDERED PERFECT. I WILL DEFEAT KATSURŌ.
WHAT?
HUH?
?
KAZU, THE GAME IS STARTING.
HURRY UP, YOU WEIRDO.
DO YOUR BEST, DAICHI.
adidas

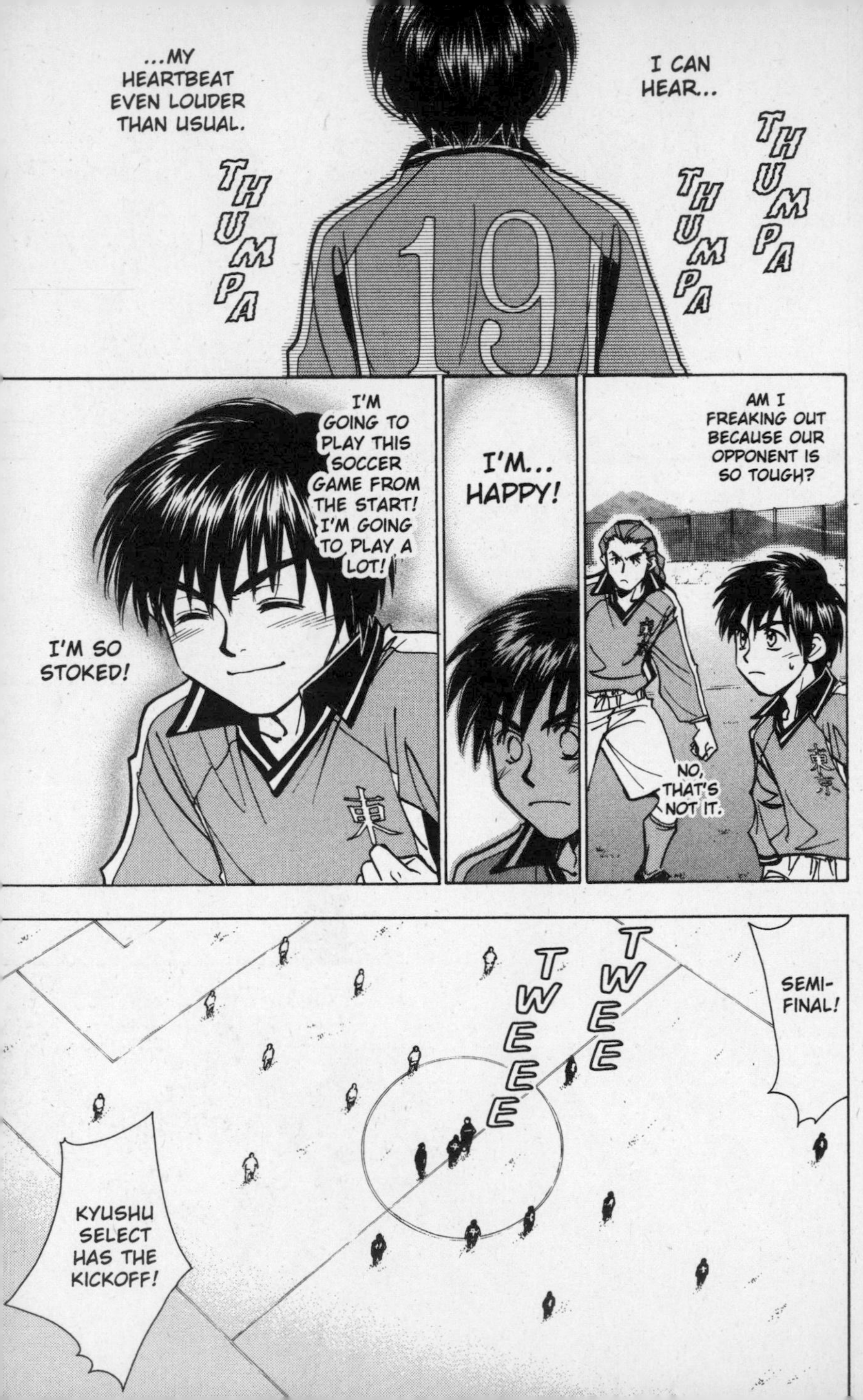
I CAN HEAR...
THUMPA
THUMPA
...MY HEARTBEAT EVEN LOUDER THAN USUAL.
THUMPA
AM I FREAKING OUT BECAUSE OUR OPPONENT IS SO TOUGH?
NO, THAT'S NOT IT.
I'M... HAPPY!
I'M GOING TO PLAY THIS SOCCER GAME FROM THE START! I'M GOING TO PLAY A LOT!
I'M SO STOKED!
SEMI-FINAL!
TWEEE
TWEEEE
KYUSHU SELECT HAS THE KICKOFF!

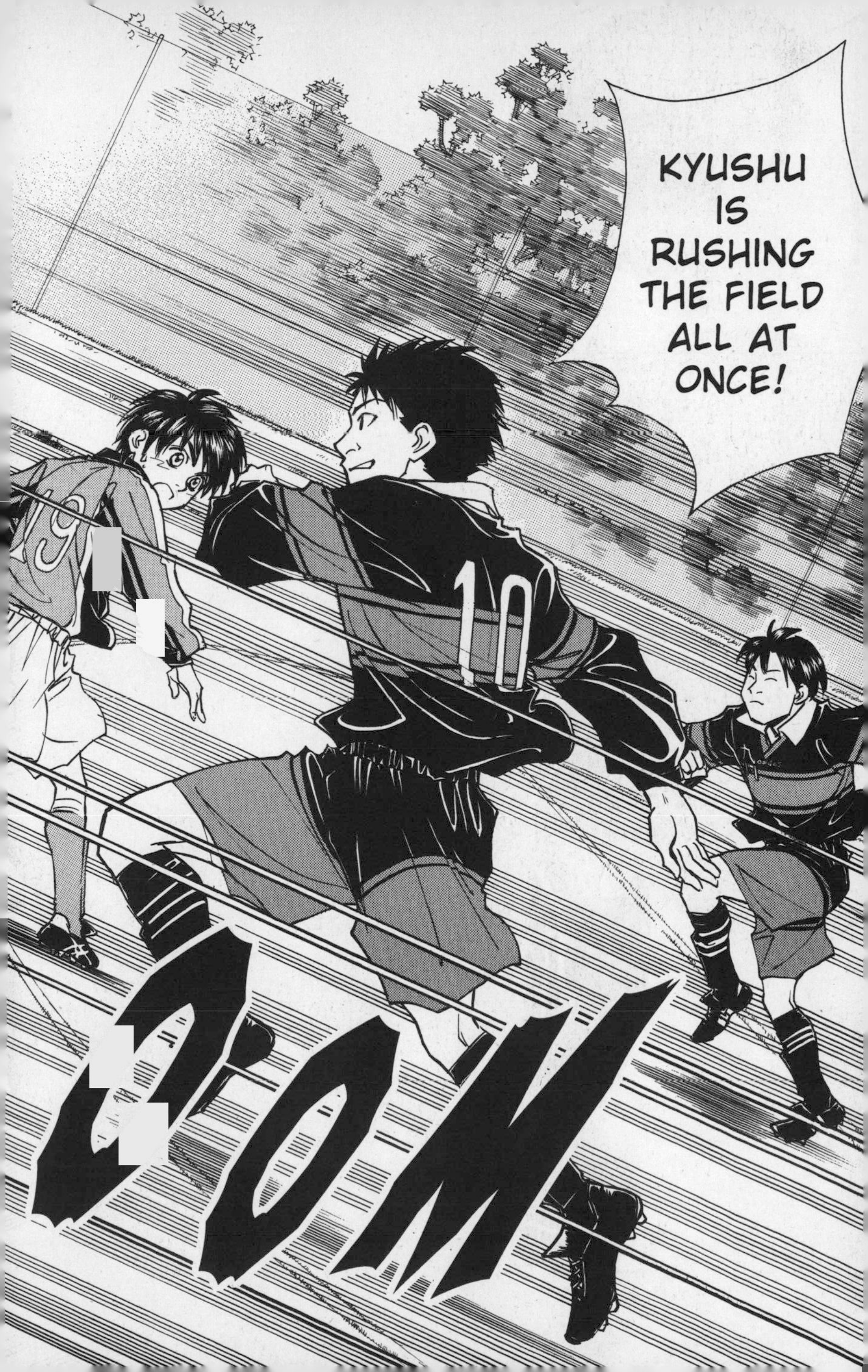
KYUSHU IS RUSHING THE FIELD ALL AT ONCE!

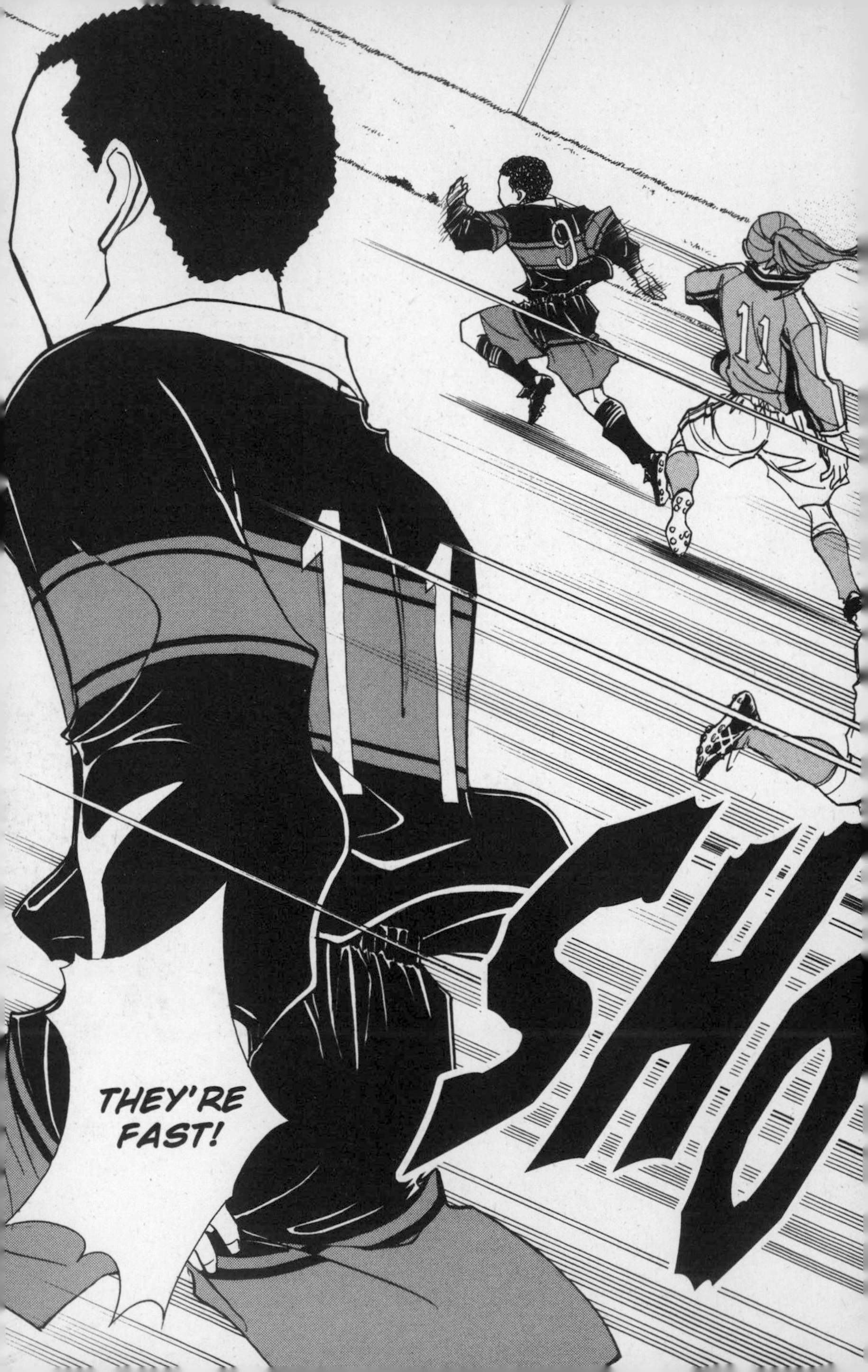
SHO
THEY'RE FAST!

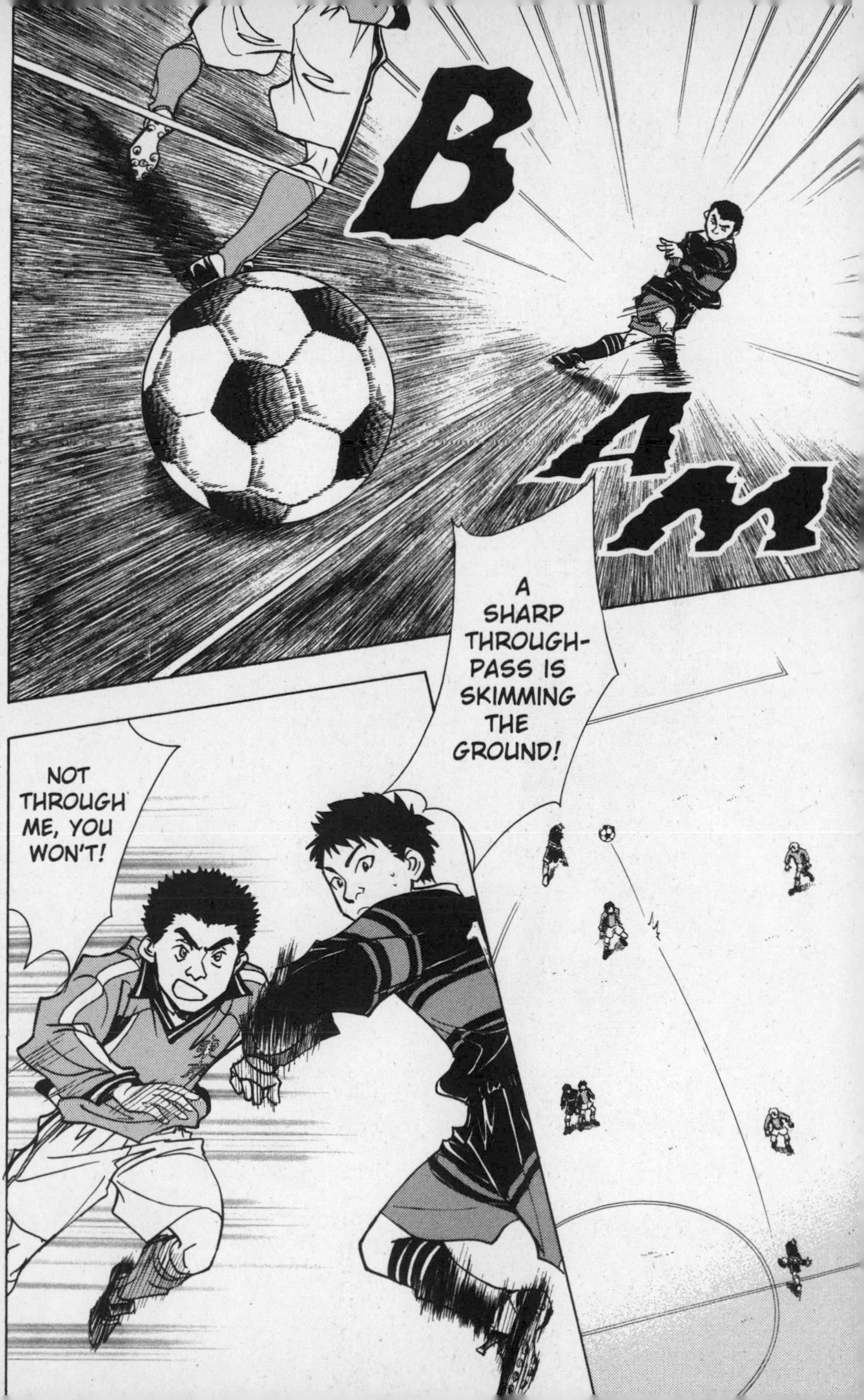
BAM
A SHARP THROUGH-PASS IS SKIMMING THE GROUND!
NOT THROUGH ME, YOU WON'T!

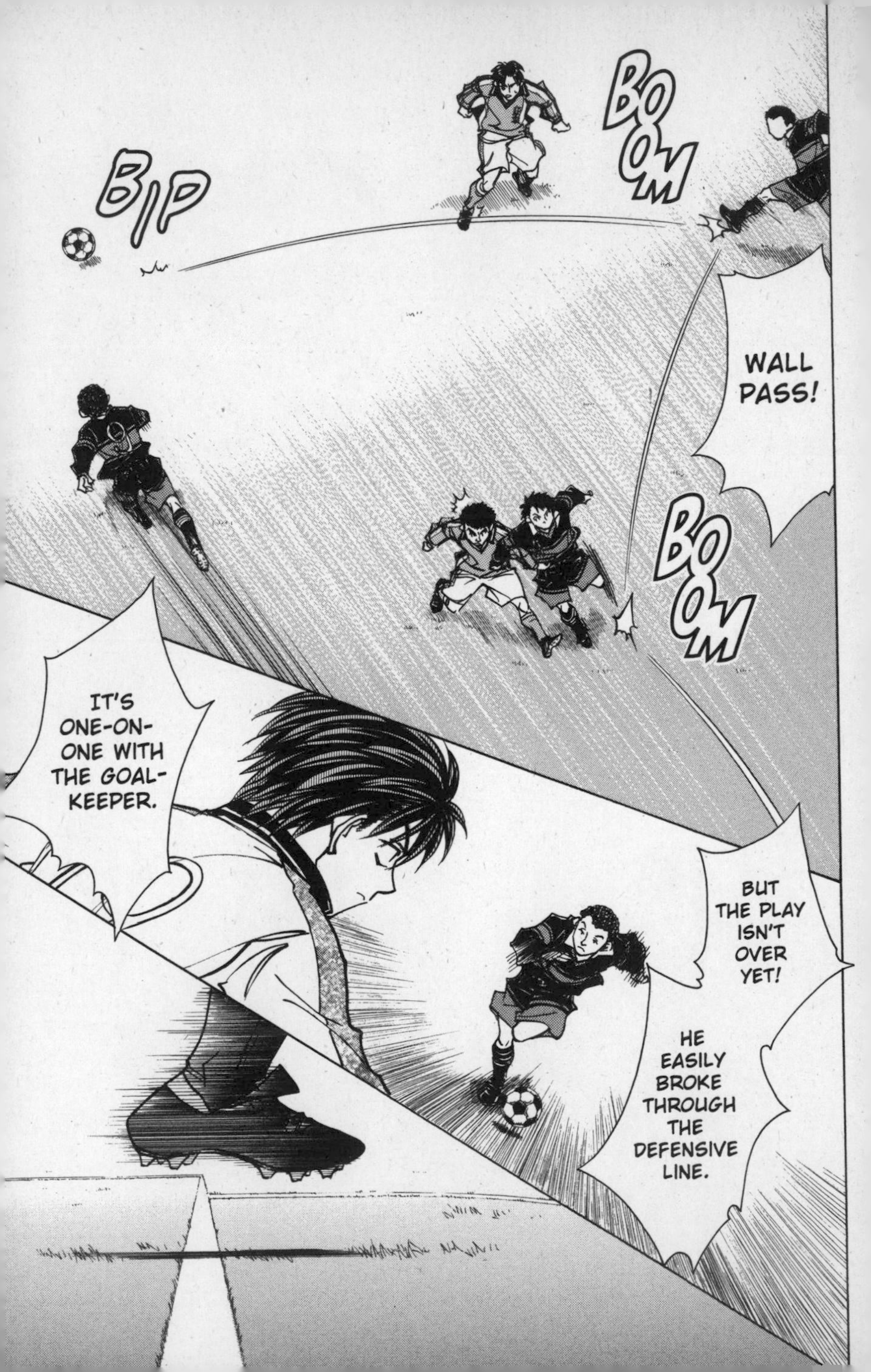
BOOM
BIP
WALL PASS!
BOOM
BUT THE PLAY ISN'T OVER YET!
HE EASILY BROKE THROUGH THE DEFENSIVE LINE.
IT'S ONE-ON-ONE WITH THE GOAL-KEEPER.

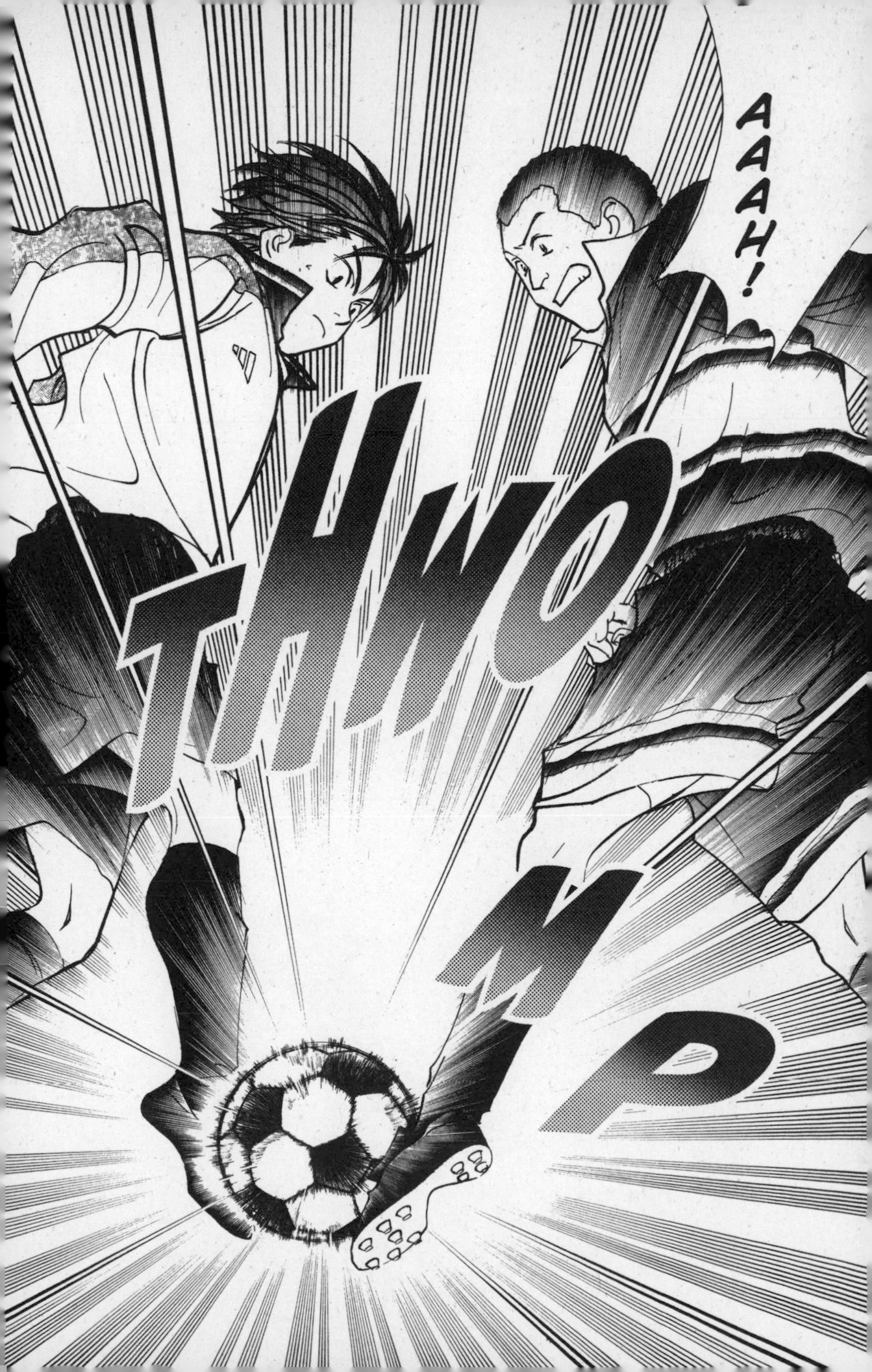
AAAAH!
THWOMP

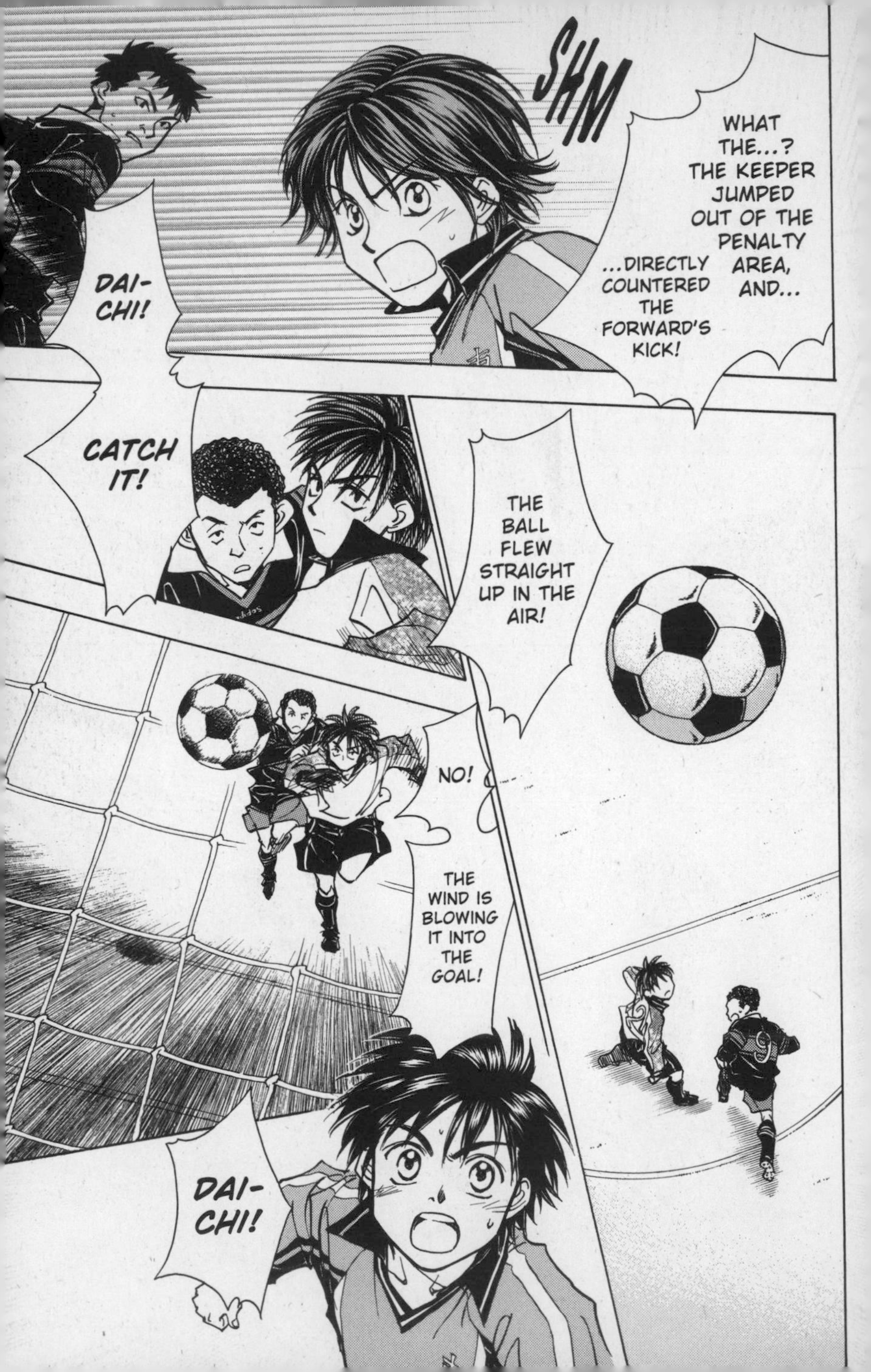
SHM
WHAT THE...? THE KEEPER JUMPED OUT OF THE PENALTY AREA, AND...
...DIRECTLY COUNTERED THE FORWARD'S KICK!
DAI-CHI!
THE BALL FLEW STRAIGHT UP IN THE AIR!
CATCH IT!
NO!
THE WIND IS BLOWING IT INTO THE GOAL!
DAI-CHI!

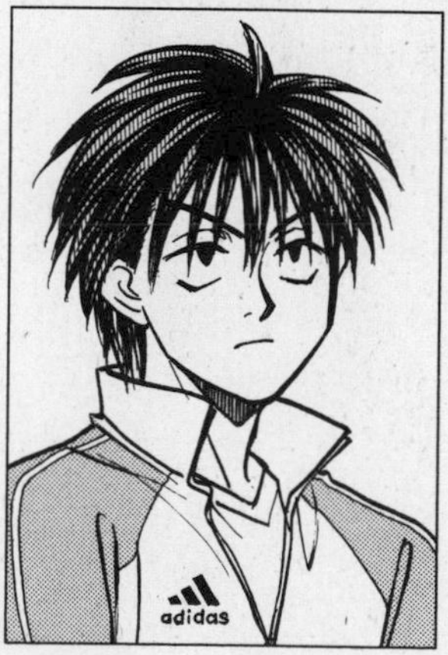
adidas

WHISTLE!

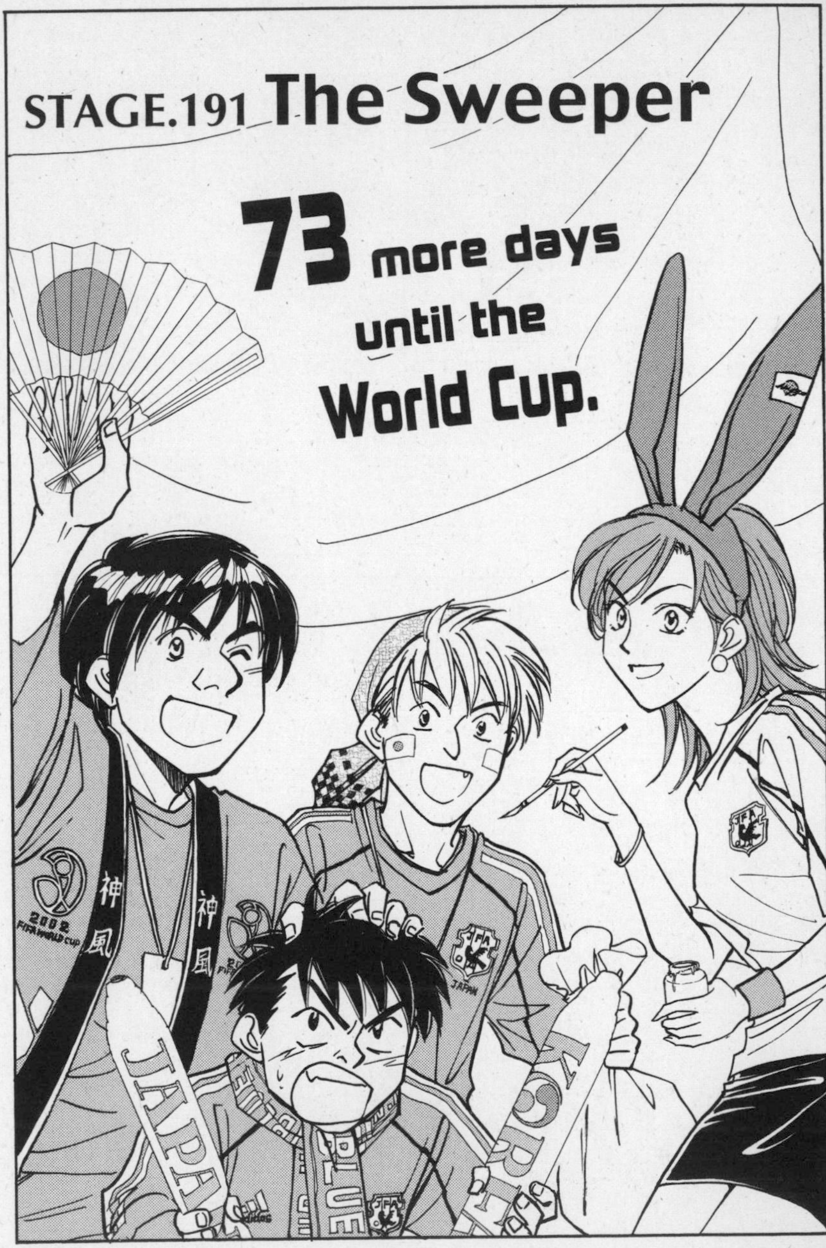
STAGE.191 The Sweeper
73 more days until the World Cup.

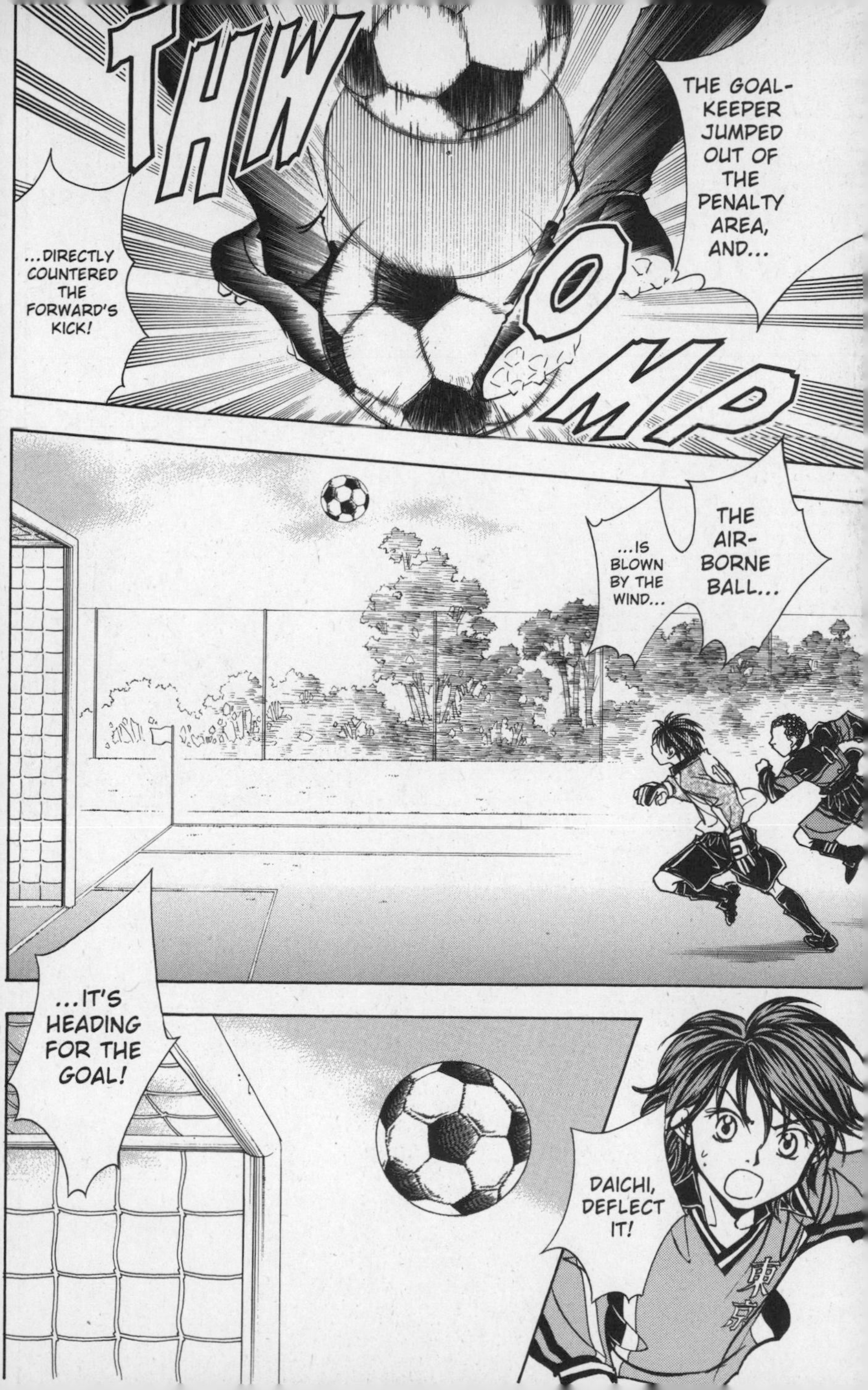
THE GOAL-KEEPER JUMPED OUT OF THE PENALTY AREA, AND...
THWOMP
...DIRECTLY COUNTERED THE FORWARD'S KICK!
THE AIR-BORNE BALL...
...IS BLOWN BY THE WIND...
...IT'S HEADING FOR THE GOAL!
DAICHI, DEFLECT IT!

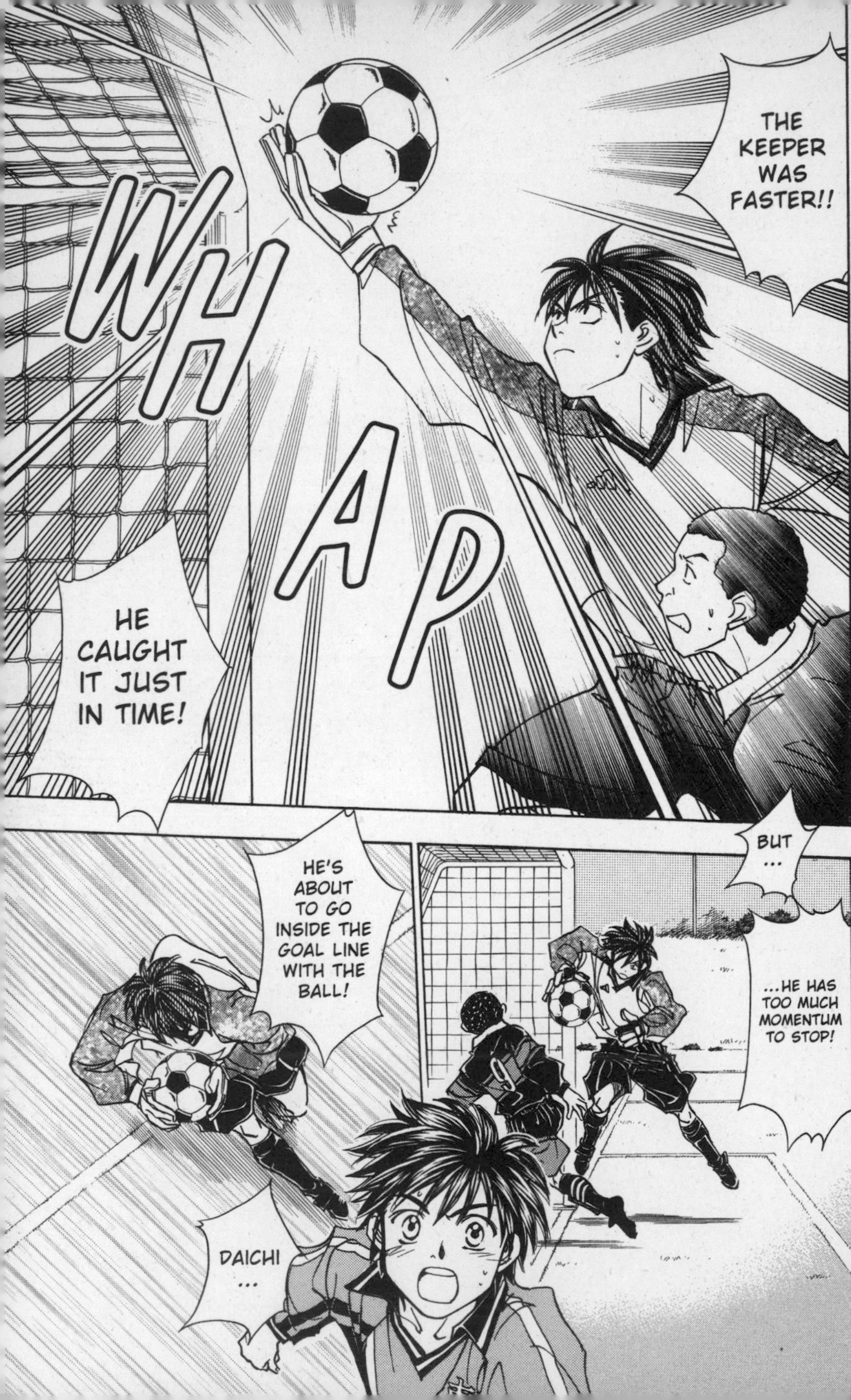
THE KEEPER WAS FASTER!!
WHAP
HE CAUGHT IT JUST IN TIME!
BUT ...
...HE HAS TOO MUCH MOMENTUM TO STOP!
HE'S ABOUT TO GO INSIDE THE GOAL LINE WITH THE BALL!
DAICHI ...

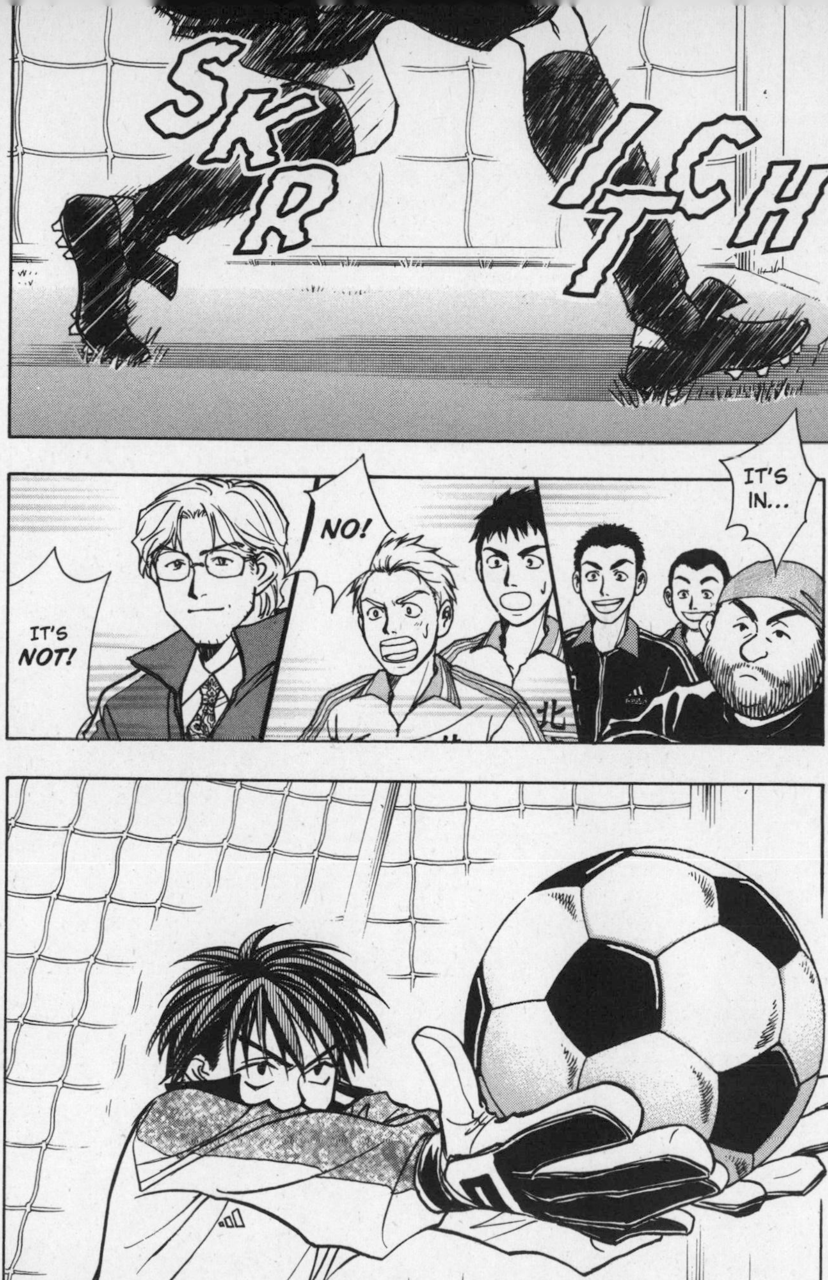
SKRITCH
IT'S IN...
NO!
IT'S NOT!

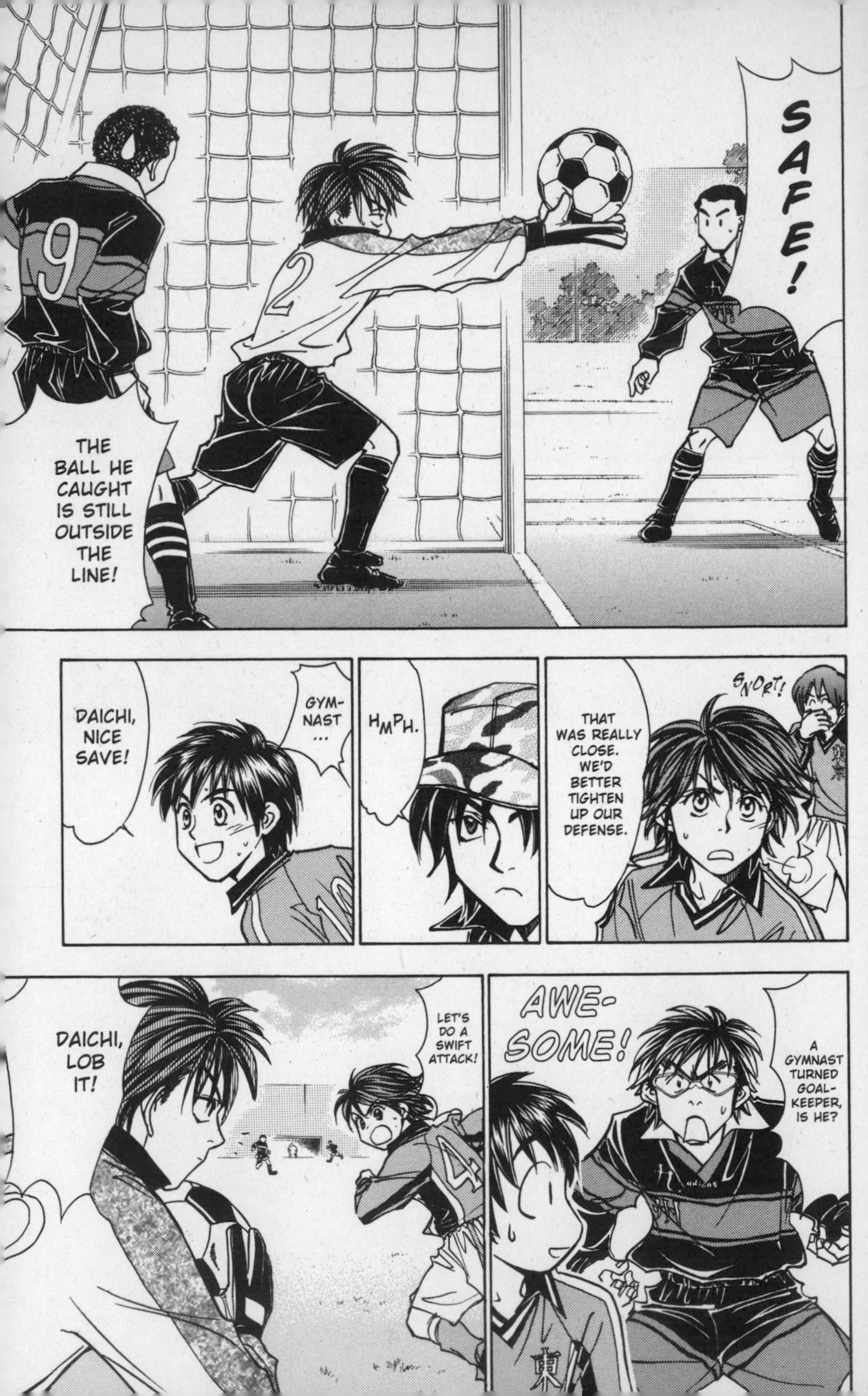
SAFE!
THE BALL HE CAUGHT IS STILL OUTSIDE THE LINE!
SNORT!
THAT WAS REALLY CLOSE. WE'D BETTER TIGHTEN UP OUR DEFENSE.
HMPH.
GYM-NAST ...
DAICHI, NICE SAVE!
A GYMNAST TURNED GOAL-KEEPER, IS HE?
AWE-SOME!
LET'S DO A SWIFT ATTACK!
DAICHI, LOB IT!

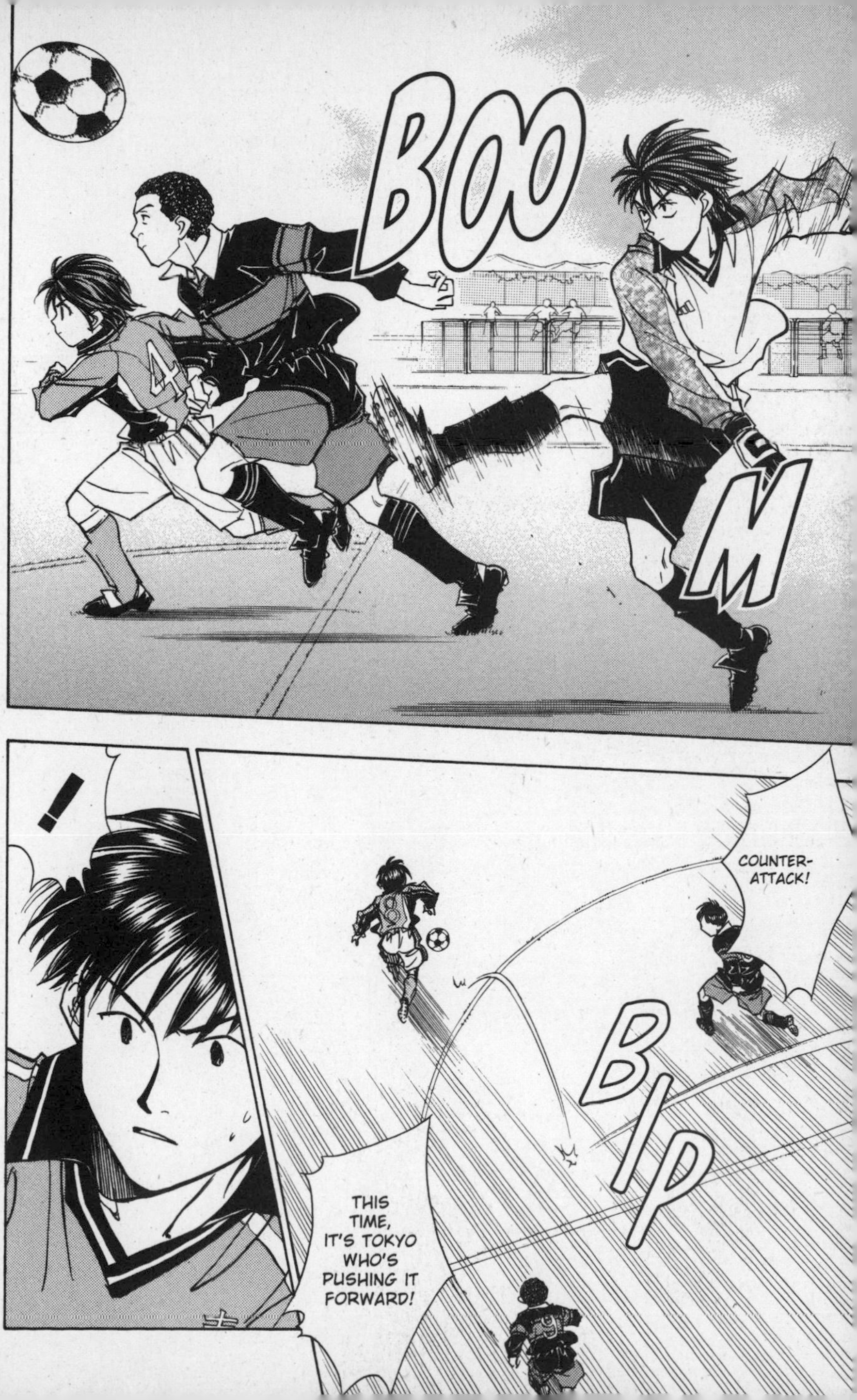
BOOM
COUNTER-ATTACK!
BIP
THIS TIME, IT'S TOKYO WHO'S PUSHING IT FORWARD!
!

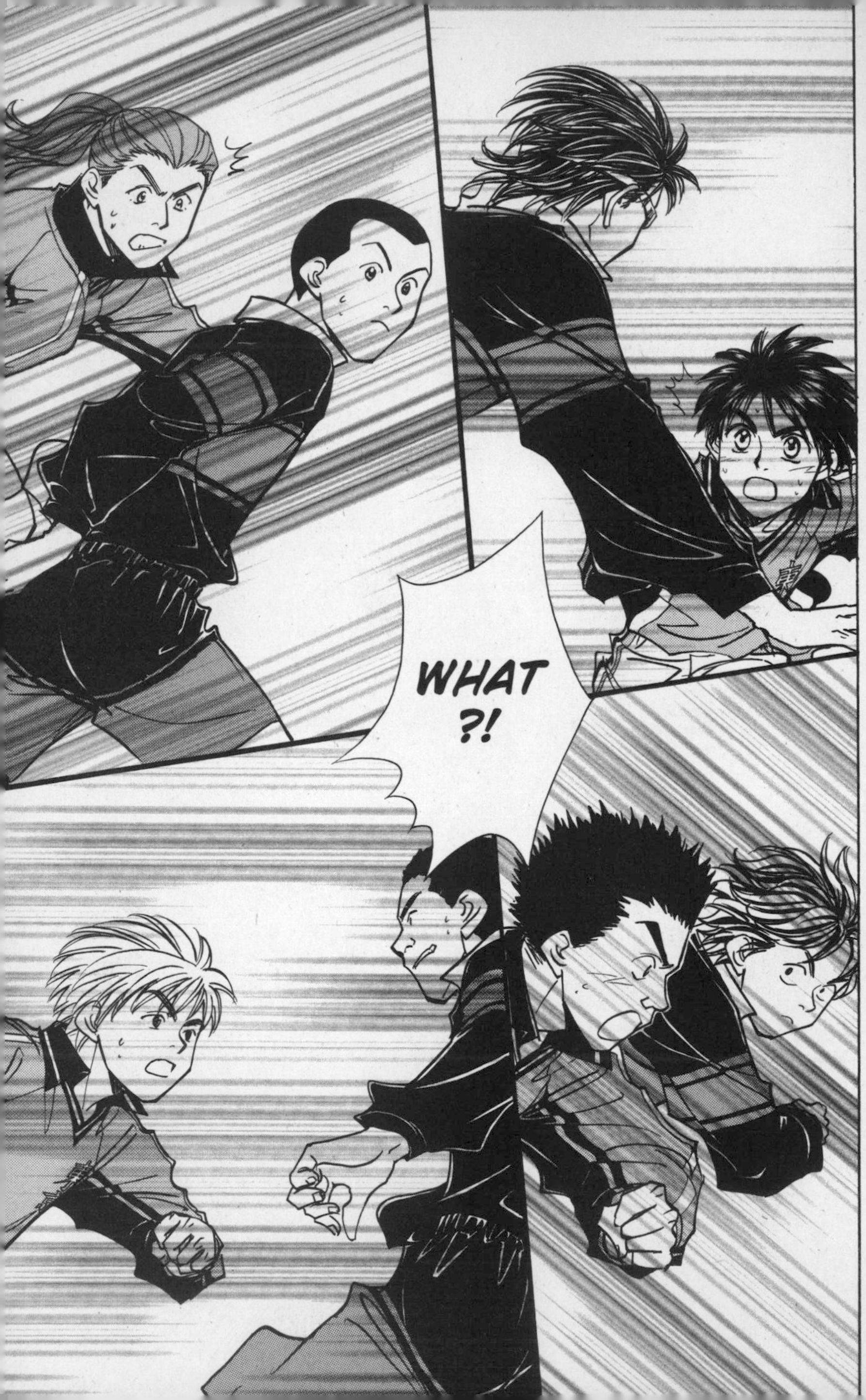
WHAT ?!

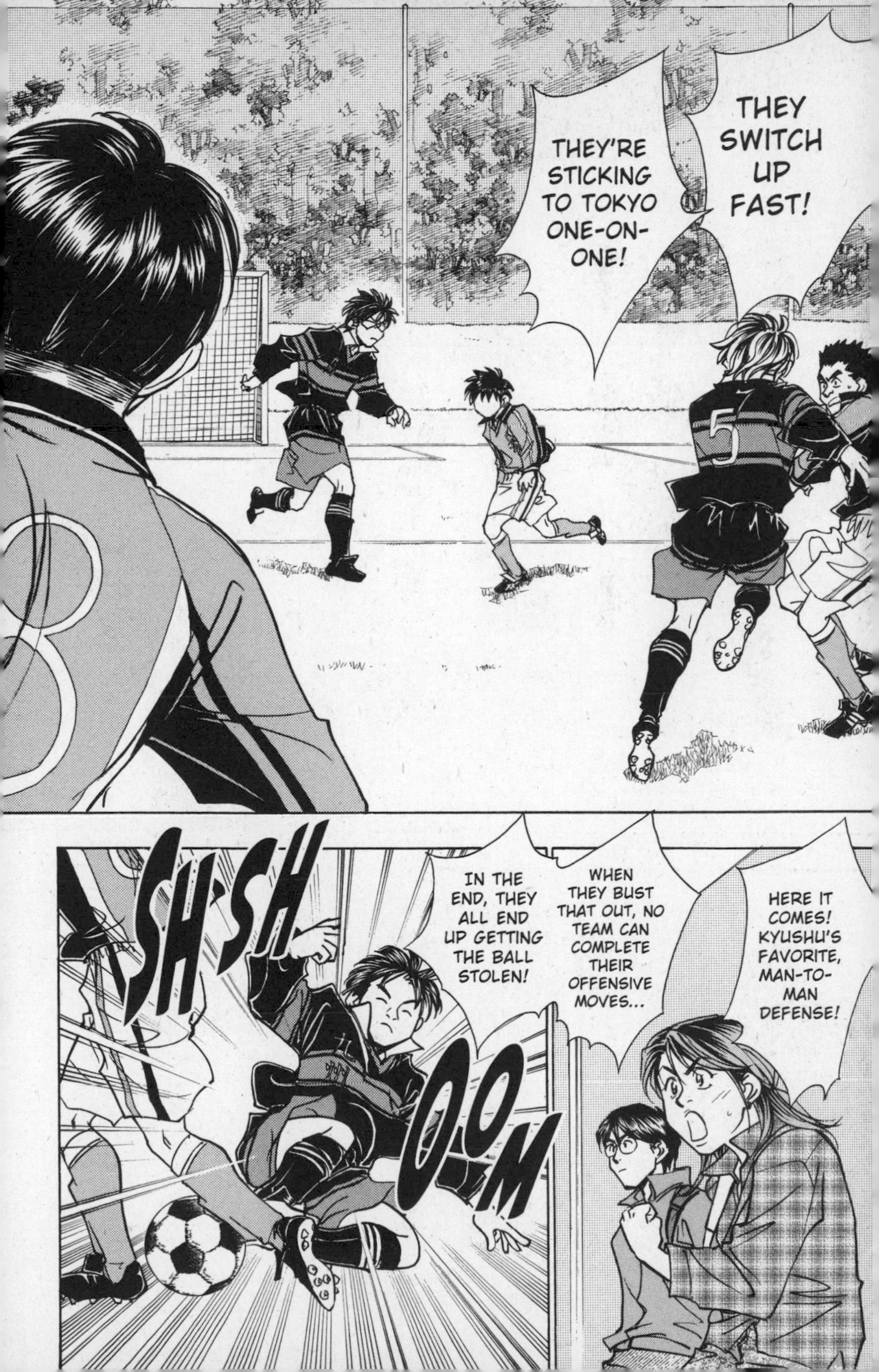
THEY SWITCH UP FAST!
THEY'RE STICKING TO TOKYO ONE-ON-ONE!
HERE IT COMES! KYUSHU'S FAVORITE, MAN-TO-MAN DEFENSE!
WHEN THEY BUST THAT OUT, NO TEAM CAN COMPLETE THEIR OFFENSIVE MOVES...
IN THE END, THEY ALL END UP GETTING THE BALL STOLEN!
SH-SH
O-O-M

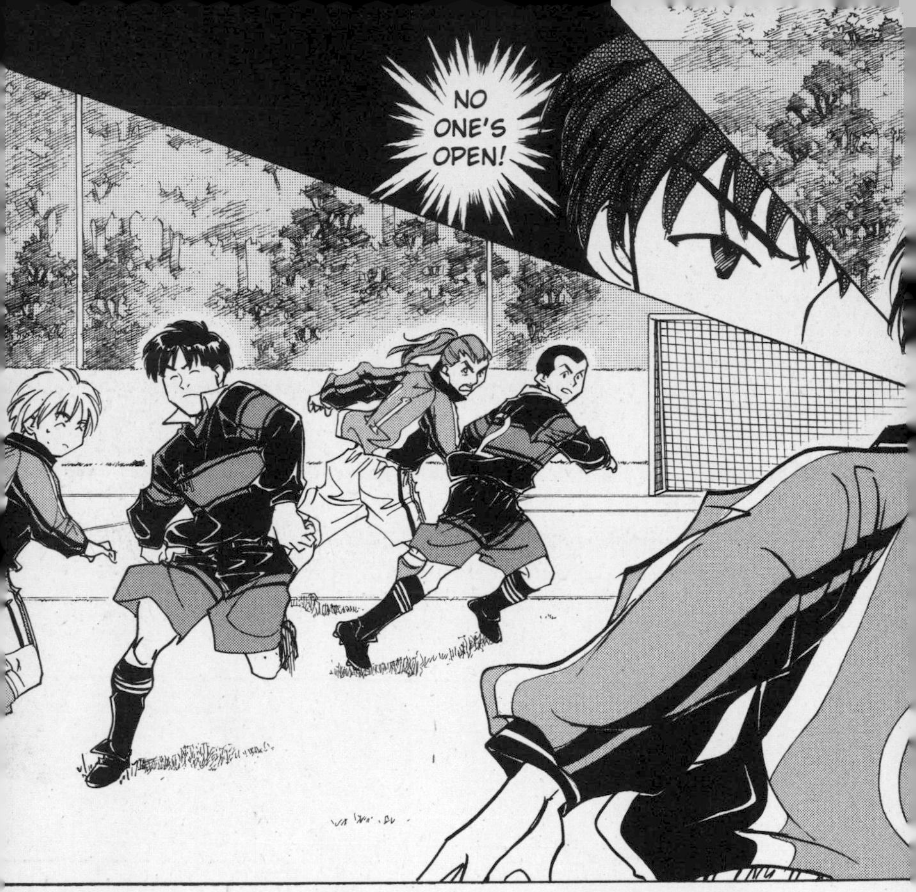
NO ONE'S OPEN!

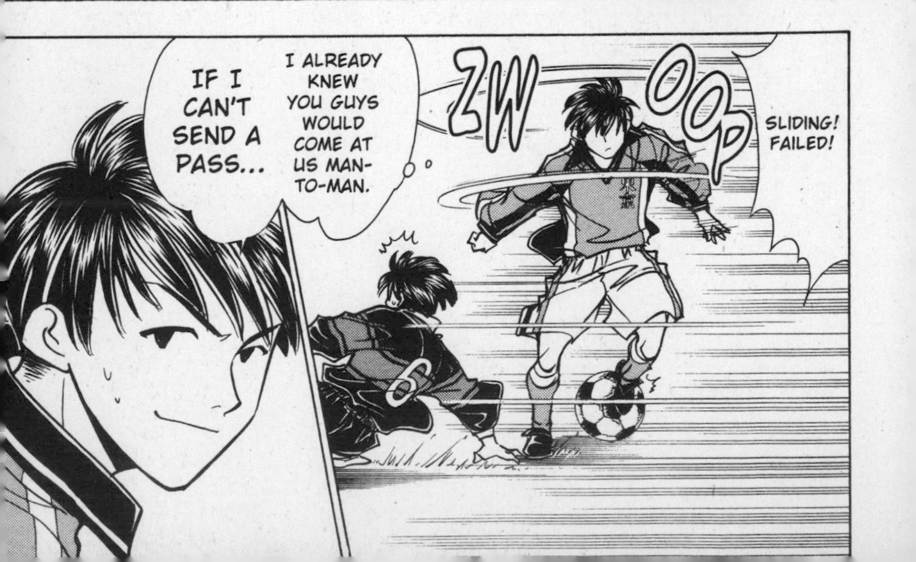
SLIDING! FAILED!
ZWOOP
I ALREADY KNEW YOU GUYS WOULD COME AT US MAN-TO-MAN.
IF I CAN'T SEND A PASS...

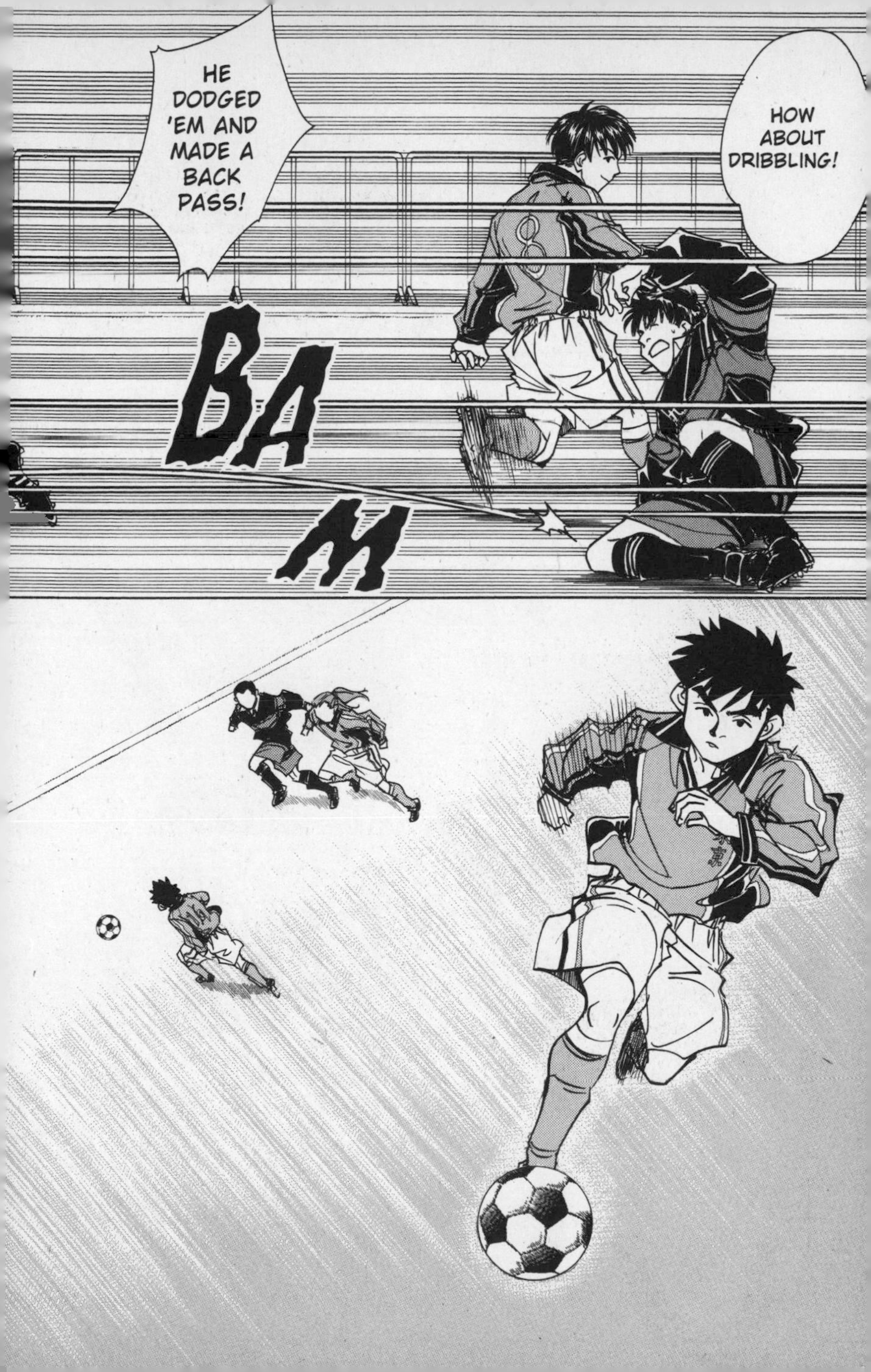
HOW ABOUT DRIBBLING!
HE DODGED 'EM AND MADE A BACK PASS!
BAM

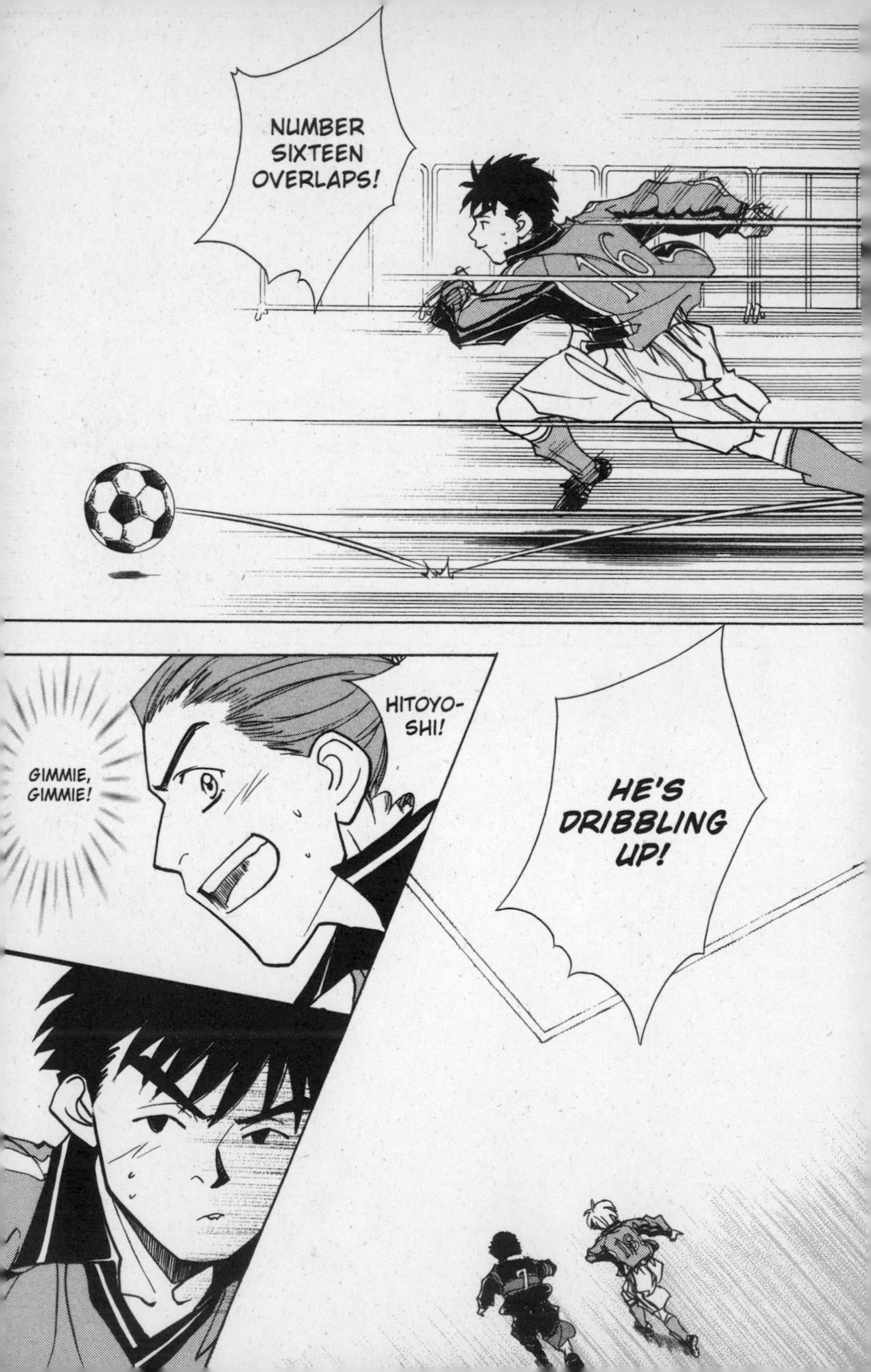
NUMBER SIXTEEN OVERLAPS!
HE'S DRIBBLING UP!
HITOYO-SHI!
GIMMIE, GIMMIE!

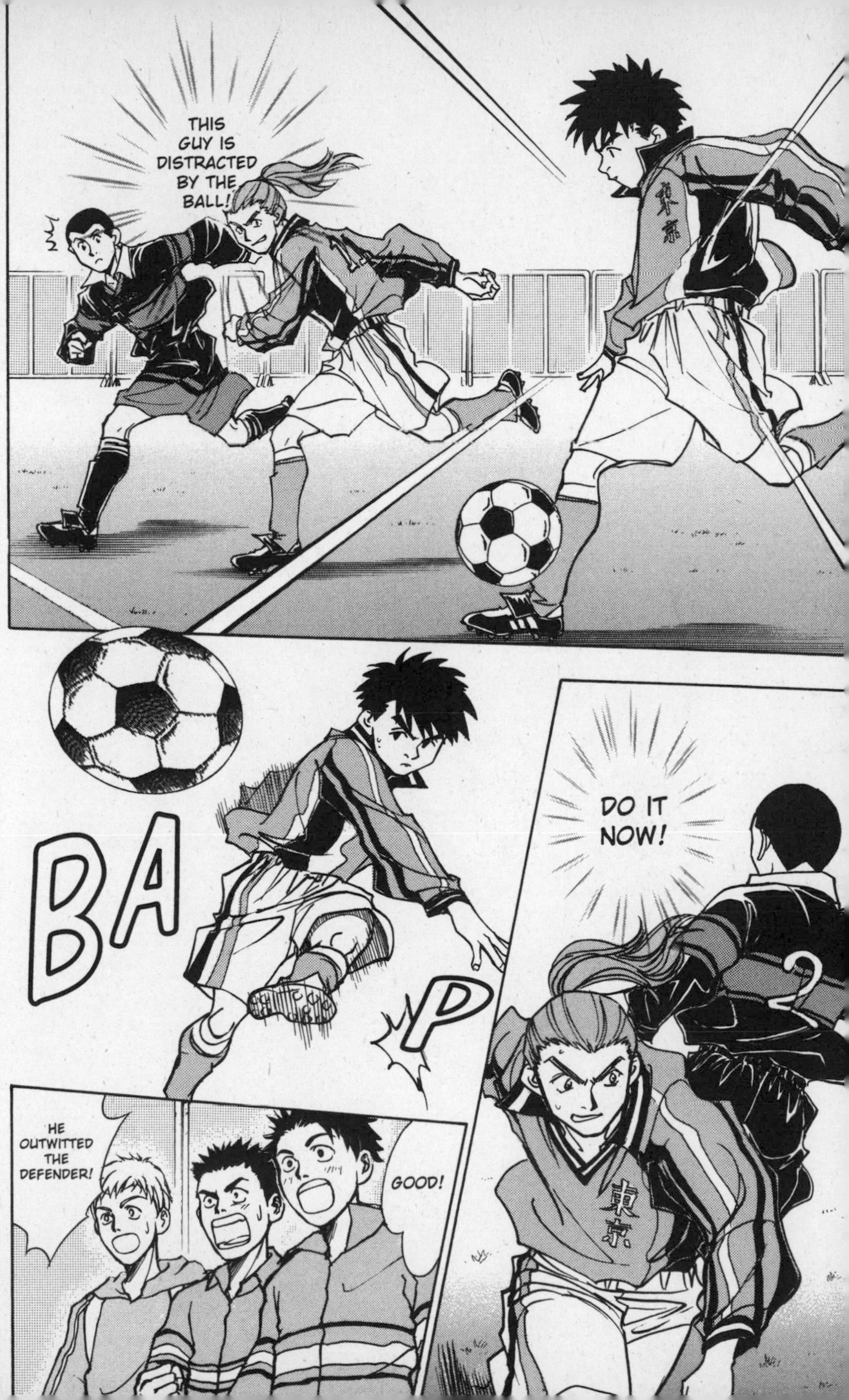
THIS GUY IS DISTRACTED BY THE BALL!
DO IT NOW!
BAP
GOOD!
HE OUTWITTED THE DEFENDER!

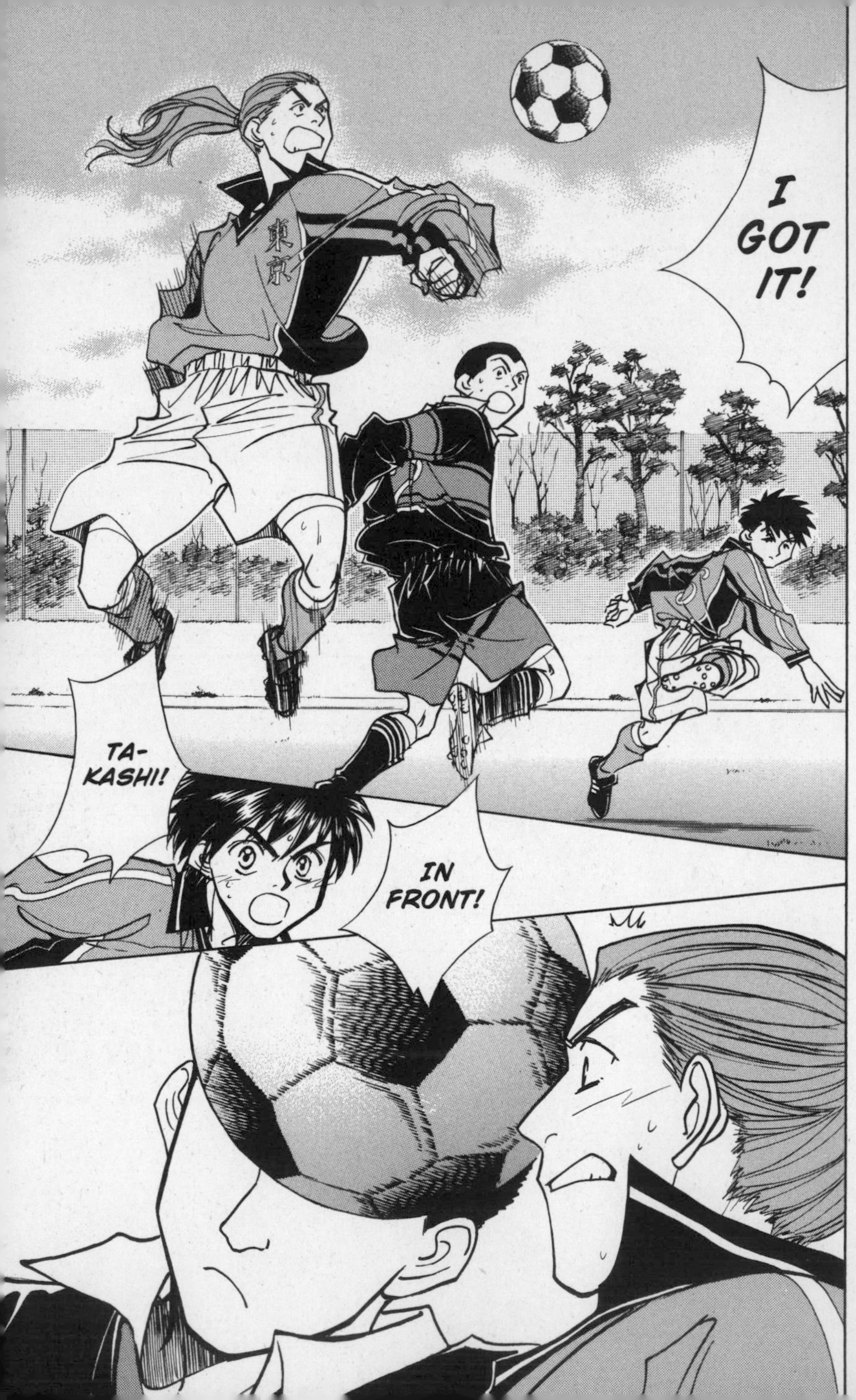
I GOT IT!
東京
TA-KASHI!
IN FRONT!

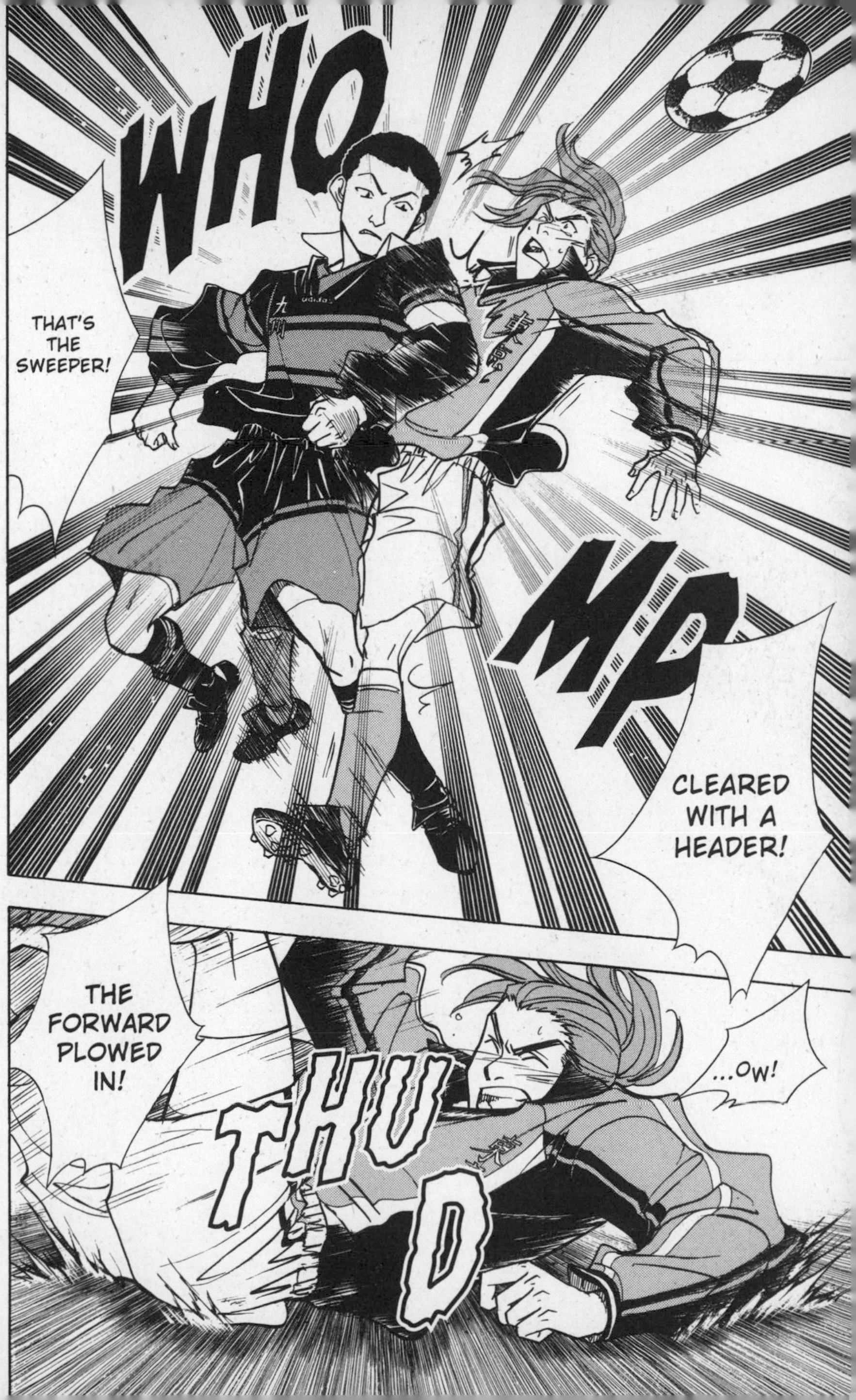
WHO
MP
THAT'S THE SWEEPER!
CLEARED WITH A HEADER!
THE FORWARD PLOWED IN!
THUD
...OW!

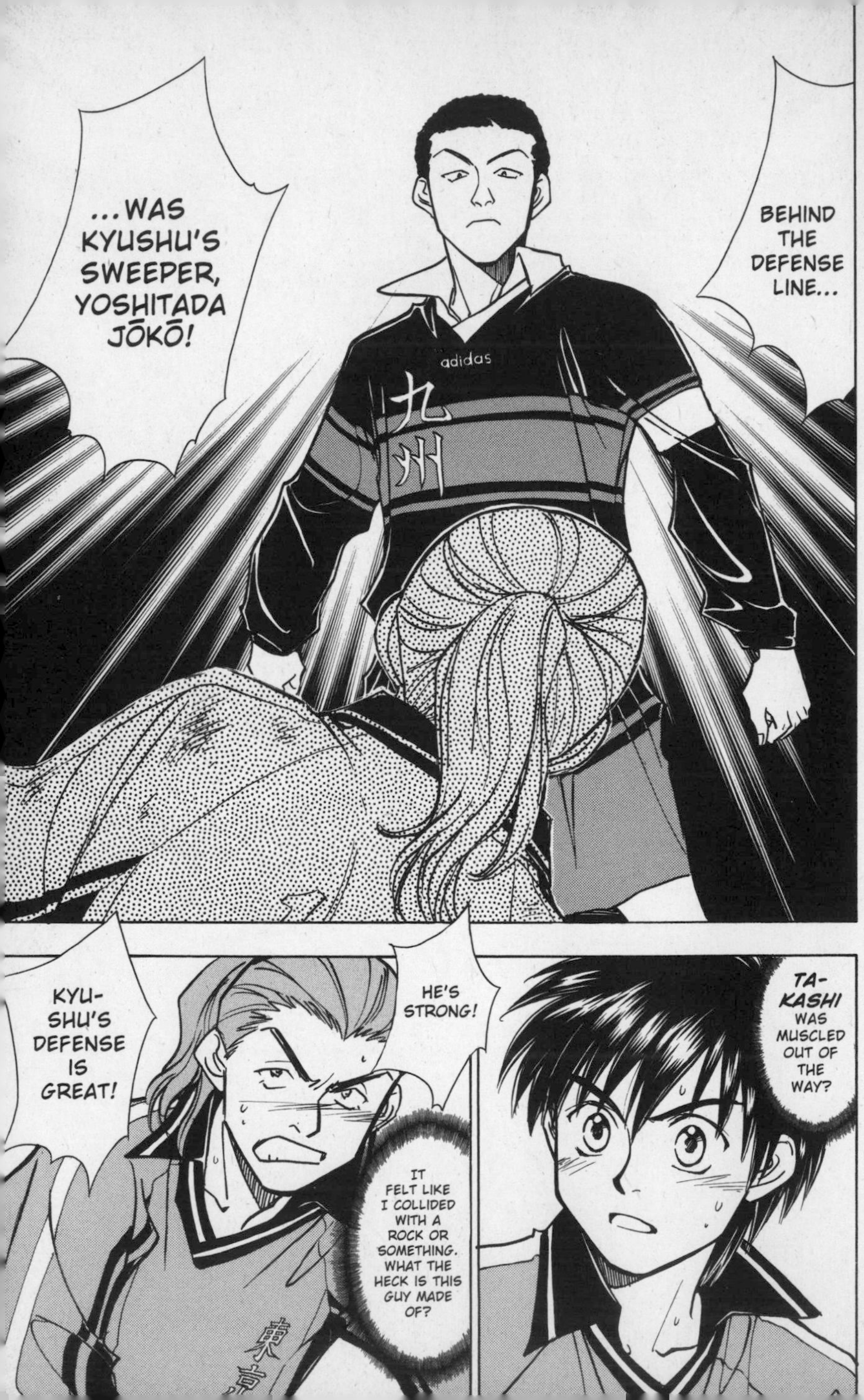
BEHIND THE DEFENSE LINE...
...WAS KYUSHU'S SWEEPER, YOSHITADA JŌKŌ!
TA-KASHI WAS MUSCLED OUT OF THE WAY?
HE'S STRONG!
KYU-SHU'S DEFENSE IS GREAT!
IT FELT LIKE I COLLIDED WITH A ROCK OR SOMETHING. WHAT THE HECK IS THIS GUY MADE OF?

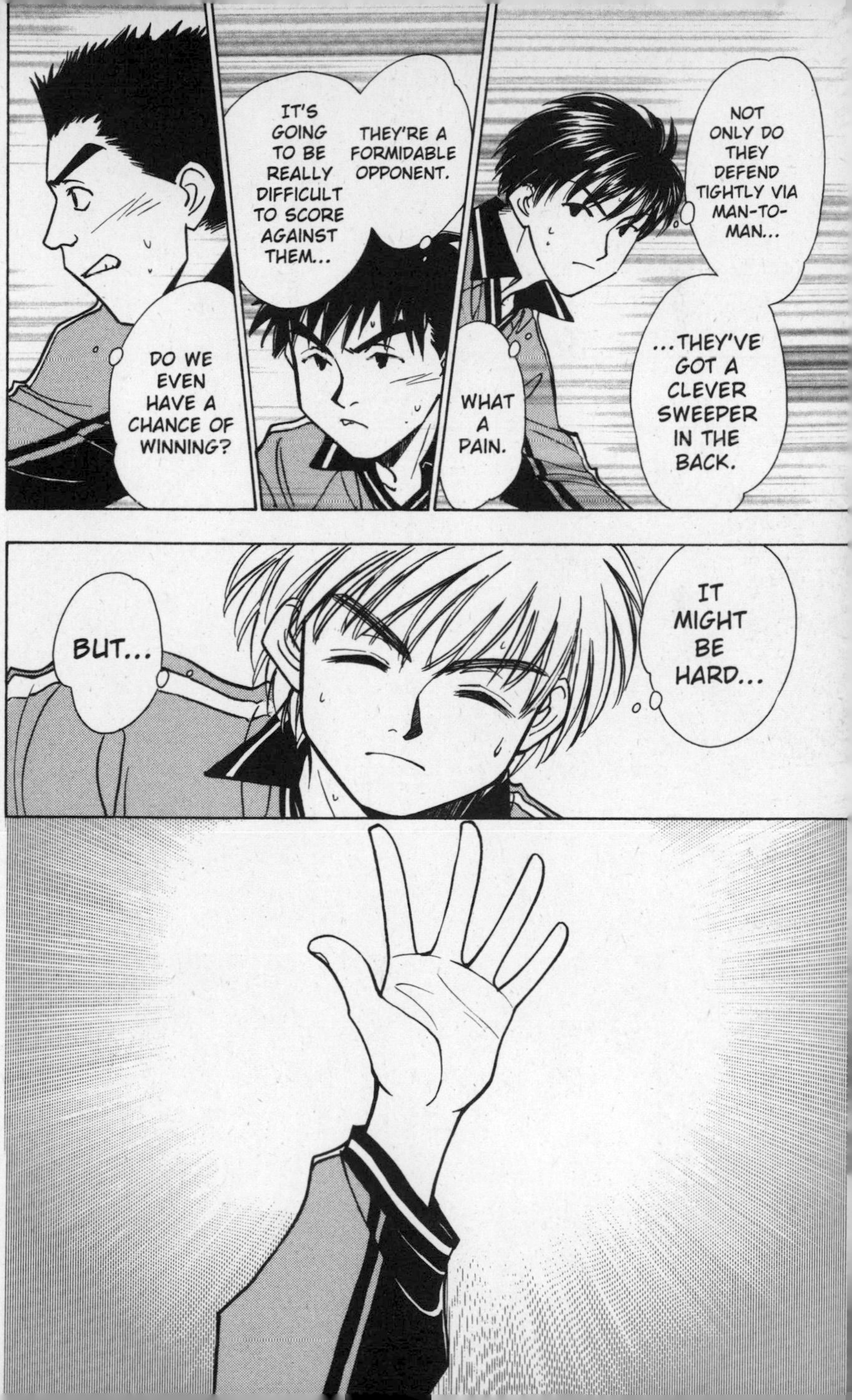
NOT ONLY DO THEY DEFEND TIGHTLY VIA MAN-TO-MAN...
...THEY'VE GOT A CLEVER SWEEPER IN THE BACK.
WHAT A PAIN.
THEY'RE A FORMIDABLE OPPONENT.
IT'S GOING TO BE REALLY DIFFICULT TO SCORE AGAINST THEM...
DO WE EVEN HAVE A CHANCE OF WINNING?
IT MIGHT BE HARD...
BUT...

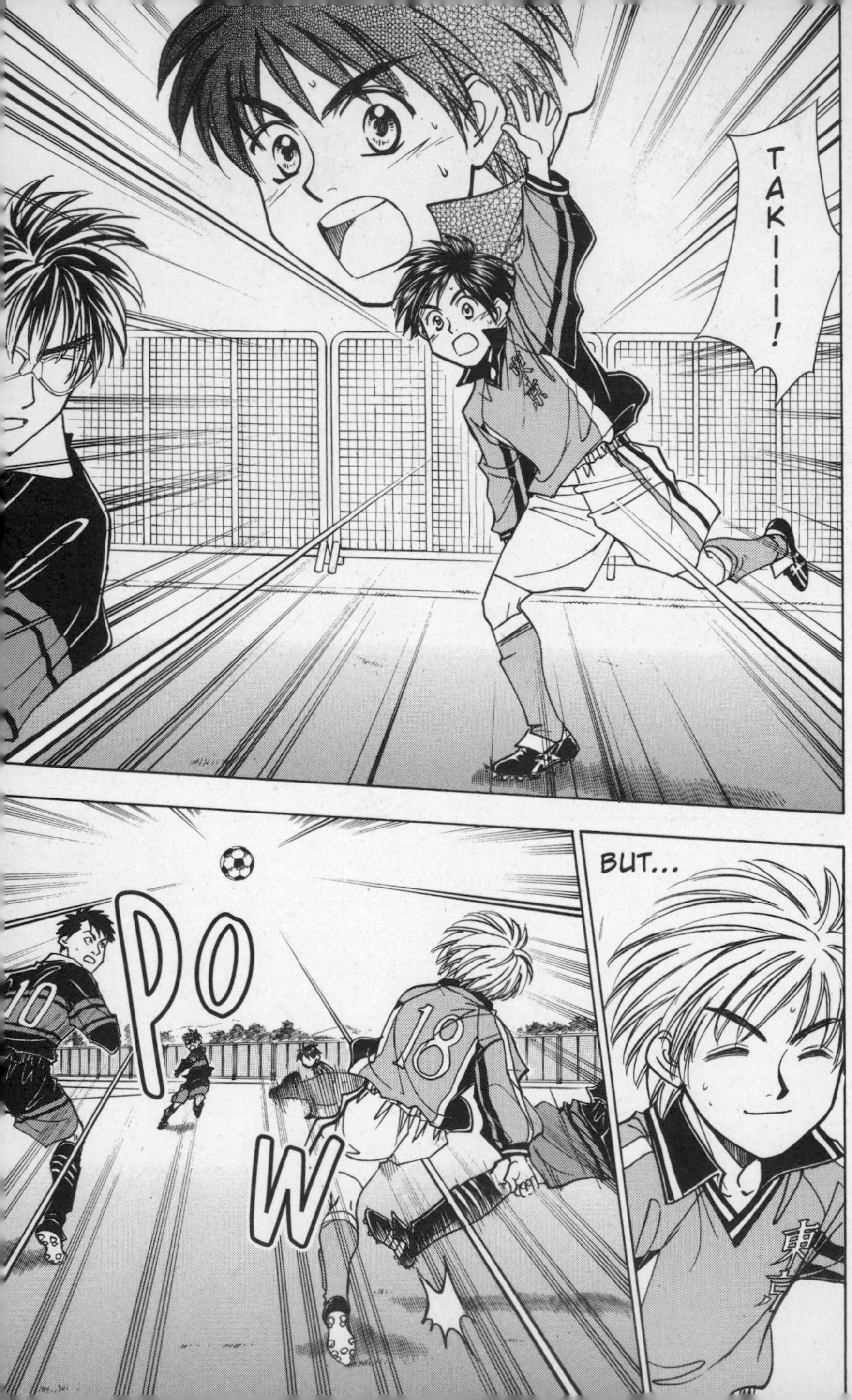
TAKIII!
BUT...
POW

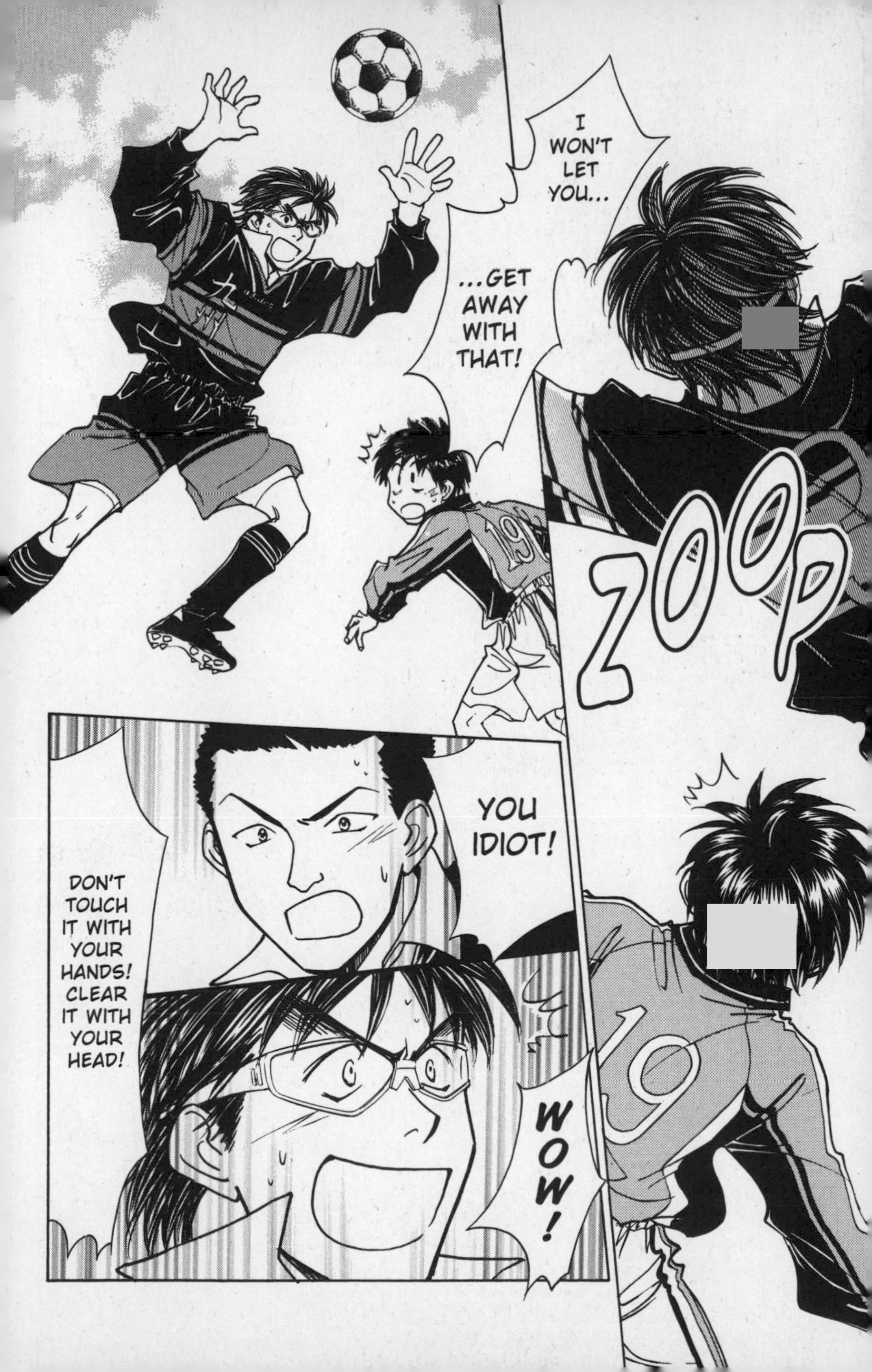
I WON'T LET YOU...
...GET AWAY WITH THAT!
ZOOP
YOU IDIOT!
DON'T TOUCH IT WITH YOUR HANDS! CLEAR IT WITH YOUR HEAD!
WOW!

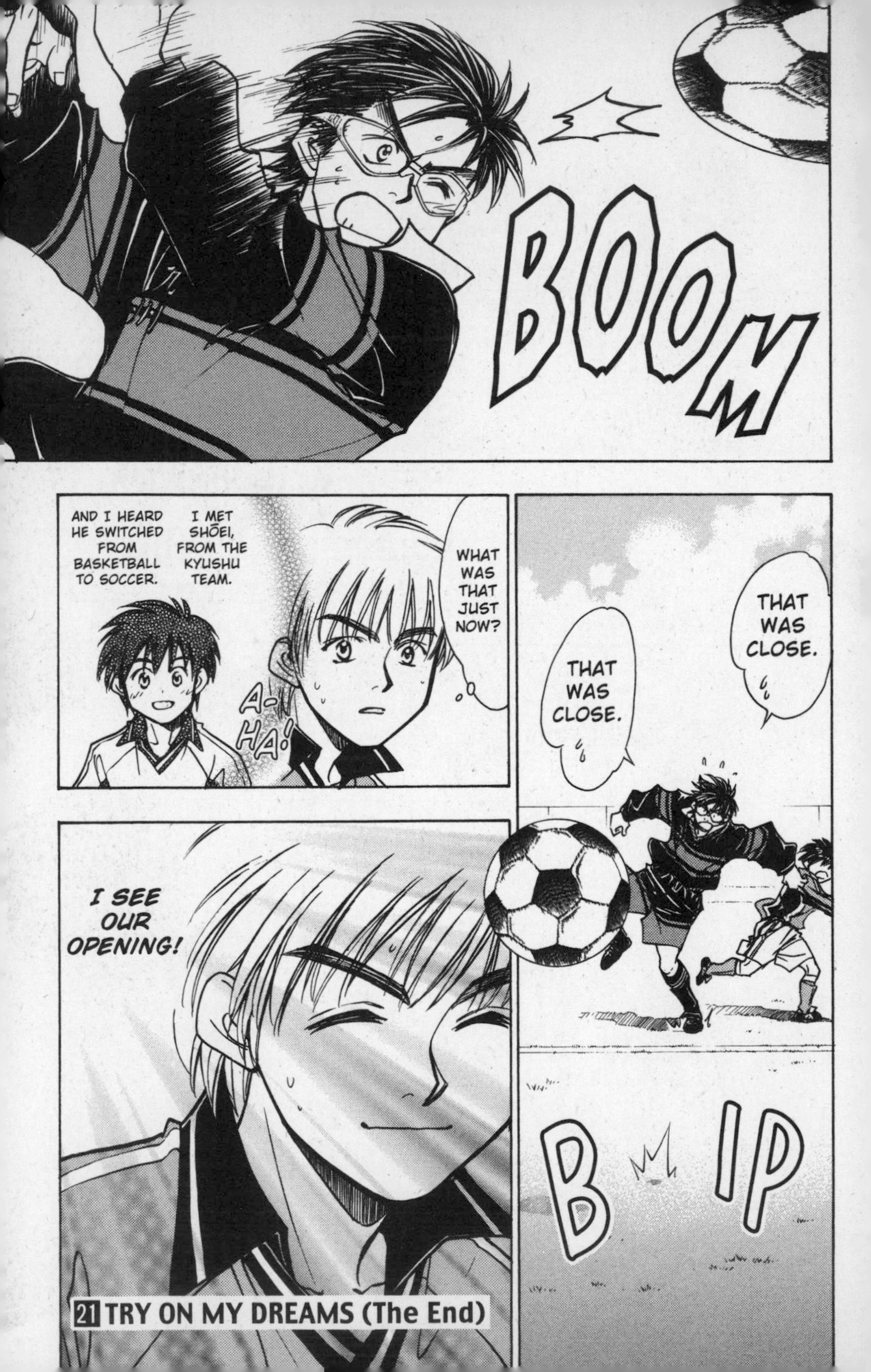
BOOM
THAT WAS CLOSE.
THAT WAS CLOSE.
B IP
WHAT WAS THAT JUST NOW?
I MET SHŌEI, FROM THE KYUSHU TEAM.
AND I HEARD HE SWITCHED FROM BASKETBALL TO SOCCER.
A-HA!
I SEE OUR OPENING!

21 TRY ON MY DREAMS (The End)

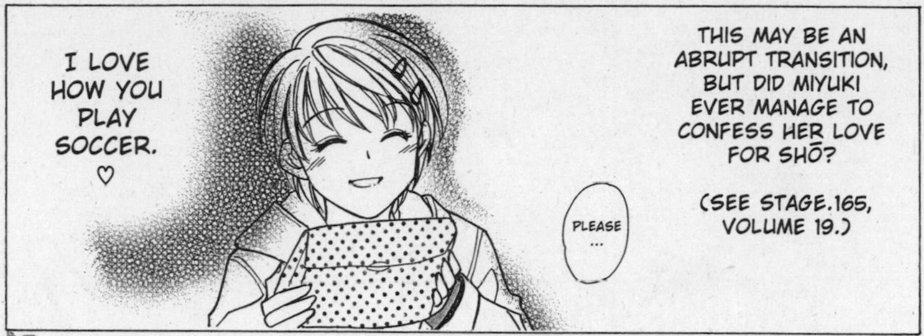
THIS MAY BE AN ABRUPT TRANSITION, BUT DID MIYUKI EVER MANAGE TO CONFESS HER LOVE FOR SHŌ?
(SEE STAGE.165, VOLUME 19.)
PLEASE...
I LOVE HOW YOU PLAY SOCCER. ♡

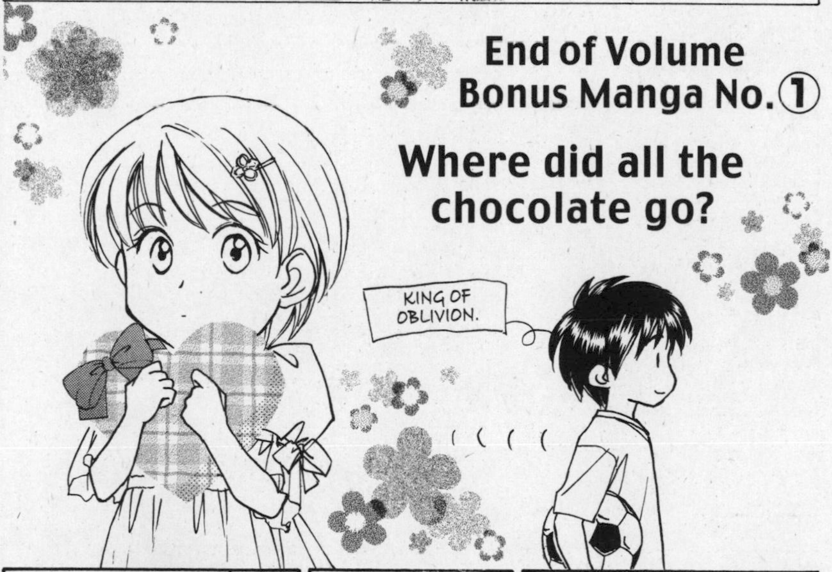
End of Volume Bonus Manga No. ①
Where did all the chocolate go?
KING OF OBLIVION.

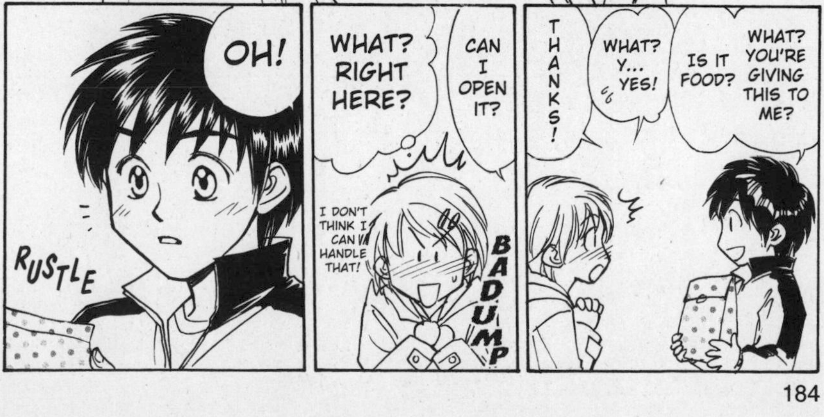
WHAT? YOU'RE GIVING THIS TO ME?
IS IT FOOD?
WHAT? Y... YES!
THANKS!
CAN I OPEN IT?
WHAT? RIGHT HERE?
BADUMP
I DON'T THINK I CAN HANDLE THAT!
OH!
RUSTLE

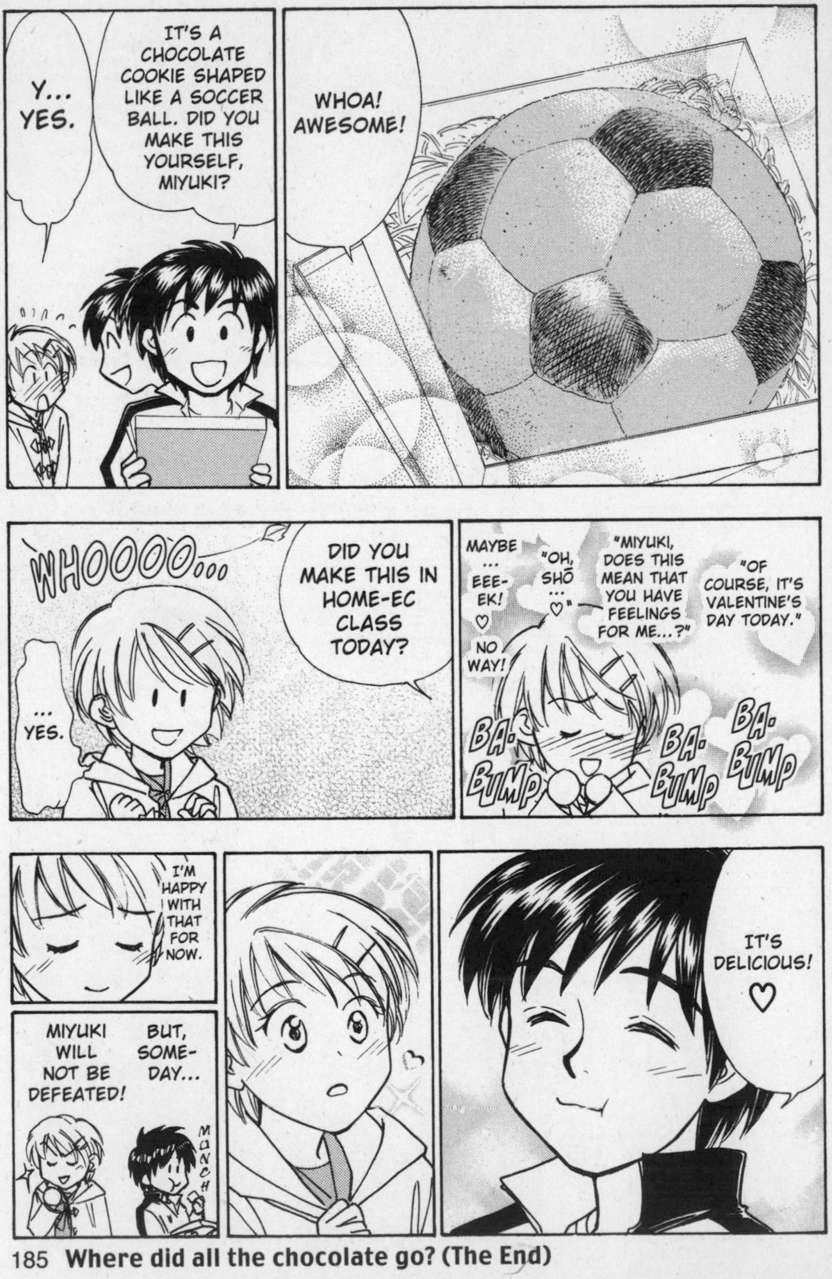
WHOA! AWESOME!
IT'S A CHOCOLATE COOKIE SHAPED LIKE A SOCCER BALL. DID YOU MAKE THIS YOURSELF, MIYUKI?
Y... YES.
"OF COURSE, IT'S VALENTINE'S DAY TODAY."
"MIYUKI, DOES THIS MEAN THAT YOU HAVE FEELINGS FOR ME...?"
"OH, SHŌ ... ♡"
MAYBE ... EEE-EK! ♡
NO WAY!
BA-BUMP
BA-BUMP
BA-BUMP
DID YOU MAKE THIS IN HOME-EC CLASS TODAY?
WHOOOOooo
... YES.
IT'S DELICIOUS! ♡
I'M HAPPY WITH THAT FOR NOW.
BUT, SOME-DAY...
MIYUKI WILL NOT BE DEFEATED!
MUNCH

 Where did all the chocolate go? (The End)

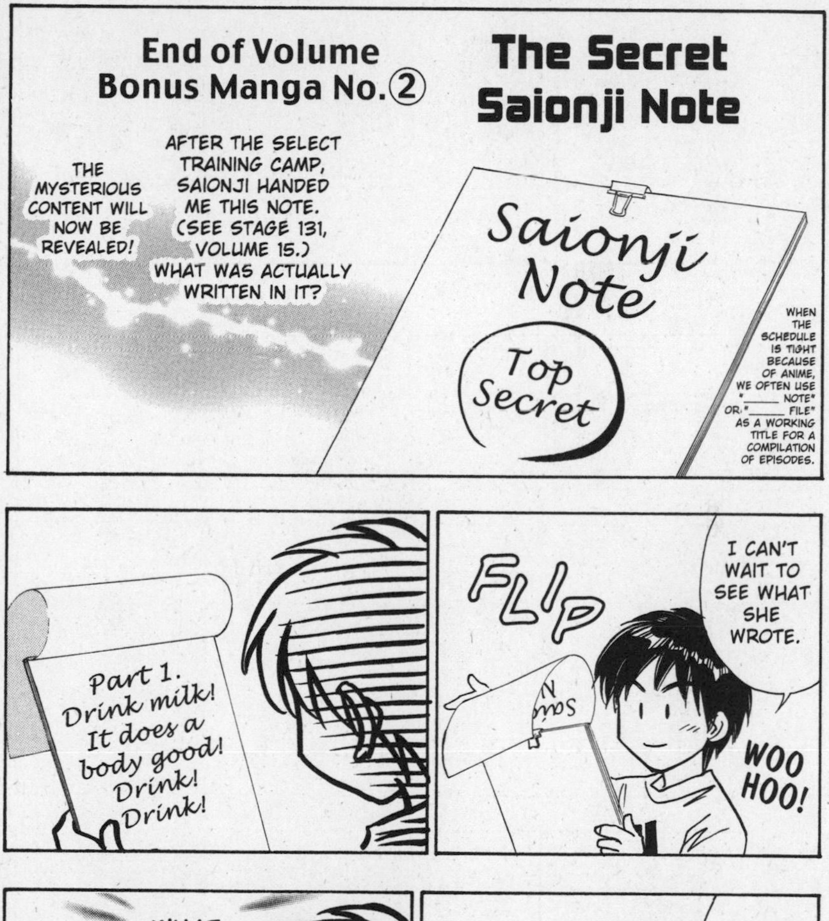
The Secret Saionji Note
End of Volume Bonus Manga No. ②
Saionji Note
Top Secret
WHEN THE SCHEDULE IS TIGHT BECAUSE OF ANIME, WE OFTEN USE "_____ NOTE" OR "_____ FILE" AS A WORKING TITLE FOR A COMPILATION OF EPISODES.
AFTER THE SELECT TRAINING CAMP, SAIONJI HANDED ME THIS NOTE. (SEE STAGE 131, VOLUME 15.) WHAT WAS ACTUALLY WRITTEN IN IT?
THE MYSTERIOUS CONTENT WILL NOW BE REVEALED!
I CAN'T WAIT TO SEE WHAT SHE WROTE.
FLIP
WOO HOO!
Part 1. Drink milk! It does a body good! Drink! Drink!
OOOKAY ... AND WHAT ELSE...
FLIP
WOO HOO ...?
WHAT IS THIS?
Obana Super Hair Attack: Blade of Death!

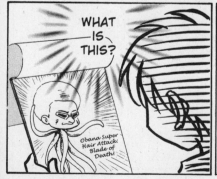

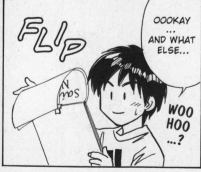

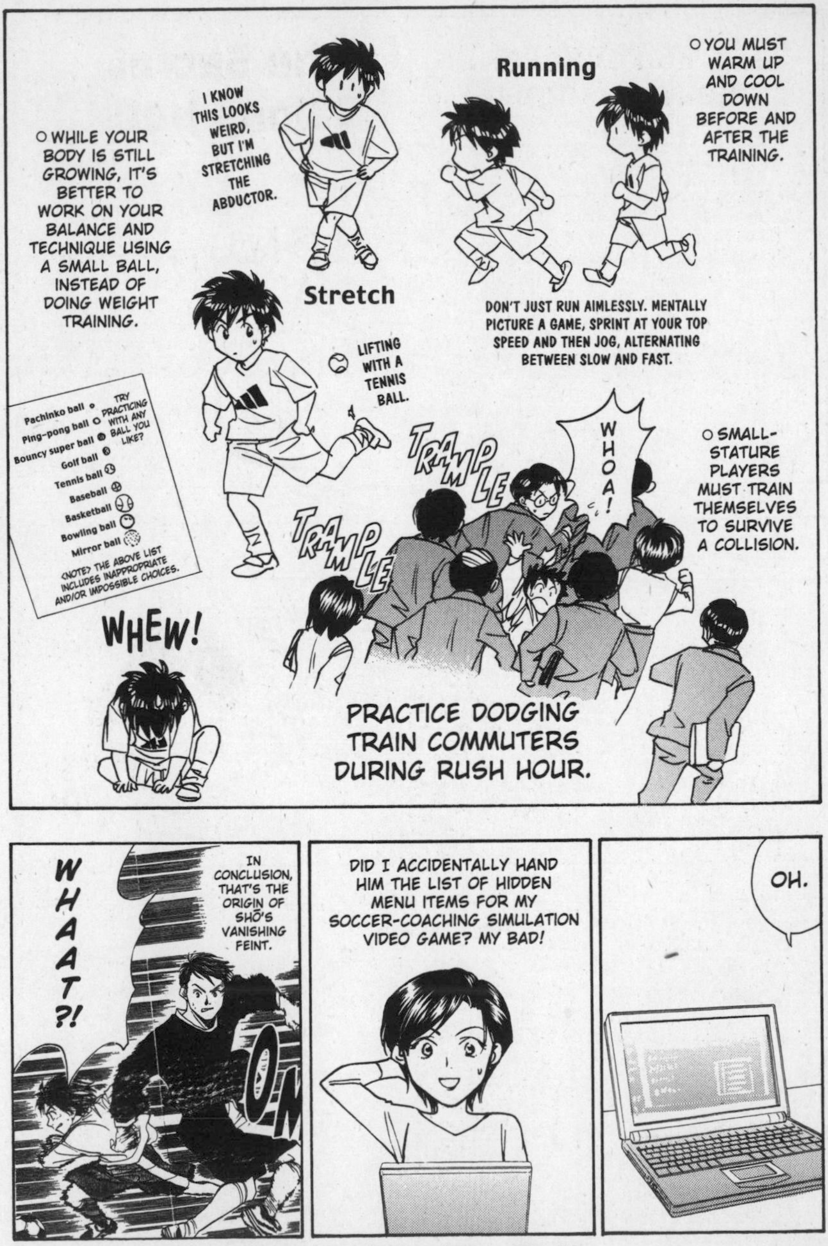
○ YOU MUST WARM UP AND COOL DOWN BEFORE AND AFTER THE TRAINING.
Running
I KNOW THIS LOOKS WEIRD, BUT I'M STRETCHING THE ABDUCTOR.
○ WHILE YOUR BODY IS STILL GROWING, IT'S BETTER TO WORK ON YOUR BALANCE AND TECHNIQUE USING A SMALL BALL, INSTEAD OF DOING WEIGHT TRAINING.
DON'T JUST RUN AIMLESSLY. MENTALLY PICTURE A GAME, SPRINT AT YOUR TOP SPEED AND THEN JOG, ALTERNATING BETWEEN SLOW AND FAST.
Stretch
LIFTING WITH A TENNIS BALL.
TRY PRACTICING WITH ANY BALL YOU LIKE?
Pachinko ball
Ping-pong ball
Bouncy super ball
Golf ball
Tennis ball
Baseball
Basketball
Bowling ball
Mirror ball
<NOTE> THE ABOVE LIST INCLUDES INAPPROPRIATE AND/OR IMPOSSIBLE CHOICES.
○ SMALL-STATURE PLAYERS MUST TRAIN THEMSELVES TO SURVIVE A COLLISION.
WHOA!
TRAMPLE
TRAMPLE
WHEW!
PRACTICE DODGING TRAIN COMMUTERS DURING RUSH HOUR.
OH.
DID I ACCIDENTALLY HAND HIM THE LIST OF HIDDEN MENU ITEMS FOR MY SOCCER-COACHING SIMULATION VIDEO GAME? MY BAD!
IN CONCLUSION, THAT'S THE ORIGIN OF SHŌ'S VANISHING FEINT.
WHAAAT?!

 The Secret Saionji Note (The End)

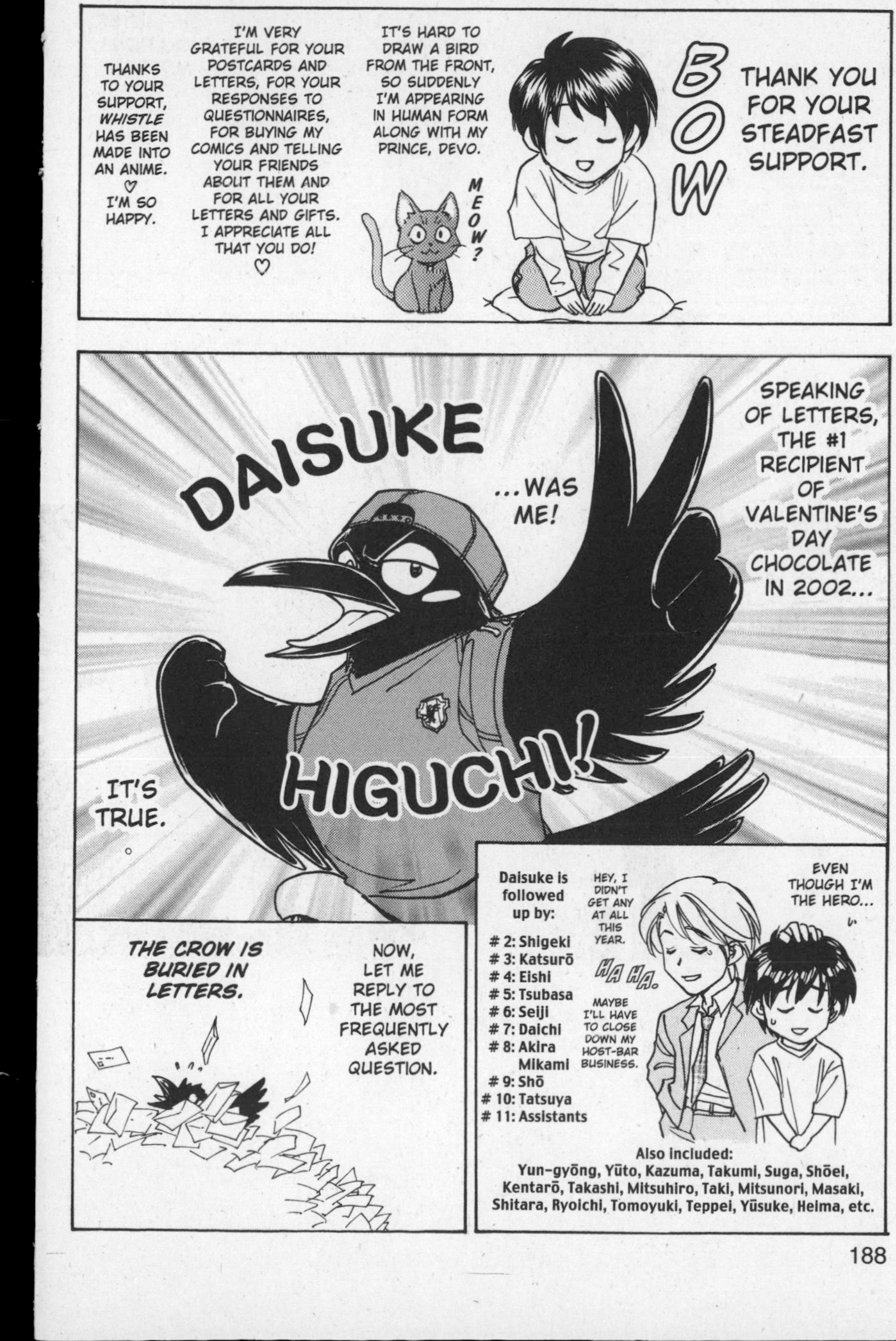
THANK YOU FOR YOUR STEADFAST SUPPORT.
BOW
MEOW?
IT'S HARD TO DRAW A BIRD FROM THE FRONT, SO SUDDENLY I'M APPEARING IN HUMAN FORM ALONG WITH MY PRINCE, DEVO.
I'M VERY GRATEFUL FOR YOUR POSTCARDS AND LETTERS, FOR YOUR RESPONSES TO QUESTIONNAIRES, FOR BUYING MY COMICS AND TELLING YOUR FRIENDS ABOUT THEM AND FOR ALL YOUR LETTERS AND GIFTS. I APPRECIATE ALL THAT YOU DO! ♡
THANKS TO YOUR SUPPORT, *WHISTLE* HAS BEEN MADE INTO AN ANIME. ♡ I'M SO HAPPY.
SPEAKING OF LETTERS, THE #1 RECIPIENT OF VALENTINE'S DAY CHOCOLATE IN 2002...
...WAS ME!
DAISUKE
HIGUCHI!
IT'S TRUE.
EVEN THOUGH I'M THE HERO...
HEY, I DIDN'T GET ANY AT ALL THIS YEAR.
HA HA.
MAYBE I'LL HAVE TO CLOSE DOWN MY HOST-BAR BUSINESS.
Daisuke is followed up by:
2: Shigeki
3: Katsurō
4: Eishi
5: Tsubasa
6: Seiji
7: Daichi
8: Akira Mikami
9: Shō
10: Tatsuya
11: Assistants
Also included:
Yun-gyōng, Yūto, Kazuma, Takumi, Suga, Shōei, Kentarō, Takashi, Mitsuhiro, Taki, Mitsunori, Masaki, Shitara, Ryoichi, Tomoyuki, Teppei, Yūsuke, Heima, etc.
NOW, LET ME REPLY TO THE MOST FREQUENTLY ASKED QUESTION.
THE CROW IS BURIED IN LETTERS.

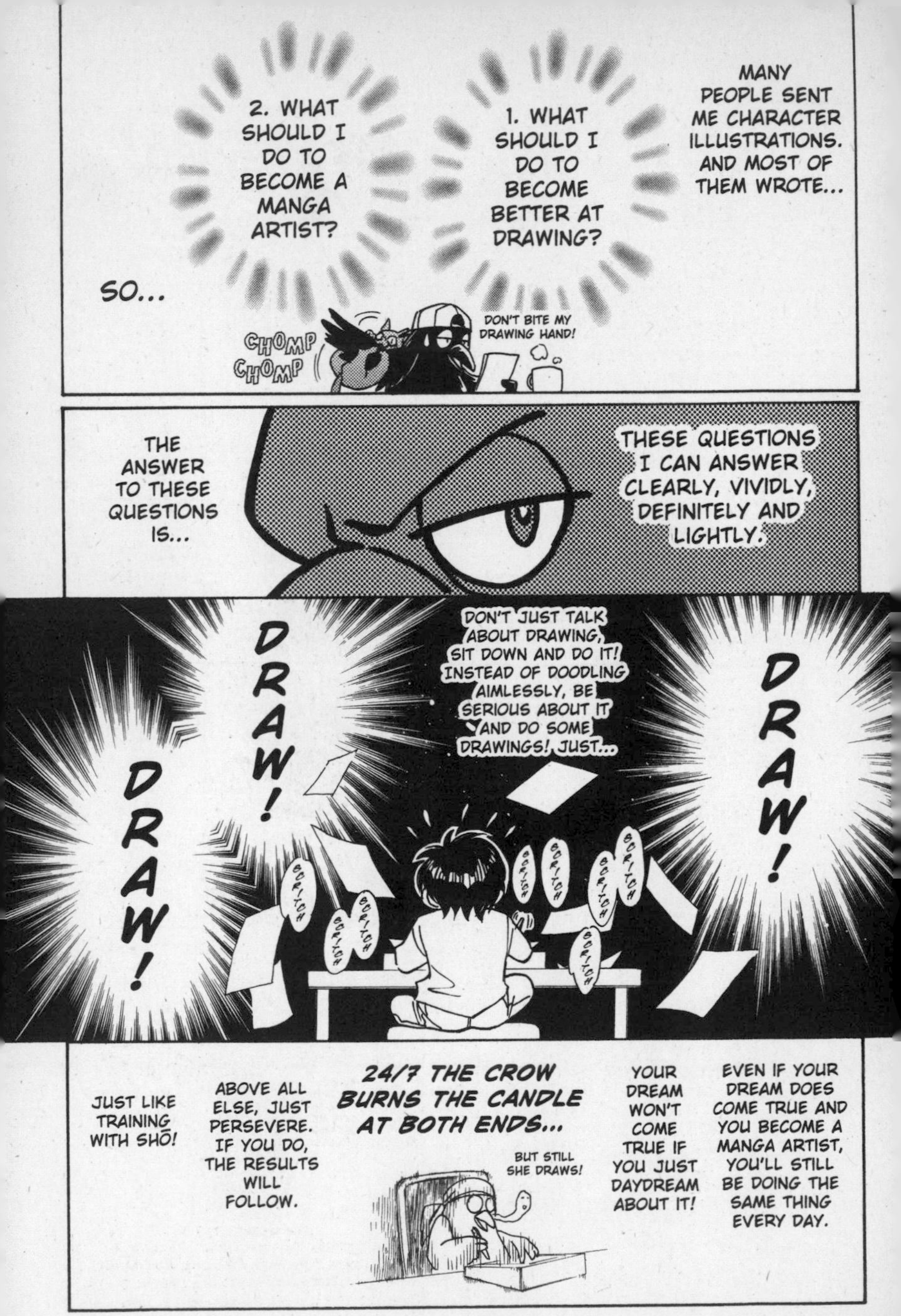
MANY PEOPLE SENT ME CHARACTER ILLUSTRATIONS. AND MOST OF THEM WROTE...
1. WHAT SHOULD I DO TO BECOME BETTER AT DRAWING?
2. WHAT SHOULD I DO TO BECOME A MANGA ARTIST?
DON'T BITE MY DRAWING HAND!
CHOMP CHOMP
SO...
THESE QUESTIONS I CAN ANSWER CLEARLY, VIVIDLY, DEFINITELY AND LIGHTLY.
THE ANSWER TO THESE QUESTIONS IS...
DRAW!
DON'T JUST TALK ABOUT DRAWING, SIT DOWN AND DO IT! INSTEAD OF DOODLING AIMLESSLY, BE SERIOUS ABOUT IT AND DO SOME DRAWINGS! JUST...
DRAW!
DRAW!
SCRITCH SCRITCH SCRITCH SCRITCH SCRITCH SCRITCH SCRITCH SCRITCH
EVEN IF YOUR DREAM DOES COME TRUE AND YOU BECOME A MANGA ARTIST, YOU'LL STILL BE DOING THE SAME THING EVERY DAY.
YOUR DREAM WON'T COME TRUE IF YOU JUST DAYDREAM ABOUT IT!
24/7 THE CROW BURNS THE CANDLE AT BOTH ENDS...
BUT STILL SHE DRAWS!
ABOVE ALL ELSE, JUST PERSEVERE. IF YOU DO, THE RESULTS WILL FOLLOW.
JUST LIKE TRAINING WITH SHŌ!

Next in Whistle!

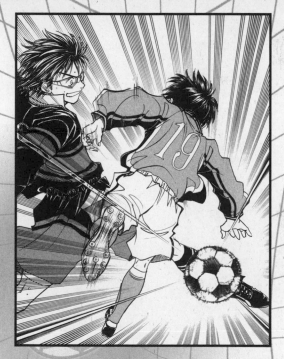

ULTRA SOUL

Shôei, the ex-basketball player, may have plenty of talent and speed, but he has very little experience with the game of soccer. So Taki decides to take advantage of it with Shô's vanishing act. Soon it becomes clear that Shôei is the hole in Kyushu's defense Taki was hoping for. Now Tokyo Select must find another way to crack Kyushu's seemingly impregnable wall and get to the goal.

Available May 2009!

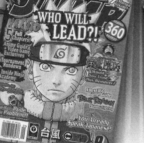
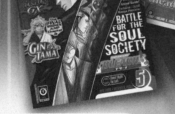

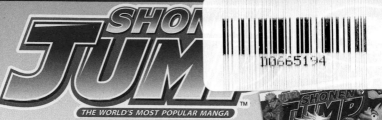
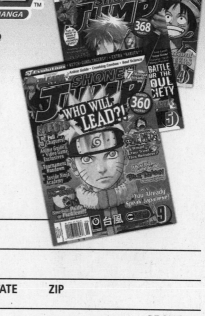